THE PRAEGER HANDBOOK
OF HUMAN RESOURCE
MANAGEMENT

The Praeger Handbook of Human Resource Management

Volume 2

Ann Gilley
Jerry W. Gilley
Scott A. Quatro
Pamela Dixon

Westport, Connecticut
London

Library of Congress Cataloging-in-Publication Data

The Praeger handbook of human resource management / edited by Ann Gilley ... [et al.].
    p. cm.
  Includes bibliographical references and index.
    ISBN 978–0–313–35015–3 ((set) : alk. paper) — ISBN 978–0–313–35017–7 ((vol. 1) : alk. paper) — ISBN
978–0–313–35019–1 ((vol. 2) : alk. paper)
1. Personnel management. I. Gilley, Ann Maycunich. II. Praeger Publishers. III. Title: Handbook of human
resource management. IV. Title: Human resource management.
HF5549.P73 2009
658.3—dc22   2008034634

British Library Cataloguing in Publication Data is available.

Library of Congress Catalog Card Number: 2008034634
ISBN: 978–0–313–35015–3 (set)
        978–0–313–35017–7 (Vol. 1)
        978–0–313–35019–1 (Vol. 2)

First published in 2009

Praeger Publishers, 88 Post Road West, Westport, CT 06881
An imprint of Greenwood Publishing Group, Inc.
www.praeger.com

Printed in the United States of America

The paper used in this book complies with the
Permanent Paper Standard issued by the National
Information Standards Organization (Z39.48–1984).

10 9 8 7 6 5 4 3 2 1

For my family and friends, who inspire me daily—especially my husband, Jerry and my mother, Connie. And for those who guide me in spirit—Ann, Richard, Sig, and Bert.
   Ann Gilley

For my best friend, Ann, and for our girls—Lakota Sioux, Pepper Lee, and Abby Rose. You are the sweetness in my life.
   Jerry W. Gilley

First, I must acknowledge my colleagues and co-editors Jerry Gilley, Pam Dixon, and especially Ann Gilley. Ann, you took on an incredibly complex project and brought it to a successful completion, and managed to remain gracious in the heat of the battle. Thanks for the opportunity to contribute to the project.
I also wish to acknowledge the academic leadership at Covenant College, specifically my Department Chair Chris Dodson, for ensuring that I had adequate course release time to take on this project.
Lastly, I dedicate my efforts on this book to my wife Jamie, and to the "Quattro, Quatro" kids—McKenna, Keaton, Hallie-Blair, and Hudson. You are the "face of God" to me.
   Scott A. Quatro

For my mother, Mary, who taught me the meaning of perseverance, sacrifice, creativity, and generosity.
   Pamela Dixon

Contents

VOLUME ONE

Preface   xv

Part I. HUMAN RESOURCE PRACTICES   1

Chapter 1. Recruiting and Selection   3
  Staffing: An Overview   3
    Ability Inventories   7
    Assessment Center   9
    Background Investigation   11
    Behavior Inventory   12
    Campus Recruiting   13
    Employee Referral Programs   15
    Employment Testing   17
    Interviewing   19
    Job Description   21
    Job Posting   24
    Negligent Hiring   26
    Polygraph Test   27
    Recruiting   29
    References   31
    Resume   33
    Selection   35
    Talent Inventory   37

Chapter 2. Employee Development   41
  Employee Development: An Overview   41
    Action Plan   42
    Appreciative Inquiry   44
    Burnout   46
    Career Planning and Development   47
    Career Resource Center   52
    Coaching   53
    Computer-Based Training   56
    Continuous Improvement Plan   58
    Corporate University   61

Cross-Training   64
Delegation   67
Emotional Intelligence   69
Goal Setting   71
Human Resource Development   73
Interactive Video Training (IVT)   76
Job Sharing   77
Maslow's Hierarchy of Needs   81
Mentoring   83
Myers-Briggs Type Indicator   85
New Employee Orientation   87
On-the-Job Training   90
Performance Aids   93
Performance Coaching   95
Productivity Improvement Plan   98
Professional Certification   102
Socialization   105
Training   108
Training Evaluation   110

Chapter 3. Performance Management   113
Performance Management: An Overview   113
Developmental Evaluations   116
Evaluation   119
Exit Interview   122
Feedback   124
Forced Ranking Evaluation   126
Motivation   129
Performance Analysis   131
Performance Appraisals   132
Performance Consulting   135
Performance Management Systems   137
Performance Standards   140
Promotion   143
Retention   144
360-Degree Feedback   146

Chapter 4. Compensation, Benefits, and Insurance   149
Compensation: An Overview   149
Absences   155
Benefits   156
Bonuses   158
Cafeteria Benefit Plans   160
Child and Elder Care   161
Compensation   163
Deferred Compensation   165
Disability Insurance   166
Domestic Partner Benefits   168

Employee Assistance Programs   170
Employee Stock Option Plan (ESOP)   171
401(k) Plans   172
Gainsharing and Profit Sharing   175
Garnishment   177
Health Care Plans   179
HIPAA   183
Insurance   184
Merit Pay   186
Pay for Performance   187
Payroll   190
Pension Benefit Guaranty Corporation   192
Pension Plans   195
Retirement   198
Salary Benchmarking   200
Scanlon Plan   203
Simplified Employee Pension (SEP)/Simple Plans   206
Severance Pay   207
Skill-based Pay   209
Unemployment Compensation   211
Vacation and Holiday Policies   213
Wellness Programs   215

Chapter 5. Employment Law   219
  Employment Law: An Overview   219
    Affirmative Action   225
    Age Discrimination in Employment Act (ADEA)   227
    Americans with Disabilities Act (ADA)   229
    Bona Fide Occupational Qualification (BFOQ)   231
    Child Labor   232
    Civil Rights Acts of 1964 and 1991   234
    COBRA   236
    Defamation   238
    Disparate Treatment/Disparate Impact   240
    Drug-Free Workplace Act   242
    Employee Polygraph Protection Act (EPPA)   243
    Employee Right-to-Know Law   243
    Equal Employment Opportunity Commission (EEOC)   245
    Equal Pay Act   246
    ERISA   248
    Fair Credit Reporting Act   249
    Fair Labor Standards Act   251
    Family and Medical Leave Act (FMLA)   253
    Fifth Amendment   255
    Four-fifths Rule   257
    Fourteenth Amendment   259
    Fourth Amendment   261

Freedom of Information Act	263
Gay Partner Rights	266
Good Faith	266
Harassment	268
H1B Visas	270
I-9 Forms	272
Immigration Reform and Control Act (IRCA)	274
Jury Duty Leave	276
Labor-Management Relations (Taft-Hartley) Act	277
Military Leave	280
Minimum Wage	281
National Labor Relations Act (NLRA)	282
Norris-LaGuardia Act	284
Occupational Safety and Health Act	285
Older Workers Benefit Protection Act	287
Pension Protection Act of 2006	288
Preferential Treatment	290
Pregnancy Discrimination Act (PDA)	292
Prima Facie	294
Privacy Act	296
Protected Classification	298
Railway Labor Act	300
Reasonable Accommodation	302
Record Retention Laws	304
Retaliation	306
Social Security Act	308
Trade Adjustment Assistance Act of 2002	310
Undue Hardship	311
Uniformed Services Employment and Reemployment Act	312
Vocational Rehabilitation Act	314
WARN Act	315
Whistle-blowing	318
Workers' Compensation	319
Workplace Privacy	323
Wrongful Termination/Discharge	325

VOLUME TWO

Part II. ORGANIZATIONAL ISSUES	327
Chapter 6. Leadership and Strategy	329
Leadership: An Overview	329
Competitive Advantage	333
Executive Coaching	335
Leadership Development	337
Leadership Theories	339

Managerial Malpractice   342
Scenario Planning   345
Short-term Executive   347
Strategic Communication   350
Strategic Planning   353
Succession Planning   354
SWOT Analysis   356
Vision, Mission, Goals, and Objectives   357

Chapter 7. Organizational Development and Change   361
    Organizational Development and Change: An Overview   361
        Change Management   368
        Innovation   370
        Internal/External Consulting   372
        Organizational Development   374
        Organizational Immune System   376

Chapter 8. Organizational Behavior   379
    Organizational Behavior: An Overview   379
        Agile Organization   380
        Community of Practice   382
        Conflict Resolution   384
        Crisis Management   387
        Culture   388
        Developmental Organizations   390
        Diversity   393
        Employee Empowerment Program   395
        Employee Relations   397
        Ethics   401
        Job Satisfaction   402
        Knowledge Transfer   404
        Learning Organizations   406
        Managerial Communication   407
        Needs Analysis   409
        Quality Circles   410
        Religion and Spirituality in the Workplace   412
        Self-directed Work Teams   415
        Sexual Harassment   417
        Talent Management   418
        Teams and Teamwork   420
        Turnover   422

Part III. GENERAL HR ISSUES   425

    General HR: An Overview   427
        Documentation   427
        Employment Agencies, Search Firms, and Headhunters   429
        Field vs. Corporate HR   431
        Forecasting   433

Homeland Security ... 435
HR Competencies ... 438
HR Compliance ... 440
HRIS ... 441
HR Metrics ... 443
HR Strategy ... 445
HR Trends ... 451
Human Capital ... 453
Innovation in Human Resources ... 455
International Human Resource Management ... 457
Interns ... 460
Job Analysis ... 462
Job Design ... 465
Knowledge Management ... 467
Mergers and Acquisitions ... 468
Organizational Design ... 472
PHR/SPHR Designations ... 475
Project Management ... 477
Safety ... 479
Work-Life Balance ... 481
Workplace Justice ... 483
Workplace Violence ... 484

Part IV. HR POLICY ... 489

Arbitration ... 491
Bargaining Unit ... 493
Collective Bargaining ... 495
Comparable Worth ... 497
Disaster Recovery Plan ... 498
Disciplinary Procedures ... 501
Dress Code ... 503
E-mail/Internet Policy ... 505
Emergency Preparedness ... 506
Employee Attitude Survey ... 508
Employee Handbook ... 509
Employment-at-Will ... 511
Exempt-Nonexempt Employee ... 513
Flextime ... 516
Grievance ... 517
Independent Contractors ... 518
Labor Unions ... 520
Layoffs and Downsizing ... 522
Mediation ... 525
Negotiation ... 526
Ombudsman ... 529
Outsourcing ... 531
Overtime ... 534

PTO (Paid Time Off) Bank   535
Security   536
Separation Agreements   538
Substance Abuse   539
Suggestion Systems   541
Surveillance   543
Telecommuting   544
Temporary/Seasonal Employees   547
Termination   549
Trade Secrets (Intellectual Property)   551
Travel   553

Part V. CHECKLISTS AND TOOLS   557

Change Management   561
Strategy   568
Performance   573
Communications/Planning   583
HR Practice   588

Part VI. RESOURCES   599

Articles   601
Books   604
Journals and Magazines   611
Organizations   613
Web Sites   618

Index   625

About the Editors and Contributors   639

Part II
Organizational Issues

Chapter 6
Leadership and Strategy

Leadership—An Overview[1]

The Contemporary State of Leadership and Leadership Development

The recent rash of high-profile corporate failures has raised a great deal of concern regarding the soundness of leadership philosophies and practices. The contemporary climate demands an investigation of these concerns. Consequently, there is a renewed focus on the means through which effective leaders are developed. Many thought leaders are calling for such investigation, soundly criticizing management education and leadership development mechanisms, be they corporate or business school-based, as conduits through which fragmented and misguided leaders are often produced.[2] Clearly, there is a call for radical reform of leadership development.

Concurrent with this is the very real need for HR to act as a driver of this reform, and as a catalyst and means through which outstanding, holistic corporate leaders are developed. Well-rounded leaders that are adept at leading in an increasingly complex business environment are sorely needed, and HR practices need to be employed to systemically develop such holistic leaders.

ACES—A Model for Holistic Leadership Development and Practice

First, while there continues to be a critical role for seminal leadership theories to play as informants of leadership practice and development (as delineated in the Leadership Theories entry of this handbook), it can be argued that leadership development programs and initiatives need to be holistic in their scope, explicitly addressing the **A**nalytical, **C**onceptual, **E**motional, and **S**piritual (ACES) domains of leadership practice and development. Such leadership development programs may ultimately help ensure that corporate leaders return to their rightful image and role as stewards of scarce societal resources and architects of business organizations that undergird a secure civil society.

These four distinct, yet interrelated, domains of holistic leadership development and practice are further delineated below:

- *Analytical*—developing leaders who are adept at understanding and managing discrete complexity. Traditionally, this has indeed been the primary focus of both corporate HR-driven leadership development initiatives and business school education programs. Analytically skilled leaders understand and manage the individual "trees" in the "forest" quite well. For example, developing a cost-benefit analysis for a new product development project requires strong analytical abilities.

- *Conceptual*—developing leaders who are adept at both understanding and managing inter-related complexity and fostering creativity. Traditionally, this has been at most a tangential focus of both corporate HR-driven leadership development initiatives and business school education programs. Leaders with strong conceptual skills understand and manage the "forest" within which the individual "trees" are growing. As an example, designing and managing a project plan for a new product development project requires advanced conceptual skills.
- *Emotional*—developing leaders who are attuned to emotional issues. Traditionally, this has not been a strong focus of either corporate HR-driven leadership development initiatives or business school education programs. Highly attuned emotional leaders are skilled at understanding and managing human emotion as an inevitable phenomenon in a corporate setting, and leveraging it as a source of energy and shaping influence on follower behavior. For example, alignment of employees around the vision for a new product development project team requires well-developed emotional skills.
- *Spiritual*—developing enlightened leaders who recognize the value and role of spirituality in the workplace. This last domain has also traditionally not been a focus of either corporate HR-driven leadership development initiatives or business school education programs. Spiritually enlightened leaders enable their followers to connect both individual tasks and the mission of the larger firm to deeply held moral, ethical, and spiritual values. As an example, leaders with advanced spiritual leadership skills openly discuss and affirm the normative spiritual beliefs and values of the employees assigned to a new product development project team.

Each of these domains of leadership development and practice are uniquely different and independently critical to leadership effectiveness. As illustrated in Figure 6.1, leaders who are practicing leadership in the analytical and conceptual domains are primarily focused on process- or product-related challenges (i.e., developing business process maps or reviewing product design concepts), whereas leaders who are focused on the emotional and spiritual domains of leadership practice are primarily concerned with people-related challenges (i.e., providing behavioral performance assessment to employees or defusing employee conflict). Further, leaders practicing leadership in the analytical and emotional domains are dealing with concrete issues (i.e., budgets, inventory levels, and market share), while leaders practicing leadership in the conceptual and spiritual domains are grappling with abstract issues (i.e., organizational mission and vision statements, organizational culture, and stakeholder analyses).

The most effective leaders recognize the unique challenges associated with leadership practice in each of the four domains, yet also the critical interdependencies that exist among each of the four domains, and demonstrate leadership practices that reflect this recognition. Thus, the most effective leaders intentionally strive to integrate all four domains into a truly holistic approach.

As a prime example, consider the development and championing of corporate mission or vision statements, a task that has been solidly established as a mandate for contemporary corporate leaders. Such statements clearly delineate both the industry and customer segments to be served by the firm, as well as the core competencies to be leveraged in so doing. Accordingly, they will reflect both the analytical and conceptual domains of leadership practice. Yet, this is where many corporate mission or vision statements appear to stop short. Holistic leaders strive to ensure that such statements engage employees at an emotional and spiritual level as well, either explicitly or implicitly.

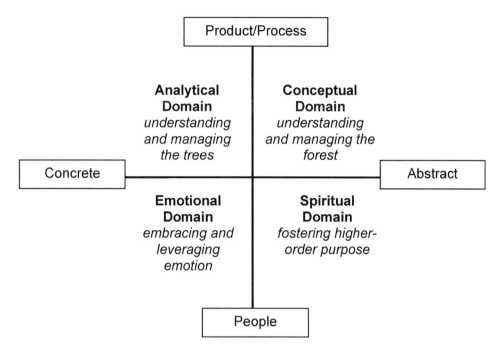

Figure 6.1   The Domains of Holistic Leadership Development and Practice

Employing Systemic Strategic HR Practices as Holistic Leadership Development Mechanisms

Secondly, a broad classification scheme of leadership development that provides a comprehensive, holistic view that includes the critical role of overarching HR practices has yet to be established. To date, the leadership development literature primarily uses formal/classroom and informal/job development classifications.[3] Formal development activities are limited to the classroom, while informal activities include development while on the job. Classifying leadership developmental mechanisms into the formal/classroom and informal/job categories works well with most activities, but these classifications do not readily accommodate the organizational mechanisms that can have an important impact, especially on the emotional and spiritual domains of leadership. There are developmental mechanisms that do not fit into the existing models. Thus, a third category, the organizational context, can be added to the leadership development categories of the classroom and job context to formulate a classification scheme that enables a more holistic view of leadership development. Adding the organizational context results in a classification scheme that enables a more systemic view of leadership development via strategic HR practices.

The addition of this third category allows us to take into account important organizational mechanisms that are often left out of existing leader development schemes. Leadership development mechanisms such as organizational culture and related core values, as well as macro HR strategies and policies that exist at the organizational level, fit neatly into this third category. Further, it can be argued that strategic HR practices are differentially efficacious for leader development across the four ACES domains, as well as fundamentally different in terms of both pedagogical design and breadth of developmental impact (as indicated in Figure 6.2), further underscoring the need for the addition of the organizational context leadership development category.

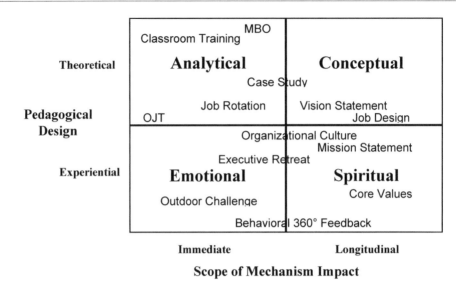

Figure 6.2 The Efficacy of Various Strategic HR Practices for Leadership Development Across the ACES Domains

For example, while classroom leadership training may be particularly effective for the immediate development of analytical abilities in leaders via theoretical exercises, organizational core values contrastingly act as long-term, experiential shapers of a leader's spiritual abilities. Moreover, organizational culture can be viewed as both an immediate and longitudinal leadership development mechanism across both the emotional and spiritual domains of ledaership practice.

Leadership Development and Contemporary HR

We must be wary of HR strategies and practices that create fragmented, narrowly focused leaders, such as performance appraisal processes that are focused primarily on meeting quantitative objectives with little or no regard for broad-based leadership development. In contrast, HR must strive to develop people in leadership positions consistent with the ACES model, thereby reinforcing leadership effectiveness in not just the analytical domain, but the conceptual, emotional, and spiritual domains as well. Such leaders are holistic in their leadership approach, and better suited to the leadership demands of today's evolving business environment.

HR must also redefine the general construct of leadership development as being larger than discrete formal training programs or on-the-job informal development, thereby championing the organizational context category for leadership development discussed herein. Related to this, HR must increasingly recognize the relevance of the spiritual domain of leadership, and foster its development via macro-level, firm infrastructure (including culture, mission, and core values) and related HR strategies or practices (e.g., performance appraisal and multisource feedback).

This last point may be particularly salient given the continuing evolution of HR as a corporate function. Traditionally, the HR function of a firm has conducted leadership training and development as an area that has been inconsistently reinforced via other HR practices. Progressively, the HR function in many firms has evolved into a more far-reaching driver of corporate direction and behavior. As the HR function takes on this broader role as a strategic partner, it becomes an asset that offers a source of hard-to-imitate, competitive advantage. As such, traditionally isolated HR practices such as leadership training and development, compensation administration, job analysis and design, and performance management, have become more tightly integrated into a coherent force that collectively can shape employee behavior in conjunction with clearly articulated statements of organizational core values, vision, and mission. In the end, those firms that have adopted this strategic view of the role of HR, and a correspondingly systemic approach to leadership development, are more capable of developing holistic leadership ACES as described here.

NOTES

1. The majority of this overview was adapted, with permission, from Scott A. Quatro, David A. Waldman, and Benjamin A. Galvin, "Leadership Development and Strategic HR at a Crossroads," in *Human Resource Management: Contemporary Issues, Challenges, and Opportunities,* ed. Ronald R. Sims (Charlotte, NC: Information Age Publishing, 2007), 349–76.

2. Warren G. Bennis, "How Business Schools Lost Their Way," *Harvard Business Review,* May 2005, 96–104; Sumantra Ghoshal, "Bad Management Theories are Destroying Good Management Practices," *Academy of Management Learning and Education* 4, no. 1 (March 2005): 75–91; Henry Mintzberg, "The MBA Menace," *Fast Company,* June 2004, 31–32.

3. Nicolas Clarke, "HRD and the Challenges of Assessing Learning in the Workplace," *International Journal of Training and Development* 8, no. 2 (June 2004): 140–56; Michael D. Enos, Marijke Thanun Kehrhahn, and Alexandra Bell, "Informal Learning and the Transfer of Learning: How Managers Develop Proficiency," *Human Resource Development Quarterly* 14, no. 4 (Winter 2003): 369–87.

Scott A. Quatro

COMPETITIVE ADVANTAGE

Competition has become more intense and widespread in recent years. No organization can ignore competition if it expects to survive. "The structure and evolution of industries, and the ways in which companies gain and sustain competitive advantage in them, lie at the core of competition."[1] Competitive advantage considers the profitability of an organization compared to its competitors in an industry. Porter identifies three types of competitive advantage: cost leadership, differentiation, and focus.[2] The latter is a niche strategy wherein a subsegment of a larger market is intentionally targeted, leveraging either a cost-based or differentiation-based competitive advantage.

Process

From a systems theory perspective, basic components of all systems include input, process, and output. Input consists of the raw materials transformed by the system. A process is "one or more tasks that add value by transforming a set of inputs into a specified set of outputs (goods or services) for another person [customer] by a combination of people, methods, and tools."[3] Output is the end product that results from a completed process.

The process level is often thought of as the pivotal link between organizational and individual performance. An organization's people, or human resources, are ultimately responsible for performing the tasks, or activities, and obtaining the expected business results. "If you want to understand the way work gets done, to improve the way work gets done, and to manage the way work gets done, processes should be the focus of your attention and actions."[4]

Value Chain

Profits are the difference between value and the cost of carrying out the activities that produce the products and services. Value is relative worth, or the amount a customer is willing to pay for a particular product or service. The value chain is a framework for examining activities and their connection to competitive advantage; that is, it provides a way to identify and assess the sources of customer value that enable a firm to sell a product or service for a premium price,[5] or the sources of efficiency that enable a firm to sell a product or service at a low cost while still realizing a healthy margin.

Cost Leadership

Cost leadership is created when an organization is able to lower its costs by carrying out its value-chain activities more efficiently than its competitors.[6] Operational effectiveness encompasses efficiency and is at the core of achieving a cost-based competitive advantage. However, competitive strategy involves either performing different activities or configuring activities differently to deliver a unique mix of value.[7] For example, Southwest Airlines has built a value-chain that overwhelmingly focuses on efficiency (e.g., flying only 737s and selling tickets only through Southwest agents or the Southwest Web site), and thereby enables the firm to achieve industry-leading profitability while still charging the lowest average ticket price in virtually every market that the firm serves. However, Southwest does not depend solely on the efficiency of their value-chain activities (i.e., operational effectiveness) for this competitive advantage. The firm also intentionally chooses to fly the shortest average routes of all major carriers, and utilizes secondary airports (where overhead costs are considerably lower) in doing so. This combination of efficiency and strategic configuration of activities enables Southwest to achieve a sustainable cost-based competitive advantage.

Differentiation

Differentiation involves creating unique, or differentiated, products and services. Uniqueness alone, however, does not equate to differentiation unless the customer perceives it as valuable.[8] Potential sources of differentiation include any value activity along the value chain and breadth of activity, or competitive scope.[9] Branding and gaining customer loyalty are also emphasized. For example, Nordstrom has achieved a differentiation-based competitive advantage by emphasizing customer service. Nordstrom associates are acculturated to see themselves as "servants" to their customers, doing everything possible to meet their wants, needs, and desires. As with cost-based competitive advantage, differentiation requires that the value-chain activities of the firm compliment and reinforce one another. To that end, Nordstrom's customer service–focused value-chain activities are reinforced by human resource management–related value-chain activities that are remarkably empowering and organic in nature. For example, historically, the Nordstrom Employee Handbook consisted of only a single 5 x 8 card including only 75 words. The few words that were included on the card essentially said two things: (1) the customer is king, and (2) do everything within your power, and within the bounds of good judgment, to satisfy the customer king. Such a customer-centric ethos and related value chain has enabled Nordstrom to command a premium price for its retail services, and has resulted in a sustainable, differentiation-based competitive advantage for the firm.

See also Strategic Planning; SWOT Analysis

NOTES

1. Michael E. Porter, *On Competition* (Boston: Harvard Business School Publishing, 1998), 2.

2. Michael E. Porter, *Competitive Advantage: Creating and Sustaining Superior Performance* (New York: The Free Press, 1985).

3. Arthur R. Tenner and Irving J. DeToro, *Process Redesign: The Implementation Guide for Managers* (Reading, MA: Addison-Wesley Publishing Company, 1997), 58.

4. Geary A. Rummler and Alan P. Brache, *Improving Performance: How to Manage the White Space on the Organizational Chart* (San Francisco: Jossey-Bass Publishers, 1990), 62.

5. Porter, *Competitive Advantage.*

6. Ibid.

7. Michael E. Porter, "What Is Strategy," *Harvard Business Review,* November 1996.

8. Ibid.

9. Porter, *Competitive Advantage.*

Alina M. Waite

EXECUTIVE COACHING

Executive coaching is a one-on-one, data-driven collaborative process that builds upon a relationship between an external or internal consultant and an executive client. This process relies upon mutually agreed ground rules, expectations, hoped-for results, and a definitive endpoint. Executive coaching comprises feedback, in-depth development, or specific content or skill building. Executive behavioral change must be sustainable and measureable within an organizational context. While personal growth and change may be a desirable outcome, effectiveness of executive coaching is demonstrated by attainment of organizational results, since the organization that pays the bills is also a client of the executive coaching process.[1]

The Process of Executive Coaching

Executive coaching can be used to enhance skills, to increase levels of performance, or to develop the potential of the executive.[2] Skills coaching is also known as content coaching,[3] where the coach is a content expert in a management field and can teach the executive a certain skill, such as in finance or marketing. Most coaching, however, involves some sort of personal behavioral change on the part of the executive.

Executive coaching generally starts with an assessment or data-gathering phase. Some sort of 360-degree-feedback instrument is usually used. This instrument evaluates the executive's behavior from the perspective of direct reports, coworkers, and supervisors. The executive coach also gathers data by observing the interaction of the executive with others. This information is then relayed to the client in a feedback session, and areas of improvement are determined.

Awareness of their behavior and acceptance of the need to change that behavior is the beginning of the change process. Behavioral change is accomplished through experimentation with the coach, copying the coach's behavior, and/or through personal reflection.[4] There is some overlap between coaching and counseling, but coaches do not provide therapy, however. If therapy is required for behavioral change, clients should be referred to a therapist.[5]

The relationship between the coach and client is extremely important.[6] Personal change can take place only when trust has been established and the client feels safe enough to be reflective and to try out new behaviors. The executive coach should be skilled in human relations as well as in organizational dynamics.[7]

Coaching Outcomes

There is no consensus on how effective executive coaching is in terms of the benefit to the organization.[8] Although behavioral change on the part of the executive can and must be measured, a direct link must also be made to organizational outcomes in order to determine how effective the executive coaching has been. Since executive coaching is so costly, organizations have begun to ask for more evidence that an intervention has been effective and has improved organizational outcomes.[9] Executive coaching should also be thought of as a way to maintain organizational health, as opposed to a last resort when there is a behavioral or skill problem.

Conclusion

Executive coaching is a process whereby executives change their behavior and/or acquire new skills to benefit both their careers and their organizations. Areas where executives need to change their behavior are identified through assessment tools and observations by the coach. Executive coaches should be able to create a safe and trusting environment for personal change to occur. Effectiveness of executive coaching is measured not only by behavioral changes in the executive, but by improved organizational metrics.

See also Coaching; Performance Coaching

NOTES

1. Barbara A. W. Eversole and Gary W. Craig, "Seeing the Elephant: Linking Theory and Practice to Integrate the Parts of Executive Coaching and Propose a Definition," *Proceedings of the International Conference of the Academy of Human Resource Development* (February 2006).

2. Robert Witherspoon and Randall P. White, "Executive Coaching: A Continuum of Roles," *Consulting Psychology Journal: Practice and Research* 48, no. 2 (Spring 1996): 87–95.

3. Liz Thach and Tom Heinselman, "Executive Coaching Defined," *Training and Development Journal* 53, no. 3 (March 1999): 34–40.

4. Donald A. Schon, *Educating the Reflective Practitioner: Toward a New Design for Teaching and Learning in the Professions* (San Francisco: Jossey-Bass, 1987).

5. Richard R. Kilburg, "When Shadows Fall: Using Psychodynamic Approaches in Executive Coaching," *Consulting Psychology Journal: Practice and Research* 56, no. 4 (Fall 2004): 246–68.

6. Jonathan Passmore, "An Integrative Model of Executive Coaching," *Consulting Psychology Journal: Practice and Research* 59, no. 1 (March 2007): 68–78.

7. Ruth L. Orenstein, "Executive Coaching: It's Not Just about the Executive," *Journal of Applied Behavioral Science* 38, no. 3 (September 2002): 355–75.

8. Terrence Maltbia, "Diversity's Impact on the Executive Coaching Process," *Proceedings of the Academy of Human Resource Development* (February 2005): 221–28.

9. David L. Dotlich and Peter C. Cairo, *Action Coaching: How to Leverage Individual Performance for Company Success.* (San Francisco: Jossey-Bass, 1999).

Barbara A. W. Eversole

LEADERSHIP DEVELOPMENT

Leadership development is an important human resources (HR) activity. Traditionally, leadership development has been concerned with providing current and future leaders with opportunities to learn, grow, change, experience, and to develop attitudes, knowledge, skills, abilities, and other characteristics necessary to function effectively in the organization. Leadership development is an aspect of organizational development that covers recruitment and assessment of executive-level employees and training them in leadership to equip them for higher positions. This process generally includes development of cognitive (thinking, idea generation, and decision making), behavioral (choosing appropriate attitudes and values), and environmental (suiting leadership style to the situation) skills.

Modern-day View of Leadership Development

The modern-day view of leadership development[1] is one that enhances an organization's effectiveness while simultaneously maintaining a competitive advantage. Underlying this view of leadership development is the assimilation of leadership development efforts with strategic planning, along with efforts to teach the more intangible aspects of leadership, market/client thinking (which is often cross-cultural), adaptability, implementation strategies, and change management. Strategically linked leadership development activities include specific on- and off-the-job assignments along with education and training. The goal is to obtain the fullest use of human resource capabilities by developing leaders to assume positions of greater responsibility. Recurring leadership development objectives for performance improvement and effectiveness include leadership of organizational change and adaptation to unique situations; reducing cycle time for virtually every major process and activity; promoting continuous learning and improvement; introducing and extending quality management principles and practices; managing cultural diversity and also cross cultural communications; and building leadership and relational skills.

Techniques and Approaches to Leadership Development

There are many on- and off-the job techniques and approaches for developing leaders. Some organizations use a narrow, limited approach. Others, such as General Electric (GE) and Hoechst Marion Roussel, Inc., have a broad, multifaceted approach to leadership development. GE has one of the oldest and most widely known leadership development centers in the world located at the John F. Welch Leadership Development Center at Crotonville, New York. GE uses a combination of course work and job experiences to develop its executives. Other programs, such as the Business Manager Course and the Executive Development Course, utilize action learning. Program participants are assigned a real problem that GE is facing and must present their recommendations to the company's CEO.

Leadership, entrepreneurship, and e-business are important topics in leadership development programs. Programs directed at developing leaders' understanding of global business issues and leading change are also parts of leadership development. Distance learning is used by many companies and universities to develop leaders. Using personal computers, leaders "attend" CD-ROM video lectures, download study aids and additional videos and audio programs and audio programs, discuss lectures, and work on team projects using computer bulletin boards, e-mail, and live chat rooms. The Internet is used to research specific companies and topics. Besides the e-learning environment, leaders spend time in traditional face-to-face instruction for several weeks at their home. Leadership development also includes traveling to attend courses or programs held in foreign or host countries.

Organizations and leadership development providers (business school or other educational institution) work together to create short, custom leadership development efforts with content designed specifically to meet the needs of the organization. MetLife and Babson College worked together to develop a course that included faculty and corporate executive participation and company project work.[2] Duke Corporate Education, a for-profit spin-off of Duke University's executive education, develops custom programs that specifically address company needs.

Formal leadership development efforts from consultants or university faculty are also supplemented with other types of training and development activities. Avon Products uses action learning for leadership development.[3] The program brings a team of employees together for six-week periods spread over 18 months. Then teams work with senior executives on a country project, such as how to penetrate a new market. The team projects are presented to Avon's top managers. Leaders who attend the Center for Creative Leadership development program in Greensboro, North Carolina, take psychological tests; receive feedback from their managers, peers, and direct reports; participate in group building activities (like adventure learning); receive counseling; set improvement goals; and write development plans.[4]

Individual Leadership Development Process

Individual leadership development plans (ILDPs) are used to improve the effectiveness and success of leadership development efforts. The overall ILDP process (1) develops an ILDP oversight committee to interpret the organization's strategic agenda into management development terms and manage the overall ILDP process (design, implementation, and evaluation); (2) develops ILDPs for all current and future leaders; (3) develops realistic job previews for all leadership jobs in the organization and make this information available to all relevant employees; (4) ensures completion of 360-degree evaluations of all leaders based on key performance dimensions linked to the strategic imperatives of the organization, with this information being used to formulate an ILDP; 5) assigns to each leader an ILDP coach and develops an individualized ILDP plan; 6) the ILDP oversight committee reviews each ILDP plan and makes recommendations and suggestions for improvement; 7) ensures ILDP coaches and leaders meet to review final ILDP plan before implementation; 8) ensures ILDP implementation begins with specific learning, growth and development activities, completion dates, and meeting dates between coaches and leaders to discuss progress (and the need to revise plans depending on organizational changes—for example, in strategic direction); 9) ensures the ILDP oversight committee meets to review progress towards achievement of each ILDP's goals (i.e., at least every six months) and assess the overall program based on established evaluation criteria; and 10) generates regular reports for senior leadership by the ILDP oversight committee on the ILDP program to keep them up to date and to identify needed changes in the program.

NOTES

1. Robert M. Fulmer and Marshall Goldsmith, *The Leadership Investment: How the World's Best Organizations Gain Strategic Advantage through Leadership Development* (Washington, DC: AMACOM, 2000); Albert A. Vicere and Robert M. Fulmer, *Leadership by Design* (Boston: Harvard Business School Press, 1998).

2. Irwin Speizer, "Custom Fit," *Workforce Management,* March 2005, 57–63.

3. Jennifer Reingold, "Corporate America Goes to School," *BusinessWeek,* October 20, 1997, 66–72.

4. Lindsey Gerdes, "Programs: Picking Up the Pace," *BusinessWeek Online,* October 24, 2005, special report on executive education, http://www.businessweek.com (accessed March 1, 2008).

Ronald R. Sims

LEADERSHIP THEORIES

There are many ways to finish the sentence "Leadership is. . ."[1] There are almost as many different definitions of leadership as there are people who have tried to define it. Leadership is a process that involves influence that occurs within a group, and it involves attainment of a goal. The noted leadership author Peter Northouse stresses the difference between management and leadership. Whereas the former exists to provide order, the latter serves to produce movement and change.

It can also be said that there are as many theories of leadership as there are those who write about it.[2] However, the major codified leadership theories include trait-factor theory, leadership style theory, leadership skills theory, situational leadership theory, contingency theory, path-goal theory, leader-member exchange theory, and transformational leadership theory. These major leadership theories are defined below and the characteristics of each are identified.

Trait-factor Theory

The first systematic attempt to study leadership was based on trait-factor theory. This research focused on "great men" and their inborn qualities that set them apart from others. Stogdill's 1948 research claimed that leadership was not a quality that individuals possessed, but a social relationship between people. Despite this, traits reappear in modern research and certain academic circles.

The strengths of the trait-factor theory include over 100 years of research. It is consistent with our perception of what leaders are, and it focuses on the leader in a leadership context. Trait-factor theory also gives us benchmarks to evaluate ourselves as leaders.

Leadership research identifies weaknesses of the trait-factor theory, such as no definitive list of traits having been published. It ignores the situational context of leadership, and researchers subjectively decide which traits are most important. Traits have not been shown to produce desired outcomes for organizations, and traits do not help us to train future leaders because we are accepting the belief that ability is bestowed upon some at birth and therefore cannot be learned.

Leadership Style Theory

The style approach examines the behavior of the leader—what they do and how they act. Leadership research notes that the style approach does not tell leaders how to behave, it merely classifies their behavior. It also reminds leaders that their actions towards others occur on a "task" and a "relationship" level. In any given situation, and with any given subordinate, one will take precedence over another.

The strengths of the style approach are that it stops us from thinking of leadership as merely an issue of personality traits, and it is supported by a wide range of studies. On a conceptual level, the style approach focuses on tasks and relationships, and it can be used to see if we are task-centered or people-centered leaders. The style approach is easy to apply, helps practicing leaders to judge themselves, and is useful for training and development workshops.

Weaknesses identified with the style approach are the lack of clarity between style and performance outcomes. Research on the style approach has failed to find a universal style suitable for all situations, and the implication that a high-task, high-relationship style is most effective has not been proven.

Leadership Skills Theory

The skills approach takes a leader-centered perspective on leadership. The skills approach differs from the previous theories as it shifts the focus away from personality characteristics, which usually are viewed as innate and largely fixed, to a focus on skills and abilities that can be learned and developed. Although personality does play an integral role in leadership, the skills approach indicates that certain knowledge and skills are needed for effective leadership.

Strengths of the skills theory include a leader-centered model that stresses the importance of developing particular leadership skills that make leadership available to everyone. The leadership skills theory approach provides a structure that is most consistent with the curricula of most leadership education programs.

However, the skills theory approach includes a breadth of skills that seems to extend beyond the boundaries of leadership. By including so many components, this theory becomes more general and less precise in explaining leadership performance. The skills approach may also be weak in predictive value, as it does not explain how variations in social judgment skills or problem-solving skills affect performance. The skills model was constructed using a large sample of military personnel and their performance in the armed services. This raises the question of the whether it can be generalized to other populations in other settings.

Situational Leadership Theory

Hersey and Blanchard developed an approach to leadership stressing that a leader must have an adaptive leadership style that mixes delegating, supporting, coaching, and directing as appropriate. The balance of these four will reflect the amount of competence and commitment subordinates have towards organizational goals (also given four classifications). The effectiveness of leaders depends on successfully diagnosing where subordinates are on the development continuum and adapting their leadership style as necessary. Because subordinates move back and forth along this continuum, leaders have to be able to move along it as well.[3]

Strengths identified with the situational approach are that it is easily understood and therefore practical, and that it is prescriptive, telling the leader what to do once he or she has classified subordinates' behaviors. The situational approach emphasizes leadership flexibility (and therefore movement), and it reminds the leader to treat subordinates as individuals.

However, research has shown certain leaders work more or less effectively with certain subordinates. Research also indicates that issues of one-to-one and group leadership are problematic; for example, how should leaders pitch their approach to an entire group?

Contingency Theory

Leadership literature describes this theory as leader-match. This means matching leaders to appropriate situations. The term "contingency" is used to reflect how well the leader's style fits the context, and effective leadership is therefore contingent on matching the leader's style to the setting. Showing similarities to style leadership theory, contingency theory describes situations as demanding either task-motivated or relationship-motivated leadership. Contingency theory argues that situations can be assessed using three factors: leader-member relations, the degree of task structure, and position power. Having assessed these three, contingency theory states certain styles will be effective in certain situations. Task-orientated leaders will do well when things are going well or there is a crisis, while relationship-orientated leaders will do well in moderate situations.

Path-goal Theory

Path-goal theory uses research on motivation to get organizational goals accomplished. The intention of path-goal theory is to enhance employee performance and satisfaction by focusing on employee motivation. While the situational approach emphasizes adaptation, and the contingency approach stresses matching the leader's style to the situation, path-goal emphasizes the relationship between the leader's style and the characteristics of the subordinates and the setting. The assumption comes from expectancy theory; subordinates will be motivated if they think they can do their work and get a favorable outcome for doing so. The leader has to use a style that best matches the subordinates' motivational needs.

Leader Member Exchange (LMX) Theory

LMX theory states that leadership is a process centered in the interaction between leaders and followers. The dyadic relationship between the two is at the center of leadership. LMX is a descriptive theory that highlights a sociological truth: we all know that our organizations have "in" and "out" groups. It is a unique theory that gives the subordinate as much importance as the leader. The importance of communication in leadership is stressed. Research supports the claim that a positive LMX equals a positive outcome for the organization. However, LMX discriminates against the out-group, and promotes the advancement of privileged individuals. LMX also fails to explain how high-quality dyads are made. Research indicates that LMX is very difficult to measure.

Transformational Leadership Theory

Transformational leadership involves values, ethics, and long-term goals. It also involves treating subordinates as "full human beings" and subsumes charismatic and visionary leadership. It can be used to describe a wide range of leadership, from specific attempts to influence followers to broad attempts to influence organizations and even cultures. While transactional leadership focuses on routine and formalized exchanges, transformational and charismatic leadership involve tapping the motives of followers in order to better reach the leader's goals. The strengths of transformational leadership are that it has been widely researched from many perspectives. The image of a transformational leader out front has popular appeal. People are attracted to transformational leadership because it makes sense to them. Transformational leaders deeply involve subordinates, as the needs of the followers are central to the theory.

However, leadership researchers believe that transformational leadership is not conceptually clear and that it has unclear perimeters. It is also viewed as one or another (transactional or transformational) rather than a point on a continuous scale. Transformational leadership is seen as a personality trait rather than behavior that people can learn, and is difficult to apply at all managerial levels. It is also open to abuse, as history shows many charismatic people who have abused leadership positions.[4]

NOTES

1. Peter G. Northouse, *Leadership Theory and Practice* (Thousand Oaks, CA: Sage Publications, 2007).
2. Bernard Bass, *Bass and Stogdill's Handbook of Leadership* (New York: Free Press, 1990).
3. Northouse, *Leadership Theory and Practice*.
4. National College for School Leadership, "What Leaders Read," United Kingdom, http://www.ncsl.org.uk/media/761/9A/randd-what-leaders-read-business-summary.pdf (accessed March 1, 2008).

Merwyn L. Strate

MANAGERIAL MALPRACTICE

Why do organizations fail to achieve or sustain high performance? The responsibility, or failure, lies within the management team. A manager is responsible for "achieving organizational objectives through the efficient and effective utilization of resources."[1] We prefer defining management as *getting results through people;* after all, the people within an organization are responsible for its success—they make things happen.

Managers, therefore, are critical members of the organizational team, coordinating the efforts of their players to achieve results. Organizational success (or lack thereof), then, is the direct result of management's talents and skills. Companies that employ managers who lack the talents and skills necessary to achieve success are guilty of managerial malpractice.

Managerial malpractice is "encouraging and supporting practices that produce unprofessional, unproductive, and incompetent managers."[2] These managers are poorly trained, misguided, or inadequately prepared for the challenges they face on a daily basis—in a word, they are unqualified. Quite simply, they lack the interpersonal skills necessary to interact appropriately with their employees and help them (and, ultimately, the firm) improve performance.

Symptoms of Managerial Malpractice

Managerial malpractice manifests itself at every echelon of the organization. People, policies, processes, and systems within firms encourage managerial malpractice at organizational and individual levels.

Organizational Symptoms

Symptoms of managerial malpractice within organizations include, but are not limited to:
- Hiring or promoting managers who lack the understanding and skills necessary to effectively manage others
- Hiring or promoting managers because they are the "best performers" or "highest producers" and without regard for their interpersonal skills
- Wasting valuable time and resources attempting to "fix" ineffective or incompetent managers
- Failing to reprimand, demote, or fire managers who are ineffective or incompetent

Individual Symptoms

Most employees have worked for an incompetent manager at one point or another. Some have worked for a multitude of poor or ineffective managers. People exhibit symptoms of managerial malpractice in a host of ways. An ineffective or incompetent manager may display any one or a combination of the following destructive behaviors:
- A superior attitude
- Indifference toward employees
- Inability to make positive change happen
- Poor communication/interpersonal skills
- Refusal to delegate
- Inability to resolve conflict
- Failure to provide feedback or evaluate employee performance in a timely, appropriate manner
- Anger, fear, or resentment of employees, colleagues, superiors, or the organization
- Displays of favoritism
- Lack of involvement in employee development
- Lack of patience
- Inability or refusal to recognize or reward others for their achievements
- Creation of a fearful or paranoid work environment
- Abusive, bullying, or harassing

Consequences of Managerial Malpractice

Managerial malpractice has been allowed to flourish within organizations since the beginning of time. Ancient battles have been lost, societies have fallen, and companies large and small have failed due to lack of managerial competence. This form of malpractice frustrates employees, negatively impacts organizational effectiveness, and creates opportunities for competitors to capitalize on the weaknesses of their foes.

The consequences to individuals and organizations of managerial malpractice are numerous and disturbing. Employees develop a distrust of management and an "us vs. them" attitude, feel little or no commitment or loyalty to the firm, and have no motivation or reason to excel, "go the extra mile," or "give 110 percent" to a manager for whom they have no respect or from whom they will receive no recognition. Incompetent managers raise levels of employee stress, fear, anger, hostility, disillusionment, paranoia, conflict, apathy, and depression while lessening their willingness to engage in personal or professional development, deliver superior customer service, work collaboratively with peers, or maximize their creativity.

Managerial malpractice causes individuals and groups to deliver lackluster performance, prevents groups from achieving "team" status and synergy, and destroys morale. Organizations guilty of managerial malpractice report greater instances of management team dysfunction and conflict, employee sabotage, resistance to change, absenteeism and turnover, litigation (employee grievances and complaints) and customer service complaints. These lead to mediocre or falling quality, efficiency, and productivity, lessened creativity, lack of competitiveness, a poor reputation as an employer, loss of goodwill, higher costs, and lower profitability. The impact on the bottom line is clear.

Eliminating Managerial Malpractice

In general, the solution to managerial malpractice is simple. "Select managers for their interpersonal skills and hold them accountable for securing results through people."[3] Strategies for reducing or eliminating managerial malpractice include:

Create a New Management Development Philosophy and Culture
Policies and procedures exist within an overriding culture and philosophical framework. In order to successfully alter current methods of practice, the underlying philosophical foundation must support the change. Leadership, which drives culture, must embrace, model, and demand adherence to a new, successful model of managerial effectiveness.

Modify the Hiring and Promotion Practices for Managers
Select new and promote existing managers for their ability to secure results through others, demonstrated specifically via exceptional interpersonal skills. Look for candidates who communicate effectively with individuals at all levels, collaborate, listen well, are able to motivate others, provide positive and developmental feedback, resolve conflict, and reward others' success.

Build Management Development Programs To Cultivate Management Talent
Create formal and informal programs to build management capacity and talent. Formal programs include training and education for aspiring or current managers regarding topics such as change management, conflict resolution, and coaching. Informal programs include activities such as mentoring and job shadowing to enhance managers' knowledge, skills, and abilities.

Coach New and Existing Managers
Life is a journey of learning and change, and who better to guide us than a coach? Successful managers understand that continuous improvement and skill enhancement is the result of repeated trial and effort, feedback, accomplishment, failure, and reflection. Star athletes do not achieve and sustain success by accident—they regularly seek the advice of a coach.

Require Managers to Function as Performance Coaches For Their Employees
Everyone needs a coach, and anyone can be a coach. Just as managers benefit from the advice and guidance of talent coaches, so too can and should managers coach their employees via training, mentoring, and development activities.

Reward Managers for Effective Behaviors

Rewards are designed to reinforce desired behavior and encourage its repetition. Rewarding effective managerial practices (e.g., coaching, growth and development, giving feedback, and so on) powerfully strengthens and communicates the values of the organization—that people are essential to the firm's success, and this success is due to the manager's skill.

Conclusion

Although managerial malpractice thrives within most organizations, it can be reduced or eliminated. Changing the way organizations choose and develop their managers is the first step toward greater effectiveness and profitability.

See also Coaching; Executive Coaching; Performance Coaching

NOTES

1. Robert N. Lussier, *Management Fundamentals* (Mason, OH: Thomson South-Western, 2006), 6.
2. Jerry W. Gilley and Nathaniel W. Boughton, *Stop Managing, Start Coaching* (New York: McGraw-Hill, 1996), 1.
3. Jerry W. Gilley, Nathaniel W. Boughton, and Ann Maycunich, *The Performance Challenge: Developing Management Systems to Make Employees Your Organization's Greatest Asset* (Cambridge, MA: Perseus Books, 1999), 9.

Ann Gilley and Jerry W. Gilley

SCENARIO PLANNING

Scenario planning is receiving increased attention as a strategic management tool. While the limits of traditional strategic planning have revealed themselves in uncertain and rapidly changing conditions, scenario planning has begun to shine because of its ability to integrate uncertainty and continuous change into the planning process. Scenario planning has been described as the most important tool for managers and HRD professionals in the coming decade because it capitalizes on learning as the key to organization strategy.[1] Longtime HR professionals know that when it comes to understanding how adults learn and reshape their thinking in organizations, they have the tools to efficiently and effectively harness that learning as a driver of organization strategy. The purpose of this entry is to provide a succinct overview of scenario planning and to describe why it is the most important emerging tool for managers and HR professionals.

Scenario planning is an iterative and continuous approach to planning that is first focused on revealing and changing the assumptions about the organization and its internal and external environments. Many organizations have had success using scenario planning as a precursor to strategic planning—using the scenario process to open up thinking, and then more traditional strategic planning tools to make decisions and implement organizational activities.

Background and Evolution of Scenario Planning

Scenario planning is about *seeing*. Pierre Wack, the undisputed "father" of modern scenario planning, along with Ted Newland and Napier Collyns, developed the technique at Royal

Dutch/Shell Oil in the 1960s and 1970s. Pierre was something of a mystic, with roots in India and Japan, where he studied extensively. Pierre was a visual thinker, and referred to his scenario efforts as the "eyes of the pack, running ahead and reporting back to Shell what he had seen."[2] In addition, Pierre recounted stories such as one about a gardener he met in Japan. "The gardener pointed to a smooth bamboo trunk as thick as a person's arm. He explained that if a small pebble was thrown at it and hit the trunk even slightly off-center, it would glance off, making hardly any sound. If, on the other hand, the pebble hit the trunk dead center, it would make a very distinctive 'clonk.'"[3] Pierre used such stories to emphasize that his goal was to strike the mental models of managers dead-center, like the bamboo stalk. If he could achieve this, he could change the basic assumptions that framed their decision-making processes. His goal was to help them *see* the world differently. In order to help them *see,* they needed to be able to learn.

Scenario planning has been defined as "a process of positing several informed, plausible and imagined alternative future environments in which decisions may be played out for the purpose of changing current thinking, improving decision-making, enhancing human and organization learning and improving performance."[4] In addition, "Scenario analysis is a disciplined way to think about the future. It demands above all an understanding of the forces that drive the system rather than reliance on forecasts."[5] Scenario planning is designed to support exploration of a constantly changing environment and uses multiple narrative stories about the past, the present, and the future to stretch the thinking inside the organization.[6] Scenarios are not about getting the future "right," nor are they tools for probabilistic prediction.

A Scenario-planning Process

There are numerous models and processes for guiding the scenario-planning effort. However, all draw on common elements. These elements include (1) a primary business issue that needs exploration, (2) assembling a team to lead the scenario project, (3) internal interviews, (4) external trends, (5) developing scenarios via several workshops with key organizational stakeholders, and (6) using the scenarios to make strategic decisions around the primary business issue.

Essentially, each scenario project is a custom one. One a project is initiated, a team is formed and that team carries out internal interviews, analyzes external trends, and leads the organization through several workshops designed to elicit the forces with the greatest potential impact on the organization and that are of the greatest uncertainty. These are obviously very subjective judgments, so the group dialogue that happens during workshops is critical. This is how mental models and assumptions are made clear and shared. Once these workshops are complete and the forces of greatest potential impact and uncertainty (key uncertainties) are identified, the team constructs four scenarios that are used to examine decisions and consider their possible outcomes. Two other key factors are that (1) scenario planning has seen its greatest success when used on an ongoing, iterative basis, and (2) scenario planning works best when there are varying points of view and should enroll members of the organization from all levels.

First- and Second-generation Scenarios

Initial scenarios rarely have an impact on managers' mental maps because they do not provide a basis on which managers can use their judgment.[7] When Pierre Wack first began using scenarios at Shell, he repeatedly had a response of "so what" from managers after they would participate in one of his scenario presentations. "What, in time, we came to learn was that these first-generation scenarios are always learning scenarios; their purpose is not action, but to gain understanding and insight."[8] Pierre therefore called these first-generation scenarios "learning scenarios." The solution was eventually found in a second round of scenario development called "second-generation scenarios," which became the "decision scenarios." Wack's insights developed when he realized that in order to affect the managers' microcosms, he needed "to make the scenarios relevant to the deepest concerns of the decision-maker in the circumstances he was facing,"[9] and that in order to accomplish this, he needed to understand the decision makers and tailor-fit the scenarios to challenge the mental models of the managers who would use them.

Conclusion

As managers and HR professionals are increasingly involved in organizational strategy, they can further leverage their roles by developing expertise in scenario planning. Because learning is increasingly valued as a driver of organizational innovation, change, and dynamic moves in competitive markets, successful organizations will be those that can outthink others. Scenario planning promotes strategic learning based on its demands that decision makers understand the forces driving the internal and external environments. Scenario planning might be thought of as an ongoing game of organizational chess—the goal being to *see* several moves ahead at any point in time. Managers and HR professionals are in a key position to promote this kind of foresight and help decision makers with the ability to consistently look "around the corner" when faced with difficult and strategic decisions.

See also Strategic Planning; SWOT Analysis

NOTES

1. Thomas J. Chermack and Richard A. Swanson, "Scenario Planning: HRD's Strategic Learning Tool," *Advances in Developing Human Resources* 10, no. 2 (2008): 129–46.

2. Hardin Tibbs, "Pierre Wack: A Remarkable Source of Insight," *Global Business Network News* 9, no. 1 (1998): 6.

3. Ibid., 8.

4. Thomas J. Chermack and Susan A. Lynham, "Definitions and Outcome Variables of Scenario Planning," *Human Resource Development Review* 1, no. 3 (2002): 376.

5. Pierre Wack, "Scenarios: Shooting the Rapids," *Harvard Business Review* 63, no. 6 (1985): 89.

6. Ron Bradfield, George Wright, George Burt, George Cairns, and Kees van derHeijden, "The Origin and Evolution of Scenario Techniques in Long Range Business Planning," *Futures* 37, no. 2 (2005): 795–812.

7. Wack, "Scenarios: Shooting the Rapids."

8. Ibid., 39.

9. Ibid., 62.

Thomas J. Chermack

SHORT-TERM EXECUTIVE

A short-term executive is a member of organizational management hired for a predefined period of time, as opposed to the standard open-ended terms of employment found with

most permanent-hire positions. The roles filled by short-term executives most often consist of the upper level, or "C-suite level" of management. It is not uncommon for businesses to bring in short-term executives to fill in as the chief executive officer, chief
operating officer, or chief financial officer. This type of arrangement also goes by many
other names, the most common of which are interim management, interim executive,
temporary management, and temporary executive.

The use of short-term executives dates back to the 1970s, when the oil-shortage crisis
triggered a wave of mergers, closings, and layoffs affecting the upper-management ranks
of businesses. This created an abundance of experienced executives available in the job
market. This abundance of supply allowed for companies to pull in previously unavailable
talent to handle specialized projects and provide leadership during periods of organizational change.[1] Thus, the short-term executive became an option available to resolve
human resources needs.

From the 1970s through the 1990s, the typical short-term executive was a white male,
over 55 years old, and financially secure due to early retirement or golden parachute packages from previous employers.[2] This has been changing since the 1990s, as more and
more young professional men and women of all races have decided to work independently
and offer their talents as short-term executives in all industries. The trend of industries has
been to look for individuals they believe will produce the best results for the organization,
with less emphasis being placed on years of experience.

The use of short-term executives has been increasing since the 1970s, with the most
notable jump in popularity occurring in the early 2000s. According to the U.S. Bureau
of Labor Statistics, temporary workers at the executive or professional levels accounted
for 7 percent of the workforce in 1998. In 2004, that percentage had climbed to
11 percent.[3] The specialized field of interim management has become a $750 million-
per-year industry in the United States.[4]

Reasons Companies Use Short-term Executives

Companies hire short-term executives for a variety of reasons, though the recurring theme
for them is to be agents of change. The most common scenarios short-term executives are
brought in to handle include:
• Restructuring an organization after catastrophic actions or behaviors of previous leaders
• Guiding a company through a period of major transition due to changing market forces
• Ushering in major changes to an organization at the request of an organization's board of
  directors, shareholders, or owners
• Handling restructuring of departments due to changes in governmental regulations and
  requirements
• Providing a placeholder of sorts while an organization searches for a permanent replacement
  for the position
• Providing specialized talent for a short-term need of the organization, much like a business
  consultant

Distinctions between Short-term Executives and Consultants

Consultants are often brought in to handle the same sort of "change agent" activities
sought from short-term executives. A consultant, though, does not become a true member
of the organization they work for, as a short-term executive does. The primary distinction

between a consultant and a short-term executive is the level of ownership a short-term executive takes in their role within the organization to which they are hired.[5]

Consultants often cannot provide the same level of dedication to their clients that a short-term executive can provide. This is because consultants generally have to balance their efforts between several different clients, while a short-term executive works exclusively for the organization they were hired by for the duration of the contract.

Hiring a Short-term Executive

Making the decision to hire a short-term executive is quite similar to the process of hiring a permanent executive. Many of the same skill sets are needed to fulfill the position, regardless of the length of commitment. Human resource professionals need to evaluate their organization's needs and existing resources, as well as the cost to the operation of not filling the perceived need, prior to deciding to go the short-term executive route.[6] As with most C-suite hiring processes, the human resources department is most involved in the initial phases, leaving orientation and training up to the existing executives to handle.

Short-term executives can be found through word of mouth, through professional networking, or by contacting a firm specializing in the placement of short-term executives. Every major metropolitan area in the United States has at least one of these firms serving regional needs of this sort. Payment to the individual depends upon the agreement and methodology of hire. There are no firm rules to follow with this type of employment, short of following federal, state, and local regulations.

One of the biggest advantages for the company and the individual pursuing the short-term executive methodology is that they both get a chance to learn more about each other. If the organization and the individual find a perfect match in philosophy, process, and culture, it is likely they will decide to make the employment arrangement permanent. This perhaps explains why over one-third of those hired on as short-term executives transition into being permanent members of management by the end of their contract.[7]

See also Employment Agencies, Search Firms, and Headhunters; Recruiting

NOTES

1. Dennis Russell and Ian Daniell, *The Interim Management: The New Career Choice for Senior Managers,* 2nd ed. (Salcombe, England: Aveton Books, 2005).

2. Ibid.

3. Martha Frase-Blunt, "Short-term Executives: Companies That Need an Executive for a Special Purpose—to Launch a Project, to Fill In during an Absence—Are Hiring Temps for the Job," *HRMagazine,* June 2004, 6.

4. Dale Buss, "More Companies Hire Temporary Executives," *Wall Street Journal: Executive Career Site,* http://www.careerjournal.com/jobhunting/strategies/20041014-buss.html (accessed October 20, 2007).

5. Marilyn Dickey, "Interim Leaders Bring Skills but No Personal Agendas to Their Tasks," *Chronicle of Philanthropy,* March 22, 2007, 11.

6. Frase-Blunt, "Short-term Executives," 6.

7. Ibid.

Adam VanDreumel

STRATEGIC COMMUNICATION

A strategy is a "long-term plan for achieving goals and objectives; specifically, it represents agreement between external opportunity and internal capability."[1] Communication is the process of transmitting information and meaning.[2] Strategic communication, therefore, is long-term, planned communication processes and tactics that enable an organization to achieve its vision, mission, goals, and objectives. These processes encompass every functional area internal to the organization as well as address all foreseeable external constituencies.

Miscommunications are commonplace in business. Frequent target issues for miscommunication at the organizational level include mergers/acquisitions, vision, mission, goals and objectives, layoffs, location closings, poor performance/financials, and any major organizational change. At the functional departmental level, miscommunications surround mission, goals, objectives, direction, new initiatives, expectations of supervisors, managers, and employees, division/department performance, team expectations, and any change. Interpersonally, common miscommunications occur with regard to goals, standards, and expectations, poor performance, terminations and demotions, changes in job responsibilities, conflict, and any change.

Just as organizations include product development, marketing, engineering, sales, and human resources in their strategic plans, so too should they include effective communication. Communication permeates all organizational levels and often determines the success of individuals, units, or initiatives. Consequently, improving communication enhances individual and organizational performance.

Costs of Miscommunication

An insurance carrier introduced a new homeowner's product, yet failed to notify its internal customer service department with predictable results. A large meat processor neglected to notify its customers that it had shipped beef contaminated with E.coli; they were later accused of a cover-up. A manufacturer attempted to conceal a warehouse fire from the public, only to be embarrassed when the story made the evening news. A small firm notified its workforce of the names of 20 employees to be laid off via company-wide e-mail on the Friday before Christmas, resulting in devastated company morale and productivity. Each of these real-world scenarios could have been avoided with effective strategic communication.

Organizational miscommunication directly, and negatively, impacts the bottom line. Costs of poor communication include (but are certainly not limited to) lower morale, lack of commitment and employee loyalty, decreases in productivity, inefficiency of processes, loss of goodwill and reputation, shareholder mistrust, and lost business opportunities.

Components of Effective Communication Plans

Communicating strategically requires systematically planning all messages to be shared in coordination with their associated events. Whether delivering information related to a company expansion, change in direction, acquisition, new product launch, lay-offs, or modification of benefits, the message must be carefully crafted. Organizations can begin by answering the following questions:

What? What (message) is to be communicated?
To whom? Which stakeholders will be affected? Employees, vendors, shareholders, the
   community? Which stakeholders take priority, if any?

By whom? Who is responsible for sending the message and possesses the necessary communication talent? The public relations (PR) department, president/CEO, a vice president, human resources, a department or unit manager? Who is most credible based on the message?

How? Which channel (or medium) is appropriate? Face-to-face (press conference, group meetings, one-on-one), e-mail, voice mail, memorandum, letter, fax?

When? Is the time line appropriate? How much advance notice do stakeholders require?

Resource needs? If the message or situation is complex, what resources are needed to ensure effective communication? Large meeting rooms, quiet office, technology?

Answers to these questions provide essential information for organizations to develop an effective strategic communication plan, regardless of the message to be delivered.

Process of Communication

The process of communication begins with a sender who has an idea, encodes a message, and transmits it through a channel to a receiver, who then decodes the message. Encoding puts the message into a form that the receiver will understand. The communication channel—the media that carries messages to receivers—may be verbal, nonverbal, or written. Decoding occurs when the receiver interprets the meaning of the message *as intended by the sender.*[3] Miscommunication typically occurs when barriers are encountered during the encoding or decoding phases.

Effectiveness of Communication Methods

Carefully selecting your channel enhances the effectiveness of the communication process. Communication channels can be verbal, nonverbal, and written. The most effective communication channel is face to face, followed by other formal channels including telephone conversations, letters and memos, and e-mail/text messages.

Verbal Communication

Verbal communication channels include face-to-face interactions (one-on-one conversations or group meetings) and telephone conversations (including voice-mail messages). Face-to-face conversations and meetings are considered the richest communication channels, as they allow participants to secure immediate feedback. By observing nonverbal cues (body language, facial expressions, eye contact) and assessing tone and inflection, the sender can immediately clarify or modify the message if necessary. Face-to-face communication is necessary when sharing information that is critical, complex, or private, and for developing and maintaining good interpersonal relations. One-on-one and group communication can be time-consuming, however, and in most cases leave no written record of the interaction.

Phone conversations allow participants to engage in personal, meaningful discussions and quick exchanges. The drawbacks, however, are that they lack the benefit of immediate feedback afforded by observation of nonverbal cues and, like some face-to-face channels, there is no documentation of the communication.

Written Communication

Letters, memoranda, reports, and newsletters represent effective means to convey general, detailed, or abundant information to a large audience. The greatest advantage to written communication is the record it provides. To the contrary, one inherent disadvantage to written communication is that it often reveals the sender's poor writing ability, which may distort the content of the message, thereby affecting the meaning. Contrary to face-to-face communication, the senders and receivers are "blind" to the other's nonverbal cues, making it difficult to provide immediate feedback. There is little opportunity here for clarification until *after* a miscommunication occurs.

E-mail and text messaging are considered poor forms of communication, despite their wide use. E-mail is a convenient, quick, low-cost, acceptable method for conveying routine information. Unfortunately, most e-mail users write too quickly, fail to proofread or review the message, and send messages that are riddled with errors and/or misconvey the sender's tone and attitude. Speed potential is a serious consideration; many an e-mail sender has regretted the inability to retrieve a poorly written message.

Communication Barriers

The relatively simple process of communication, when combined with the complexity of individuals and organizations, often yields disappointing results. Numerous barriers impede communication at the individual (personal) level as well as the organizational level.

Interpersonal Barriers

Human beings are complex creatures whose behaviors manifest the sum of their varied experiences (or commonly referred to as life experience). This life experience includes our education, work life, family history, and so on. Thus, the barriers that inhibit our communication occur when there are discrepancies, or differences, in our life experience surrounding education, family, gender, perceptions, history, age, etc. These differences may result in biases, stereotypes, distrust, negative emotions, poor listening skills, misuse of slang, personal filters, information overload, or omission, all of which leads to interference with message transmission or interpretation.

Organizational Barriers

Within organizations, we compound our personal barriers with those encountered in a group or work setting. In addition to our own self-imposed obstacles, on the job we encounter additional barriers, including information overload or omission, lack of communication skills among supervisors, peers, and subordinates, poor group dynamics, dysfunctional organizational culture, diversity challenges, approximation and ambiguity, power and status constraints, peer pressure, and industrial or organizational slang. With these barriers in mind, organizations would be well served to take a proactive approach and develop a clear, strategic communication plan.

Strategically Planned Communication

Failure to plan results in planned failure. Communication is no exception. Approaching communication strategically, like any other business function, improves the degree of success and, ultimately, organizational results. By ignoring the importance of communication in the strategic planning process, organizations will find that more often than not, miscommunication will be the rule when it should be the exception.

See also HR Strategy; Managerial Communications

NOTES

1. Robert Kreitner, *Foundations of Management: Basics and Best Practices* (Boston: Houghton Mifflin, 2005).

2. Robert N. Lussier, *Management Fundamentals: Concepts, Applications, Skill Development,* 3rd ed. (Mason, OH: Thomson South-Western, 2006).

3. Dan O'Hair, Gustav W. Friedrich, and Lynda Dee Dixon, *Strategic Communication in Business and the Professions,* 5th ed. (Boston: Houghton Mifflin, 2005).

Ann Gilley, Brenda E. Ogden, and Jerry W. Gilley

STRATEGIC PLANNING

Strategic planning is the process of developing long-term (greater than one year) goals, objectives, and tactics. Organizational leaders, primarily top-level executives, are responsible for strategic planning, which includes crafting an organization's vision and mission.

Operational planning, in contrast, is the process of developing short-term (one year or less) goals, objectives, and procedures. Middle and frontline managers typically create and/or implement operational plans that govern day-to-day business activities.

Strategic Levels

Strategic planning occurs at three strategic levels—corporate, business, and functional. Corporate-level strategy sets the direction for the entire firm and its multiple lines of business. Top-level executives at organizations such as General Motors, 3M, Starbucks, and Hewlett-Packard determine the overall strategic directions for their firms. Business-level strategy involves planning for one particular line or product of the firm. The Saturn division of General Motors is an example, as is the Homeowner's Insurance division of State Farm. Functional-level strategy focuses on one area of business, such as design, marketing, operations, human resources, or customer service.

Competitive Strategies

Approaches to strategic planning focus heavily on competitiveness and dominance in the marketplace. Three effective corporate-level competitive strategies are operational efficiency, product leadership, and customer intimacy.[1] Once a company has determined its strategy, the firm should devote its resources to excelling in that area in order to be successful, even world class.

Operationally efficient companies offer lower prices to attract customers. These firms maximize the efficiency of their operations via technology and economies of scale. They then pass their cost savings on to their customers. Wal-Mart and Dell Computers are examples.

With a product leadership strategy, a company focuses its resources on delivering the best products in terms of quality, innovation, and technology. These firms invest heavily in quality initiatives, research and development, and technological advances to provide clients with products that are considered state-of-the-art or of superior quality or prestige. Sony and Rolls Royce are examples.

Customer-intimate firms develop relationships with their clients to uncover their unique wants and needs. These companies then develop customized solutions for their customers. Consulting firms, custom home builders, and physicians are examples.

SWOT Analysis

One of the first steps in strategic planning entails determining the capabilities of the firm given the constraints of its internal and external environments. SWOT analysis provides a tool by which firms assess their environments in terms of strengths, weaknesses, opportunities, and threats (SWOT).

Strengths and weaknesses are components of the internal environment and those factors over which the organization has control. Examples include workforce talent, technology, well-known brands, the firm's reputation, quality of leadership/management, availability of resources, manufacturing processes and patents, and so forth. Identification of strengths and weaknesses enables a company to focus its resources on maximizing its capabilities and minimizing or overcoming its limitations.

Opportunities and threats are posed by the external environment, yet influence the company and its operations. Opportunities and threats include the economy, competitors, legislative environment, societal trends, changing technology, industry forces, and more. Although a firm has no control over the external environment, it must be keenly aware of potential opportunities to be exploited or threats to be avoided.

Vision, Mission, Goals, and Objectives

Strategic planning entails crafting an organization's vision, mission, goals, and objectives. The *vision* represents the ideal, the epitome of what the firm desires to become (often the "best," or "world class"). The *mission* reveals what the company will do to achieve its vision—who it will serve, what it will produce, and so forth. Goals and objectives support the broader vision and mission by specifying how an organization will accomplish its tasks via quantity and quality measures. Effective goals and objectives are SMART—that is, specific, measurable, agreed upon, realistic, and time bound.[2]

See also Competitive Advantage; SWOT Analysis

NOTES

1. Michael Treacy and Fred Wiersema, *The Discipline of Market Leaders* (New York: Basic Books, 2005).
2. Jerry W. Gilley and Ann Gilley, *Strategically Integrated HRD: Six Transformational Roles in Creating Results Driven Programs* (Cambridge, MA: Perseus Publishing, 2003).

Ann Gilley and Jerry W. Gilley

SUCCESSION PLANNING

Succession planning is a talent management process that enables an organization to ensure its future prosperity. The process is used to identify, assess, and develop employees who are viewed as having potential to succeed in management positions. The outcome is a plan that identifies employees who have the potential to be developed and groomed to someday manage a department, manage a division, or become CEO of an organization. Why the need for succession planning? There is a demographic shift in the workforce that is primarily driving the need for succession planning; the exodus of baby boomers from the workforce. Leaders, specifically those in the C suite (e.g., CEO, CFO, CIO) in organizations are becoming eligible for retirement within the next decade. The decisions regarding succession planning have a direct impact on long-term organizational profitability and sustainability.

The succession planning process can be used for all levels of management in the organization, but it is more typically applied to upper-level management positions. While there is no one right way to design a succession plan, there are generally five steps involved:[1]

1. Identify potential successors
2. Develop a formal development plan for the successor
3. Determine a timetable
4. Create a transition plan for the incumbent
5. Transfer the successor into the role (prior to the incumbent's departure so that coaching and mentoring can be incorporated into the development plan)

Candidates and the respective development plans should be reviewed semiannually. Developmental progress, outcomes achieved, and observation of day-to-day performance should be discussed with regard to readiness for expanded developmental projects or responsibilities.

Other Types of Succession Strategies

Given that many industries are faced with rapidly and continuously changing markets, organizations may choose to use "succession management,"[2] which is geared toward developing a group of employees who have demonstrated the competencies required for management through on-the-job-experiences in the organization.

Fast-track programs, or replacement planning, are also used in organizations. These succession strategies are used to prepare for circumstances where there is an immediate need for a qualified backup in key management positions. The emphasis is placed on identifying a qualified candidate vs. employees with development potential, which is the focus of succession planning. Further, the time frame for replacement planning tends to be less than one year, whereas succession planning typically lasts between one and three years.

Regardless of the succession strategy used, it is imperative that an organization have preestablished criteria in place for selection of high-potential or qualified candidates. Further, the process used should not exclude employees based on protected characteristics such as age or gender. Caution should also be taken with regard to reactions from employees who are not selected as "high potential." There can be resentment or a feeling of favoritism if the plan is not communicated and implemented with careful thought.

Conclusion

Change is a constant for organizations today. A change that is driving the need for succession planning is the mass departure of baby boomers within the next decade. Retirement of senior managers and the C suite (e.g., CEO, CFO, CIO) in organizations will create a large gap in leadership talent. Succession planning is about sustaining the organization throughout constant change.

See also Recruiting

NOTES

1. Jon M. Werner and Randy L. DeSimone, *Human Resource Development* (Mason, OH: Cengage Learning, 2009).
2. Ibid.

Pamela Dixon

SWOT ANALYSIS

One of the best ways to prepare for a human resource planning activity or talent inventory is to conduct an internal and external environmental analysis. Upon completion, HR professionals and managers have identified the strengths and weaknesses of employees (internal environment) and the opportunities and threats (external environment) facing the firm, which determine the future human capital required to remain competitive in the marketplace. This analysis is often referred to as a SWOT analysis. SWOT stands for strengths, weaknesses, opportunities, and threats.

Strengths and weaknesses (SW), which are internal, are completely under the company's control. For example, a firm's strengths or weaknesses may be due to its leadership, policies, procedures, strategy, assets, employee talent, product mix, reputation, and so forth. Opportunities and threats (OT), in contrast, are external to the firm and *beyond its control,* yet may influence the firm's business. Opportunities and threats may be posed by competitors, laws and regulations, the economy, weather and natural disasters, changing consumer preferences, trends, and the like.

SWOT analysis information is useful in making adjustments in human resource forecasts and utilization, and taking corrective actions necessary to overcome weakness and address threats. This information also helps organizations build on strengths and capitalize on opportunities.

Internal Environmental Analysis

Several questions and statements are useful when conducting an internal environmental analysis:

1. What is the financial condition of the organization?
2. What are the aptitudes and abilities of managers and employees?
3. What is the current condition of facilities?
4. What is the current state and quality of technology?
5. What is the quality and quantity of internal human and material resources?
6. How is the organization structured?
7. Describe the organizational culture.
8. Describe the work climate within the organization.
9. Describe the managerial practices within the organization.
10. Identify the policies and procedures that enhance or impede organizational performance, effectiveness, and development.
11. Describe organizational leadership
12. Identify the organization's mission and strategy.
13. Describe the organizational learning system.
14. Describe the compensation and reward system.

15. Describe the performance appraisal and coaching process.
16. Does the organization advocate employee growth and development?
17. Is organizational renewal and competitive readiness important to the organization?
18. What performance gaps exist within the organization?
19. What organizational effectiveness gaps exist?
20. What is the current state of human resource practice within the organization?[1]

Once these questions are addressed, HR professionals and managers are able to describe each in relationship to its strengths, weaknesses, and impact on long-term human resource planning

External Environmental Analysis

External environmental analysis reveals the health of an organization, its values, political climate, use of technology and resources, competitive rank within its industry, overall image, and areas requiring improvement.[2] Such information will be invaluable to HR professionals and developmental organization leaders when making decisions regarding the allocation and utilization of human resources.

Several questions that will assist in examination of the external environment include:

1. What are the economic conditions of the nation, region, and local community?
2. What social and cultural values predominate within the industry and its geographic region?
3. What quantity and quality of technology does the organization employ to achieve business results?
4. What external human resources are available?
5. What is the quantity and quality of external human resources?
6. What is the organization's image in the marketplace?
7. What is the company's competitive rank within the industry?[3]

Identifying the opportunities and threats facing an organization allows HR professionals, managers, and organizational leaders to avoid costly mistakes common when conducting human resource planning activities and talent inventories. Both are extremely important to the long-term competitiveness of an organization and, ultimately, their success.

See also Competitive Advantage; Strategic Planning

NOTES

1. Jerry W. Gilley and Ann Maycunich Gilley, *Strategically Integrated HRD: Six Transformational Roles in Creating Results Driven Programs* (Cambridge, MA: Perseus Publishing, 2003).
2. Ibid.
3. Ibid, 100.

Jerry W. Gilley and Ann Gilley

VISION, MISSION, GOALS, AND OBJECTIVES

A vision statement conveys the purpose and value of an organization. A vision statement reveals a company's reason for existence and should drive its performance. It provides insight on where the company is headed and what it wishes to become. A firm's vision drives its mission and goals.

Mission statements explain who a company serves in terms of stakeholders—customers, shareholders, employees, and the community. A mission statement supports the vision. Goals further define how a company will achieve its vision and mission. A vision statement describes "what" the firm hopes to become, the mission describes "who" it will serve, and goals/objectives explain "how." The vision drives a firm's mission and goals, while goals and mission support the vision.

Purpose

Vision statements are sometimes confused with mission statements, although each has a distinct purpose. An organization's vision and mission statements together reveal its overall strategy. The *vision* statement represents what the firm strives to eventually become and how it wants to be perceived by others. The vision is the ideal that guides the firm's long- and short-term actions. Vision statements often assert the firm's desire to be "number one," "the leader," or "world class." The vision should powerfully rally the organization and its members around a common cause. Top-level executives envision the firm's future and must empower their followers to achieve it. The vision, therefore, must be clearly articulated to, understood, and embraced by all individuals within company.

The vision drives the *mission* statement, which identifies what the company will do, what it will produce, and who it will serve (customers, employees, shareholders, society, the community, and other stakeholders) in its quest to achieve the vision. For example, mission statements commonly report that the firm will provide (1) quality, innovative products to its customers, (2) a healthy, safe working environment for employees, (3) a fair rate of return for shareholders, and (4) support or service to the community. Mission statements support the vision and are the basis for goals and objectives.

Vision

Creating the vision is the first step in strategic planning. A vision is a broad yet succinct statement that describes the direction of the company, and reveals what the company aims for in the long term, which is typically to be the best in what it does. This is often stated in the desire to be "#1" or "world class." The vision draws upon the desire of an organization to be the best, and drives the mission, goals, and objectives of a company. An appropriate vision is not generic to an industry; it is specific to the organization. The company's values and priorities are an important consideration when developing its vision.

When writing a vision, companies want to make sure that it is future-oriented, focuses on one purpose, is specific to the company, and that it is no more than one or two sentences. Effective visions capture the spirit of the organization's desire to be the best and guide employee behavior at all levels. It becomes a source of pride as well as an important goal.

Although the executive leadership team often develops the vision, input from employees increases their understanding of and commitment to it. Organizational leaders are responsible for communicating the firm's vision to all employees and rallying their support. A vision ceases to be effective when organizational employees are unaware of it.

Mission

A firm's mission describes who it will serve in its quest to be the best. Creating the mission is the second step in strategic planning. The mission should support the vision.

Effective mission statements clearly and concisely explain who the firm serves and how. The stakeholders of a company include any individual or firm that has an interest in its success. These constituent groups may include employees, customers, vendors, shareholders, the community, and others.

An effective mission statement addresses the following concepts:
— Ethical position of the company
— Description of target market and desired public image
— Product/service description
— Geographic domain[1]

An example of typical wording of a mission statement is: "We will provide our employees with a healthy, motivating work environment; our customers with high-quality products and services; and our shareholders with a competitive rate of return; while being enthusiastic supporters of the community." Again, a firm's mission supports its vision to be the best.

Goals and Objectives

Goals and objectives are specific statements of results a company wishes to achieve in both the short term and long term. Goals are built upon what is stated in the vision and mission, and provide details as to "how" it will achieve short- and long-term success. Short-term goals are those which can be achieved in a year or less. Long-term goals are those that exceed a year; these typically promote a firm's lengthy viability. Preoccupation with profits can lead to short-term thinking at the expense of long-term success. Broader goals that support the mission include market standing, productivity, management and worker performance, innovation, and public responsibility. Objectives indicate specifically what is to be accomplished and the level of performance to be achieved.[2] For example, an organizational goal might be to increase sales this year; the objective might be by 8 percent.

When writing goals the SMART criteria should be kept in mind:

Specific—goals should be clear and precise, not broad
Measurable—quantifiable, not vague
Achievable—realistic and attainable, while still challenging
Results-oriented—productive, must support meeting of goals
Time-based—a specific time period must be given in which to meet goal[3]

Within organizations, each person, unit, department, and division often has its own specific goals. These should, ultimately, support the mission and vision of the organization at large. Individual performance evaluations, for example, over time are often altered to the point that they fail to support the broader goals of the firm and cease to be truly effective in helping it achieve its mission and vision. Care must be taken, then, to ensure continuous alignment of individual, group, departmental, and divisional objectives with organizational focuses.

Ambiguous, open-ended goals serve little purpose and often go unmet. Motivating, successful objectives clearly specify what is to be accomplished, the measurement criterion, are agreed upon by those responsible for achievement, are attainable, and subject to a time frame. "Be friendlier" is a broad goal. "Receive three satisfactory to exemplary customer evaluation cards each month" represents a realistic objective when established collaboratively with the person who will be held responsible for its achievement.

Conclusion

A visions reveals what a company wants to be, a mission states who the company serves, and goals explain how a company will achieve success. Each step builds upon the other.

NOTES

1. "Mission Statement," Business Resource Software, Inc., November 30, 2006. http:// businessplans.org/Mission.html (accessed August 18, 2008).

2. Robert N. Lussier, *Management Fundamentals,* 3rd ed. (Mason, OH: Thomson South-Western, 2006).

3. Jerry W. Gilley and Ann Gilley, *Strategically Integrated HRD: Six Transformational Roles in Creating Results Driven Programs* (Cambridge, MA: Perseus Publishing, 2003).

Maria Valladares

Chapter 7

Organizational Development and Change

Organizational Development and Change: An Overview

Centuries ago Plato said, "Change takes place no matter what deters it." This statement still rings true. The dynamic world in which we live forces individuals and organizations to routinely engage in change. A firm's long-term viability depends more and more on its ability to change and continuously grow, develop, and reinvent or renew itself. Many companies report that they undergo moderate organizational change at least once a year, and major changes every four to five years.[1] And yet, fewer than 40 percent of change efforts produce positive change, while nearly one-third of major change efforts do not work or actually make the situation worse.[2] What can be done to improve the rate of successful change within firms? Organizational development is one approach.

Organizational Development

Organizational development (OD) is planned, continuous, incremental change intended to improve a firm's performance. When regular, incremental change occurs over time, OD becomes a way of life.[3]

Organizational development is both a philosophy and a process of organizational improvement. Developing innovative approaches to problem solving and establishing a "survivalist attitude" in a continuously evolving environment of cultural change and technological advancement improves overall organizational effectiveness. OD encompasses a systemwide process of data collection, diagnosis, action planning, intervention, and evaluation. The result is enhanced alignment between organizational structure, processes, strategy, people, culture, development of new and creative organizational solutions, and increased organizational self-renewing capacity.[4]

Organizational development draws from many different fields and types of initiatives to achieve its goals. Organizational design/redesign, leadership/management development, strategic planning, change management, team building, internal training/coaching, and performance management systems are among a few. OD practitioners, whether members of the management team or housed in HR, constantly seek new ways to improve the human part of the system and, thus, focus on humanistic rather than behaviorist strategies. Although the field relies on theory from psychology and organizational behavior, the results are practical, relevant, and critical to business success.

Benefits of Organizational Development

Organizational development and change yield a wealth of benefits to all levels and for all members of a firm. Benefits to the organization include improved culture, communications, teamwork, quality, creativity and innovation, loyalty, decision making, and goal achievement. Individuals note improved work climate, morale, support from management, involvement, creativity, respect, communications, and job security, to name a few.

Organizational development provides opportunities for employees to develop to their fullest potential while helping the firm achieve its strategic goals and objectives. An exciting, challenging work environment nurtures creativity while tapping the complex set of skills, values, and needs held by each contributor, regardless of title or level within the firm. Creativity and informed risk-taking combine with effective information gathering to produce new solutions or solve problems in innovative ways. As individuals are empowered to influence their work via involvement and support, valuable contributions are made to organizational performance and long-term viability.

Principles of Organizational Development and Change

The heart of organizational development is change; thus OD and change are often combined into ODC (organizational development and change). To understand the complexity of organizational development, one must understand change.

Types of Change. At the corporate or macro level, common organizational development and changes enhance strategy, structure, and culture, often involving different leadership or reporting lines, acquisitions, expansion or downsizing, or incorporation of new technologies.

Change is often defined as transitional, transformational, or developmental. *Transitional* change, the most common and basic, represents continuous management-driven efforts to enhance the current state by modifying structure, policies, or procedures, utilizing technology, or increasing staffing levels. *Transformational* change radically shifts from the current state, involving personal behaviors and mind-sets. Transformational changes alter the culture, formulate new, drastically different strategy, or involve being acquired by another firm and being forced to conform to its ways.

Developmental change, the foundation of organizational development, is an overall philosophy of continuous growth and development for individuals and organizations. Developmental organizations continually scan their internal and external environments for opportunities, making regular, incremental changes along the way. Motivating, healthy work environments encourage innovation, personal growth and development, renewal, involvement, partnering, and a sense of ownership and commitment among organizational members by incorporating manageable changes gradually, and avoiding large-scale, radical change.

Change Audits. The first step in approaching change is to complete a change audit, which assesses a firm's past experiences with and present approach to change, along with future capabilities.[5] Change audits examine the firm's culture with respect to change, types of changes that occurred in the past (e.g., small, moderate, large-scale), who was responsible, when change efforts occurred, how changes were implemented, barriers at the time (e.g., culture, poor management or communications, insufficient resources), and success or failure rates (results).

Evaluating the current state of readiness for change reveals attitudes toward change (e.g., resistance, fear, etc.), status of current change efforts, types of change in progress, implementation techniques, willingness and ability of participants, barriers, and conditions that will be necessary for successful change. A thorough internal analysis assesses company strengths and weaknesses including leadership talent, level of cultural dysfunction, effectiveness of structure, policies and procedures, resource availability, and so forth.

A change audit concludes with an action plan that specifies what must happen for change to successfully occur. How can gaps in ability be lessened, barriers be reduced or eliminated, and willingness enhanced? An action plan details how success will be measured (e.g., based on impact on people or processes, profitability, congruence with organizational mission and goals, etc.), who should lead future changes and why, how change should be implemented, resource needs, how to overcome obstacles, and how success should be celebrated.

Change Implementation

Implementing change requires understanding the impact of change on people and their organizations, as well as skill in change techniques. Continuous ODC demands expertise on the part of individuals throughout the firm. A culture of change exists when all organizational members understand, appreciate, and are involved in current and future change efforts.

HR plays a critical role in change by educating and training managers in the fundamentals of change. Mentoring, observations, workshops, seminars, and collaborative teaming sessions allow HRM professionals to assess individual talents and capabilities with respect to change, and create appropriate change expertise growth and development plans.

Change Management. Change management models attempt to guide organizations and their people through change. Early change models offered a simple three-step process that evaluated and prepared a firm for change, engaged in the change, and solidified the change into the daily operations of the firm. Lewin's classic model, for example, consists of *unfreezing, movement,* and *refreezing.*[6] Unfreezing assesses and readies individuals and organizations for change; movement occurs when individuals engage in the change process; and refreezing anchors the new way into the daily routine, behaviors, and culture of the organization.

More extensive, multistep change frameworks include components of leadership, employee involvement, rewards, and communication, to name a few. Kotter and Ulrich for example, each developed models that include vision, empowerment, guiding coalitions, commitment, "selling" the change, and more.[7] Although these models provide valuable guidelines for planning and implementing change, they assume that change will occur successfully if all of the steps are followed in sequence. This assumption fails to understand and accommodate natural human resistance, or overcome obstacles to change. A more realistic, in-depth, comprehensive guideline for change implementation suggests that change leaders:

1. Understand that change is immensely complex.
2. Understand individual and organizational responses (resistance) to change, and how to deal with these responses.
3. Create a culture that supports change.
4. Establish a vision for ongoing change.
5. Build a guiding coalition for the change.

6. "Sell" the need for continuous change to individuals at all levels of the organization; help people understand that the change is necessary, urgent; teach that change is good, desirable.
7. Remove barriers to action.
8. Involve employees at all levels of the organization in change processes (including initial decision making, planning, implementation, monitoring, and rewarding).
9. Communicate proficiently; solicit input and share information with those impacted by the change; lack of information breeds fear.
10. Prepare for and plan responses to resistance; treat resistance to change as an opportunity; understand that resistance is a symptom of a deeper problem (e.g., poor management or strategy, ineffective communication, etc.).
11. Deal with employees and their reactions individually, not as a group.
12. Execute ongoing changes in small increments.
13. Constantly monitor progress of change initiatives and refine/adjust as needed.
14. Reward individuals and groups for engaging in change.
15. Celebrate short- and long-term wins.
16. Solidify changes in the newly emerged culture.[8]

People and Change. Individuals approach, react to, and accept change in different ways and at varying rates. Predisposition toward change is a component of ones personality. *Acceptance Rates of Change:* According to Rogers, individual acceptance rates of change vary greatly and depend on the degree of newness as perceived by the individual.[9] Acceptance of change is described in stages such as *awareness* of the change, *interest* in the change, the *decision* to quit or continue, and *adoption* of the change into one's life. Five categories of individuals have been identified based on their general acceptance of change as innovators, early adopters, early majority, late majority, and laggards.

Innovators: 2.5 percent of population; thrive on change and take pride in being the first to accept change.
Early adopters: 13.5 percent of population; like challenges and are supportive of change.
Early majority: 34 percent of population; prefer to observe the impact of change on innovators and early adopters; are deliberate accepters of change.
Late majority: 34 percent of population; skeptical of change, often succumb to peer pressure or change only as a last resort.
Laggards: 16 percent of population; resist change and attempt to hold on to the past, often reject change completely.

Rogers' research implies that approximately half of employees are more accepting of change, while half are more resistant. Those who accept change more readily exhibit certain personality characteristics, such as a more favorable attitude toward change, a more rational approach, have higher aspirations, are better able to cope with ambiguity and risk, are more knowledgeable of change, and have more contact with change agents. Nearly half of the population is predisposed against change, which will present a challenge to those responsible for ODC. Additional personal attention, communication, or meetings to uncover fear or explore opportunities may be necessary to increase their comfort levels with impending change.
Phases of Response to Change: Individuals respond to change in one of four ways: denial, resistance, exploration, or commitment.[10] Each phase represents unique and specific perceptions, emotions, and reactions of those facing change. Helping people work through the phases of change and to commitment is a critical role of leaders, managers, and anyone responsible for organizational development and change.

Denial, a common initial reaction to change, surfaces when people are naïve in the belief that the change will have little, if any, impact on them personally. Symptoms of denial include lack of engagement in the change, an unrealistic enthusiasm relative to the change, and statements such as, "This won't involve me," or "No big deal." Moving past denial and facing change more honestly involves increasing their understanding of their role in change and how it will impact them personally, involving them in the change process, providing adequate information relative to the change, and encouraging feedback.

Resistance occurs when the proposed change has become personal and is perceived as negative. People doubt the change or its benefits to them as a result of receiving additional information—accurate or not—regarding the looming change. In this phase, individuals realize the difficulty, inconvenience, or personal hardship they will face, and some begin to actively resist. Symptoms of resistance include withdrawal, blaming, arguing, negativism, gossip, refusal to attempt change, slowdown of work, sabotage, and increased absenteeism, to name a few. Commonly heard statements include, "They can't make me change," "It won't work," or "The old way is better."

Exploration, which is phase three, reflects progress in acceptance of the proposed change. In this phase, people are hopeful and seek positive outcomes of the change. Although cynicism and fear do not completely disappear, individuals recognize the eventuality of or necessity for change on a personal level. Symptoms of exploration consist of questions pertaining to potential benefits, a greater willingness for personal involvement, and employees helping each other with specific tasks or change related issues. Employee statements include, "This might work," "How can I...," and "Show me..."

Commitment is characterized by acceptance of the change as positive and incorporation of changed behaviors into daily organizational life. Symptoms of the fourth phase include employee support of the change and involvement in managing its implementation. Commonly heard statements include, "It's working," and "Let me help with that."

Some people navigate quickly through the change process, while others need more time, stall, or vacillate between phases. Understanding human reactions to change and responding appropriately are the keys to leading people through the change process and to acceptance. Providing information, soliciting feedback, and encouraging involvement help individuals overcome their natural resistance and work through change. People desire information, being involved, making a difference, conquering a challenge, and being rewarded for their efforts.

Organizations and Change. Organizations are simply collections of people. Therefore, as individuals change or resist, so do their organizations. "Individual and organizational behaviors and reactions are remarkably similar...individual behaviors manifest themselves as organizational actions—the two cannot be separated."[11]

People resist change physically as well as cognitively. The human body's immune system is a complex network that protects the body by: (1) identifying and destroying infectious agents (such as bacteria and viruses) that cause disease, (2) recognizing and fighting its own cells growing out of control (e.g., cancer cells), and (3) detecting and attacking non-biological intruders (e.g., slivers).[12] A key immune system cell, the macrophage, monitors every portal of entry to the body—including eyes, nose, and lungs—and thus is known as the *sentinel of the immune system.*[13] This gatekeeping cell, which is constantly on the move, searches for and destroys or engulfs invading or foreign entities such as bacteria, viruses, cancer cells, or nonbiological materials (e.g., slivers).

On occasion, the body's immune system misjudges a threat, works too well, or misidentifies a cell and overreacts (with occasionally disastrous results). The nonselective nature of the immune system ignores the source or purpose of the intrusion and simply responds in survival mode, seeking to destroy any intruding cells. Rejections of organ implants or tissue grafts are common examples, as is the body's response to AIDS.

Organizations, similarly, have their own immune systems with parallel aims—to protect the status quo and thwart change. Informally and often not consciously, employees at all levels (including executive) act as gatekeepers who routinely monitor organizational conditions, sometimes overreacting to proposed change, failing to recognize impending threats posed by competitors or market conditions, or refusing to embrace technological advances. The individual's response is often a self-protective, defensive move that fails to consider the overall well-being of the organization.

People in organizations are similar to the immune system's macrophage cells in that both are gatekeepers positioned at every portal of entry to the system, ready to attack any perceived threat (change). Just as macrophages engulf or destroy objects in the body, people reject or attack new ideas or change initiatives. The body responds to situations in which a threat may be real or perceived. Likewise, organizational change may be viewed by employees as a real threat, even when the change is potentially positive. The challenge lies in overcoming this inherent response and encouraging people to realize the positive consequences of change. The organization's immune system reflects attitudes and actions held by people throughout the firm; thus, strategies for reducing resistance and encouraging change must focus on all levels of the organization, from executive to front-line. Effective organization-wide ODC interventions include management/leadership training and development (with emphasis on change skills), communication, employee involvement, stress management techniques, conflict resolution, and negotiation.

Resistance to change must be understood and managed on a personal level in order to be implemented organization-wide. ODC agents are responsible for understanding individual and organizational responses to change (particularly resistance), identifying organizational resisters, preparing for inevitable resistance, addressing each individual's specific reasons for resisting change, harnessing the strengths of group/team dynamics, seeking employee input, involving individuals in the change process, and helping all organizational members work through change toward a successful end.

Barriers to Change

"Change is inherently messy and always complicated."[14] Change, by definition, disrupts the balance with which we are familiar. Common barriers to change are rooted in the organizational system, leadership/management, and people in general.

System barriers include a dysfunctional culture, the immune system, ineffective policies or procedures, insufficient resources or support, and internal conflicts. *Leadership/management* barriers are due to their inability to deal with resistance to change, lack of change management skills, lack of trust between management and employees, faulty assumptions regarding change (e.g., change is easy), refusal to involve employees in change decision-making, insufficient communications, and lack of rewards for change, to name a few.

Individual barriers are varied. The most daunting obstacle is our inherent resistance to change. People often fear change and the resulting disruption to our comfortable routines. Change may be perceived as threatening to our security, identity, sense of control, or need for clarity or order. Negative individual reactions to change manifest themselves in lack of engagement in discussions or actions that involve risk or the unknown, longing for the "good old days," desire to protect the status quo, and negative comments relative to the change or those pursuing it.

Overcoming Barriers to Change

Barriers to change are as personal as the individual and as complex as the organization. Overcoming obstacles to change, as a result, requires deep understanding of individuals and their organizations. Individual personalities, talents, weaknesses, and predisposition to change to change combine with thorough knowledge of organizational culture, leadership skills, procedures, capabilities, and history of change to frame strategies for successful change implementation and long-term organizational development. Strategies for leaders, managers, and HRM professionals in overcoming obstacles to change are:

- Enhance your change skills.
- Determine what should be changed.
- Know your people and their predispositions toward change.
- Model the change.
- Remove obstacles in the system.
- Understand and plan for resistance.
- Involve people at all levels in all stages of the change.
- Communicate, communicate, communicate.
- Provide resources and support.
- Reward change efforts and celebrate successes.
- Create a culture of organizational development and change.

Conclusion

Organizational development and change efforts equip firms in their fight for survival. A planned, ongoing process of change, ODC provides a framework through which individuals and their organizations engage in well-planned change initiatives that have a greater chance of success. Organizations do not change—their people do. Yet ODC yields a host of personal and company-wide benefits including improved work culture and conditions, growth and development opportunities, innovation, quality, communication, and efficiency.

NOTES

1. Steve A. Allen, "Organizational Choice and General Influence Networks for Diversified Companies. *Academy of Management Journal,* September 1978, 341.

2. J.J. Porras and P.J. Robertson, "Organization Development: Theory, Practice, and Research," in *The Handbook of Industrial and Organizational Psychology,* vol. 3, ed. M.D. Dunnette and L.M. Hough (Palo Alto, CA: Consulting Psychologists Press, 1983); R.S. Bibler, *The Arthur Young Management Guide to Mergers and Acquisitions* New York: J. Wiley, 1989); and Michael Beer, R.A. Eisenstat, and B. Spector, "Why Change Programs Don't Produce Change," *Harvard Business Review* 68, no. 6 (1990): 158–66.

3. Jerry W. Gilley, Steven A. Eggland, and Ann Maycunich Gilley, *Principles of Human Resource Development.* 2nd ed. (Cambridge, MA: Perseus, 2002).

4. Michael Beer, "What Is Organizational Development," in *Training and Development Sourcebook,* ed. L.S. Baird, C.E. Schneiner, and D. Laird (Amherst, MA: HRD Press, 1983).

5. Ann Gilley, *The Manager as Change Leader* (Westport, CT: Praeger, 2005), 98–99.

6. Kurt Lewin, *Field Theory in Social Science* (New York: Harper, 1950).

7. John P. Kotter, *Leading Change* (Cambridge, MA: Harvard Business School Press, 1996); and David A. Nadler, *Champions of Change: How CEOs and Their Companies are Mastering the Skills of Radical Change* (San Francisco: Jossey-Bass Publishers, 1998).

8. Gilley, *The Manager as Change Leader,* 36.

9. Everett M. Rogers, *Diffusion of Innovations,* 5th ed. (New York: The Free Press, 2003).

10. C.D. Scott and D.T. Jaffe, "Survive and thrive in times of change," *Training and Development Journal,* April 1988, 25–27.

11. Gilley, *The Manager as Change Leader,* 29.

12. Ann Gilley, Marisha L. Godek, and Jerry W. Gilley, "The Organizational Immune System: Individual and Organizational Responses to Change" (2004), unpublished mss.

13. M.J. Auger and J.A. Ross, "The Biology of the Macrophage," in *The Macrophage,* ed. C.E. Lewis and J.O'D. McGee (Oxford: Oxford University Press, 1992), 1–12.

14. Nadler, *Champions of Change,* 3.

Ann Gilley and Jerry W. Gilley

CHANGE MANAGEMENT

Organisms that do not evolve or change eventually die. The same holds true for organizations. Thus, knowledge of change and change management are critical in today's hyper-competitive, rapidly evolving world. As a result, managers have found that their primary job is to make change happen through their people, and expertise in change management is a necessary skill.

Change, according to the *American Heritage Dictionary,* is defined as "to cause to be different; alter; a transition from one state, condition, or phase to another." Change management, therefore, we will define as "planned facilitation of change," which requires knowledge and understanding of the forces of change, obstacles and human reactions to change, and ways to overcome barriers and desired make change happen.

Forces of Change

What causes change to occur? In many cases, change occurs slowly and incrementally as individuals and organizations respond to gradual modifications of their internal and external environments. Changes in internal policies and personnel or shifting societal trends and legislation, while occasionally unpleasant, are often foreseen and may be planned for.

Conversely, certain incidents occur quickly and without warning. Natural disasters, death of a leader, war, and some technological advances can act as catalysts of rapid, even radical change.

Obstacles to Change

Individual and organizational barriers inhibit or entirely prevent desired change. Individual obstacles to change include our inherent resistance, personality (including predisposition toward or against change), fear, intolerance of ambiguity and/or risk, and lack of coping skills.

Fear is a natural and predictable response to change. People fear change and its consequences, real or perceived. Other reasons why individuals resist change include:

— Fear of the unknown
— Fear of failure

- Intolerance of conflict
- Perceived lost of security, power, status, or control
- No incentive to change
- Peer pressure
- Lack of input into the change
- Mistrust of management
- Lack of guidance or clarity[1]

  Organizational obstacles to change are even greater in number, including:
- Poor leadership/management
- Lack of management support for change
- Insufficient resources allocated for change
- Internal conflict for resources
- Dysfunctional culture
- Lack of trust between managers and employees
- Lack of commitment to change
- Lack of benefits or rewards for change
- Lack of consequences for refusal or failure to change
- Poor policies and procedures
- Intolerance of conflict
- Punishment of risk-takers
- Poor communications[2]

Consequences

Organizations whose people or systems erect multiple barriers to change report numerous negative symptoms such as lower morale, frustration/anger among employees, lost productivity, cost overruns, increased stress, poorer customer service, lessened commitment, and failure to meet goals (individual and organizational).

Overcoming Resistance and Managing Change

Successfully implementing change requires that impacted parties understand the processes of change along with human reactions (e.g., resistance). The four phases of response to change are denial, resistance, exploration, and commitment.[3]

Denial, often one's initial response to an impending change, occurs when an individual believes that the change will not affect him or her. Denial typically surfaces when information about the change is lacking. *Resistance,* the second phase, arises when people receive some information that leads them to perceive that the change will impact them negatively (e.g., they may lose their jobs or may be forced to take on additional work responsibilities, etc.). The third phase, *exploration,* reflects some progress in the change effort as individuals begin to seek or recognize personal benefits associated with the change. *Commitment,* the last phase, is manifested in ones acceptance of and support for the change.

Helping others through the process of change and managing its outcome proves more successful when: (1) those impacted by the change are involved in its conceptualization, design, and implementation, (2) open, honest communications and feedback occur at each phase, (3) management visibly and substantially supports the change and provides the resources necessary to be successful, (4) individuals are rewarded for engaging in change, and (5) problems are anticipated and planned for.

Change Models

Numerous models address the complexities of managing change, from Lewin's classic yet simplistic *unfreeze-move-refreeze*[4] to multistep approaches that address resistance, culture, and rewards such as the following change model:[5]

Acknowledge that change is immensely complex.
Understand individual and organizational responses (resistance) to change, and how to deal with these responses.
Create a culture that supports change.
Establish a vision for change.
Build a guiding coalition for the change.
Sell the benefits of change to individuals at all levels of the organization.
Remove barriers.
Involve employees at all levels of the organization in the change process.
Communicate, communicate, communicate.
Prepare for and plan responses to resistance.
Deal with employees and their reactions individually, not as a group.
Execute the change in small increments.
Constantly monitor progress of the change and refine/adjust accordingly.
Reward individuals and groups for engaging in change.
Celebrate short- and long-term wins.
Solidify the change in the newly emerged culture.

Conclusion

Change is inevitable. Understanding its complexities and change management techniques enables individuals and organizations to face the challenges posed by an uncertain future.

See also Organizational Development and Change: An Overview

NOTES

1. Ann Gilley, *The Manager as Change Leader* (Westport, CT: Praeger, 2005).
2. Ibid.
3. C.D. Scott and D.T. Jaffe, "Survive and Thrive in Times of Change," *Training and Development Journal*, April 1988, 25–27.
4. Kurt Lewin, *Field Theory in Social Science* (New York: Harper, 1951).
5. Gilley, *The Manager as Change Leader*, 35.

Ann Gilley

INNOVATION

Given the extraordinary changes occurring today with regard to economics, technology, and demographics, organizations are attempting to remain competitive through continuous and transformational change. Transformational change requires innovation.[1] Innovation is applied to products and services, as well as technology, organizational structure and processes, and an organization's business model.[2] From this perspective, innovation can be viewed as the engine that drives transformational change.

Regardless of where efforts are focused, innovation requires disruptive growth; not just getting better at what they do, but changing to the extent that an organization differentiates itself. However, even though the importance of being innovative is clear, only a few organizations achieve transformational change. A primary reason is that innovation requires a culture and work environment conducive to the application of creativity, which is lacking in many organizations. Creativity has been described as the emergence of novel ideas, and innovation has been described as the implementation of these ideas.[3]

Multiple elements within an organization's culture serve to enhance or inhibit innovation. Poor managerial support and work climate limit the impact of creativity in terms of influencing idea implementation, leading to innovation.[4] Leaders can influence the culture and climate by focusing on cognitive, as well as behavioral, approaches.

As complex adaptive systems, organizations' ability to generate new ideas, grow, renew, and change requires the capacity to quickly respond to novel problems or situations in the external market.[5] In order to support adaptability and capacity building, organizations rely on initiatives that support continuous learning and performance improvement. Further, organizations demonstrate agility by changing the structure and/or processes. In turn, structures and processes are manifested by underlying patterns of thinking regarding relationships, information sharing, and behaviors. Therefore, it can be inferred that both cognitive and behavioral approaches are critical to ensuring innovation. The cognitive approach manifests itself as "intellectual capital."

Cognitive Approaches

Creativity must be viewed in the context of the organization. It is driven by intellectual capital, "which is the knowledge that people have and that will increase in worth."[6] It has been suggested that noticing generic structures (e.g., mental models, scripts, and cultural norms) is important to enabling intellectual capital.[7] Being aware of generic structures enables invention, through seeing relationships or connections between seemingly disparate concepts. Essentially, remaining unaware of generic structures becomes an obstacle for innovation. In order to create or invent, an individual must have the ability to look beyond the generic structures that are their current frame of reference. This requires time and reflection, which, in the normal course of the day in most organizations, is not embraced.

Behavioral Approaches

In terms of behavioral approaches, innovation requires leadership to move beyond the command-and-control mode of managing, which supports maintenance of the status quo. Rather, innovation requires the use of an array of communication techniques. Specifically, communicating to the organization the risks in clinging to the status quo and the potential rewards of embracing a radically different future. Also, enabling the flow of ideas is critical. This is done by allowing time for reflection and creative thought. Leaders must work purposefully to convert creative, yet impractical and wild ideas, into innovations. Leaders should approach innovation knowing that new ideas will seem impractical and that there is no way of telling the silly ideas from the stroke of genius—both look equally impossible at first glance. Further, innovations that arise from genius, rather than from purposeful and organized work, cannot be replicated and simply remain brilliant ideas—they are rarely acted upon. Therefore, cultivating a work environment conducive to creativity is imperative.

Conclusion

Organizations can remain competitive through continuous and transformational change, which requires innovation. Innovation is the result of the creative thought of employees, and action on the part of leaders. Without a culture and work climate that enables creative thought, innovation will not occur. Therefore, it is imperative for organizations to place emphasis on both cognitive approaches and behavioral approaches in order to cultivate creativity and achieve innovation.

NOTES

1. Steve Denning, "Transformational Innovation," *Strategy & Leadership* 33 (2005): 11–16.
2. International Business Machines, *Expanding the Innovation Horizon: The Global CEO Study* (Somers, NY: IBM Global Business Services, 2006).
3. Max Zornada, "Stroke of Genious?" *Manager,* June–July 2006, 28–29.
4. Kamal Birdi, "No Idea? Evaluating the Effectiveness of Creativity Training," *Journal of European Industrial Training* 29 (2004): 102–11.
5. Fikret Berkes, Johan Colding, and Carl Folke, "Rediscovery of Traditional Ecological Knowledge as Adaptive Management," *Ecological Applications* 10 (2000): 1251–62.
6. Robert Haskell, *Reengineering Corporate Training: Intellectual Capital and Transfer of Learning.* (Westport, CT: Quorum Books, 1998)
7. Ibid., 285.

Pamela Dixon

INTERNAL/EXTERNAL CONSULTING

The term "consultant" describes a myriad of services provided by a myriad of providers. Consulting, in the business context, means the giving of advice for pay. Consulting is an advisory service contracted for and provided to organizations by specially trained and qualified persons who assist, in an objective and independent manner, the client organization to identify organizational problems (and opportunities), analyze such problems (and opportunities), recommend solutions to these problems, and help, when requested, in the implementation of solutions. Such a definition helps an internal consultant to be engaged in the management process (not simply in problem definitions) with a client system.

Management consulting (which comprises strategy consulting and operations consulting) refers to both the practice of helping organizations to improve performance through analysis of existing business problems and the development of future plans or opportunities. Management consulting may involve the identification and cross-fertilization of best practices, analytical or diagnostic techniques, change management and coaching skills, technology implementations, strategy development, or operational improvement.

Internal Consulting

Internal consulting is frequently used to develop and implement corporate strategies, propagate new management practices across divisions, train managers and staff, perform management audits, assist in the correction of the problems discovered, and, in general, to improve performance of the organization. Internal consultants are already members of the organization (e.g., a top executive; a manager of human resources or organization development; or simply an organization member who initiates change) who perform tasks that are similar to those performed by external consultants, except that they generally do this within the boundaries of their host organization.

Internal management consultants, like their external counterparts, are also considered as change agents with a role to influence and advise people, and to persuade them and help them to do things differently. Internal consulting makes available to the manager a specialist resource with deep knowledge of the organization to assist in identifying and studying problems and opportunities; preparing recommendations; and assisting in the implementation of these recommendations, if requested.

Internal consulting is a particularly apt solution when the special skills are needed only periodically, or when problems cut across divisional boundaries within an organization. The function is of particular importance to small- and medium-sized organizations that cannot afford to keep a large staff of specialists, as well as to large organizations to assist them in improving organizational objectives, structures, operations and processes, productivity and quality.

The distinctive advantage internal consultants have over their external counterparts is their familiarity with the internal cultures and political systems of the organization, and thus the relative ease with which they can help an organization change.[1] Because internal consultants are often considered "overhead," many value-driven companies such as Anheuser-Busch, American Express, General Electric, Sara Lee, Pepsico, and Sony compel their internal consultants to market their services both internally and externally.

External Consulting

External consultants are not members of the organization (e.g., not on the company's payroll) and work on specific projects for limited periods because of a particular expertise that is unavailable internally, to bring a different viewpoint and, potentially, a more objective perspective. Using external consultants is necessary under the following circumstances: the organization needs specialized help not available on staff; the company faces time pressure to find a solution and the staff is already under stress; the nature of the problem or the company's political atmosphere means that solutions presented by an unbiased, apolitical outsider will have greater credibility and acceptance; and the organization requires a fresh perspective on a problem.

There are certain kinds of assignments for which the external consultant is uniquely qualified. The benefits of external consulting include their objectivity about the organization's problems (and opportunities) and their independence from the organization's power structure. An external consultant is also not dependent on a single client for his or her livelihood and not afraid to criticize the client company politics, approaches, and processes. The external consultant is free to leave the company and/or reject the assignment. External consultants as outside specialists may have more influence with the client-organization, which could consider him or her as an "expert" who has more varied experiences and a broader perspective from working in many companies. Among thousands of external consultants, it is always possible to find unique expertise, and the best expertise, to solve the client's problems. Certain jobs could be done better by outside consultants such as executive recruiting, market studies, intercompanies' experience transfer, etc.

The Internal and External Consulting Team

Both internal and external consultants are helpers. In this sense, they have similar roles. They must get their job done through others who do not report to them organizationally. They do not have "power" as line managers. They work with and through client-organization members using forms of influence other than formal authority. They can both play multiple consulting roles.

There are certain advantages and disadvantages of internal and external consulting. The best potential lies in forming a powerful combination in undertaking the joint work of internal and external consultants. The external-internal consulting team is the most effective consulting approach. Effective organizational executives use internal and external consultants in a complementary manner. The organization can also call for an outside opinion on a major decision in addition to the internal consultant's recommendations.

The internal and external consultant brings to the consulting team complementary resources—that is, advantages and strengths that offset the disadvantages and weaknesses of the other. The external consultant brings expertise, objectivity, and new insights to organization problems and opportunities. The internal consultant, on the other hand, brings detailed knowledge of organization issues and norms, a longtime acquaintance with members, and an awareness of strengths and weaknesses.[2] External consultants are preferred in situations in which an internal consultant does not meet the criteria of impartiality and confidentiality, or lacks expertise. Joint teams of external and internal consultants can use complementary consulting skills while sharing the workload and possibly accomplishing more than either would be operating alone.

NOTES

1. Charles J. Fombrun and Mark D. Nevins, *The Advice Business: Essential Tools and Models for Management Consulting* (Upper Saddle River, NJ: Pearson Prentice Hall, 2003).

2. Philip Hunsaker, "Strategies for Organizational Change: The Role of the Inside Change Agent," *Personnel,* September–October 1982, 10–28.

Ronald R. Sims

ORGANIZATIONAL DEVELOPMENT

Organizational development (OD) is a comprehensive or systematic approach to planned change that is designed to improve the overall effectiveness of organizations, including improved quality of work life and increased productivity, and is designed to work on issues of both external adaptation and internal integration. HR professionals and others use OD to successfully respond to and manage change to improve performance in organizations of many types, sizes, and settings. It includes a set of tools with which any HR professional who is concerned about achieving and maintaining high levels of productivity needs to be familiar. Because of its comprehensive nature and scientific foundations, OD is frequently implemented with the aid of an external consultant.

Action-research Foundations of OD

Action research is the process used by HR professionals and others to systematically collect data on an organization, feed it back to the members for action planning, and evaluate results by collecting and reflecting on more data after the planned actions have been taken. Action research is a data-based and collaborative approach to problem solving and organizational assessment. When used in the OD process, action research helps identify action directions that may enhance an organization's effectiveness. In a typical action-research sequence, the sequence is initiated when someone senses a performance gap and decides to analyze the situation systematically for the problems and opportunities it represents. The process continues through the following steps: data gathering, data feedback, data analysis, and action planning. It continues to the point at which action is taken and results are evaluated. The evaluation or reassessment stage may or may not generate another performance gap. If it does, the action-research cycle begins anew.

Open Systems Framework

The open systems framework assists HR professionals in accomplishing the required diagnoses. At the organizational level, effectiveness must be understood with respect to forces in the external environment and major organizational aspects, such as strategy, technology, structure, culture, and management systems. At the group level, effectiveness is viewed in a context of forces in the internal environment of the organization and major group aspects, such as tasks, membership, norms, cohesiveness, and group processes. At the individual level, effectiveness is considered in relationship to the internal environment of the workgroup and individual aspects, such as tasks, goals, and interpersonal relationships.

The action-research process engages members of an organization in activities designed to accomplish the required diagnoses and to develop and implement plans for constructive change. Action research, data collection, and the diagnostic foundations come together through the choice and use of OD interventions. An intervention is a specific action that HR professionals and others who are responsible for change take to focus the change process. With less formality, many of these techniques are used by HR professionals to help them understand and improve their own operations.

Organizational Development Interventions

Although intervention has a generally used meaning, it has a specific meaning in the context of OD, where it refers to a formal activity. Choice of a particular intervention depends on the nature of the problem that the organization's leadership and HR professionals have diagnosed. As change agents, HR professionals along with other organizational members determine which alternative is most likely to produce the desired outcome, whether it is improvement in skills, attitudes, behavior, or structure. OD interventions have different effects on organizations, groups, and individuals. OD interventions include: human process, technostructural, human resource management, and strategic interventions.

Human Process Interventions

Human process interventions (individual and group relations) focus on people within organizations and the processes through which they accomplish organizational goals in order to enhance their overall organization. These interventions help people gain individual skills and knowledge, interpersonal competence, work through interpersonal conflicts, develop effective groups or teams or departments, as well as on relations between groups, teams, or departments. Human process interventions include coaching, training and development, process consultation, third-party intervention, team building, organization confrontation meeting, intergroup relations, and large-group interventions.[1]

Technostructural Interventions

Technostructural interventions (structures and technologies) focus on improving the performance of organizations (productivity and organizational effectiveness) primarily by modifying structures, technologies, operations, procedures and roles/positions in the organization. These interventions include approaches to employee involvement, as well as methods for designing organizations, groups, and jobs. An intervention involving work-technology might be the introduction of e-mail to improve employee communication. An intervention involving an organization-design change might be making an organization less centralized in its decision making. Technostructural interventions include total quality management/employee involvement, reengineering, downsizing, and structural design.[2]

Human Resource Management Interventions

Human resource management interventions (individual and group performance management) focus on enhancing overall organizational performance by improving the performance of individuals and groups within the organization. These interventions concern performance management and developing and assisting employees and include goal setting, performance appraisal, reward systems, career planning and development, managing workforce diversity, employee stress, and wellness.[3]

Strategic Interventions

Strategic interventions (organization and its external environment) focus especially on the organization and its interactions with its external environment, and often involve changes to many aspects of the organization, including employees, groups, technologies, products and services, etc. These interventions are organization-wide and bring about a better fit between an organization's strategy, structure, culture, and the larger environment. Strategic interventions include mergers and acquisitions, culture change, organizational learning, and knowledge management.

See also Organizational Development and Change: An Overview

NOTES

1. T.G. Cummings and C.G. Worley, *Organization Development and Change,* 8th ed. (Cincinnati, OH: South-Western College Publishing, 2005); and A. Kinicki and B. Williams, *Management: A Practical Introduction,* 3rd ed. (Burr Ridge, IL: McGraw-Hill/Irwin, 2006), 329.

2. J.M. Werner and R.L. DeSimone. *Human Resource Development,* 4th ed.). (Mason, OH: Thomson-SouthWestern).

3. Cummings and Worley, *Organization Development and Change,* and Kinicki and Williams, *Management: A Practical Introduction.*

Ronald R. Sims

ORGANIZATIONAL IMMUNE SYSTEM

Change, although constant in organizations, often proves a painful process. One major deterrent to a firm's ability to change lies in its immune system, which mirrors the human body's immune system. An immune system is designed to protect the body against harmful intrusions (foreign entities). An organization's immune system is the collection of people, policies, procedures, and processes that prevent change without regard for its consequences, positive or negative.

Organizations, like the human body, are systems.[1] The body consists of many interrelated subsystems just as organizations are comprised of multiple departments and functions. Healthy, dynamic systems respond to change positively. Dysfunctional systems—those whose immune systems are out of control—react negatively to change and reject it without consideration.

The immune system protects the body by identifying and subsequently removing or isolating any foreign entity (e.g., a sliver, a cell growing out of control). A misjudged threat, however, can be catastrophic. Failure to identify viruses or disease may result in infection, illness, or death. Or, the immune system may reject healthy tissues or organs when the body mistakenly perceives that they are foreign and proceeds to destroy them.[2]

Similarities between the Human Body and Organizations

In the body, one key immune system player is a cell called the macrophage. Macrophages reside at every portal of entry to the body, such as the eyes, nose, and mouth, and thus are known as the *sentinels of the immune system*.[3] The circulating form of the macrophage continually moves throughout the body in search of invading or foreign entities (e.g., bacteria, tumor cells, surgical implants).[4] Within organizations, sentinels attempting to preserve the status quo exist at all levels. They may be in the executive suite, among seasoned staff members, embedded within policies, procedures, and processes, or dispersed within the framework of a dysfunctional culture.

Upon encountering a foreign entity, the macrophage attempts to separate it from the body by engulfing or attaching to it, part of the body's natural response. In the case of surgical implants designed to augment or replace a host function, and thus a beneficial addition to the body, macrophage cells may still react in a negative fashion, a process called the "foreign body response." In essence, the body responds in survival mode—similar to the rejection of new ideas in an organizational setting. The individual's response (like the cell's response) is often a knee-jerk reaction to an intrusion or change without consideration of the overall well-being of the system (the organization).

The body's macrophages are similar to many organizational members. Macrophages are gatekeepers, positioned at every portal of entry to the system, ready to attack any invaders of the body. Organizations, too, have their own watchful gatekeepers, skeptics, and defenders. Just as macrophages surround or engulf (ingest) objects, people encounter new ideas that they then attack or suppress. Just as the body responds based on the initial response of the macrophage to a real or perceived threat, so too, do organizational members perceive change as a real threat, even when the outcome is potentially positive.

Policies, procedures, and processes prevent change and contribute to the immune system by encouraging or requiring control, continuity, and standardization measures that inhibit creativity and innovation while providing temporary security for organizational members. This temporary security fuels a dysfunctional culture and immune system that lead to organizational inertia at the expense of needed change that supports long-term firm viability.

Overriding the Immune System

Organizations continually search for viable means through which to tolerate, even embrace change. Preventing rejection and encouraging people to accept desired change requires overriding the immune system and enabling change to occur. Strategies for enabling change include (1) altering cellular (human) behaviors so that the change can be tolerated, (2) concealing the change from the immune system, and (3) disarming the immune system.

Alter Behavior

Means by which to help individuals cope with change include creating a culture of change, promoting win-win change situations, communicating that the change is beneficial, providing training, involving employees in decision making regarding changes, and rewarding change efforts.

Conceal Change from the Immune System

Changes that occur gradually, incrementally, even imperceptibly will be better tolerated by people.

Disarm the Immune System

The immune system may be mitigated by reducing or eliminating barriers to change (poor leadership, lack of support, etc.), maximizing the influence of organizational change agents, identifying and neutralizing the effects of greatest resisters, and through appropriate communications.

Conclusion

Organizations, like the human body, possess immune systems that shield the entity from harm by resisting change. Understanding the human body's immune system enables us to better understand and manage the organizational immune system.

See also: Change Management; Culture; Organizational Behavior: An Overview

NOTES

1. Jerry W. Gilley and Ann Maycunich Gilley, *Strategically Integrated HRD: Six Transformational Roles in Creating Results-driven Programs,* 2nd ed. (Cambridge, MA: Perseus Publishing, 2003).

2. Janis Kuby, "Transplantion immunology," in *Immunology,* ed. Richard A. Goldsby, Thomas J. Kindt, and Barbara A. Osborne, 4th ed. (New York: W. H. Freeman and Co, 2000), 517–38.

3. M. J. Auger and J. A. Ross, "The Biology of the Macrophage," in *The Macrophage,* ed. Claire E. Lewis and Bernard Burke, 2nd ed. (Oxford: Oxford University Press, 1992), 1–72.

4. Janis Kuby, "Cells and Organs of the Immune System," in *Immunology,* ed. Richard A. Goldsby, Thomas J. Kindt, and Barbara A. Osborne, 4th ed. (New York: W. H. Freeman and Co, 2000), 27–60.

Ann Gilley, Marisha L. Godek, and Jerry W. Gilley

Chapter 8
Organizational Behavior

Organizational Behavior: An Overview

Organizational behavior can be defined as the study of how individuals and groups act in organizations.[1] The study of organizational behavior is multidisciplinary and focuses on individual behavior, interpersonal behavior, group behavior, and the behavior of "whole systems" within organizations.[2] Organizational behavior encompasses a wide range of topics, including:

- Social systems
- Motivation
- Leadership
- Employee participation
- Interpersonal communication
- Teams
- Conflict management

Management practices utilized today are driven by six major forces that have had a great impact on organizations:[3]

- *Human resources*—The projected shortage of skilled workers and the increasing importance placed on human capital.
- *Globalization*—Increased growth in world trading for goods and services.
- *Diversity*—The U.S. workforce is becoming more culturally diverse.
- *Change*—Increased rate of change requires managers to adapt quickly and to be skilled at managing multiple changes at once.
- *Psychological contract*—The expectation of lifetime employment in one organization no longer exists. Today, the new unspoken contract consists of employees who expect opportunities for development (employability); flexibility in terms of balancing all aspects of life, including family; and having employers place greater emphasis on employee well-being, both physical and mental health.
- *Technology*—Organizations use technology to get work done. Information and communication technology have provided options for working across the globe in a synchronous or asynchronous manner. Work can be completed by virtual teams from different countries, all communicating and transferring information via networks at increasing speeds.

The results obtained from employee performance are the building blocks to organizational performance. Leaders in organizations must manage in a way that addresses the forces noted above. Failure to do so could result in costly increased turnover, lack of commitment, poor quality, lower productivity, and worker dissatisfaction.[4]

At its foundation, an organization consists of its leadership's values, vision, and objectives, which in turn influence the organizational culture. An organization's culture establishes the communication, group dynamics, and the degree to which individuals are integrated within the organization. Employees perceive this as the quality of work life, which influences their motivation and level of commitment. Managers can design jobs, develop working conditions, and create working relationships with employees that enhance quality of work life. This results in the degree to which superior performance (output) is achieved at the individual, group, and organizational levels.

Conclusion

Elements of organizational behavior address the needs of employees and the employer in the work relationship. An organization's leaders, utilizing interpersonal skills and other management practices highlighted in studies of organizational behavior, have the power to drive performance and influence the achievement of individual, group, and organizational goals.

NOTES

1. John W. Newstrom, *Organizational Behavior: Human Behavior at Work* (Boston: McGraw-Hill, 2007).
2. Ibid, 9.
3. John M. Ivancevich, Robert Konopaske, and Michael T. Matteson, *Organizational Behavior and Management* (Boston: McGraw-Hill, 2008).
4. Ibid.

Pamela Dixon

AGILE ORGANIZATION

An agile organization is one that can change rapidly to remain competitive in today's fast-paced world of business. Accordingly, organizational leaders trust the talent of the group to make decisions and adjustments to continuously improve processes. This allows the organization to remain competitive and achieve goals quickly in the changing market.[1]

Organizational Structure in an Agile Organization

Traditional organizations are bureaucratic and very rigid, with specified and prescribed work rules. This bureaucracy creates an environment that is slower to change than the marketplace demands. The recent emphases on "sustainable competitive advantage"[2] and the shortages of talent in the market have put pressures on organizations to restructure. Often, these become agile organizations, which are structured to provide opportunities for improved information sharing with employees. This creates avenues of communication that encourage shared decision making. Additionally, the new structure increases the flow of information and promotes peer-to-peer sharing of ideas to achieve organizational goals.

Organizations that demonstrate these kinds of self-organizing, complex, and emergent performance effects are of particular scientific interest. Agile organizations do not have any characteristic scale and can thus exhibit the full range of behavioral options within the system restraints, giving them a position of optimal flexibility. This allows employees to unite to perform a particular task. Employees are not directed by anyone outside the group. This is not the same as "self-management," as no manager outside the group dictates that employees should belong to a specific group and do not dictate what they should do or how it should be done. Group members choose to come together, and they decide what they will do and how it will be done. Another feature of such groups is that they are informal and often temporary. Enabling agile organizations can often be a source of innovation.[3]

Employees in an agile organization are more like networks designed to get the current job completed and have the ability to shift team members with each new objective.[4] Therefore, communication is key so that everyone knows the status of each project and employees are interchangeable resources. Agile organizations broaden roles and responsibilities, which can improve the effectiveness of the entire organization. Employees report that they enjoy their work more if they are fully engaged and part of the process.[5]

Communication

Communication is crucial in an agile organization to keep a constant flow of information throughout the corporation. Telecommunications, including e-commerce, e-mail, and the Internet, are tools that allow structural changes and efficiencies for team members to remain in contact with achievement of goals to sustain market flexibility. Virtual communication structures need to be a significant administrative focus as a competitive strategy to support the flexibility of the agile organization.[6]

Leadership

The leader in an agile organization must be able to establish the vision and an atmosphere of trust in which the team members have the opportunity to achieve that vision.[7] Trust is crucial in the development of an agile organization, as each individual has to be trusted to know what is required, and to be rewarded accordingly.[8] Agile organizational leaders will require skills in envisioning, enabling, and energizing employees to create a flexible team environment. Leaders are responsible for creating a clear vision of the future with challenging, plausible, and meaningful goals and outcomes for the organization. The picture needs to be one in which employees can see themselves as an integral part of reaching the destination and are excited at the prospects of the journey. Facilitation and empowerment are also necessary to support individuals so that they are able to accomplish goals effectively and meet the challenges of the rapidly changing marketplace. Empowerment allows employees to identify changes within the organization, team, or external environment and allows them to make those changes quickly in order to remain competitive in the market. Leaders no longer dictate actions of the group but, rather, have the opportunity to energize the organization through enthusiasm and vision to achieve a competitive edge.[9]

The world of business has become more competitive and moves more quickly because of technologies than ever before in history. In order to remain competitive in this global market, organizations must have the ability to change rapidly throughout every level of the organizational structure. "While not all change will be successful, inertia or incremental change in the face of altered competitive arenas is a recipe for failure."[10] The agile organization has the potential to create a sustainable and innovative position in the ever-changing world of business.

See also Culture; Developmental Organizations

NOTES

1. "The HR Mandate: Creating an Agile Organization," in *HR Spectrum, CAHRS Center for Advanced Human Resource Studies,* May–June 2000, http://www.ilr.cornell.edu/depts/cahrs/downloads/PDFs/hrSpectrum/HRSpec06-00.pdf (accessed February 15, 2008).

2. Simon Reay Atkinson, "The Agile Organization: From Informal Networks to Complex Effects and Agility," in *Department of Defense Command and Control Research Program* (Washington, DC: U.S. Department of Defense, July 2005), 32–33.

3. Juhary Ali, Chew Thong Giap, and Tang Tuck Cheong, "Knowledge Management in Agile Organizations," *Sunway College Journal* 1 (2004): 13–20.

4. Steven E. Prokesch, "Mastering Chaos at the High-Tech Frontier: An Interview with Silicon Graphic's Ed McCracken," *Harvard Business Review,* November–December 1993, 134–44.

5. Atkinson, "The Agile Organization," 37.

6. Steven A. Morris and Denise Johnson McManus, "Information Infrastructure Centrality in the Agile Organization," *Information Systems Management,* Fall 2002, 8–12.

7. Wendell L French, and Cecil H. Bell Jr., *Organizational Development: Behavioral Science Interventions for Organization Improvement,* 5th ed. (Englewood Cliffs, NJ: Prentice Hall, 1995).

8. Atkinson, "The Agile Organization," 83.

9. David A. Nadler and Michael L. Tushman, "Beyond the Charismatic Leader: Leadership and Organizational Change," *California Management Review,* Winter 1990, 77–97.

10. Ibid.

Debora A. Montgomery-Colbert

COMMUNITY OF PRACTICE

A community of practice is a group of individuals who share a common interest, passion, or curiosity for an activity or endeavor, and, through regular interaction, improve their knowledge, skills, and abilities related to it.[1] A community of practice may be distinguished from other organizational structures on the basis of membership (typically voluntary, and may incorporate people external to the organization) and purpose (to create, expand, and exchange knowledge, and to develop individual competencies and capabilities).[2]

Common Characteristics

A community of practice will typically have members who acquire knowledge, skills, and abilities within a participational framework, not an individual mind. A community of practice will typically contain both novice, or "apprentice" members and more senior, experienced, or "master" members, but with a modern twist. Although apprentices may acquire more knowledge relative to more experienced or senior members, masters also continue to learn as a direct result and consequence of their participation within the community. Since membership within a community of practice is usually voluntary, it is the ability and desire to continue to learn, to share experiences, and to engage in the activities and endeavors of interest that maintain solidarity, continuity, and a sense of *esprit de corps* among participants.

A community of practice (and the corresponding "master-apprentice" relationships) can be very beneficial for those activities and occupations demanding high levels of skill, knowledge, and expertise, and include a wide, diverse array of disciplines (medicine, law, teaching, professional sports, the arts, industrial trades). Occupations that are staffed by "professionals," allowing for the management of greater task complexity with more highly skilled workers (rather than through the division of tasks among skill-differentiated workers with a more limited repertoire and range), capable of deploying their knowledge, skills, and abilities with a high degree of flexibility, independence, and discretion under uncertain or ambiguous circumstances,[3] are prime candidates for capitalizing upon a community of practice.

A community of practice is usually (but not always) an informal, natural, or organic[4] structure that coexists within the formal, rational structure of an organization. As such, they frequently reflect the "fault lines" along which an organization naturally (as opposed to rationally) operates.[5]

Role within an Organization

A community of practice is a very specific type of social structure with an equally specific purpose.[6] By linking those with a common interest, passion, or curiosity within an organization, individuals with functionally similar or equivalent responsibilities and duties are better able to interact, to capitalize on the learnings of others, even if they report to different managers, units, or divisions within an organization. As such, a community of practice is capable of providing horizontal linkages between employees, and better facilitates the flow of information in such a manner. A community of practice also plays an important role within the domain of a firm's knowledge management strategy, or those practices used to identify, create, harvest, and distribute knowledge as necessary both within and external to the organization.

The activities occurring within a community of practice can also enable improved organizational performance when the knowledge they create is translated into codified, repeatable, and refined procedures that others can use when carrying out their work. This often occurs through formal "lessons learned" or "best practice" documents, allowing for permanence within the organization. Communities of practice also may facilitate companies when linking together in value chains or networks.[7] A naturally occurring value chain in business involves an organization's suppliers at one end and distributors and retailers at the other. Similarly, an organization choosing to participate in (or abstain from) a merger, joint venture, or alliance is likely to confront opportunities and challenges requiring the processing of unique, complex, and nuanced information.[8] The upside potential of such relatively recent organizational forms may be increased by having communities of practice in critical areas, as knowledge present in the separate organizations may be more readily accessed and exploited by the new entity.

Challenges Confronting Communities of Practice

A community of practice, typically being an informal, natural, or organic structure, may have difficulty gaining legitimacy, recognition, and permanence within an established organization. Despite the advantages that can develop through communities or practice, they are also somewhat resistant to supervision and cooptation by an organization.[9] A community of practice may be most vulnerable to the "poverty of time" that many individuals in organizations increasingly experience. As an organization increasingly constrains an individual's time, an activity that does not receive organizational legitimacy, or one in which the role, purpose, and deliverables are somewhat abstract and ambiguous, is more likely to be "crowded out" and not attended to. The internal relationships existing within a community of practice are not immune to various organizational pathologies, including imperialism, narcissism and factionalism.[10,] Additionally, a community of practice is most likely to thrive in an organizational climate that promotes trust, and in which the culture is oriented towards the work and tasks at hand. However, the conditions necessary to facilitate the successful utilization of communities of practice, and the climate and culture present within an organization, are often not the same. Unless such issues are properly addressed, communities of practice are not likely to produce any substantive progress or benefits, and will likely not realize their potential.

NOTES

1. Etienne Wenger, "Communities of Practice—A Brief Introduction," http://www.ewenger.com/theory/index.htm (accessed October 22, 2007).

2. Etienne Wenger, Richard McDermott, and William Snyder, *Cultivating Communities of Practice* (Boston: Harvard Business School Press, 2002).

3. W. Richard Scott, *Organizations: Rational, Natural, and Open Systems* (Upper Saddle River, NJ: Prentice Hall, 2003).

4. Etienne C. Wenger and William M. Snyder, "Communities of Practice: The Organizational Frontier," *Harvard Business Review,* January–February 2000, 139–45.

5. Scott, *Organizations;* Paul Wright, "Emerging Trends in New Product Development and R&D," *Knowledge Management Review,* July–August 1998, 12–15.

6. Wenger, McDermott, and Snyder, *Cultivating Communities of Practice.*

7. Rein Juriado and Niklas Gustafsson, "Emergent Communities of Practice in Temporary Inter-Organisational Partnerships," *The Learning Organization,* January 2007, 50–61.

8. Wenger, McDermott, and Snyder, *Cultivating Communities of Practice.*

9. Wenger and Snyder, "Communities of Practice."

10. Wenger, McDermott, and Snyder, *Cultivating Communities of Practice;* Jon Pemberton, Sharon Mavin, and Brenda Stalker, "Scratching Beneath the Surface of Communities of (Mal)practice," *The Learning Organization,* January 2007, 62–73.

Steven J. Kerno Jr.

CONFLICT RESOLUTION

Conflict exists everywhere—personal relationships, work relationships, and everywhere in between. It is unavoidable. Conflict can be defined as "a situation in which interdependent people express (manifest or latent) differences in satisfying their individual needs and interests, and they experience interference from each other in accomplishing their goals."[1] Another definition states that "conflict arises when a difference between two (or more) people necessitates change in at least one person in order for their engagement to continue and develop. The differences cannot coexist without some adjustment."[2] This adjustment necessitates resolution. People can resolve conflict in a variety of ways, including avoidance, violence, or legal processes. Conflict resolution or management, however, has become a field of study and practice unto itself, and in this realm, it involves problem solving in order to attempt to achieve a win-win solution.

Conflict resolution can be handled by those who are in conflict or with the help of a third party, such as in mediation. In any instance of conflict resolution, insight as to why the conflict exists, an individual's conflict style, and the utilization of skills that promote dialogue are important.

Causes of Conflict

A variety of theories and models exist that provides frameworks for understanding the causes of conflict. The Circle of Conflict model[3] provides six categories of conflict:

- Value conflicts: different ideologies, different criteria for evaluating
- Relationship conflicts: misperceptions, repetitive negative interactions
- Data conflicts: lack of information, different interpretations
- Structural conflicts: unequal power, environmental barriers, time constraints
- Interest conflicts: competing emotional, procedural, or substantive needs.

Value and structural conflicts are typically the most difficult to resolve, as these deal with either an individual's core beliefs or constraints that the parties in conflict are not able to change or alter.[4] Determining which of these causes exist in a conflict assists in determining appropriate interventions.

Attribution theory provides a useful lens for interpreting conflict and its roots. This theory purports that when we are involved in a negative event or harm is done to us, we attribute the cause to the situation, circumstances beyond our control, or to the other people involved.[5] When other people are involved in negative events, however, we then attribute the cause directly to them, such as their bad character or inappropriate actions, rather than to external circumstances or simply the situation.[6] This bias toward the other has a large effect on trust and, in turn, could cause one person to exaggerate or make assumptions about another's behavior,[7] and hence further affect their relationship and their ability to interact effectively.

A third model, the Triangle of Satisfaction, is related to the Circle of Conflict and the category-of-interest conflicts. Essentially, people in conflict have wants and needs and according to this model, those "interests" can be categorized as:

- Result/substantive interests: the outcome, the final decision, the "what."
- Process/procedural interests: the process by which an outcome is achieved, the "how."
- Emotion/psychological interests: emotional needs such as wanting to be heard, to save face, wanting an apology.[8]

This model can be used to determine what is most important to someone at any given time during a conflict as people's interests change.[9] Additionally, it can be used as a three-way test once it appears that a conflict has been solved. Conflict participants have to feel as if all three of these interests were met or feel fair in order for the conflict to be truly resolved. Otherwise, conflict may resurface, for example, due to someone not feeling as if the process was fair or if they did not feel heard and validated during the resolution process.

These theories and models represent just a few of the many frameworks that exist for analyzing conflicts, assessing causes, and determining appropriate interventions. They can be used by conflict intervenors, such as mediators, informal third parties, or anyone who attempts to help others in conflict. These models can also be utilized by those in conflict. Being personally involved in conflict can be emotional and causes people to see things subjectively and according to their biases. If a person was able to analyze his own conflict using these models, he would gain a more objective view, be able to understand that another side/perspective exists, and hence damper his own emotions and be more likely to achieve a win-win solution.

Conflict Styles

An individual's ability to utilize these models in her own conflict could be influenced by her conflict style. The five conflict styles are:[10]
- Avoidance: denial of or ignoring the conflict, changing topics, joking, being noncommittal
- Competition: "power over" style, uncooperative or aggressive, trying to "win"
- Compromise: moderately assertive, gives us some to get some
- Accommodation: passive, gives in
- Collaboration: assertive, balances own needs with those of others.

A collaborative style is the most conducive for conflict resolution, as it demonstrates a concern for self and a concern for the other.[11] This style strives to have the needs of all involved be met as much as possible and to preserve relationships. A competition style helps one to achieve one's goal, but relationships may be ruined in the process and hence further conflict will result. Avoidance and accommodation styles result in one's goals not being met as well as relationships not necessarily being strengthened. A compromise style is a healthy style, as it helps to meet the goals of all those involved and preserve relationships; however, a collaborative style uses more creativity and problem solving to attempt to meet people's needs without having to sacrifice some of what they want. Moreover, an individual with a collaborative style would be more likely to be introspective and analyze her part in the conflict and objectively analyze the other person's actions and needs.

Skills for Resolution

Dialogue skills are an essential part of the collaborative style and hence successful conflict resolution. Isaacs promotes four skills or practices for dialogue:[12]
- Listening: really listening and hearing the other person as well as listening to yourself and your own reactions
- Respecting: seeing the other person as a whole being, honoring them
- Suspending: giving up having to be right, suspending your opinion, attempting to gain a larger perspective
- Voicing: finding the right words, voicing your opinion assertively and with care.

These skills enable those in conflict to hear the places where they agree versus the places where they disagree. Debate is concerned with the latter; whereas dialogue encourages the finding of common ground.

Conflict Management

One of the previous conflict definitions stated, "differences cannot coexist without some adjustment."[13] Conflict theories, a collaborative conflict style, and dialogue skills are crucial aspects of conflict resolution. They are tools, or adjustments, that assist people in coexisting with their differences and managing their conflicts.

NOTES

1. William W. Wilmot and Joyce L. Hocker, *Interpersonal Conflict* (Boston: McGraw Hill, 1998), 33.
2. Ibid.

3. Christopher W. Moore, *The Mediation Process: Practical Strategies for Resolving Conflicts* (San Francisco: Jossey-Bass, 1996).

4. Ibid.

5. Gary T. Furlong, *The Conflict Resolution Toolbox: Models and Maps for Analyzing, Diagnosing, and Resolving Conflict* (Mississauga, Ontario: John Wiley & Sons Canada, Ltd., 2005).

6. Ibid.

7. Ibid.

8. Ibid.

9. Ibid.

10. Wilmot and Hocker, *Interpersonal Conflict.*

11. Ibid.

12. William Isaacs, *Dialogue and the Art of Thinking Together: A Pioneering Approach to Communicating in Business and in Life* (New York: Doubleday, 1999).

13. Wilmot and Hocker, *Interpersonal Conflict,* 33.

Shay Bright

CRISIS MANAGEMENT

A crisis may be any situation that causes a significant disruption of business, and may impact revenue and income sources, operations, competitiveness, safety and security, or any value creation process within the firm. A crisis (1) poses a threat to the organization and its stakeholders, (2) has the element of surprise, and (3) allows for only a short decision time.[1] Crises are inevitable and force managers at all organizational levels to plan or react to them on a daily basis.

Types of Crises

The four types of organizational crises are sudden, smoldering, bizarre, and perceptual. Sudden crises include natural disasters, incidents of workplace violence, death of the leader, and so forth. Smoldering crises are problems that start small and gradually build, typically because no one recognized or paid attention to the problem. Bizarre crises represent unique occurrences that occasionally defy even the most stringent planning, such as when someone tampered with Johnson and Johnson's Tylenol by adding cyanide, resulting in the deaths of seven people in 1982. Perceptual crises may be long-term issues, such as the image problems Exxon continues to face due to its *Valdez* oil spill off the Alaskan coast in 1989.[2]

Crisis Management Planning

Crisis management is the systematic attempt to avoid organizational crises or manage those crises that occur.[3] The first step in crisis management is planning, for although crises may be unexpected, they will happen. The questions are how, when, where, and why.

Models of crises management offer guidelines for effective planning and response, stressing the need to:

• Define scenarios that constitute a crisis.

• Develop plans that will best manage a crisis.

• Trigger crisis management response mechanisms.

• Create communications to deal with reality and perceptions during and after the crisis.[4]

A crisis management framework begins with identification of the possible crises that may impact a firm, internally or externally. While identification of all potential crises is unrealistic, common themes can be isolated (e.g., likely disasters or safety events, product or service issues, competitive changes, etc.) and planned for.

Contingency plans, drafted in advance, help an organization appropriately prepare for a crisis by identifying people, responsibilities, and actions necessary during the event. Any plan must clearly stipulate chain of command, roles and responsibilities, order of functions, backup in case of failure of a function or process, and communications and information flow. Rehearsals and drills help crisis management teams perfect their responses with speed and efficiency.

Resources:

Dictionary.com. "Documentation." *WordNet® 3.0*. Princeton University. http://dictionary .reference.com/browse/documentation (accessed November 28, 2007).

NOTES

1. M.W. Seeger, T.L. Sellnow, and R.R. Ulmer, "Communication, Organization, and Crisis," *Communication Yearbook* (1998): 21, 231–275.

2. Larry Smith and Dan Millar, *Before Crisis Hits: Building a Strategic Crisis Plan* (Washington, DC: AACC Community College Press, 2002).

3. C.M. Pearson and J.A. Clair, "Reframing Crisis Management," *Academy of Management Review* 23 (1998): 59–76.

4. A. Gonzalez-Herrero and C.B. Pratt, "How to Manage a Crisis Before or Whenever It Hits," *Public Relations Quarterly* 40 (1995): 25–30.

Ann Gilley

CULTURE

When asked about the culture of their organizations, most people respond with a list of adjectives such as laid back, easy going, supportive or structured, rigid, or formal. However, when asked what culture is, specifically, responses typically include "the atmosphere in the company" or "just how things are done." Culture, and changing the culture within organizations, have been hot topics in business since the early 1980s.

Culture is very easy to formally define, yet less easy to explain. Culture, as defined in Webster's Dictionary, is the customary beliefs, social forms, and material traits of a racial, religious, or social group.

Basis of Organizational Culture

The basis of organizational culture flows from its vision and values; what it does and what it aspires to be. These attributes lay a foundation, so to speak, for culture.

Ultimately, culture is the personality of an organization, including how it is viewed by its employees as well as the outside world. Just as people's personalities vary, so too do cultures vary between organizations. For example, the culture in nonprofit organizations is much different than that of for-profit firms. The organizational culture of a hospital may differ greatly from that of a law firm. Corporate cultures also vary greatly based on the culture in the country where they are based. Organizational culture directly affects how employees deal with stakeholders, including other employees, customers, suppliers, and the community. When an organization's culture is clearly defined, employees know what to expect and what is, in turn, expected of them.

Influencers of Culture

Organizational culture is shaped by both internal and external forces. Internally, the hierarchical structure, different personalities, attitudes of leaders, and even organizational history influence culture. When leaders and managers make decisions with regard to the culture and what will mesh with it, success comes more easily. When decisions are made without consideration for the culture, success is more difficult to achieve. Different personalities in people inherently make up any workforce. Those differences also shape and reshape culture. History, myths, and legends within an organization that are passed down through generations of employees or espoused also by executives influence culture.

Externally, societal norms, laws, and even competition have influence. If competition is fierce, an organization's culture may represent high pressure to perform or focus more on producing a quality product. The global society and global competition are placing more demands on corporate culture to be flexible, to bend and change more frequently than ever before.

Role of Culture

Culture plays a strong role in organizations. The culture of an organization dictates how it operates, innovates, and welcomes change. It influences a company's strategic plan, employee relations, and corporate image. In an open culture, employees may be encouraged to express new ideas for improvement. In a closed culture, it may be more difficult for a subordinate employee to introduce new ideas. Most organizations that are based in technology or research and development are very open and adaptable to change. It is in their nature to embrace the opportunity to try new things and become more efficient. Manufacturing and financial institutions are usually less ready to accept change because of the basis of the business they conduct, which is inherently procedural. Rituals and routines, like weekly meetings or certain reports (even those that are nonproductive), often become habitual and more difficult to change or eliminate because organizational culture sometimes dictates "the way things are done around here."

Culture influences dress code, the chain of command, even how the furniture is arranged or what office one occupies. Culture shapes symbols such as logos, letterhead, and even less traditional symbols like parking spaces. In turn, symbols are shaped by the culture.

Organizational subcultures evolve in different divisions, departments, and work teams. For instance, the engineering department may have a more open and innovative culture, while the accounting department's culture may be more closed and rigid.

The presence of a strong culture provides guidance to employees, often unifying their work toward achieving the same goal. Strong cultures are often present in older, larger organizations. It is more difficult to initiate and complete change when strong cultures exist because culture is ingrained. Weaker cultures, often found in companies that are smaller with less history, are much easier to change and are better able to adapt.

Implications for Managers

As a decision maker or manager, having a clear understanding of the culture of one's organization is paramount to success. Initiating change that goes against the grain of the current culture could be disastrous. Success is easier found when employees have an incentive to change the culture. When interviewing potential new employees, hiring managers should evaluate the fit between a candidate's personality and the organizational culture. Ensuring this compatibility will ultimately make the transition into the new job easier and create the likelihood of a longer-lasting employee. New employees make an effort to fit in and acclimate to a firm's culture. They also try to change it to suit them.

Care must be taken in mergers and acquisitions to lessen the clash of corporate cultures. It is often perceived that the acquiring company's culture will override that of the acquired company, creating the necessity for change and often a greater deal of stress for the acquired company. Clear communication of the combined cultural objective in this new union is necessary to create highly functioning work teams.

Culture changes slowly over time. Corporate cultures are cultivated and must be actively developed, monitored, and maintained. Recognizing the importance of culture is a requirement of effective leadership to allow the company to change and progress. The culture in an organization enables or hinders, stifles or inspires, and affects how employees feel about going to work. Culturally savvy executives understand the importance of culture and use it to their advantage to motivate, increase productivity, and effectively manage their workforce.

The importance of a healthy corporate culture is apparent—it promotes more effective employee interaction, celebrates tradition, allows the organization to adapt, and creates unity throughout.

See also Agile Organizations; Developmental Organizations; Leadership: An Overview
Resources:
Hofstede, Gerte. *Cultures and Organizations: Software of the Mind.* London: McGraw-Hill, 1991.
Schein, Edgar. "Organizational Culture." *American Psychologist* 45, no. 2 (February 1990): 109–19.

Kerry Schut

DEVELOPMENTAL ORGANIZATIONS

"An organization is a coordinated unit consisting of at least two people who function to achieve a common goal or set of goals."[1] Three types of organizations are identified in the literature: traditional, learning, and developmental. The distinguishing characteristics are described according to the emphasis on employee growth and development and an organization's capacity for renewal and desire to improve competitive readiness.[2] A developmental organization consistently performs at a high level in all areas, whereas a traditional organization places less emphasis on such practices.

Types of Organizations

Traditional Organization

A traditional organization is generally characterized by a hierarchical structure and autocratic leadership. Although the organization often achieves satisfactory business results, its full potential is never realized. A traditional organization could stand to gain increased effectiveness, but it fails to recognize the need to evolve to a higher order. Effectiveness describes the ability to deliver products and services to customers in relation to their needs or expectations.[3] Effectiveness is increased by improving the products and services so they offer greater value to customers. A traditional organization (1) does not place the same importance on its people, or human resources, as it does on financial and physical resources, (2) typically assumes training alone will enhance the organization, (3) focuses developmental activities on knowledge acquisition resulting in comprehension, (4) looks short-term at quarterly profits and losses and consequently has a low capacity for organizational renewal, and (5) lacks the ability to respond to environmental forces to remain competitive in periods of economic decline.[4]

Learning Organization

In contrast with a traditional organization, a learning organization holds a long-term shared vision and "is continually expanding its capacity to create its future. For such an organization, it is not enough merely to survive."[5] A learning organization is oriented toward learning and is structured accordingly to promote individual and group or team learning. Learning communities are offered as an alternative to the "expert" model.[6] The expert model represents experts, or people who purportedly have all the answers, and learners. The model implies a unidirectional flow of information, which limits the opportunity for experts to learn from learners and learners to learn on their own. Conversely, experts and learners in learning communities further their curiosity and learning together.

Transactional and transformation leaders acknowledge the importance of developing human resources.[7] Employee growth and development are fostered in a nurturing environment whereby mistakes are thought of as learning opportunities. A learning organization focuses developmental activities on application and reflection, leading to both personal mastery and self-awareness, respectively.[8] A learning organization considers continuous lifelong learning critical to increasing organizational effectiveness and adapts to environment forces to remain competitive through feedback employed by systems thinking. Senge (1990) identified five learning disciplines needed to successfully transition from a traditional organization to one that embraces learning; they are personal mastery, mental models, building shared vision, team learning, and systems thinking.[9]

Developmental Organization

As important as learning is to transition a traditional organization to a learning organization, it has been suggested that learning itself does not guarantee employee or business growth and development.[10] Moreover, they state this approach neither directly links to organizational performance nor provides a framework for improving performance. What is beyond the learning organization lies a developmental organization, which represents the evolutionary pinnacle of organizational transformation, and offers an approach to integrate organizational performance with organizational learning and change.[11] Development is defined as "the gradual advancement through progressive stages."[12] In the context of human resource development, the idea is to bring individuals and the organization up to another threshold of performance. "Development of people refers to the advancement of knowledge, skills, and competencies for the purpose of improving performance within an organization."[13] Its longer-term aim is to provide individuals with avenues for professional advancement, or career development. A comprehensive career-development process can help create a development culture that encourages employees to advance their development options.[14] Development of people within an organization is self-directed by the organization. The short-term goal for organizations is to achieve increased efficiency, effectiveness, and ultimately profitability to remain competitive (performance management); the longer-term goal is to reinvent itself as needed by continually enhancing the culture.[15]

Developmental champions and transactional and transformation leaders share similar qualities, but in addition, a developmental organization needs a leader "who realizes that organizational renewal and competitive readiness are totally dependent on employees prepared for future challenges, new work assignments, ever-increasing competition, continuous lifelong learning and change, and continuous growth and development."[16] Ten principles of leadership are required to successfully transform a learning organization into a developmental organization.[17] In addition to the new type of leader, a paradigm shift also necessitates employees to transition from being self-directed learners to enhancers of development, and human resources professionals to shift their roles from program provider to change agent. A distinguishing characteristic of a developmental organization is a genuine concern for employee growth and development. As employees improve their personal renewal and performance capacity, the organization benefits by increasing its aggregate renewal and performance capacity.[18]

See also Change Management; Community of Practice; Leadership: An Overview; Learning Organizations; Quality Circles

NOTES

1. James L. Gibson, John M. Ivancevich, James H. Donnelly Jr., and Robert Konopaske, *Organizations: Behavior, Structure, Processes,* 12th ed. (New York, NY: McGraw-Hill/Irwin, 2006), 5.

2. Peter M. Senge, *The Fifth Discipline: The Art and Practice of the Learning Organization* (New York: Doubleday, 1990), 14.

3. Jerry W. Gilley and Ann Maycunich, *Beyond the Learning Organization: Creating a Culture of Continuous Growth and Development through State-of-the-Art Human Resource Practices* (Cambridge, MA: Perseus Books, 2000), 62.

4. Ibid.

5. Arthur R. Tenner and Irving J. DeToro, *Process Redesign: The Implementation Guide for Managers* (Reading, MA: Addison-Wesley Publishing Company, 1997).

6. Ibid.

7. Gilley and Maycunich, *Beyond the Learning Organization,* 62.

8. Ibid.

9. Tenner and DeToro, *Process Redesign: The Implementation Guide for Managers.*

10. Gilley and Maycunich, *Beyond the Learning Organization,* 62.

11. Ibid.

12. Senge, *The Fifth Discipline,* 14.

13. Stephanie Ryan, "Learning Communities: An Alternative to the "Expert" Model," in *Learning Organizations,* ed. Sarita Chawla and John Renesch (Portland, OR: Productivity Press, 1995), 278–91.

14. Jerry W. Gilley and Ann Maycunich, *Organizational Learning Performance and Change: An Introduction to Strategic Human Resource Development* (Cambridge, MA: Perseus Publishing, 2000).

15. Oxford English Dictionary Online, "Development" (New York: Oxford University Press), http://lib.colostate.edu/databases/permlink.php?id=601 (accessed November 30, 2007).

16. Jerry W. Gilley, Steven A. Eggland, and Ann Maycunich Gilley, *Principles of Human Resource Development,* 2nd ed. (Cambridge, MA: Perseus Publishing, 2002), 5.

17. Gilley and Maycunich, *Beyond the Learning Organization,* 62.

18. Peggy Simonsen, *Promoting a Development Culture in Your Organization: Using Career Development as a Change Agent* (Palo Alto, CA: Davies-Black Publishing, 1997).

Alina M. Waite

DIVERSITY

The definition of diversity has traditionally focused on the areas of race and gender. In fact, governmental standards such as the Affirmative Action Program require certain employers to monitor employee demographic information and to demonstrate efforts to maintain acceptable levels of races and genders. Several companies, however, see benefits in all areas of diversity. Dick Kovacevich, president and CEO of Wells Fargo, states, "Diversity is an important business strategy. Life in the business world is about people —caring, committed, diverse, people who reflect the diversity of our markets."[1]

In this vein, the Society of Human Resource Management[1] provides a list of opportunities for recognizing and embracing diversity (Table 8.1):

Business Case

Hewitt and Associates[2] point out how increasing diversity is expected to make an impact on the workplace:

- *Greater diversity in the workplace*—by 2008, women and minorities will represent 70 percent of the new labor force entrants, and by 2010, 34 percent of the workforce will be non-Caucasian
- *An aging workforce*—by 2010, the U.S. workforce will have an increase of 29 percent in the 45–64 age group, a 14 percent increase in the 65+ age group, and a 1 percent decline in the 18–44 age group.
- *Globalization*—in the next decade, 75 percent of new workers will likely be from Asia, while North America and Europe will have 3 percent of the world's new labor force.

Thus, organizations must become increasingly equipped to embrace this increasingly diverse workforce. It is simply a fact-based imperative.

Related to this, the marketplace is experiencing a similar transformation. Thus, it is fast becoming a market-dictated mandate for organizations to become better equipped to serve an increasingly diverse customer/client base. To that end, the SHRM Diversity Forum provides the following examples of how embracing diversity supports business objectives:

- Diversity initiatives can improve the quality of an organization's workforce and can be the catalyst for a better ROI in human capital.
- Businesses can capitalize on new markets; customer bases are becoming even more diverse than the workforce.

Table 8.1   Opportunities for Recognizing and Embracing Diversity

Internal	External	Organizational
Age	Geographic location	Functional level
Gender	Income	Work content/field
Sexual orientation	Personal habits	Division/department/unit
Physical ability	Religion	Seniority
Ethnicity	Education	Work location
Race	Work experience	Union affiliation
	Parental status	Management status
	Marital status	

- Recognized diversity initiatives and diversity results will attract the best and brightest employees to the company.
- Diversity encourages creativity.
- Flexibility ensures survival.

Attracting and Retaining Diverse Candidates

Attracting diverse candidates is the initial step in many diversity initiatives. However, it is not the only step, nor is it typically the most difficult. Once candidates have been sourced, interviewed, and hired, the organization must ensure that the infrastructure (e.g., corporate climate, rewards system, etc.) is set to welcome and integrate diversity candidates.

Sourcing

Each organization will differ in budgetary allowances and overall strategy as it pertains to diversity sourcing and recruiting. SHRM research indicates that the most effective programs for diversity recruiting are college/university internships, targeted college/university recruiting, leadership development programs, mentoring programs, scholarship programs, and high school work-study programs. An organization's strategy should also consider how its partnership with staffing agencies and internal referral bonuses can be enhanced to encourage diverse candidates. Lastly, new partnerships with diverse professional organizations should be considered and evaluated.

Retaining

To ensure effective and efficient integration of diverse candidates, steps should be taken to prepare the organization's infrastructure to welcome and appreciate such integration. The following areas of opportunity are of paramount importance in such integration:
- *Leadership Support*—a unified sense of commitment and a shared vision across all levels of the organization especially at the top levels of the organization must be in place for the integrations to take roots.
- *Goals and Objectives*—in additional to traditional business goals such as increased sales, decreased costs, etc., a company that is serious about incorporating diverse candidates will need to examine it's reward systems to ensure it is rewarding the correct behavior (diversifying it's workforce). If the organization, a division, or an employee's goals do not take into account its diversity efforts, the initiative has little opportunity for success.
- *Training and Education*—the company must carefully consider all the stakeholders and draft a communication plan that educates and prepares such stakeholders for the diversification process. Often such an initiative can impact the way an employee does their job. The company must consider how it addresses the "why are we doing this" questions as well as manage issues that may arise from stereotyping. Such educational processes must begin at the front end of the initiative as well as during the actual integration. Often a company may find that they did not anticipate all the issues that could come up and find themselves reworking their training and education efforts.

See also Affirmative Action; Employment Law: An Overview

NOTES

1. G. Pascal Zachary, "Why Wells Fargo Bank Is Different" (June 2006), http://money.cnn.com/2006/06/09/magazines/business2/bankdifferent/ (accessed September 7, 2008).

2. Joseph P. Johnson III, PHR, Creating a Diverse Workforce (*SHRM Information Center, August 2003*)

3. Hewitt Associates, "Preparing the Workforce of Tomorrow" (February 2004), http://www.hewittassociates.com/Intl/NA/en-US/KnowledgeCenter/ArticlesReports/ArticleDetail.aspx?cid=1734 (accessed August 20, 2008).

Pat Schneider

EMPLOYEE EMPOWERMENT PROGRAM

Your employees will treat your customers the same way you treat your employees. If ever there was a rationale for looking very hard at the concept of employee empowerment, it is this "golden rule" of employee engagement. It is a truism that has been proven in many organizations and has been part of their success or an element of their downfall.

Employee Empowerment Defined

Employee empowerment can be defined as the enlargement of employees' spheres of influence, giving them greater responsibility and "authority to make decisions about their work without supervisory approval," thereby creating value for the ultimate customer.[1]

Employee empowerment has been linked to total quality management (TQM), which can be defined as the "never-ending process of continuous improvement that covers people, equipment, suppliers, materials and procedures...so that every aspect of an operation can be improved...and the end goal is perfection, which is never achieved but always sought."[2]

In the empowerment methodology, people are considered the primary resource for furthering productivity. Employees are encouraged to take the initiative in identifying problems and proposing solutions. Through participation in teams, people at all levels offer their unique expertise in a cooperative, problem-solving process.

Employee Empowerment Process

While the title of this entry is "Employee Empowerment Program," it may be more accurate to call this effort of empowerment a *process* rather than a *program*. Employee empowerment is an effort that includes creating a culture of trust within the organization, and building trust is always a process. We will use the term *program,* however, because this empowerment process includes specific and intentional steps, which must be implemented as if they were part of a program.

Strategies and Examples

Employee empowerment programs are as varied as the organizations that implement them, and there are specific nuances to any shared strategy. The following are just a few examples of strategies used by organizations to empower their employees:
• Flattening organizational pyramids
• Using team management and self-conducted teams
• Profit sharing
• Employee stock option plans (ESOPs)
• Helping employees set up their own freestanding companies within the corporation (e.g., Chicago-based Hyatt Hotels Corporation)

- Allowing employees to spend a certain percentage of their time working on any new idea they want
- Ongoing career counseling for employees
- Employee-directed benefit packages
- Training employees with problem-solving tools

Benefits of Employee Empowerment

Employee empowerment can be a powerful tool to increase the effectiveness of any organization. Some of the benefits include:

- Increased efficiency
- Reduction in overhead
- More time for leadership to dedicate to overall directional issues
- The shared knowledge of a greater number of employees
- Greater customer service
- Greater level of employee job satisfaction
- Employee personal growth

When employee empowerment is implemented correctly, it is a "win-win-win" situation: customers benefit from authorized and responsible employees; organizations benefit from satisfied customers and employees; and employees benefit from improving their confidence and self-esteems.[3]

A Key to Effective Employee Empowerment

As stated earlier, trust is foundational for effective employee empowerment, and trust is built on communication. For an organization to practice and foster employee empowerment, the management must trust and communicate with employees. Employee communication is one of the strongest signs of employee empowerment; honest and repeated communication, from elements of the strategic plan, key performance indicators, and financial performance, down to daily decision making. Because clear communication is so important, it must be an intentional part of implementing an effective employee empowerment program.

Dangers of Poorly Implemented Employee Empowerment

When carefully implemented, employee empowerment can produce significant results, but there are some pitfalls to avoid in the process, for example:

- Poorly defined power and authority structures.
- Poorly defined expectations and responsibilities.
- Managers unwilling to give up necessary power.
- New employee responsibility seen as a threat by the employee.
- Poorly trained employees given responsibility and authority too quickly.
- Lack of trust in the organization.
- Impatience when the process seems to be taking a long time.
- Resorting to former hierarchal structure in a pinch.
- Managers abdicating all responsibility and accountability for decision making.
- Lack of understanding of what employee empowerment means.

Employee Empowerment Begins at the Top

Employee empowerment begins with an organization's senior-level executives, because it must be owned at all levels, with a consistent philosophy and approach backed up with observable behaviors. Through clear and consistent communication, the employee empowerment program can be implemented and sustained, resulting in the above benefits, and will raise the employee commitment level. If an organization wants a greater level of commitment to the organization from the employee, then the organization must take the first step in demonstrating a greater level of commitment to the employee. Therefore, any employee empowerment program must begin with the leadership of the organization.

NOTES

1. Louis E. Boone and David Kurtz, *Contemporary Marketing* (Fort Worth, TX: The Dryden Press, 1998).

2. Jay Heizer and Barry Render, *Principles of Operations Management* (Upper Saddle River, NJ: Prentice-Hall, 1999).

3. Connie Sitterly, "Empowering Others Improves Workplace Quality," *Business Press* 11, no. 22 (1998).

Brad M. Jensen

EMPLOYEE RELATIONS

Employee relations are the steps an organization takes to ensure day-to-day business practices consider the welfare of employees when making decisions. As defined in the Society for Human Resource Management's (SHRM) online glossary of HR terms, employee relations is "a broad term used to refer to the general management and planning of activities related to developing, maintaining and improving employee relationships by communicating with employees, processing grievances/disputes, etc."[1]

Employee relations is a traditional human resources role, but has developed depth to cover many areas over the years. It encompasses the life cycle of an employee upon entry into an organization through end of employment. This includes the on-boarding process, HR policies, performance management, corrective action, recognition, employee feedback systems, retention, relationship with managers, and the exiting process.

On-boarding Process

The on-boarding process includes orientation, on-the-job training, and assimilation. The on-boarding process starts as soon a candidate accepts an offer of employment and becomes an employee. Many companies provide information about the organization, company polices and the employee handbook to new employees before they start their first day. Typically, an employee's first day includes an orientation lasting a few hours to a full day, depending on the company's resources and structure. Orientation should include three main areas:

1. Things that affect an employee personally—e.g., attendance policy, where to park, job expectations
2. Things that affect an employee as a member of a department—e.g., team goals, team meetings, department organization chart
3. Things that affect an employee of an organization—e.g., culture, diversity, strategic goals, vision

After orientation, an employee may receive formal training or move right into on-the-job training. On-the-job training is provided to employees by their managers and/or experienced peers; it is conducted by actual performance of the job tasks, and the supervisor or peer observes the task and provides feedback to the employee. The assimilation process may be covered by the supervisor, or an employee may receive a buddy (mentor). During the assimilation process, an employee observes company culture, communication, decision making, employee involvement, and recognition. It is important for a new employee to review these areas with her supervisor or mentor.

Human Resources Policies

The human resources policies are provided to employees through the employee handbook. The employee handbook is a written or electronic document containing summaries of the employer's policies and benefits, designed to familiarize employees with various matters affecting the employment relationship. The employee handbook is provided on or before the employee's first day and is reviewed in orientation or with the employee's manager. The employee handbook may not cover all of the human resources polices. It typically covers the company's policies on discrimination, sexual harassment, time and attendance, corrective action, standards of conduct, business attire, dispute resolution and the performance review process.

Performance Management

The performance management process includes goal setting, continuous feedback on performance, formal reviews, and recognition. Goal setting is established annually or within 30 days of a new employee's first day. Continuous feedback enables the employee to know how she is progressing against her goals and make adjustments if needed. Managers may provide ongoing feedback on progress against goals weekly, monthly, or quarterly; if an employee is working on a long-term project, the feedback may be on an as-needed basis. The formal performance review process should accomplish five objectives:

1. Provide feedback to employees on their performance
2. Discuss goals that may need to be changed or adjusted
3. Discuss areas in need of improvement
4. Discuss new, more challenging goals
5. Provide key areas of focus for the remanding review period

The formal review may be conducted annually or semiannually and is scheduled on a common review date or from hire date. As an employee progresses against her goals, it is important for the manager to recognize the employees' achievements and provide monetary rewards, if applicable. The human resources department is generally very involved in the process and provides direction and support.

Corrective Action

There are many different processes for corrective action based on the culture of an organization. The piece that is similar is the result of performance improvement or a change in behavior or conduct. Corrective action is successful when the manager addresses the issue with the employee in a timely manner, asks the employee how he would like to resolve the issue, agrees on a time line, follows up with the employee, and provides recognition on improvements. Conversations are documented by recapping a summary of the conversation or providing a formal warning. If the employee does not improve his performance or change his behavior or conduct, the last step is termination. By the time a manager is ready to meet with an employee to terminate, the employee should not be surprised by the termination.

Recognition

The purpose of an employee recognition program is to say "thank you," "well done," "we value you as an employee." Employee recognition can be classified as formal or informal. For either form of recognition to be effective, the manager needs to be specific about the reason why the employee is receiving the recognition. Examples of formal recognition are company stock, bonuses, or gift certificates. Informal recognition is low cost or no cost. Examples include acknowledging an employee in a meeting in front of peers, saying thank you for a job well done, or acknowledging a specific trait or quality that stands out. Other examples are sending an employee to a meeting in your place, which shows you trust him or her; inviting an employee to be on a task force or committee; or sending the person to a special training class. Even small gestures can make an impression—for example, treating the employee to lunch or awarding a certificate of accomplishment. It is also important for managers to recognize employees when they improve their performance. The amount of employee recognition a manager can give is unlimited, and it does not have to be time or resource consuming.

Employee Feedback Systems

Understanding how employees feel every day when they walk through the door is understood through employee feedback systems. Employee feedback can lead to improvements in workplace practices, employee engagement, and retention. Many employers hold annual satisfaction surveys to gauge the climate of the organization. Other forms of feedback systems are new hire surveys, on-boarding (60–90 days) surveys, change management surveys, career development surveys, manager effectiveness surveys, exit surveys, and suggestion systems. There are many ways to learn what employees are thinking. To develop an effective system, employers need to gather results, determine the gaps, develop an action plan, communicate the plan to employees, execute action items and follow-up, and make adjustments as needed.

Retention

One of the top reasons retention is tracked by business leaders is the cost. The Saratoga Institute estimates the average cost of losing an employee to be equivalent to that employee's annual salary. This means that a company with 300 employees, an average salary of $35,000, and a voluntary turnover rate of 15 percent per year is losing $1,575,000 per year in turnover costs alone.[2]

Other reasons to look at retention is the effect it has on attracting talent and employee engagement. If an organization is known for employee turnover, talent may be hesitant to pursue opportunities there until things change. Managers tend to think employees leave or stay mostly for money. A Saratoga Institute survey revealed that 80–90 percent of employees leave for reasons not related to money but to the job, the manager, the culture, or the work environment.[3] If employees are struggling with their manager, job, or work environment, they may become disengaged. Disengaged employees are uncommitted, marginally productive, and frequently absent.[4] The cost of absenteeism alone, a signal of disengagement, is estimated to be $40 billion per year.[5] It is imperative that organizations see the cost factor of turnover and the need to train their managers to understand the importance of improving the culture and keeping their employees engaged.

Relationship with Manager

Frontline managers have a critical impact on employee relations in any organization. Too frequently, managers lack the experience, skills, or information they need to succeed in this area. It is the organization's responsibility to take the appropriate steps. The first step is to place the right manager in the role for the right reasons. Secondly, train managers on policies, practices, and leadership. Next, clearly define the expectations of their role, commit to providing them ongoing feedback, continuous training, and development, and utilize a 360-degree survey for leadership development. Lastly, help them become a career coach and developer of talent. Managers should be trained to assess talent and recognize everything.

Exiting Process

Having an exit interview process is a way to learn important aspects about your culture. When an employee leaves your organization, you have an opportunity to gain insight about that employee's experience with you from a variety of perspectives. It is important to inform all managers that your organization has an exit interview process and to convey the value the organization places on the feedback received during this process. In addition, make sure that employees know that their feedback is valued at any time during their tenure. The exit interview should come to be viewed as just another stage in the "life cycle" of employment. By managing employees' expectations about the process, they will be less likely to be taken by surprise by the request for an exit interview and, hopefully, more thoughtful about their responses. Develop a method for compiling the information you receive to identify trends that may be leading to turnover and communicate the results with senior management.

See also Disciplinary Procedures; Employee Attitude Survey; Employee Handbook; HR Policy: An Overview; Performance Management: An Overview; Retention; Staffing: An Overview

NOTES

1. "Online Glossary of HR Terms," Society of Human Resource Management, http://www.shrm.com (accessed August 20, 2008).

2. Leigh Branham, *The Seven Hidden Reasons Employees Leave* (New York: American Management Association, 2005).

3. Ibid.

4. Ibid.

5. Ibid.

Cyndi Stewart

ETHICS

In the broadest definition, ethics focuses on the branch of philosophy concerned with intent, means, and consequences of moral behavior. Derived from the Greek word "ethos," ethics refers to a person's fundamental orientation toward life or inner character. Ethics and morals are respectively akin to theory and practice. Moral behavior refers to what is right and wrong, good and bad, with emphasis on overt behavior-acts, habits, and customs. Levels of moral reasoning include preconventional morality, based on avoiding punishment and striving for pleasure; conventional morality, based on pleasing others and doing one's duty as prescribed by authorities; and postconventional morality, based on mutual consent and personal convention.[1]

Defining what ethics is *not* adds to the bounding of the definition. Ethics are not doing what feels right. Ethics and law are not always the same. Ethics are not necessarily doing whatever society finds acceptable. Many people believe that if you do not break the law, then you are behaving in an ethical manner, but ethics goes far beyond the law. Ethical standards for the most part apply to behavior not covered by law. Although current laws often reflect minimum moral standards, not all moral standards are codified into law. The morality of aiding a drowning person, for example, is not definitively specified by law.

Business Ethics

Business ethics focus on the area of *applied* ethics as organizations examine moral and ethical issues in their (business) environments and develop applicable ethical principles and standards. High ethical standards require both businesses and individuals to conform to sound moral principles. However, some special aspects must first be considered when applying ethics to business.

First, to survive, a business must earn a profit. If profits are realized through misconduct, however, the life of the organization may be shortened. Many firms, including Arthur Anderson and Enron, ultimately went bankrupt or failed because of the legal and financial repercussions related to their ethical misconduct. Businesses must balance their desires for profits against the needs and desires of society. Maintaining this balance often requires compromises and trade-offs. To address these unique aspects of the business world, society has developed rules, both legal and implicit, to guide businesses in their efforts to earn profits in ways that do not harm individuals or society as a whole. Whether a specific action is right or wrong, ethical or unethical, is often determined by investors, employees, customers, interest groups, the legal system, and the community. Although these groups are not necessarily "right," their judgments influence society's acceptance or rejection of a business and its activities.

Research demonstrates that building an ethical reputation among employees, customers, and the general public provides benefits that include increased efficiency in daily operations, greater employee commitment, increased investor willingness to entrust funds, improved customer trust and satisfaction, and better financial performance. The reputation of a company has a major effect on its relationships with employees, investors, customers, and many other parties, and thus has the potential to affect its bottom line.[2]

Leadership and Ethics

Ethical behaviors in organizations are developed and strengthened primarily through leadership behavior. Leaders influence ethical behavior through their personal ethical values and the connection of those deeply held values to organizational goals. Employees learn about the ethical values of the organization from watching the leaders. Leaders generate a high level of trust and respect from employees, based not just on stated values, but on the courage, determination, and self-sacrifice they demonstrate in upholding those values. When leaders are willing to make personal sacrifices for the sake of values, employees become more willing to do so as well.

For organizations to be ethical, leaders need to be openly and strongly committed to ethical conduct. In addition, ethical leaders uphold their commitment to values during difficult times or crises. Leaders have to discover their own personal ethical values and actively communicate values to others through both words and actions. When faced with difficult decisions, values-based leaders know what they stand for, and they have the courage to act on their principles. In addition, by clearly communicating the ethical standards they expect others to live by, leaders can empower people throughout the organization to make decisions within that framework.[3]

Conclusion

Internationally recognized leadership expert, speaker, and author John Maxwell responded very clearly to a question about business ethics. He stated, "There's no such thing as business ethics—there's only ethics. People try to use one set of ethics for their professional life, another for their spiritual life, and still another at home with their family. That gets them into trouble. Ethics is ethics. If you desire to be ethical, you live it by one standard across the board." Living an ethical life may not always be easy, but it need not be complicated.[4]

NOTES

1. George Manning and Kent Curtis, *The Art of Leadership* (Boston: McGraw-Hill, 2007).
2. O.C. Ferrell, John Fraedrich, and Linda Ferrell, *Business Ethics: Ethical Decision Making and Cases* (Boston: Houghton Mifflin, 2005).
3. Richard L. Daft, *The Leadership Experience* (Mason, OH: Thompson, 2008).
4. John C. Maxwell, *There's No Such Thing as Business Ethics* (New York: Warner Books, 2003).

Merwyn L. Strate

JOB SATISFACTION

Job satisfaction is defined as one's feelings or state of mind regarding the nature of one's work. The level of job satisfaction can be linked to an outcome of an increase or decrease in employee engagement, production, absenteeism, and turnover.

According to the SHRM 2007 Job Satisfaction Survey Report,[1] compensation and benefits continue to be the top contributors to employee satisfaction. After those two requirements are met, employees are seeking job security, work/life balance, communication between employees and their manager, recognition of job performance, opportunities to use skills/ability, and autonomy. Managers have the choice to create an environment in which employees feel satisfied.

Job Security

Job security will probably continue to be high on the satisfaction scale as off-shoring, restructuring, mergers, and layoffs increase, and as workplace skills change. Employers cannot guarantee jobs, but they can create of culture of continuous learning so employees can obtain the skills to move into new and different positions and adapt to changes in their current positions. Counter to this, it is becoming more common to hold positions with many companies, and job security tends to be less important for younger generations.

Work/Life Balance

As businesses become more global, work hours are varying and commutes are becoming longer. With the improvement in workplace technology, employees are looking for ways to sustain their performance while concurrently increasing job flexibility. Studies have shown an increase in job satisfaction, productivity, and retention from employees who telecommute. Relatively few companies offer telecommuting, yet the need is rising.

Communication

Employees seek two-way communication with their managers. Employees feel like their opinions do not matter when there is limited communication, or they hear an update from a peer who works for a different manager. Lack of communication can also be viewed as a lack of respect. In addition, without regular communication, employees tend to fill in their own blanks, and then rumors are created. Creating a culture of holding regular manager/ employee meetings, company-wide employee meetings, e-mails, and maintaining a company Web page will improve communication and reduce workplace rumors.

Recognition

Recognition ranks among the top five indicators of employee satisfaction. It is cost-effective and informal, yet few managers practice it regularly. Recognition can be as simple as providing praise for a job well done, saying "thank you," offering an award, or buying a latte. If a manager is unsure what kind of recognition would be effective, he can solicit ideas from his employees through a survey or in individual meetings.

Opportunities to Use Skills/Having Autonomy

Employees feel good about their work when they have opportunities to use their unique skills, when they believe they are contributing to the organization, and when they have a sense of autonomy. Unique skills can be used and improved by cross-training, covering a meeting for the manager, or assigning an employee to lead a task force or outreach project.

Assessing Job Satisfaction

Employee surveys and exit interviews are the most common methods used by organizations to assess job satisfaction. Other common practices include holding focus groups, speaking with employees one on one, implementing suggestions systems, ask-the-president e-mails, addressing and tracking employee complaints, attendance, turnover, and performance for trends. Keep in mind that employee feedback loses its value if you do not report back the results and work on improving areas of concerns.

See also Compensation: An Overview; Employee Attitude Surveys; Employee Relations; Managerial Communications; Retention; Turnover; Work-Life Balance

NOTE

1. SHRMs 2007 annual employee satisfaction survey, http://www.shrm.org/hrresources/surveys _published/2007 Job Satisfaction Survey Report.pdf.

Cyndi Stewart

KNOWLEDGE TRANSFER

Knowledge transfer is a process whereby one individual or team conveys information accumulated over time to another individual or team who will then internalize and apply the information to their current work. Successful transfer of knowledge relies on many factors. Whether the knowledge is formal or informal, tacit or explicit, the extent to which an individual can internalize information and transform it into knowledge can be influenced by learning style, motivation, practice, reflection, and experience. Because of the growing importance of knowledge as a driver for innovation and competitive advantage in modern organizations as well as the continuously changing dynamics of the workforce, organizations are integrating knowledge transfer practices into their knowledge management strategies to speed innovation, mitigate risk, improve performance, and preserve wisdom.

Defining Knowledge Is Difficult

Knowledge transfer may be better understood by first discussing the complexity of knowledge itself. Knowledge has many definitions and interpretations. While Plato believed that the key requirements for knowledge was that it must be "justified, true, and believed,"[1] the Oxford English Dictionary defines it simply as "expertise, and skills acquired by a person through experience or education."[2] Knowledge can be represented formally as that which is documented in books, manuals, documents, and training courses. But what may be more important to the knowledge transfer process is informal knowledge, such as ideas, facts, assumptions, meanings, questions, decisions, guesses, stories, and points of view. This knowledge is more ephemeral and thus is more difficult to capture and keep.

Knowledge Work and Knowledge Transfer

In a modern organization, knowledge is now perceived as the new currency of the workforce. Management theorist and consultant Peter Drucker initiated many of the current ideas about the growing value of knowledge in organizations. He coined the term "knowledge work," and named those who perform a large part of this work as "knowledge workers."[3] Unlike the blue-collar or even the traditional white-collar worker, the knowledge worker is an expert or specialist who in contemporary organizations routinely comes together with other knowledge workers to solve complex problems in teams. Thus, such workers must also have strong collaboration skills. The productivity of a knowledge team depends on its ability to efficiently and effectively communicate and learn from one another. To this end, knowledge workers must also be able to incorporate new information into knowledge and be able to apply it quickly.

Factors Influencing Knowledge Transfer

An individual's learning style can influence the process of knowledge transfer. For example, hands-on learning has been found to be especially effective. Motivation is also an important factor and has not only been linked to the likelihood of transfer but also to the success of the organization (through mastery and performance). Through the process of reflection and interpretation, the factors of experience and success also influence the effectiveness of knowledge transfer.

But effective knowledge transfer is also an interactive process. Research has shown that managers learn most of their skills informally. Of these informal skills, interaction was cited as the activity used most frequently to develop both core leadership skills and the proficiency needed to complete their work tasks. Peer support through social networking is also important and has the highest correlation with knowledge transfer. Within an organization, knowledge transfer occurs from implicit sharing in such informal activities as mentoring or storytelling, internal and external blogs, and the collaborative efforts of wikis, as well as more formal efforts such as action learning projects.

Considering the individual components of the process, knowledge is effectively transferred through both implicit and explicit exchanges with the organization and social networks, resulting in the development of deeper knowledge, which is then transferred back to the organization and social networks. As the cycle continues and collective understanding and competency further develop, creative ideas and insights are shared, and innovative ideas emerge. As knowledge grows, wisdom can develop, and that collective wisdom is the key to the sort of continuous innovation that can sustain organizational growth.

Conclusion

Despite every effort to establish effective knowledge transfer strategies, organizational knowledge is fragile. Competencies can shift due to transition of resources (inbound and outbound mobility, downsizing, retirement), shifting investments by the organization, or just become stale or lost due to lack of use. Recently, a new term called "knowledge continuity management" has emerged, which is defined by Hamilton Beazley (chairman of the Strategic Leadership Group in Arlington, Virginia) as "effective methods for transferring employee know-how." It involves establishing communication practices to methodically pass on knowledge to peers. Fundamental to its success is an organizational environment and culture which is deeply committed to supporting the interactions of knowledge transfer.

See also Knowledge Management

Resources:

Anis, Mahmud, Steven Armstrong, and Zhichang Zhu. "The Influence of Learning Styles on Knowledge Acquisition in Public Sector Management." *Educational Psychology* 24, no. 4 (August 2004).

Burrow, Jim, and Paula Berardinelli. "Systematic Performance Improvement—Refining the Space between Learning and Results." *Journal of Workplace Learning* 15, no. 1 (2003).

Cross, Rob, Wayne Baker, and Andrew Parker. "What Creates Energy in Organizations?" *MIT Sloan Management Review,* Summer 2003.

Enos, Michael D., Marijke Kehrhahn, and Alexandra Bell. "Informal Learning and the Transfer of Learning: How Managers Develop Proficiency." *Human Resource Development Quarterly* 14, no. 4 (Winter 2003).

Holton, E.F., III. "The Flawed Four-level Evaluation Model." *Human Resource Development Quarterly* 7, no. 1 (1996): 5–25.

Kinman, Gail, and Russell Kinman. "The Role of Motivation to Learn in Management Education." *Journal of Workplace Learning* 13, no. 4 (2001).

NOTES

1. Wikimedia Foundation, Inc., "Knowledge,"http://en.wikipedia.org/wiki/Knowledge (accessed August 20, 2008).

2. Catherine Soanes and Angus Stevenson, eds., *Oxford English Dictionary* (Oxford: Oxford Dictionaries, 2005).

3. Ikujiro Nonaka, *The Knowledge-Creating Company: How Japanese Companies Create the Dynamics of Innovation* (New York: Oxford University Press, 1995).

Pamela Dixon and Alison Thero

LEARNING ORGANIZATIONS

A learning organization is a broad term used to describe organizations that emphasize the expansion of learning capacity, at all organizational levels, in order to generate results, creativity, patterns of thinking, and an environment in which all employees of the organization aspire to learn.[1] Learning organizations are further defined by their drive to implement initiatives and strategies designed to improve the effectiveness of the organization through the development of employee qualities, capabilities, and expertise.[2] A learning organization is constantly recreating itself by encouraging the interrelationship between organizational learning and the processes of organizational change. This type of adaptability is created by the organization's ability to build capacity by motivating individuals to want to learn and develop professionally.

Learning organizations foster transformational learning and typically encourage a culture based on human values, a set of practices that generate coordinated action, and the capacity to work with the dynamic interrelations of systems.[3] In order to develop these practices and systems, learning organizations often employ a common language to communicate the terminology, categories, and concepts necessary to define the strategies the organization plans to utilize in order to build upon its organizational learning capacity. A learning organization's longevity depends upon an organization's adaptability and commitment to continually research and act upon opportunities that build learning capacity and produce results for the organization.[4]

Disciplines of Learning Organizations

Arguably, Peter Senge has had the most profound influence on the contemporary business world relative to the concept of organizational learning. In his seminal work Senge outlines the following core disciplines of learning organizations:[5]

- *Mental models*—learning organizations encourage open dialogue as a means of surfacing the individual and shared presuppositions that shape individual and corporate behavior.
- *Shared vision*—learning organizations employ open dialogue regarding shared mental models to develop a shared vision of the desired future state of the organization.

- *Personal mastery*—learning organizations reinforce individual employee excellence and accountability without fear of failure.
- *Team learning*—learning organizations leverage shared vision and individual excellence to achieve synergy via team structures.
- *Systems thinking*—learning organizations constantly reinforce the big picture and getting to the root cause of all things.

Conclusion

As the world's most developed nation-states move toward more services-based economies (65 percent of the GDP of the United States is now accounted for by services-based industries and organizations), organizational learning will become a more important source of competitive advantage. In services-based organizations, the employees are essentially the "product," and their individual and aggregate learning greatly influences organizational performance and ongoing vitality.

See also Developmental Organizations; Knowledge Management

NOTES

1. Peter M. Senge, *The Fifth Discipline: The Art and Practice of the Learning Organization* (New York: Currency Doubleday, 1990), 371.

2. Richard Pettinger, *The Learning Organization* (Oxford: Capstone Publishing, 2002), 2.

3. Fred Kofman and Peter M. Senge, "Communities of Commitment: The Heart of Learning Organizations," in *Learning Organizations: Developing Cultures for Tomorrow's Workplace,* ed. Sarita Chawla and John Renesch (Portland, OR: Productivity Press, 1995), 14–43.

4. Peter M. Senge, "The Leader's New Work: Building Learning Organizations," in *Sloan Management Review,* Fall 1990, 7–23.

5. Senge, *The Fifth Discipline,* 371.

Matt Neibauer

MANAGERIAL COMMUNICATION

Managerial communication is the verbal and nonverbal/written methods of exchange of information between management and employees, and the effectiveness with which it is transmitted, integrated, and perceived. It may be used to build partnerships and intellectual resources, or to promote an idea, product, or service in order to create value for the organization.[1]

Communication within the management arena may include one-on-one interaction with an employee or another management member, an oral presentation given to a group, correspondence via letter or e-mail, or written instructions and policies. Since all organizations consist of people, effective interpersonal communication skills, including listening, speaking, and writing, are vital for success.

Elements of Communication

Communication is comprised of a sender, a message, a receiver, and an interpretation. The sender is the person who has a message to convey. The message is the information the sender delivers either verbally, via nonverbal cues, or in writing. The receiver is the person to whom the message is directed. The interpretation is how the receiver evaluates the message according to his/her standpoint, life experiences, frame of reference, and personal assumptions. Individual differences in the levels of communication development and competence can affect information exchanges.[2]

Elements of Managerial Communication

The diversity of today's workforce—more elderly, a growing foreign population with language barriers, the handicapped, and so forth—requires a manager to communicate with an awareness of the variety of components unique to each employee.

Communication in a business organization provides the critical link between core functions.[3] Management should aim to develop communication patterns between individuals and groups that are meaningful, direct, open, and honest.[4] Many factors are involved in this process, one of the most important of which is listening. Managers who listen to their employees, considering their views and concerns, are in a better position to receive positive responses, cooperation, and work effort. Communication in any environment, especially a professional one, should function with the idea that one "speaks in a way that makes it possible for others to listen, and listens in a way that makes it possible for others to speak."[5]

Effective managerial communication involves considering the perspective and communication skills of the receiver and constructing competent messages. Benefits of good communication skills can include anticipation of problems within the workplace; coordination of workflow; management of employee knowledge, ideas, and creativity; creation of a clear organizational vision; and energizing employees.[6]

In recent studies of characteristics of effective managers, employees list "communications" as one of the most important skills a manager can possess.[7] The communication climate that management models and embraces affects an organization's function and success. For example, the manner in which a manager portrays his/her status or authority and/or the manner in which the employee interprets that portrayal can potentially affect communication and, thus, productivity.[8] Consequently, perfecting one's communication skills and practices will be essential for managers and their organizations.

NOTES

1. Vadim Kotelnikov, "Effective Business Communication," http://www.1000ventures.com/business_guide/crosscuttings/biz-communication (accessed September 7, 2007).

2. John F. Cragan, David W. Wright, and Chris R. Kasch, *Communication in Small Groups: Theory, Process, Skills* (Belmont, CA: Thomson-Wadsworth, 2004), 177.

3. Marty Blalok, "Listen Up: Why Good Communication is Good Business," http://www.bus.wisc.edu/update/winter05/business_communication.asp (accessed July 23, 2007).

4. "Communication Skills: Conceptual Model," http://www.accel-team.com/communications/busComms_00.html (accessed July 23, 2007).

5. Em Griffin, *A First Look at Communication Theory*, 5th ed. (New York: McGraw-Hill, 2003), 77.

6. Ibid.

7. Ann Gilley, Pamela Dixon, and Jerry W. Gilley, "Characteristics of Leadership Effectiveness," paper presented at the Midwest Academy of Management Conference, Kansas City, MO, 2007.

8. Charles E. Beck, "Review of *Managerial Communication: Bridging Theory and Practice,* by Zhu Yunxia," *Business Communication Quarterly* 66, no. 4 (2003): 125–28.

Julianne Daniels

NEEDS ANALYSIS

A needs analysis process involves a series of activities conducted to identify problems or other issues in the workplace, and to determine root causes and opportunities. This information is then used to determine possible solutions. The needs analysis is necessary as a first step in the change process, as it aids in the identification of gaps that exist between the current state and the desired state. For example, internal or external consultants can conduct needs analyses as part of a larger training and development initiative, with the ultimate objective being the identification of knowledge, skills, and attitudes in which employees are currently deficient.[1]

Rationale

Several circumstances warrant a needs analysis, each of which has variable benefits and risks to the organization. Such scenarios include:
• An annual assessment.
• The introduction of a new leader to a department, division, or company.
• Addressing performance problems.
• The potential addition of a new system, task, or technology.
• The potential to benefit from a new opportunity.

Benefits

Conducting a needs analysis prior to making organizational plans is helpful for a number of reasons. It allows the organization to:
• Identify training needs.
• Identify developmental needs for individuals and groups.
• Prioritize training needs.
• Recognize areas of strength.
• Set clear objectives.[2]

Consequences of Not Conducting a Needs Analysis

The consequences of not performing a needs analysis, or performing the needs analysis incorrectly, include:
• Training is misapplied.
• Missed opportunities.
• Poor performance continues.

Performing the Needs Analysis

The steps in a needs analysis are sequential in nature, as one step builds on the previous step and provides the organization with valuable insight necessary in determining the next logical step. During this process, it is imperative that the needs analysis consultants remain objective, not allowing their perceptions to influence the direction of the analysis.

Steps in the Needs Analysis

The classic action research model focuses on planned change as a cyclical process in which initial research about the organization provides information to guide subsequent action.[3] Each step in the process requires collaboration and discussion to ensure the process fits the needs of the organization, as well as to ensure there is common agreement on the meaning behind the data collected. Specific steps of the action research model include:

- Problem identification
- Consultation with a behavioral science expert
- Data gathering and preliminary diagnosis
- Feedback to the key client or group
- Joint diagnosis of the problem
- Joint action planning
- Action
- Data gathering after action

Data Collection

Consultants have numerous options to choose from to aid in the gathering of data during the needs analysis. These data collection options include:

- *Surveys*—a series of verbal questions or a questionnaire used to gather data about employee attitudes, behaviors, skills, etc.
- *Interviews*—an interview is a conversation between two or more people where questions are asked to obtain information about the interviewee.
- *Unobtrusive data analysis*—data not obtained from subjects but from available sources, such as company records and reports.
- *Observations*—obtaining data from simply observing subjects or tracking the occurrences of specific behaviors.
- *Focus groups*—a qualitative research technique in which 8 to 12 subject participants are gathered in one room for a discussion under the leadership of a trained moderator. Discussion focuses on a problem, product, or potential solution to a problem.

Often it is prudent to utilize a sequential combination of two more of these techniques, and it is common to consider all of the techniques if they are available.

See also Training; Training Evaluation; Employee Development: An Overview; Performance Management: An Overview

NOTES

1. Jerry W. Gilley and Ann Gilley, *Strategically Integrated HRD* (Cambridge, MA: Perseus Publishing, 2003).
2. Malcolm Carlaw, Peggy Carla, Vasudha K. Deming, and Kurt Friedmann, *Managing and Motivating Contact Center Employees* (New York: McGraw-Hill Companies, 2003).
3. Thomas G. Cummings and Christopher G. Worley, *Organization Development and Change* (Mason, OH: Thomson South-Western, 2005).

Pat Schneider

QUALITY CIRCLES

Quality circles are groups of volunteer employees who work together to solve productivity problems. It is a technique whereby employees participate in how their work is performed by discussing, analyzing, and solving work issues.[1] Very popular in Japan, quality circles were first used by Lockheed Missile and Space Company in the 1970s.[2] Since then, quality circles became very popular in the United States as well, with one estimate that by the

1980s, 90 percent of Fortune 500 companies had quality circles.[3] Quality circles were a component of Deming's quality program, and later became part of total quality management (as quality improvement teams), and later evolved into self-managed work teams.[4] Although the use of the term is in decline in the United States, these programs are based on the same participative group problem-solving techniques. Quality circles are one of the first manifestations of employee empowerment in the United States.

How Quality Circles Work

Quality circles are formed by employees who volunteer to meet in a group for the purpose of making suggestions to improve the quality of the company's products and increasing the productivity of work processes by studying problems. But they are generally not given any information about the overall strategy or performance of the organization.[5] Quality circles meet on company time to discuss ways to improve production processes, generally using statistical quality control methods.[6] Occasionally, quality circles are allowed to also implement their recommendations, but generally they are formed primarily to make suggestions or recommendations for improvement.

Quality circles may or may not be effective. The effectiveness of quality circles depends on many factors: individual (skills, knowledge, self-esteem, feelings of accomplishment) differences, group (cohesion, dynamics, rewards) differences, and/or organizational (type, jobs, quality program existence, organizational, and management support and recognition) differences.[7]

Advantages and Disadvantages of Quality Circles

Quality circles have advantages and disadvantages. Most advantages are the result of employee involvement in problem solving and cost reductions, while disadvantages have to do with the way the quality circles are managed in the organization.

Advantages of Quality Circles

The main advantage of quality circles is that they can help an organization to reduce costs by improving work processes and productivity, while increasing or maintaining product quality.[8] A secondary benefit may be that employees' job satisfaction is enhanced due to their having an opportunity to participate in decisions involving their work. There is no general consensus, though, as to whether or not participation in a quality circle increases an employee's job satisfaction, morale, or attitude.

Disadvantages of Quality Circles

One disadvantage of quality circles is that they were sometimes not focused on particular problems and/or did not understand their goals.[9] Management failed to communicate important information, plan appropriately, and provide training for the circles. Another disadvantage of quality circles was that they sometimes targeted unimportant objectives and ran out of steam.[10] One solution of this problem is to have managers decide what projects should be improved. In any case, by 1988, quality circles no longer existed at 80 percent of the Fortune 500 companies that had adopted them earlier.[11]

Conclusion

Quality circles were developed as a way to increase employee participation by allowing them to form groups to solve work problems. Product quality was increased, costs reduced, and work processes improved as a result of quality circles. However, problems such as a lack of management communication, commitment, and planning, and/or a lack of training of quality circle members, often resulted in poor outcomes. Nevertheless, the principles of worker participation in solving production process problems and increasing product quality has endured in the form of total quality management, self-directed work teams, and employee empowerment programs.

See also Continuous Improvement Plan; Self-directed Work Teams; Teams and Teamwork

NOTES

1. Paul E. Spector, *Industrial and Organizational Psychology: Research and Practice* (Hoboken, NJ: John Wiley, 2006).

2. George R. Gray, "Quality Circles: An Update," *S.A.M. Advanced Management Journal,* Spring 1993, 41–48.

3. Thomas Li-Ping Tang and Edie Aguilar Butler. "Attributions of Quality Circles' Problem Solving Failure: Differences Among Management, Supporting Staff, and Quality Circle Members," *Public Personnel Management,* Summer 1997. 203–25.

4. Jane Whitney Gibson, Dana V. Tesone, and Charles W. Blackwell, "Management Fads: Here Yesterday, Gone Today?" *S.A.M. Advance Management Journal,* Autumn 2003, 12–59.

5. Richard A. Harman, Damodar Y. Golhar, and Satish P. Deshpande, "Lessons Learnt in Work Teams," *Production Planning and Control,* June 2002, 362–69.

6. Gloria M. Pereira and H.G. Osburn, "Effects of Participation in Decision Making on Performance and Employee Attitudes: A Quality Circles Meta-Analysis," *Journal of Business Psychology,* July 2007, 145–53.

7. Ibid.

8. J.M. Juran and F.M. Gryna, *Quality Planning and Analysis: From Product Development through Use,* 3rd ed. (New York: McGraw-Hill, 1993).

9. Jane Whitney Gibson and Dana V. Tesone, "Management Fads: Emergence, Evolution, and Implications for Managers," *Academy of Management Executives,* November 2001, 122–33.

10. Arthur R. Tenner and Irving J. DeToro, *Process ReDesign, The Implementation Guide for Managers* (Reading, MA: Addison-Wesley, 1997).

11. E. Abrahamson, "Management Fashion, Academic Fashion, and Enduring Truths," *Academy of Management Review,* January 1996, 616–19.

Barbara A. W. Eversole

RELIGION AND SPIRITUALITY IN THE WORKPLACE

The topic of spirituality in the workplace has exploded onto the contemporary business scene and related literature over the last 12 years. It is perhaps one of the most compelling and least understood forces driving organizational theory and practice today. Much has been written about the increasingly spiritual nature of work.[1] However, HR professionals have been largely resistant to embracing the phenomenon. The obvious plurality of perspectives represented by the religion/spirituality movement has restricted the comfort with which HR practitioners have championed the phenomenon, for fear of becoming entangled in a web of philosophical and religious differences and legal complexities. However, the movement has gained such momentum that it has been suggested that HR practitioners can no longer avoid recognizing it as a legitimate influence on employee behavior and HR practice.[2]

Catalysts of the Religion/Spirituality in the Workplace Movement

The last two decades have witnessed a tremendous advancement in the fundamental nature of the world economy. In short, globalization is increasingly driven by services-based and technology-based industries and firms that require a more highly educated and evolved workforce than at any other point in history. Concurrent with this pattern has been a significant increase in the relative affluence of the citizens and employees in the world's most developed nations. As a result, many employees are no longer motivated by lower-order needs, but rather operate as a workforce in search of aggregate self-actualization.[3] As such, they are increasingly desirous of reconciling their daily work-lives with their spiritual or religious beliefs.

The Harmony and "Doctrine" of the Religion/Spirituality in the Workplace Movement

Despite concerns regarding irreconcilable differences, there is, in reality, a great deal of philosophical and even doctrinal harmony among the varied spiritual and religious traditions. This is especially true as those doctrinal elements relate to management and leadership practice, as delineated in Table 8.2. The normativity of belief and morality expressed by the passages shown in Table 8.2, each attributed to either a major world religion or spiritual philosophy, is clear. It is also clearly applicable to embrace these spiritual and religious beliefs in conjunction with HR practice, as employees increasingly strive to connect their individual and corporate work lives to such religious/spiritual imperatives.

Table 8.2   The Normativity of the Golden Rule

Good people proceed while considering what is best for others is best for themselves. (*Hitopadesa,* Hinduism).
Thou shalt love thy neighbor as thyself. (*Leviticus* 19:18, Judaism).
By embracing spiritual transformation and kindness, we wind up in a personal universe of Blessed. As this spiritual revolution of Kabbalah increases in the world, a critical mass will be achieved, and the chaos of life will vanish forever like a long-forgotten dream. Therefore, love thy neighbor as thyself. All the rest is mere commentary. Now go and learn. (*Yehuda Berg,* Kabbalah).
Therefore all things whatsoever ye would that men should do to you, do ye even so to them. (*Matthew* 7:12, Christianity).
When you become detached mentally from yourself and concentrate on helping other people with their difficulties, you will be able to cope with your own more effectively. Somehow, the act of self-giving is a personal power-releasing factor. (*Norman Vincent Peale,* Humanism).
Hurt not others with that which pains yourself. (*Udanavarga* 5:18, Buddhism).
No one of you is a believer until he loves for his brother what he loves for himself. (*Traditions,* Islam).

Table 8.3   The Practices, Values, Beliefs, and Norms that Comprise the Doctrine of the Contemporary Organizational Spirituality Movement

Shared and intentional mission/vision/values—the formal articulation and integration of mission, vision, and core values into every aspect of the organizational system is of the utmost importance.
Individual and group transparency—open, honest, and non-defensive communication is valued and expected at all levels of the organization, and is not limited to work matters.
Equity and justice—fairness, particularly surrounding performance management, compensation, and employee discipline, is of critical importance.
Personal consciousness and accountability—awareness of individual and aggregate group/corporate behavior and related consequences (both positive and negative) is continually reinforced throughout the organization.
Ethical clarity and soundness—the ethical code of the organization is unequivocally clear and consistent with natural and moral law (i.e., the "golden rule").
Task significance—the organization constantly reinforces the "higher-order" purpose of the organization, and the individual and corporate tasks completed therein.
Individual/organizational/societal interconnectedness—the belief that organizational life is not a "zero-sum" game is widely propagated throughout the organization, reinforcing the symbiotic nature of open organizational systems.
Inclusiveness—the organization intentionally embraces and leverages people from all walks of life, without unnecessary regard for individual personal differences surrounding race, national origin, gender, age, or spirituality/religion.
Servanthood—the ideal of leadership as servantship is widely embraced and embodied by the senior management of the organization.
Empowerment and shared governance—employees at all levels of the organization are engaged in the planning, conceptualization, and design activities traditionally performed only by management.
Active individual and organizational religious/spiritual practice and expression—the organization fosters and welcomes individual, group, and even corporate practice and expression of religion/spirituality in the regular course of daily organizational life.

Moreover, the codified practices, values, beliefs, and norms associated with the movement are widely embraceable, and even normative in terms of contemporary HR practice. That is, many HR practitioners are already proponents of the movement without recognizing as such. Collectively, these practices, values, beliefs, and norms (delineated in Table 8.3) can be viewed as representing the "doctrine" of the religion/spirituality in the workplace movement.[4]

Compelling Statistics Related to Employee Religious/Spiritual Background and Motivations

Lastly, from a pragmatic standpoint, it may be sobering for HR practitioners that continue to resist the religion/spirituality in the workplace movement to reflect on the fact that fully 78 percent of the world's population claim to be adherents of the five world religions referenced in Table 8.2, 95 percent of Americans consider themselves to be spiritual, and

80 percent of Americans desire to experience spiritual integration and growth in conjunction with their daily work lives.[5] Thus, continued resistance to the phenomenon may be unfounded inasmuch as this resistance may be based upon the assumption that most employees are not religious/spiritual, or the further assumption that employees do not view the corporate workplace as an appropriate setting for living out their religious/spiritual beliefs. Clearly these demographics and descriptive statistics squarely challenge such assumptions.

See also Motivation; Maslow's Hierarchy of Needs; Job Satisfaction; HR Strategy

NOTES

1. Robert A. Giaclone and Carole L. Jurkiewicz, ed., *Handbook of Workplace Spirituality and Organizational Performance* (Armonk, NY: M.E. Sharpe, 2003).

2. Scott A. Quatro, "HR-Minded Leadership: Five Critical Areas of Focus for Contemporary Organizational Leaders," in *Leadership: Succeeding in the Private, Public, and Not-for-Profit Sectors,* ed. Ronald R. Sims and Scott A. Quatro (Armonk, NY: M.E. Sharpe, 2005): 280–96; and Scott A. Quatro, David A. Waldman, and Benjamin M. Galvin, "Developing Holistic Leaders: Four Domains for Leadership Practice and Development," *Human Resource Management Review,* December 2007, 427–41.

3. Paul R. Abramson and Ronald Inglehart, *Value Change in Global Perspective* (Ann Arbor, MI: University of Michigan Press, 1995).

4. Scott A. Quatro, "New Age or Age Old: Classical Management Theory and Traditional Organized Religion as Underpinnings of the Contemporary Organizational Spirituality Movement," *Human Resource Development Review,* September 2004, 228–49.

5. These statistics were derived from several sources, including the International Database (IDB) developed by the U.S. Census Bureau, the Universal Almanac, and the Gallup Organization.

Scott A. Quatro

SELF-DIRECTED WORK TEAMS

Self-directed work teams (SDWTs), also known as self-managed teams, self-designing teams, and autonomous work teams, are teams that work together to achieve a common purpose but with the additional responsibility and authority to make decisions and manage themselves. In the best-case scenario, the SDWT "owns the task" or project at hand.[1] If companies think that teams, in general, create challenges for management, SDWTs create a whole new set of challenges. With contemporary organizations becoming increasingly more global and collapsing the traditional hierarchical structure to achieve efficiency across internal and external boundaries, SDWTs provide several advantages. They do not, however, come without costs. Therefore, organizations must take appropriate measures to ensure the success of SDWTs.

Advantages for Organizations

While benefits of SDWTs can vary between organizations, most agree on a few fundamental advantages. The ability to make quick decisions without outside approval, ability to set team policies within organizational limits to leverage member efficiency (vacation, work hours, etc.), and increased buy-in to team goals are inherent in SDWTs. Additionally, some have identified a much more specific set of advantages, including increased commitment among members, increased morale and productivity, increased potential for innovation, and increased opportunity for organizational learning and change.[2]

To make an informed decision, organizations need to weigh these benefits against the costs associated with using these autonomous teams.

Disadvantages Inherent in SDWT

Again, there are some obvious disadvantages to using SDWTs, one of which is the perception that these teams are "leaderless."[3] While the leadership role may change depending on the project, these teams are far from leaderless. They are, however, time-consuming, have great potential for conflict, and can be very expensive to develop.[4] In fact, many SDWTs fail because members did not have the necessary knowledge, skills, or abilities to ensure success.[5] Fortunately for organizations, there are precautionary measures they can take to leverage advantages of these teams and ensure a better chance for success.

Leveraging the Benefits of SDWTs

Implementing the concept of the SDWT should be a well-thought-out decision for organizations that have much to gain by innovation, quick decision making, and flexibility in the face of globalization and change. Keys to successful implementation are centered around the top management team and organizational culture. If SDWTs are not supported from the top, and the culture fails to lend credence to their autonomy and resulting decisions, the concept is doomed for failure. Organizations, at the very least, need to make a commitment to provide clear vision for these teams and how they "fit" with strategic goals, provide resources necessary for training and development for skills as well as internal team issues (conflict management, communication, etc.), and provide clear expectations and constructive feedback to these teams. While this is not an exhaustive list of measures, and organizations can take many short-term actions to help SDWTs in day-to-day operation, these are the most critical to ensure their success in the long term.

Conclusion

The concept of SDWTs is becoming more popular as organizations erase internal and external borders. There are no guarantees as to the success of these teams, but making the organizational commitment to support SDWTs in theory and practice goes a long way towards ensuring increased productivity, innovation, and lower costs in the long run. These teams can present the greatest challenges; they can also produce the greatest results.

NOTES

1. H. van Mierlo, C.G. Rutte, J.K. Vermunt, M.A.J. Kompier, and J.A.M.C. Doorewaard, "Individual Autonomy in Work Teams: The Role of Team Autonomy, Self-Efficacy, and Social Support," *European Journal of Work and Organizational Psychology* 15, no. 3 (September 2006): 282–99.

2. Leigh L. Thompson, *Making the Team: A Guide for Managers* (Upper Saddle River, NJ: Pearson Prentice Hall, 2004).

3. Thomas Capozzoli, "How to Succeed with Self-Directed Work Teams." *Supervision,* February 2006, 25–26.

4. Thompson, *Making the Team: A Guide for Managers.*

5. Capozzoli, "How to Succeed with Self-Directed Work Teams."

Brenda E. Ogden

SEXUAL HARASSMENT

Sexual harassment is a form of discrimination prohibited by Title VII of the Civil Rights Act, which prohibits discrimination due to one's gender. Sexual harassment is any attempt to coerce a person into a sexual relationship, subject a person to unwanted sexual attention, or punish a refusal to comply with sexual demands. Sexual harassment may include unwelcome sexual advances, requests for sexual favors, or other verbal or physical conduct of a sexual nature. Sexual harassment manifests itself in two ways, in quid pro quo and/or a hostile work environment.

Quid Pro Quo

Quid pro quo literally means "this for that." This type of harassment occurs when there is the threat or promise of an employment action, such as hiring, promotion, demotion, or firing, in exchange for sexual favors. Ultimately, one's employment security is contingent upon exchange of sexual favors, thus one may be subject to economic injury.

Hostile Work Environment

A hostile work environment occurs when unwelcome sexually related behavior creates an intimidating, demeaning, hostile, or offensive work setting. Objectionable behaviors that contribute to a sexually hostile work environment include visual or written materials with vulgar, lewd, or graphic content (e.g., posters, magazines, handouts, e-mails, etc.), inappropriate verbal comments (e.g., lewd comments, dirty/sexual jokes, whistling, intrusive questions about personal life, etc.), and unwanted physical conduct (e.g., patting, grabbing, hugging, pinching, staring, caressing, etc.). Although the recipient suffers no economic harm, the behavior interferes with the work environment and can lead to psychological injury from a stressful work setting.

Consensual Relationships

Consensual relationships may give rise to claims of sexual harassment when third parties are adversely affected due to perceptions of favoritism, the relationship creates a hostile or intimidating work environment for others (particularly when the relationship sours), or the relationship ends, and one person continues behavior that the other has made clear is now unwelcome. Supervisors should advise those involved in a workplace consensual relationship of potential repercussions should the relationship begin to negatively impact the workplace, and intervene if the relationship does create problems.

Responsibilities of Supervisors

To ensure compliance with the law, supervisors and their organizations should (1) clearly articulate the firm's sexual harassment policy, federal, state, and local related laws, and reporting procedures, (2) maintain a harassment-free environment, (3) immediately address complaints brought to their attention, (4) engage in timely, fair investigations of allegations that protect the privacy of the accused and accuser, and (5) prevent retaliation. To limit their liability, supervisors are advised to notify their human resources department and/or their immediate superior when allegations of sexual harassment occur.

Filing Complaints

Formal complaints of sexual harassment may be filed with the employer's internal HR department or with an external agency. Managers and HR professionals should encourage employees to utilize their company's harassment reporting procedures, which should include a means by which to bypass an immediate supervisor and procedures for dealing with victims and alleged perpetrators. It is in the company's best interest to create an environment in which employees feel comfortable and trusting of those to whom they report harassment, and confident that the harassment will be stopped. Further, the HR department should be informed of any allegations of harassment so that they may intervene or deal with the harasser, or refine/develop appropriate training and development programs that deal with harassment.

In spite of an organization's internal harassment policies, employees may still feel compelled to contact the EEOC, the U.S. Department of Education's Office of Civil Rights, a state or local civil rights office, or an attorney with complaints of harassment. This is particularly the case when management or the HR department is perceived as part of the problem of harassment and not the solution. Employees may file external complaints with the EEOC at 800-669-4000, the U.S. Department of Education's Office for Civil Rights at 816-880-4200, and/or their state civil rights office.

See also Civil Rights Acts of 1964 and 1991; Harassment

Resources:
Civil Rights Act of 1964, Title VII (42 USC 2000) http://www.eeoc.gov/policy/vii.html.

Amanda Easton and Ann Gilley

TALENT MANAGEMENT

Talent management is a concept and strategy that integrates human resources and systems to improve processes for developing and managing human resources. It aligns talent with business strategy and includes participation across all departments and levels of an organization.

Contrary to some perceptions, talent management does not just focus on specific positions or on recruiting and retaining employees. Putting the right people at the right time in the right job is a critical component of managing talent, but it also involves managing employees at all levels to their highest potential, as demographics and business trends have proven that talent can be a critical advantage.

History of Talent Management

The term "talent management" first emerged in the late 1990s and was popularized when a study completed by researchers within McKinsey & Company revealed that it was not the "best HR practices" that distinguished high performing companies but it was a pervasive talent management mind-set.[1] The research found that on average, companies that did a better job of attracting, developing, and retaining talented employees earned 22 percentage points higher return to shareholders. But there is nothing new about companies wanting to secure the best talent. The East India Company, founded in 1600, used competitive examinations to recruit the best and the brightest. GE, Capital One, IBM, and American Express are examples of companies that have developed successful talent management strategies for developing their people. What is new is that organizations are now ready to embrace the whole concept and not just pieces of it. Technology has contributed to the success of talent management strategies with the automation of processes, but it is the strategic component that allows successful organizations to gain the advantage.

Talent Management as a Strategic Approach

Talent management is a strategic approach for both human resources and business planning with the goal of improving organizational effectiveness. As human resources (HR) has gained credibility and partnered with the operational management of organizations, the talent management strategy is no longer considered just an "HR initiative." It is the potential of the people who can make a measurable difference to the organization. As most organizations claim that people are their most valuable asset, it is the actions developed and taken within a talent management strategy that proves the difference. Talent management aims to produce enhanced performance at all levels of the workforce and to allow all individuals to reach their potential.

When talent is aligned with the business strategy, it is a fluid process so that as the business drivers change within an organization, so will the definitions of talent.[2] It is important for systems to be designed and implemented that improve the processes for attracting, developing and retaining employees. Succession planning is also a component of talent management strategy. In order to drive performance and create sustainable success, organizations must have the appropriate talent in place and be ready to deploy and change it at any time. Talent management must be built into and integrated within the overall business strategy.

Talent Management and the Role of Human Resources

Since talent is the key asset of an organization, HR has a tremendous role within an organization to ensure that talent management is always well positioned and considered by the top decision-makers. HR is the strategy architect that needs to be able to identify business trends, roadblocks, and opportunities.[3] It is the ability to locate the differentiator on the people side. It includes attracting, developing, and retaining employees as well as implementing performance and workforce management systems. But organizational culture, engagement, and leadership must also be integrated into the talent management strategy.[4] These other factors also impact how a business can achieve success.

Companies such as IBM are restructuring HR so that talent management is part of the core business.[5] Companies are building talent factories where the talent processes support the strategic and cultural initiatives.[6] HR must be the business partner with all management levels to infuse the culture with the strategy, or it will fail. Companies such as Proctor & Gamble and HSBC Group have created talent factories for current and future needs.

Conclusion

Talent management is a strategy that encompasses not only recruitment, development, and retention, but focuses on maximizing human capital so organizations can achieve growth and sustain success. Change will continuously occur, but developing people at all levels to react to this type of dynamic environment can result in increased organizational performance. The culture, engagement, and leadership must be integrated with the strategy; for without talented human resources, the success and performance of a firm remains at risk.

See also Human Capital; Career Planning and Development; Performance Management: An Overview; Recruiting; Retention

Resources:

Boudreau, John W., and Peter M. Ramstad. "Talentship and the New Paradigm for Human Resource Management: From Professional Practices to Strategic Talent Decision Science." *Human Resource Planning,* no. 2 (2005): 17–26.

 Lewis, Robert E., and Robert J. Heckman. "Talent Management: A Critical Review." *Human Resource Management Review,* June 2006, 139–54.

NOTES

1. Ed Michaels, Helen Handfield-Jones, and Beth Axelrod, *The War for Talent* (Boston: Harvard Business School Press, 2001).

2. Chris Ashton and Lynne Morton, "Managing Talent for Competitive Advantage," *Strategic Human Resources Review,* July–August 2005, 28–31.

3. Robert J. Grossman, "New Competencies for HR," *HR Magazine,* June 2007, 58–62.

4. Nancy R. Lockwood, "Talent Management Driver for Organizational Success," *HR Magazine,* June 2006, 1–11.

5. Robert J. Grossman, "IBM's HR Takes a Risk," *HR Magazine,* April 2007, 54–59.

6. Douglas A. Ready and Jay A. Conger, "Make Your Company a Talent Factory," *Harvard Business Review,* June 2007, 68–77.

Susan Sweem

TEAMS AND TEAMWORK

The use of teams is fairly well established, and using a team-based structure can help organizations improve quality and productivity, enhance customer service, provide for increased flexibility and adaptability needed in the global marketplace, and enrich the quality of work life for employees. A "team" can be defined as a collection of individuals who share responsibility for completion of specific organizational goals. One of the hallmarks of teamwork is interdependence, whereby members must share their knowledge, resources, and expertise to successfully accomplish the task at hand. Teams typically have the ability to manage their own work and internal processes.[1]

Teams may be structured with varying degrees of freedom and authority, ranging from being predominantly manager-led to self-managing or completely autonomous. Using teams, however, is not a panacea, and organizations need to consider if interdependence is truly required for goal attainment. If work is accomplished by individual efforts with little need for collaboration, working in teams may not be necessary.

Traditional studies in group dynamics have shown that all teams progress through various stages of development. Early on in the life of a group, little "real work" gets done as members get to know each other (*form*), resolve conflict and address leadership issues (*storm*), and decide how they want to work together (*norm*). Once issues are resolved, the group can then begin to make real progress on the task at hand (*perform*).[2] Simply putting individuals into teams and expecting them to work effectively does not ensure that they will do so.

To be successful, teams need ongoing support and coaching. Knowing that difficulties can be expected can help the manager prepare for them, and plan for intervening when needed. There are three distinct opportunities for coaching: at the beginning, to effectively "launch" the project, establish expectations, and set direction; during the middle, when significant conflict or storming arises and the need for behavioral readjustment becomes evident; and upon project completion, to celebrate accomplishments and cement "lessons learned."[3]

Some practical ways to enhance teamwork include:[4]

- *Limit the number of members.* The larger the team, the more difficult it is to communicate, schedule meetings, and come to a consensus on issues. As a rule of thumb, membership should be limited to 10 individuals or fewer.
- *Have an agenda.* Members need a clear sense of where they are going. An agenda helps keep the group on track and provides a way to structure their time together.
- *Train members together.* This provides an opportunity for members to coordinate their efforts, get to know each other better, and build trust. Members may need training on effective communication, conflict resolution, group problem solving, and decision making.
- *Practice.* If teamwork is a fairly new concept and members have been accustomed to working independently, it will take practice for them to work collaboratively. After every encounter, members should reflect together on the quality of their process so that they can learn from each other and continuously improve their collective experience over time.
- *Minimize links in communication.* It is better for members to directly communicate with each other rather than communicating indirectly through others.
- *Set clear performance standards.* Clear objective goals at the individual level as well as the team level are imperative for effective performance. In addition, members should receive feedback on their contribution to minimize ineffective behavior, social loafing and free riding. Both individual as well as collective rewards should be a part of the performance management process.

Virtual Teams

As technology plays an increasingly larger role in shaping the character of the workplace, it is no longer necessary for all workers to collaborate in the same place at the same time in order to complete a project. Trends such as virtual teaming are becoming more commonplace. In the virtual team, members primarily use technology such as e-mail, the Internet or an intranet, virtual conferences, or discussion forums to accomplish their task.

Although the use of technology increases efficiency, virtual team members may have more difficulty with human interaction and group process issues than those teams that meet in one place. It is suggested that members destined to be part of virtual teams spend some time together early on to get to know each other first, create a sense of connection, clarify roles, build relationships, develop norms, and establish a group identity. It is imperative that the virtual team have a clear purpose from the beginning. Members must also be aware that using electronic communication may create misunderstanding because verbal and nonverbal cues normally used to clarify meaning in normal face-to-face interactions are lost.[5]

See also Self-directed Work Teams; Quality Circles

NOTES

1. Leigh Thompson, *Making the Team: A Guide for Managers* (Upper Saddle River, NJ: Pearson Prentice Hall, 2004).

2. Bruce Tuckman, "Developmental Sequence in Small Groups," *Psychological Bulletin* 63 (1965): 384–89.

3. J. Richard Hackman and Ruth Wageman, "A Theory of Team Coaching," *Academy of Management Review* 30 (2005): 269–87.

4. Thompson, *Making the Team.*

5. Wally Bock, "Some Rules for Virtual Teams." *Journal for Quality and Participation,* Fall 2003, 43.

Cynthia Roberts

TURNOVER

Turnover is the measurement of how many employees leave an organization. The opposite of turnover is retention. A high turnover rate means that the organization has to replace its employees frequently, whereas a lower turnover rate means that an organization retains, or keeps, most of its employees. An acceptable rate of turnover can be a factor of the industry in which an organization exists. Service organizations tend to have very high turnover (56.4 percent per year), while the average turnover rate is around 23 percent.[1] When assessing an organization's turnover compared to other organizations, care must be taken to look at what is the average for the industry. There are many causes of high turnover, and turnover tends to be costly, as it is expensive to replace employees.[2]

Causes of High Turnover

Turnover can be due to a variety of factors. Employees leave for a variety of reasons, such as retirement, resignation, or termination. Generally, a company would prefer to keep high-performing, talented employees while only losing employees that are underperforming. One estimate of an appropriate turnover rate is 10–12 percent,[3] depending on the industry. Unfortunately, often when a company experiences difficulties leading to high turnover, the best employees are often the first to go, because they have plenty of opportunities to move on.

Factors Leading to High Turnover

It has often been stated that employees do not leave companies, they leave their managers. Employees these days are also less loyal, due to an erosion of the employment contract. Due to demographics, many baby boomers are retiring. Organizations with an aging workforce will find their turnover high due to retirement. Alternately, those with a large percentage of younger workers may find their turnover higher because younger workers have less loyalty and are more likely to change jobs to further their careers.

Factors Leading to Low Turnover

Organizations with highly engaged employees tend to invest in training and development and have effective succession planning. Ways to keep your talented employees include finding out why they leave (exit interviews); offering financial incentives to stay (performance management or pay-for-performance); offering more challenging work; and showing you value your employees by providing support for sabbaticals, flexible work arrangements, and/or developmental experiences.[4]

Measuring Turnover and Its Costs

Turnover is usually measured as the ratio of employees who have left the company (for any reason) to the number of employees returning in a year, expressed as a percentage. Estimates of turnover costs range from 150 to 250 percent of the annual compensation of the employee who has left.[5] These costs include recruiting costs, retraining costs, and loss of productivity. This productivity cost includes the lower productivity of the unhappy employee who intends to leave, which can also affect the productivity of other employees.

Conclusion

Turnover is the number of employees who have left the company divided by the employees who remain, expressed in a percentage. It can be very costly, almost double the leaving employee's annual salary, due to recruiting, retraining, and lost productivity. Causes of high turnover include job dissatisfaction, often caused by a poor supervisor. It is worthwhile for an organization to carefully manage its turnover, and be able retain talented workers while losing only underperforming workers.

See also Compensation: An Overview; Employee Development: An Overview; Employee Relations; Job Satisfaction; Managerial Malpractice; Performance Management: An Overview; Retention

NOTES

1. Rudy Karsen, "Calculating the Cost of Turnover," *Employment Relations Today,* Spring 2007, 33–36.

2. Ibid.

3. "Take Talent Management to the Next Level," *HR Focus,* November 2007, 13–15.

4. Dave Ulrich and Wayne Brockbank, *The HR Value Proposition* (Boston: Harvard Business School Press, 2005).

5. "Take Talent Management to the Next Level."

Barbara A. W. Eversole

Part III
General HR Issues

General HR: An Overview

The challenges facing organizations and their members are many, often defying attempts to categorize their effect or impact via simple themes. The topics addressed in this section represent a broad range of subjects concerning employers and workers, from documentation to HR competencies to workplace violence.

Each topic in this section helps frame human resource management, while each in turn is also shaped by emerging trends in society and the competitive business environment. Recent and evolving "hot" HRM issues include subjects such as homeland security, HR metrics, innovation in HR, knowledge management, work-life balance, and workplace justice. These are increasingly important areas of concern to managers at all organizational levels and to the HR professionals with whom they partner to enhance results.

DOCUMENTATION

Documentation is defined as "confirmation that some fact or statement is true through the use of documentary evidence."[1] It is imperative that facts are documented because it protects a business and its employees from legal issues, disputes of fact, or interruptions to its operations.

Required Employment Documentation

Employers are required to keep numerous records on their employees, including federal, state, and employer-specific information. For example, the Immigration Reform and Control Act of 1986 requires that employers verify a candidate's legal ability to work in the United States. Necessary employment information records to be kept include an Employment Eligibility Verification form (I-9), along with a copy of the worker's passport or driver's license, Social Security card, birth certificate, or other approved identification listed on the I-9; and federal and state income tax withholding forms (W-4).

Companies typically keep a copy of the worker's employment application and/or resume, results of employment tests (e.g., health screening, skills and abilities inventories), and verification of educational degrees. Company-specific records may also include, but are not limited to:

- Employment contracts
- Conflict of interest forms

- Noncompete agreements
- Direct deposit forms
- Benefits choices
- Emergency contact information
- Loyalty form
- Alcohol/substance abuse form
- Performance evaluations and employment actions

Performance Appraisals and Employment Actions

It is of the utmost importance to document evaluations and employment actions to protect the firm against frivolous lawsuits or allegations of discrimination or illegal activity. In particular, firms involved in legal cases will be compelled to present evidence that an adverse decision (e.g., termination, denial of promotion, etc.) made regarding an employee was made legally (e.g., not based on discrimination). Proper documentation and notification to the employee of performance problems protects the organization.

Regular performance appraisals provide organizations with a legal defense for employment-related decisions. Although courts decide each case based on its own merits, legally defensible performance evaluations tend to exhibit certain characteristics.

- Employees were involved in establishing criteria and standards for their positions.
- Position requirements and standards are relevant to the essentials of the job.
- Requirements and standards are documented in writing and provided to the employee.
- Employees are informed of and understand the critical requirements and expectations of the job, and verify their understanding (by signing off).
- The evaluation system should not be based on comparisons between employees.
- The performance evaluation occurs regularly (e.g., at least annually) and performance discussions are properly documented.
- Employees are allowed and encouraged to include comments and responses in performance appraisal documentation.
- Managers who conduct performance appraisals have been trained in evaluation.
- Employees are informed of performance problems or issues in advance of the formal review and are given the opportunity to correct any problems.[2]

These documented evaluations should be as objective as possible and quantify both the strengths and weaknesses of an employee. Performance problems must be clearly explained by the evaluator and understood by the employee. Further, a plan of action to remedy the unacceptable performance should be created that thoroughly explains the expectations of performance, support to be provided by the evaluator, and time frame for follow-up and desired results. Between formal evaluations, documentation in the form of e-mails or memoranda between the evaluator and employee may prove valuable. Written documentation such as this will help ensure the company's integrity, verify the facts and clarify confusion, and deter a lawsuit.

Daily Operations

The importance of documenting daily operations is evident to the well-being of any business. Records such as hours worked, supplies used, injuries, turnover rates, and customer feedback enables companies, divisions, and even HR departments to determine their efficiency, fees to be charged, supplies to be ordered, new products to be developed, and so forth. Information supports knowledge and greater understanding of one's internal and external environments, enabling improvement of people, policies, and processes. In addition, it will allow employers to reward or discipline employees in accordance to their performance, maintain stability in operations, and allow materials, costs, and manpower to be properly allocated.

Conclusion

Managers and HR professionals are responsible for documenting all aspects of their business and its employment of personnel, including selection decisions, performance, adverse actions, and daily operations. Record keeping and documentation confirm facts and protect both an organization and its employees from misunderstandings and subsequent legal actions. Facts and events that are not properly documented may be subject to varied interpretations.

See also Employment Law: An Overview; I-9; Immigration Reform and Control Act of 1986; Performance Appraisals; Record Retention Laws

NOTES

1. "Documentation," Dictionary.com, *WordNet® 3.0,* Princeton University, http://dictionary .reference.com/browse/documentation (accessed November 28, 2007).

2. "What Factors Make Performance Appraisals Legally Defensible?" http://performance -appraisals.org/faq/reviewlegal.htm (accessed May 13, 2008).

Chris Armstrong

EMPLOYMENT AGENCIES, SEARCH FIRMS, AND HEADHUNTERS

The terms "employment agency," "search firm," and "headhunters" are used to refer to distinct types of personnel and staffing services. Each is considered separately below.

Employment Agencies

Employment agencies may work on behalf of either job seekers or employers, may be private or public, and may specialize in service to specific or target groups of people, and thus have eligibility requirements.[1] Employment agencies may also offer services to job seekers, including placement assistance, job search assistance, and career planning assistance. An employment agency may have a list of open positions for an employer and thus have the responsibility of recruiting, screening, and referring qualified applicants for further consideration. Employment agencies may concentrate or specialize in temporary, permanent, contract, or temp-to-hire, or be sufficiently large and diversified to include staffing abilities in several categories. Their size may range from providing staffing services to a relatively small geographic location, all the way to a national network of offices. Alternately, employment agencies may specialize in specific trades, skills, or occupations, including finance, accounting, information technology, human resource management, and sales. An increasingly important consideration for employment agencies (particularly for those specializing in permanent or long-term positions) is whether or not a prospective hire will fit a certain corporate culture. Employment agencies may also keep employees on shorter-term work assignments on their payrolls and provide such benefits as health and disability insurance, vacation time, holiday pay, and other benefits. Employment agencies can be particularly useful for companies that have a longer-term employment need, leading to the deployment of "permanent temporaries," or for those desiring to "try before they buy" the services of someone.[2] Employment agencies typically receive payment for finding a suitable employee to hire only when a company selects a candidate. This payment may, depending upon the position, be either a fixed amount or a percentage of the first year's salary.

Employment agencies provide many companies with a higher degree of flexibility regarding their staffing, and give temporary workers the opportunity to tailor specific knowledge or skills to the work arrangement they find most satisfying, whether for personal or professional reasons. However, it is advisable to consult the various local, state, and federal laws governing the employment of temporary workers before committing to such a work arrangement.

Search Firms or Headhunters

Headhunters, or executive search firms, derive their name from the fact that they typically attempt to place people who are currently employed, and who may, in fact, not even be searching for another position.[3] Headhunters are often hired by companies to fill critical-need vacancies, such as middle management positions up to the CEO's office. Most positions headhunters are seeking to fill are not advertised or widely known, and the prospects or candidates who are qualified may be equally invisible or inaccessible to employers.[4] As such, headhunters serve as a very important "confidentiality buffer" between companies and potential candidates.[5] Headhunters also are more personally involved in the matching of candidates with companies, as the positions for which they recruit tend to be both higher paying and longer term, with the potential for significant impact (financially and otherwise) not only upon employees but upon other firm stakeholders as well, such as customers, shareholders, and suppliers.

Headhunters not only keep an extensive proprietary database of information related to a candidate's relevant knowledge, skills, and abilities, but also attempt to discern fit between a prospect and the culture of the hiring company. They will often go beyond the accomplishments and previous positions listed on a resume to determine the personal drivers, lifestyle expectations, and geographic proximities that can often differentiate equally qualified and competent individuals.[8] Accordingly, headhunters will be equally honest and forthright with candidates in describing the culture of the hiring company—good, bad, and otherwise.[9] Additionally, headhunters will usually take an active role in such activities as preparing candidates for interviews, and salary and bonus negotiations once a suitable person has been determined.

Depending upon the position in question and the professional standing of the headhunter (individual or company), payment for services may be either on a retainer or a contingency basis. Top-tier headhunters will often receive one-third of their fee up front as a retainer, the second third after a predetermined amount of time once the search commences (typically 30 or 60 days), and the remainder after a candidate is hired. If a candidate does not work out, headhunters will typically conduct a free replacement search. The duration of such guarantees may range from 90 days to one year after placement.[10] Headhunters also work on a contingency basis, receiving payment only after someone is successfully placed.[11] For both retained and contingent searches, the fees are typically a percentage of the hired candidate's first-year salary and bonus, and this percentage will correspondingly rise with the importance of the duties and title conferred (with a normative range being from 25 percent for middle management roles to 50 percent for senior executive roles).

To be of optimal value to a company wanting to use the services of a headhunter, it is necessary to conduct proactive due diligence. Reputable headhunters will welcome the opportunity to provide references, will want to know as much as possible about the company and its culture, the position for which the search will be conducted, and may even meet with the CEO and relevant members of the board of directors, as well as functional department heads. Although using a headhunter can be a relatively expensive proposition initially, the services of one capable of matching the "right person for the right seat on the right bus"[10] can pay for itself within a matter of months.

See also: Employee Referral Programs; Job Posting; Recruiting

NOTES

1. Idaho Department of Labor, "Creative Job Search: Employment Agencies." http://cl.idaho.gov/cjs/cjsbook/process6.htm (accessed November 24, 2007).

2. Staff Report, "Employment Agencies vs. Executive Search Firms," *Atlanta Business Chronicle,* March 29, 1999, http://atlanta.bizjournals.com/atlanta/stories/1999/03/29/smallb11.html (accessed November 24, 2007).

3. Raymond A. Noe, John R. Hollenbeck, Barry Gerhart, and Patrick M. Wright, *Human Resource Management* (New York: McGraw-Hill, 2003).

4. Steve Brooks, "Getting a Hand Hiring Top Talent," *Restaurant Business,* October 2007, 22–26; and Claire Gagne, "Search & Employ," *Canadian Business,* January 16, 2006, 62–63.

5. Beverly Nazmi, "How to Get the Best from a Headhunter," *Management Services,* Spring 2006, 42–43; and Noe, Hollenbeck, Gerhart, and Wright, *Human Resource Management.*

6. Nazmi, "How to Get the Best from a Headhunter."

7. Gagne, "Search & Employ."

8. Brooks, "Getting a Hand Hiring Top Talent."

9. Gagne, "Search & Employ."

10. Brooks, "Getting a Hand Hiring Top Talent."

Steven J. Kerno Jr.

FIELD VS. CORPORATE HR

Many organizations have both a corporate and a field component to their human resource (HR) capacity. There are inherently different functions that these positions serve. Whether you call a satellite organization a field office, a research and development center, a manufacturing location, or a distribution site, the differences between the two competing needs are often not acknowledged or properly understood.

Corporate Strategy vs. Field Needs

Field HR organizations are more tactical in delivery. Often the HR professional at a field office deals with a myriad of topics, issues, and levels of individuals ranging from executives to line workers needing advice. Although many of the people in these roles may not start out as HR generalists, they ultimately assume the role and responsibilities. There is an emphasis on "problem solving, high visibility and day-to-day operations."[1] In the field, doing whatever is needed to make the business run efficiently is the order of business. Inherent in this type of work is the ability to "thrive on hands-on work, enjoy new challenges every day and have a knack for reading situations and resolving problems, influencing people, building consensus and finding solutions quickly.[2] Two major traits are the ability to build relationships with workers and share data.

Corporate HR is more strategic. A corporate HR group is focused on anticipating the future. What will need to be in place two to five years out? Critical to this orientation is the need to focus on the business almost obsessively, identifying implications for the business.[3] Corporate HR tends to have more specialized functions, such as compensation, benefits, or learning.

Working Together

Conflict occurs when corporate HR has certain objectives that they need to implement and field HR must take on the responsibility to carry out those objectives. Neither side generally has anything against pitching in; it is often how objectives are communicated that serves as a sore point for one or the other. Without effective communication, field locations often will "fill in the blanks." Watson Wyatt recommends developing a constant communication channel complete with face-to-face meetings as much as possible.[4] The exact amount of communication needed between field and corporate HR depends on the size of the organization, type of business, culture, and budget. During an interview for a recent organizational study, a field HR representative described corporate as operating like a "Sea-gull." "They often swoop in and leave us with some unpleasant things then they go back to corporate."[5] Their corporate counterparts were actually trying to create a corporate reporting system in which they could gain an accurate head count globally without having to request it each month from the field. There clearly was a good reason to be the "Sea-gull," but the field offices only saw what they were leaving and that they incurred additional costs as a result. Clear communication with detailed benefits would have solved this misunderstanding on both sides.

Technology has made HR communications much easier and faster to communicate with employees, management and other HR professionals. Online tools such as e-mail provide an obvious advantage to relaying information; however, be wary of utilizing e-mail as the only means of information. Employees and other HR professionals can be left feeling the distance between locations. Personal interaction, whether by phone or face to face, is critical to a successful partnership between corporate and the field.

Conclusion

The HR professional supports the goals and objectives of an organization and advances the strategic business plan. The field HR representative is an expert on the design of work systems in which people contribute. The corporate HR representative is a strategic partner who works with the management team to influence the organization's direction. Communication between field HR and corporate HR is essential to manage any overlapping responsibilities and coordinate activities.

NOTES

1. Carolyn Hirschman, "Out of Sight, Not Out of Mind," *HR Magazine* 45, no. 2 (February 2000): 72–77.
2. Ibid.

3. Ibid.
4. Susan Wells, "The Path Taken," *HR Magazine* 48, no. 6 (June 2003): 50–55.
5. Confidential source, interview by Lisa Brinkman, June 20, 2005.

Lisa Scott Brinkman and Alina M. Waite

FORECASTING

Managing Operations

Organizations have many tools available to them to use in managing their operations. The basic financial tool that is most often used to plan operations is the budget. Budgets are great guides that cover various periods of time. Typically this is for a year, but may be incorporated into a strategic plan that extends five years or more.

The big downfall of a budget is that no one has a crystal ball to predict the future. Thus, budgets are not always accurate. No one wants to plan for, predict, or expect poor performance. Although a financial executive can prepare an accurate budget, it requires a lot of insight into everything that can affect the operations over the budget period, plus a degree of luck. Budgets crafted too conservatively can make an organization appear as if it had a great year by "meeting and exceeding" budget when, in fact, it may have had only mediocre performance and could have done better.

In the governmental segment, budgets drive the administrative function. Unfortunately, this leads to much planned and excessive, or even unnecessary, spending. In simple terms, governmental budgeting encourages operational inefficiency due to the mind-set that prevails—if it is budgeted and not spent, we will lose the money for next year; hence the process is inefficient and leads to uncontrolled spending.

Forecasting Defined

What, then, is a better tool to use in the financial and operational management of an organization? Forecasting is a much more accurate and efficient method of predicting and planning for an organization's performance.

What is a forecast? In comparing a forecast to a budget, a budget is typically a short- or long-term financial plan, based on history, with an idea or hope as to what will happen in the future. A budget is usually developed significantly before the budgeted period begins (e.g., this calendar year's budget may have been developed and approved last July). In contrast, a forecast is a financial and operational plan rooted in the present that uses current market information to predict what is expected to happen in the future from both a financial and operational standpoint. This is where the benefit of a forecast is best utilized. A forecast is a "living document" as opposed to a basic plan because it is designed and expected to change and adapt to actual occurrences and events; it is not "set in stone" as a budget tends to be.

Developing Forecasts

The first step in developing a forecast is to determine how often you want to revise the forecast and how far out from the present you want to predict. A three- or four-month forecast is the most reasonable and accurate time period. A four-month forecast, for example, allows you to work in the present month and plan for the next three. The "rolling method" enables you to update the forecast monthly and show the current month plus the next three. Continually revising forecasts each month increases accuracy of predicted performance. For example, in February, you may forecast operations for the next three months, March, April, and May. When March arrives, the February forecast is dropped, while June is added after updating predictions for April and May.

Once the desired forecasting time periods are determined, data is gathered. In a manufacturing organization, for example, actual trends for the past three to six months are examined and critical questions asked. If trends have been steady or constant, is it reasonable to expect these trends to continue? Have there been fluctuations—minor or severe—that must be accounted for? What has happened in the marketplace? Have there been any events that would impact the organization either positively or negatively? Have there been events that will affect the needs of customers?

The next step is to discuss the data with relevant contacts, such as your field sales force, production staff, or customer service, to name a few. These individuals have the best "feel" as to what will happen over the coming months and will help develop an accurate picture of what sales, revenues, or other key factors will be. When examining expenses, you are then faced with determining the other operational costs incurred. The fixed costs, monetary and nonmonetary, are easy to identify and plan for. Included among these categories are salaries, insurance, and depreciation, for example. The variable costs should be somewhat predictable based on historical data. You may also have to account for cyclical cost fluctuations such as heating, cooling, or water usage; these bills may be higher during certain times of the year. After compiling the financial data, then you can determine the bottom-line performance.

Another component to consider is staffing. Of all of the expenses an operation incurs, staffing seems to be the easiest to control because it stems totally from the election of management as opposed to an external source. Although compensation is directly affected by external forces, it is not the same as purchasing external supplies or services. An organization's staffing is totally at the discretion of its management and should be based on what is required to operate efficiently. A store manager, for example, will have history and corporate information for similar stores. The challenge usually comes seasonally, with the need to staff the store with temporary personnel at Christmas. Forecasting for this need allows the manager to plan for the changes, staff increases, and planned release of temporary employees.

Planning or forecasting the needs of full-time or part-time staff can be crucial to an organization. It is critical to have adequate staff to handle job functions. From a financial standpoint, however, there are distinct differences between full-time and part-time employees. In any organization, staffing of full-time employees typically means extra costs in the form of benefits and taxes of as much as 100 percent of the compensation paid. Accurate forecasting based on known needs and external observations and analysis will allow any organization to properly staff for their specific operation. Doing so enables firms to avoid the severe fluctuations in staffing and layoffs.

Conclusion

Forecasting is an invaluable tool for an organization's management team. While a budget can be a good guide, a living document such as a forecast constantly takes into account all of the internal and external factors that affect an organization's performance over a given time, and is a much more valuable tool in guiding the outcomes of that organization.

James Steven Beck

HOMELAND SECURITY

The words *Homeland Security* conjure up images of armed military and law enforcement personnel manning checkpoints with bomb-sniffing dogs and high-tech scanning devices. In a post-9/11 world, homeland security has taken on far greater connotations, and the ramifications for businesses and organizations can be significant. The fact that the economy itself is a target for terrorism is no longer refuted by experts. Add natural disasters such as Hurricane Katrina and concerns about issues such as flu pandemics, and it is easy to see that homeland security is not just about terrorism.

To the general public, and most likely the average business owner or manager, homeland security is an issue for the government to handle. Issues such as border security, transportation security, intelligence gathering, and other such issues for the most part do fall to government agencies. From a business or corporate perspective, the issues surrounding homeland security can cross lines with other already familiar issues such as workplace violence, employee safety and training, OSHA regulations, federal and state employment guidelines, and other issues that the average business owner/manager would not necessarily consider homeland security issues. Businesses are strongly encouraged to examine what role and responsibility they may have in dealing with homeland security issues. There is potential for significant liability, both in real costs and from litigation, for businesses and corporations that choose to ignore this issue.

Potential Impact on Organizations

Regular examples in the media demonstrate the changes that have come about as a result of homeland security–related issues. Large corporations have been raided during the workday by federal law enforcement and have had hundreds of employees arrested for being in the country illegally. The losses to corporations in terms of productivity and revenue have the potential to be staggering. Corporations and managers also face the potential of criminal prosecution for failing to comply with federal guidelines pertaining to employing undocumented workers.

New regulations driven by a concern for homeland security also have the potential to impact the bottom line of businesses both large and small. Federally mandated security measures in industries such as chemical research and production, privately owned transportation companies, and import and export businesses, to name just a few, will have an impact on operating expenses. Banking and information industries have had unprecedented layers of regulation and demands from the government as it pertains to not only security, but also the sharing of customer information, data, financial transactions, and other such issues. The burden to these industries in real costs is significant.

There is also a potential for new liability issues. For instance, the same banking and information industries have been in court for both complying and failing to comply with new government regulations and demands. Privacy issues in an Internet age have created an ever-changing minefield for businesses to navigate. Other industries, such as construction and manufacturing, are now trying to anticipate the potential liabilities as a result of terrorism and natural disasters. Prior to 9/11, the thought of constructing a building that would be able to withstand the impact of a commercial airliner was not a very realistic consideration. Developers now have to consider such scenarios. The bombing of the Alfred P. Murrah Building in Oklahoma City was accomplished by detonating, among other things, a fertilizer commonly used and widely available to farmers. The impact was immediate, as government regulation made the fertilizer harder to purchase and more expensive.

Natural disasters have impacted many industries and how they do business. Accordingly, the insurance industry is attempting to limit its business in the Gulf region as a result of losses incurred by Hurricane Katrina. Lawsuits because of coverage disputes between property owners and insurance companies could result in significant government regulation. State governments are threatening legislation to force insurance companies to sell policies in areas where the insurance companies no longer want to do business. Hospitals, nursing homes, and other private entities were held liable for not being prepared to deal with a natural disaster that most could not have foreseen. There were serious ramifications, both civilly and criminally, specifically because of a lack of emergency preparedness planning by organizations and companies. The resulting litigation, government regulation, and changes in industry practices will impact businesses and their customer bases for decades to come.

Organizational Response

What does all of this mean to the private sector manager? It means that concerns and issues that were previously the purview of government managers now fall on the private sector. In dealing with homeland security issues, the federal government has identified what it calls "Critical Infrastructure and Key Assets."[1] These are areas, both private and public, that the government deems absolutely critical to the stabilization and recovery of the country and/or a geographic area in the event of a significant disaster, whether man-made or natural. The Homeland Security Act of 2002 defines critical infrastructure as

> [S]ystems in assets, whether physical or virtual, so vital to the United States that the incapacity or destruction of such systems and assets would have a debilitating impact on security, national economic security, national public health or safety, or any combination of those matters.

These areas will include, but are not necessarily limited to, the following:
- Agriculture
- Food
- Water
- Public health
- Emergency services
- Government
- Defense industrial base
- Information and telecommunications
- Energy
- Transportation
- Banking and finance
- Chemical industry
- Postal and shipping

These areas cover almost every aspect of daily life. Government mandates are not just targeting the public sector, but are also meant to target the private sector. The majority of these categories are foundationally supported by private entities. The government regulates many industries, although the ability to actually perform most functions under the above headings falls to the private sector. This makes homeland security in the private sector critical.

To that end, governments on federal, state, and local levels are actively encouraging businesses to prepare plans for dealing with homeland security issues. Businesses need to be able to get back up and running as soon as possible after an emergency. The Department of Homeland Security has links on its main Web page that direct private-sector managers to informational sites designed to help them formulate response plans to disasters, both natural and man-made. The sites give step-by-step recommendations as to how businesses should prepare. The issues dealt with include, but are not limited to, the following:

Continuity Planning—What are the essential resources and assets needed to get a business up and functioning as soon as possible after the disaster, and how does a business protect those resources and assets?

Emergency Planning/Supplies—Information is given as to what is necessary for a successful emergency plan and how such a plan is formulated. Outlines are available on how to identify critical issues such as emergency communications, evacuation, and protection of life. Suggestions are made as to how to identify what types of resources and supplies should be kept on site.

Employee Preparedness/Education—Highlights the importance of employee education in planning and supporting emergency response plan. These plans include preparing for and dealing with the disaster as it occurs as well as the aftermath, including employee health issues and dealing with employees' personal lives after such an event.

Every state has its own department of homeland security, and most of these organizations also have resources for the private sector. Some resources are actually more practical in scope because they look at emergency preparedness from a private-sector perspective. For instance, the state of Utah has a "12 Point Program to Business Continuity Planning." This guide is a practical overview that addresses most aspects of emergency preparedness from any business point of view. This comprehensive overview covers topics ranging from assessing risks and hazards to having proper insurance coverage and protecting vital records. It also helps the business assist employees in creating individual preparedness plans. It builds on the federal plan mentioned above but in some ways is more practical and detailed.

As in every other area, there are paid consultants who will develop emergency response plans and train organizations to deal with such plans. Many industries are also creating resources for their members to address industry-specific plans. Trade associations and professional organizations should be contacted as probable resources for emergency preparedness plans.

Organizations and businesses should not panic at the thought of creating emergency response plans. Like business plans for growth or market change, emergency preparedness plans are simply another one of those changes that the private sector has to adapt to if it wants to survive in a world economy that is impacted by many things other than normal market forces.

See also Emergency Preparedness; Occupational Safety and Health Administration; Safety; Security

NOTE

1. John Moteff and Paul Parfomak, "Critical Infrastructure and Key Assets: Definition and Identification," CRS Report for Congress (Washington, DC: Congressional Research Service, 2004), http://www.fas.org/sgp/crs/RL32631.pdf.

Jim Byrne

HR COMPETENCIES

Human resource (HR) management is a fast-changing discipline whose strategic importance for impacting bottom-line organizational profitability has grown over the last 20 years. HR has become more important to business leaders as they have seen the tangible, sustained competitive advantage that the intangibles of human capital (talent and capability) can deliver. Given this robust dynamic, the HR function must continue its maturation to providing solutions to one of the most critical issues facing modern business; namely, building sustained organizational capability.

While HR's role in building organizational capability is not new, changes in workplace demographics, technology, globalization, legislation, employee expectations, customer demands, and access to information, among other things, have had dramatic implications on human resource practices and strategies. An organization's competitive capability has been described as a combination of the collective learning of its employees and their ability to apply that knowledge to business.[1] HR can and must greatly influence this body of strategic work.

Unfortunately, most HR functions are not rising to the challenges of being the strategic partner HR should be. According to a Corporate Leadership Council study, fewer than one in six CEOs assign strategic importance to HR, and only one in four rate HR's performance favorably. Therefore, it is critical to build the competencies of HR practitioners in order to live up to their potential as value-added business partners.

HR Competencies Identified

Competencies have been defined as the characteristics—knowledge, skills, mind-sets, thought patterns, and the like—that, when used either singularly or in various combinations, result in successful performance.[2] But on which competencies should HR focus? There is not one standard HR competency model that is universally accepted. However, there are several leading authorities in the field of HR competency research and several common themes among most HR competency models.

Two leaders in HR competency model research are the RBL Group and the Ross School of Business at the University of Michigan. They have jointly conducted the *Human Resource Competency Study* five times over the last 20 years. The global study has surveyed more then 40,000 HR leaders and their business partners in determining what knowledge, skills, and abilities are most valued and required of HR professionals. The fifth round of the *Human Resources Competency Study* identified six HR competencies:

1. *Talent manager/organization designer:* Focuses on attracting, developing, retaining, and upgrading the talent in an organization, while ensuring the organization can perform at high levels because appropriate organizational structure, processes, and policies exist.
2. *Strategy architect:* Focuses on HR's role in establishing organizational strategy.

3. *Operational executor:* Focuses on the flawless delivery of HR platform activities and administrative operations.
4. *Business ally:* Focuses on business acumen and understanding to be able to contribute to driving high levels of business performance.
5. *Culture and change steward:* Focuses on shaping the organization's culture and developing disciplines to shape individual employee and organizational behaviors in a way that is aligned with the organization's goals.
6. *Credible activist:* Focuses on the leadership attributes required of HR professionals to be both respected and fully engaged in the business.

Common Themes of Other HR Competency Models

A review of various other HR competency models reveals additional common themes of competencies. Competencies that were commonly identified included:
- *Talent*—including workforce planning, talent attraction and selection, turnover management, employee development, and succession planning.
- *Performance*—including change management, employee engagement, project management, and performance management.
- *Organizational capability*—including organizational design, organizational effectiveness, and organizational development.
- *Platform*—including compensation, benefits, policy management, compliance, HR systems, and vendor management.
- *Credibility*—including business acumen, influence, and initiative.

What to do Next: The Three Rs

More important than creating the "ideal" competency model is creating a framework for your HR organization to own and develop its capability to best meet the needs of business leaders. The key principles to consider in any basic competency framework are:

Relevant—addressing pertinent issues of concern to the business.
Rigorously implemented—embedded into the business as sustainable business processes.
Results-oriented—delivering value and positively impacting the performance of the business.

Building a solid framework with the right HR competencies enables organizational capability for truly impacting business performance. Through the creation of sustained competitive advantage, the HR organization will be recognized as a true, value-added business partner.

See also Forecasting; HR Metrics; HR Strategy

Resources:

Corporate Leadership Council. *Defining Critical Skills of Human Resources Staff, Chief Human Resources Officer View of HR Function and Staff Effectiveness.* Ann Arbor, MI, 2006.

Ulrich, David, and Dani Johnson. *Human Resources Competency Conference.* Ann Arbor, MI, 2007.

NOTES

1. C.K. Prahalad and G. Hamel, "The Core Competencies of the Corporation," *Harvard Business Review* 90, no. 3 (1990): 79–91.
2. D.D. Dubois, *The Competency Case Book* (Amherst, MA: HRD Press Inc., 1998).

Robert Paxton and Tim Reynolds

HR COMPLIANCE

Human resources (HR) compliance is a necessity for every business regardless of the number of employees. HR compliance refers to adhering to all state and federal employment laws, including Title VII of the Civil Rights Act of 1964, the Americans with Disabilities Act, antidiscrimination laws, and the federal Fair Labor and Standards Act (FLSA). Therefore, business owners have to know the state and federal laws and apply all of the laws that affect all employees.

Employee Handbook

An employee handbook, which includes policies on military leave, sexual harassment, breaks, appropriate behavior, Internet use, whistle-blowing, preemployment and drug testing, smoking, and any other policy items, is recommended for all organizations.[1] The handbook needs to be carefully written to include applicable federal laws as well as state laws in which the organization will be doing business. Some organizations may have several versions of the employee handbook, depending upon their location(s).[2] Accordingly, policies need to be communicated and integrated into the culture of the organization.[3]

Managers need to be educated on the complex HR laws or have appropriate good legal representation, since such laws are constantly changing. The handbook needs to be regularly updated and should be reviewed by legal counsel. Managers and employees need to understand the policies contained in the handbook in order to comply. Communication is the key to instituting policies in the handbook, which include any consequences for noncompliance.[4]

Equal Employment Opportunity Regulations

Business owners, regardless of the size of the organization, need to be in compliance with all equal employment opportunity laws (EEO). There are four major EEO laws, which employers need to understand. The four major EEO laws are:
- *Title VII of the Civil Rights Act of 1964* prohibits employment discrimination based on race, color, religion, sex, and national origin. This act applies specifically to those businesses that have 15 or more employees on the payroll at any given time.
- The *Age Discrimination in Employment Act of 1967 (ADEA)* prohibits age discrimination against individuals who are 40 years of age or older. This act applies specifically to businesses with a minimum of 20 employees on the payroll at any given time.
- *Title I of the Americans with Disabilities Act of 1990 (ADA)* prohibits employment discrimination against qualified individuals with disabilities. This act applies to employers with a minimum of 15 employees.
- The *Equal Pay Act of 1963 (EPA)* prohibits wage discrimination between men and women in substantially equal jobs within the same establishment. All employers should take special note of this act, as it applies to any business with a minimum of one employee.[5]

State and federal equal opportunity Laws need to be posted within the organization for employees' access.

See also Age Discrimination in Employment Act; American Disabilities Act; Civil Rights Acts of 1964 and 1991; Employee Handbook; Equal Pay Act; Harassment

NOTES

1. Sally Anne Morris, "Human Resource Compliance is for Every Business" (Blethen Maine Newspapers Inc., 2004), http://www.hrtutor.com/en/news_rss/articles/2004/Human_Resource_Compliance_for_Business.aspx (accessed February 16, 2008).

2. Barry Gross, "Determining Which Federal, State, and Local Employment Laws Are Applicable to Your Business," http://www.allbusiness.com/governemnts/emloyment-regulations/11996-1.html (accessed February 17, 2008).

3. "Developing an Effective HR Compliance Program," http://www.allbusiness.com/human-resources/wrokplace-health-safety/979-1.html (accessed February 11, 2008).

4. Ibid.

5. "The EEOC and Small Business: Complying with Equal Opportunity Regulations," http://www.allbusiness.com/government/employment-regulations-u-s-equal-employment/11896-1.html (accessed February 17, 2008).

Debora A. Montgomery-Colbert

HRIS

Human resource information systems (HRIS) are organized systems for collecting, storing, maintaining, retrieving, and validating data needed by an organization about its current or potential future employees. A typical HRIS system can range from a small informal payroll application to a larger all-inclusive package that integrates the information technology (IT) department with the human resources (HR) department. Larger applications tend to coordinate strategic management with employee data collection, providing an enterprise-wide solution that may contain advanced reporting and forecasting capabilities.[1]

Human Resource Management Challenge

As global marketing challenges expand, human resource managers are asked to play a more strategic role in the success of an organization. Managing the duty of maximizing return on investment on human capital is an overwhelming task. These challenging responsibilities may force HR professionals to seek out additional tools that help save funds, manage resources, and provide organizational charting.

HRIS can provide HR professionals with a decision support tool that can present data in a format that is easy to understand and can assist in the identification of specific patterns, bottlenecks, or lags in a company's workflow. A typical HRIS is specialized software for implementing, monitoring, and benchmarking these HR processes. A business may acquire an HRIS software application, or it may work with IT technicians to develop a proprietary system that fits their corporate or governmental reporting requirements.

Importance of HRIS

The importance of the HR department is sometimes underestimated. With corporations merging and acquiring new subsidiaries, the HR department is forced to manage a signification amount of data. Management of this data is not a fixed process, as employees may transfer between divisions or other entities owned by the corporation. Employees may also change job titles or be terminated, forcing managers to shift duties to other individuals. The HRIS can manage this data, providing HR professionals and other administrative leaders with the reports required to maintain a productive environment. Effective communication of departmental resources to all entities involved can facilitate an efficient workflow and improve company performance.

The HRIS may manage these significant tasks:

1. Floating charges—phones, computers, wireless handheld devices, vehicles.
2. Extra pay, insurance, and benefits.
3. Termination time—charges, salary, and benefits cease.
4. New employees.
5. Management and control of payroll errors.
6. Staffing—predicting busy or down times.
7. Contractors and outsourcing.

Develop an "In-house" HRIS or Purchase One?

Many different vendors market proprietary HRIS applications. Many of these vendors develop applications specific to a company's or industry's needs—for example, Spectrum Human Resource Systems Corporation develops HRIS applications for the health care industry.[2] This system has been developed to manage HR processes for health care organizations, providing them with detailed reporting or specialized formatting required by their organizational standards.

When choosing an HRIS for an organization, HR professionals will want to examine organizational needs before choosing between vendors or before building an "in-house" application. Getting an HRIS approved through budgetary procedures is a challenge. HR professionals will need to convince the administration that an HRIS will contribute to the management of human resources and may save the company money in the long term.

To accomplish this task, HR professionals should start by analyzing organizational needs. A good place to start would be to outline current HR activities within the business. Hagel & Company provides a listing of questions that might start this process:[3]

- What information are people requesting?
- How do you, line managers, the chief executive officer, and the chief financial officer obtain needed personnel information?
- How long does it take you to respond to a new request for information?
- What HR management needs are not being addressed and handled properly?
- How effective is your support to the budgeting and planning processes?
- Where do you stand in complying with COBRA, ERISA, FLSA, OSHA, and other statutes and regulations?
- What tasks are you being asked to do today? How well are you performing these tasks?
- What programs, services, and management support must you provide to help your organization meet its goals?
- What are the major tasks that you intend to accomplish and the results you plan to achieve in order to have a successful HR operation?

Once HR professionals have established organizational needs, they should work toward justifying the development or purchase of the appropriate system. By aligning their requirements with those for meeting corporate goals, HR professionals will have a better chance of convincing management of an HRIS's importance to the company.

See also HR Strategy; Human Capital; Payroll

NOTES

1. William Jones and Robert C. Hoell, "Human Resource Information System Courses: An Examination of Instructional Methods," *Journal of Information Systems Education,* Fall 2005.

2. Spectrum, "Healthy HRIS," Spectrum Human Resource Systems Corporation, http://www.healthyhris.com/ (accessed October 23, 2007).

3. Hagel & Company, "Choosing an HRIS," Hagel & Company Software for HR Professionals, http://www.hagel.net/pdf_files/HRIS_checklist.pdf (accessed October 31, 2007).

Lori Nicholson

HR METRICS

HR and its place within organizations is changing. Organizations rely more heavily on knowledge workers today than ever before and, as a result, HR's ability to measure aspects of the organization is at a higher profile. No longer are metrics such as time to fill and benefits cost per employee[1] enough to provide management with data about talent as a competitive advantage.[2]

What Are HR Metrics?

HR metrics have historically been measures that speak to satisfying business goals: a benchmark that delineates a path, and the organization's progression along it. Metrics are the compilation of data that measure any number of areas, such as employee satisfaction, voluntary turnover, training spending per employee, and recruiting cycle time in days. HR metrics provide organizations with a window into the people side of the business. A metric at its simplest level is a calculation, not a cause. It is a numerical representation of a number of activities and events, some occurring externally, that have occurred previous to collecting and calculating the metric.[3] Table 9.1 provides a representative sample of the kinds of key HR metrics that are increasingly driving HR-related strategic decision making in contemporary organizations.

HR Metrics and a Wider Financial Picture

Critical to HR's future is its ability to transform into the strategic partner that business needs to compete in the marketplace today. Metrics are no longer about only telling what happened last month, last quarter, or last year, but about providing the business with optimization and predictive models and forecasts to prepare the business for the future, such as those metrics delineated in Table 9.1.[4] Talent is at the top of the agenda for many executives, and HR must lead the organization's drive to maximize competitive advantage through its human capital.[5] Impact in the area of a financial picture means "demonstrating a link between what HR does and tangible effects on the organization's ability to gain and sustain competitive advantage."[6]

Creating HR Metrics

Conceptually, the process for developing HR metrics is not dissimilar to the development of other business metrics, and includes traditional accounting categories (e.g., cost, time, volume, income, quality, and stakeholder reaction), computational methods (e.g., rate,

Table 9.1   Representative Strategic HR Metrics

Metric	Definition	Usage
Cost per hire	Reflects average investment for one hire. Equal to total staffing costs divided by the number of hires.	Plan and manage staffing initiatives.
Yield ratio	Reflects number of original applicants required to yield one hire. Equal to the number of candidates from a given source divided by the number hired from that source.	Evaluate the productivity of various candidate sources.
Training ROI	Reflects direct return on investment for a training initiative. Equal to the direct economic outcome of a training initiative divided by the total cost of that training initiative.	Prioritize training investment based upon economic value-added.
Market value per employee	Reflects the market-value generation capacity of a publicly traded firm's human capital. Equal to the result of the number of shares outstanding multiplied by the price per share, then divided by the total number of employees.	Assess equity-market value generation of human capital vis-à-vis peer organizations.

ratio, composition, and indices), and a variety of possibilities for cutting or cross-sectioning the data.

In terms of accounting categories, *cost* is formally defined as a sacrifice (in terms of time or money) incurred to obtain a benefit or service. Cost is a direct measure guaranteed to get the attention of an organization's management team. *Time* is considered a resource under individual control that is sufficient enough to accomplish a given task. With the abundance of technology available, work is expected to be performed faster, and organizations are expected to have quicker response times. Organizations that efficiently perform faster than their competition achieve a differentiating competitive advantage. *Volume* is a measure of output, tangible or intangible. Volume is traditionally measured in units produced, in the number of customers served, or in the frequency of events. *Income* is a measure of the money that is received as the result of normal business activity. It encompasses the revenues and profits of the organization. *Quality* is a measurement of people, processes, and systems to ensure that predetermined standards are met. Quality measurements are often manifested in product returns and customer satisfaction reports, in addition to the traditional scrap and rework measures. Finally, *stakeholder reaction* is the response of the organization's constituent groups. Measures of stakeholder reaction are found internally (e.g., satisfaction, engagement) and externally (e.g., market-share price).[7]

In terms of computation methods, *rate* is the proportion of one or more parts to the whole. Rate is traditionally expressed as a percentage or frequency. *Ratio* is the proportion of one number to the other, and is often expressed as a fraction. *Composition* is the classification of the whole into its parts, with a percentage of the whole allocated to each part.

An *index* is the weighted combination of distinct data into one number relative to a scale or defined anchor. These four basic methods or formulas can be used by organizations to calculate and compare measures across human resource processes.

Finally, metrics are subject to an almost infinite number of cross-sectional analysis possibilities. Such possibilities provide organizations with additional data manageability. The data can be sectioned in any number of combinations, depending upon the constituent group that the organization wishes to analyze. Some options for cross-sectional analysis are (1) by organization division, (e.g., department, location, product line); (2) sociodemographics (e.g., age, gender, marital status, parental status); (3) employment status (e.g., full time, part time, per diem); (4) job type (e.g., exempt or nonexempt, management or line staff); and (5) longevity or tenure (e.g., time in position, time with organization).

Conclusion

HR metrics are utilized to create accountability tools (e.g., scorecards, dashboards), as well as for decision making, problem solving, mapping business strategies, and determining the alignment of organization processes to achieve efficiency, effectiveness, and maximum firm performance.

See also HR Competencies; Human Capital

Resources:

Fitz-enz, Jac. *How to Measure Human Resources Management.* New York: McGraw-Hill, 1984.

Phillips, Jack J. *Investing in Your Company's Human Capital.* New York: AMACOM, 2005.

Phillips, Jack J. and Patricia P. Phillips. *Proving the Value of HR.* Alexandria, VA: Society for Human Resource Management, 2005.

Phillips, Jack J., Ron D. Stone, and Patricia P. Phillips. *The Human Resources Scorecard: Measuring the Return on Investment.* Boston: Butterworth Heinemann, 2001.

Sullivan, John. *HR Metrics the World Class Way* Peterborough, NH: Kennedy Information, 2003.

NOTES

1. "What Is the 'Most Important' Metric? (Cover Story)," *HR Focus* 85, no. 2 (2008): 1–15.
2. Richard W. Beatty, Mark A. Huselid, and Craig Eric Schneier, "New HR Metrics: Scoring on the Business Scorecard." *Organizational Dynamics* 32, no. 2 (2003): 1007–21.
3. Jac Fitz-enz, *The ROI of Human Capital: Measuring the Economic Value of Employee Performance* (New York: AMACOM, 2000.
4. "How to 'Make over' Your Hr Metrics," *HR Focus* 84, no. 9 (2007): 3–4.
5. "Top Trends for 2008: Leadership, Talent, & Metrics Will Be Key," *HR Focus* 85, no. 1 (2008): 8.
6. Edward E. Lawler III, Alec Levenson, and John W. Boudreau. "HR Metrics and Analytics: Use and Impact." *Human Resource Planning* 27, no. 4 (2004): 27–35.
7. Eric G. Flamholtz, *Human Resource Accounting: Advances in Concepts, Methods and Applications* (Boston: Kluwer Academic Publishers, 1999).

Lisa Scott Brinkman, Heather S. McMillan, and Michael Lane Morris

HR STRATEGY

HR professionals are challenged to develop strategies to improve their organizations. Nine strategies are available to HR professionals to improve their effectiveness in organizations.

Strategy 1: Establish Credibility

Some HR programs falter because they are not based on the needs of the organization or are not results-oriented, while others fail because HR professionals do not properly communicate the value and benefits of their programs, interventions, and initiatives to decision makers within the organization. Although all of these are contributing factors, most HR programs fail because clients' business and performance needs are not satisfied; thus, HR is not perceived as important. When clients believe that HR is unable to help improve their performance, quality, efficiency, or productivity, they view HR as nonessential in accomplishing the strategic business goals and objectives of the organization. In other words, HR professionals lack credibility within the organization, and their programs are destined to fail.

Improved credibility results from HR professionals' ability to demonstrate professional expertise as well as their understanding of organizational operations and culture. In this way, HRD professionals provide real value to the organization.

HR professionals need to demonstrate several behaviors in order to enhance credibility. Accordingly HR professionals need to:

1. Be accurate in all HRD practices.
2. Be predictable and consistent—dependable and reliable so that decision makers have confidence in their actions and recommendations.
3. Meet their commitments in a timely and efficient manner.
4. Establish collaborative client relationships built on trust and honesty.
5. Express their opinions, ideas, strategies, and activities in an understandable and clear manner, and at the most appropriate times.
6. Behave in an ethical manner that demonstrates integrity.
7. Demonstrate creativity and innovation.
8. Maintain confidentiality.
9. Listen to and focus on executive problems in a manner that brings about mutual respect.[1]

Others believe that HR professionals establish credibility within their organizations by demonstrating the ability to solve complex problems that satisfy client needs and expectations; exhibiting professional expertise combined with understanding of organizational operations and culture; demonstrating integrity by delivering results; and networking with organizational decision makers. In essence, credibility must be earned.[2]

Strategy 2: Understand Business Principles and Practices

An awareness of how business principles and practices are executed is essential for HR professionals, and enables them to think like their clients. This includes knowledge of business fundamentals, systems theory, organizational culture, and the organization's philosophy, mission, and goals. HR professionals also demonstrate business understanding via knowledge of stockholder needs and expectations. This knowledge enables them to adapt their practices, procedures, products, innovations, and services, which allows them to better serve their clients. Further, business understanding also requires knowledge of how things get done and how decisions are made inside an organization. HR professionals who have an understanding of such principles and practices are better able to facilitate change without disrupting the organization's operations. Consequently, HR professionals need to gain experience in functional areas such as marketing, finance, operations, or sales to generate pertinent, practical solutions for their clients.

Strategy 3: Reengineer the HR Function

Beyond business understanding, the HR function must to be reengineered to become a business partner in the organization. The following are some major characteristics that the HR function must have in order to perform accordingly. To be specific, the human resource function needs to:

- Be staffed by individuals who understand the business as well as change strategy.
- Be a valued member of management teams by contributing to business strategy and operations decision making.
- Effectively use outsourcers as a way to reduce the cost of the human resource development function and to draw on expertise that is not easily built into the organization.
- Retain control over setting the strategic direction for the organization's human resource systems, while using outsourcers when appropriate.
- Have high levels of competency in designing human resource systems and in managing their implementation.
- Effectively utilize information technology to support the development of organizational capabilities and competencies and of individuals' careers.
- Develop computer-based human resource management systems that free the human resource organization from the day-to-day management and administration of the human resources in the organization.[3]

Strategy 4: Establish Priorities

Research has shown that there are seven priorities of HR. Each must be addressed in order to identify appropriate HR strategies. They include helping their organization reinvent/redesign itself to compete more effectively; reinventing the HR function to be a more customer-focused, cost-effective organization; and attracting and developing the next-generation/twenty-first-century leaders and executive. Additionally, HR professionals should be contributing to the continuing cost containment/management effort; continuing to work on becoming a more effective business partner with their customers; rejecting fads, quick fixes, and other HR, fads; sticking to the basics that work; and addressing the diversity challenge.[4]

Strategy 5: Create Value by Achieving Results

HR professionals can choose between two strategies: activity or results. These strategies differ in their focus and in their contribution to the organization.

Many HR strategies do not focus on deliverables. Rather, they focus on function or process. Far too many HR functions provide programs that are not based on employees' needs. Little attention is paid to employees' needs as long as HR professionals are staying active. This can referred to as the activity strategy of HR. HR professionals who embrace the activity approach report the number of programs offered, transactions completed, or training classes offered to justify their value. Activity-based HR professionals believe that the more activity that occurs, the better the organization will perform.[5]

What is value? Value is that measure by which stakeholders within an organization perceive worth. HR processes should begin to focus on delivering valuables (as deemed worthy by the stakeholders) rather than focusing on transactions. "Everyone knows what HR does, but what does it deliver?" is a great question.[6] HR professionals can begin to mold their strategies to focus on deliverables, thus becoming part of the strategic process within the organization. Known as a results strategy,[7] it is an approach HR professionals use to improve organization performance through performance improvement interventions and change initiatives. The focus is not on many programs, transaction, or training classes but on the results obtained through their performance and change efforts. HR professionals who use this approach report on outcomes as a means of validating the HR function.

Six principles have been identified to help HR professionals in creating value through HRM. They are as follows:

- Human resource strategy must be anchored to the business strategy.
- Human resource management is not about programs; it is about relationships.
- The human resource department must be known as an organization that embraces change and understands what is necessary to implement it.
- HR should be an outspoken advocate of employee interest, yet it must understand that business decisions have to balance a range of factors that often conflict with one another.
- The effectiveness of HR depends on its staying focused on issues rather than on personalities.
- Human resource executives must accept that constant learning and skill enhancement are essential to their being a contributor to the business.[8]

Strategy 6: Facilitate and Manage Change

HR professionals, acting as change agents, must turn knowledge about change into know-how for accomplishing change, and success factors for change into action plans for accomplishing change.

The first step is to have a clearly defined change model. Such a model identifies the key factors for a successful change as well as the essential questions that must be answered to put the model into action. Specific questions determine the extent to which key success factors exist within an organization. The seven key success factors are:

- *Leading change:* Having a sponsor of change who owns and leads the change initiative.
- *Creating a shared need:* Ensuring that individuals know why they should change and that the need for change is greater than the resistance to change.
- *Shaping a vision:* Articulating the desired outcome from the change.
- *Mobilizing commitment:* Identifying, involving, and pledging the key stakeholders who must be involved to accomplish the change.
- *Changing systems and structures:* Using HRD and management tools (staffing, development, appraisal, rewards, organization design, communication, systems, and so on) to ensure that the change is built into the organization's infrastructure.
- *Monitoring progress:* Defining benchmarks, milestones, and experiments with which to measure and demonstrate progress.
- *Making change last:* Ensuring that change happens through implementation plans, follow-through, and ongoing commitment.[9]

Facilitating and managing change means transforming the seven key success factors from a theoretical exercise into a managerial process. Using the following questions, the seven factors' capacity for change in a given organization can be profiled. Thus, HR professionals assigned to integrate change should answer these questions to ensure that the resources needed for making change happen will be available.

- To what extent does the change have a champion, sponsor, or other leader who will support the change? (Leading change)
- To what extent do the people essential to the success of the change feel a need for change that exceeds the resistance to the change? (Creating a need)

- To what extent do we know the desired outcomes for change? (Shaping a vision)
- To what extent are key stakeholders committed to the change outcomes? (Mobilizing commitment)
- To what extent have we institutionalized the change through systems and structures? (Changing systems and structures)
- To what extent are indicators in place to track our progress on the change effort? (Monitoring progress)
- To what extent do we have an action plan for getting change to happen? (Making change last).[10]

HR professionals as change agents do not implement change, but they must be able to *get the change done.*[11] By identifying and profiling key factors for change, they lead teams through the steps necessary for increasing change capacity.

Strategy 7: Define the Impact of HR Investments

Defining and creating the scope of how investing in HR practices can help the organization to improve or become more effective requires HR professionals to:
- Define the impact of investments in HR practices and business performance
- Present a capability-based view of the organization that shows the "why" and the "how" of the bridge connecting investment in HR and business performance
- Review critical capabilities that may link HR and performance
- Suggest implications of these capabilities for HR functions and professionals.[12]

Strategy 8: Become an Employee Champion

HR professionals are in a unique position to serve as employee champions because they help employees identify legitimate work demands and thus help workers set priorities.[13] By doing so, they help employees balance work demands through the proper allocation of resources. Accordingly, HR professionals identify creative ways of leveraging resources so employees do not feel overwhelmed by what is expected of them.

There are 10 questions that help HR professionals determine whether employees and organizations are responding appropriately to demand situations:

1. Do employees control key decision-making processes that determine how work is done?
2. Do employees have a vision and direction that commits them to working hard?
3. Are employees given challenging work assignments that provide opportunities to learn new skills?
4. Do employees work in teams to accomplish goals?
5. Does the work environment provide opportunities for celebration, fun, excitement, and openness?
6. Are employees compensated and rewarded for work accomplishments?
7. Do employees enjoy open, candid, and frequent information sharing with management?
8. Are employees treated with dignity while differences are openly shared and respected?
9. Do employees have access to and use of technology that makes their work easier?
10. Do employees have the skills necessary to do their work well?[14]

Positive responses to these questions enable an organization to determine the adequacy of employee control, commitment to the organization, the type of challenging work provided to employees, the degree to which collaboration and teamwork are employed, the adequacy of organizational culture, quality of the compensation and reward system used, quality and quantity of organizational communications, concern for due process, adequacy of technology, and employee competence.[15] When serving as employee champions, HR professionals devote a majority of their time helping their organization positively answer each of the above 10 questions. Doing so enables them to increase their influence within the organization, which positively impacts its business results.[16]

Strategy 9: Adopt the Outcomes of a Strategically Integrated HR Function

By applying the principles, techniques, and strategies of the strategically integrated HR approach, HR professionals should be able to:

1. Develop a philosophy of HR that will help organizations achieve their business results.
2. Adopt a strategic approach to improving organizational performance and development.
3. Think responsively but responsibly about client requests.
4. Develop an understanding of an organization and its business.
5. Design, develop, and implement organizational transformation tools and techniques.
6. Develop a systems approach to organizational change and development.
7. Develop performance management systems.
8. Develop strategic business partnerships.
9. Link HR interventions and initiatives to an organization's strategic business goals and objectives.
10. Adopt a customer service approach with internal clients.
11. Help managers develop their employees.
12. Cultivate management development partnerships.
13. Help managers link performance appraisals to performance *improvement.*
14. Help managers develop performance coaching skills.
15. Implement organizational development partnerships.
16. Make the transition from trainer to organizational development consultant.
17. Identify organizational and performance needs.
18. Use organizational and performance needs as the foundation of all HR interventions and initiatives
19. Design and develop performance improvement and change interventions.
20. Create a learning acquisition strategy.
21. Eliminate barriers to learning transfer.
22. Implement learning transfer strategies.
23. Measure the impact of HR intervention.
24. Improve the image and credibility of HRD within organizations.
25. Develop a promotional strategy for an organization's HRD program.[17]

See also HR Competencies; HR Metrics

NOTES

1. David Ulrich and Wayne Brockbank, *The HR Values Propositions* (Cambridge, MA: Harvard Business Press, 2005).

2. Jerry W. Gilley and Ann Maycunich Gilley, *Strategically Integrated HRD: Six Transformational Roles in Creating Results Driven Programs* (Cambridge, MA: Perseus Publishing, 2003).

3. Ibid.

4. C.J. Ehrlich, "Human Resource Management: A Changing Script for a Changing World," in *Tomorrow's HR Management: 48 Thought Leaders Call for Change,* ed. David. Ulrich, M.R. Losey, and G. Lake (New York: Wiley & Sons, 1997), 163–70.

5. R. Eichinger and David Ulrich, *Human Resource Challenges* (New York: The Human Resource Planning Society, 1995).

6. Dave Ulrich and Wayne Brockbank, "HR's New Mandate: Be a Strategic Player" (June 20, 2005), http://hbswk.hbs.edu/archive/4861.html (accessed August 20, 2008).

7. Ulrich and Wayne Brockbank, *The HR Values Propositions*.

8. Gilley and Gilley, *Strategically Integrated HRD*.

9. Ulrich and Brockbank, *The HR Values Propositions*.

10. Ibid.

11. Ibid.

12. Jerry W. Gilley and Ann Maycunich, *Organizational Learning, Performance, and Change: An Introduction to Strategic HRD* (Cambridge, MA: Perseus Publishing, 2000).

13. Randall S. Schuler and Susan E. Jackson, *Strategic Human Resource Management,* 2nd ed. (San Francisco: Blackwell Publishing, 2007).

14. David Ulrich, *Human Resource Champions* (Boston: Harvard Business School Press, 1997), 135.

15. Ibid., 136.

16. Gilley and Gilley, *Strategically Integrated HRD*.

17. Ibid.

Jerry W. Gilley and Paul Shelton

HR TRENDS

In a Society of Human Resource Management executive survey, executives were asked, "Which of the following trends do you think will most significantly alter the workforce in the next decade?" Their responses:

- Baby boomer retirements—47 percent
- Global business interactions—31 percent
- Outsourcing—11 percent
- Remote work arrangements—5 percent
- Other—6 percent[1]

Top 10 Trends in Human Resource Management for 2007

The Society of Human Resource Management recently surveyed top executives who identified the following as the most critical trends facing human resource management:

1. *Rising health care costs.* Health care costs to employers are rising dramatically. In a recent study conducted by the National Coalition on Health Care, health care costs rose 6.9 percent during 2007. This rate is twice the current rate of inflation.[2] This rising cost is dramatically affecting the organization's ability to pay for its employees' health care coverage. Many organizations have moved to a cost-share method of health care, which has the employee paying for a portion of the health care costs.

2. *Increased use of outsourcing (off-shoring) of jobs.* Outsourcing, also known as off-shoring, is becoming more and more prevalent. In a recent survey of 500 senior executives, cost was identified as the biggest factor when deciding to go offshore with job tasks (92 percent).[3]

3. *Increased health care/medical costs.* The rising costs of health care are having a negative effect on the profitability of most organizations.[4] While health care costs are increasing, organizations must begin to look elsewhere to limit costs to increase a competitive margin. Leveraged costs such as health care premiums increase the necessary profit margin.

4. *Increased demand for work/life balance.* Organizations are now focusing not only on an employee's work, but the employee's off-work time as well. A recent study showed that work/life balance is a major factor in employment decisions from businessmen and women.[5] Even the federal government has stepped in to address the issue of work/life balance by instituting the Family Medical Leave Act, which mandates employers to allow employees up to 12 weeks of leave for certain reasons, such as the birth of a child, ill relative, adoption, or sickness.[6]

5. *Retirement of large numbers of "baby boomers" (those born between 1945 and 1964).* There are likely to be a number of issues shaping the future of HR and the workforce, but for today's organizations, one stands out above the rest. Nearly half of the senior executives (47 percent) surveyed said baby-boomer retirements will have the greatest impact on the workforce over the next decade.[7] Between 2000 and 2010, the number of U.S. workers ages 45–54 is projected to grow by just over 20 percent, while the number of those ages 55–64 is projected to grow more than 50 percent. In contrast, the number of workers ages 35–44 is projected to decrease by 10 percent.[8] Further, the annual growth rate of the traditional working-age U.S. population (ages 15–64), is projected at 0.3 percent. The comparable rate for ages 65 and over is projected at 3.1 percent. Almost 90 percent of the net increase in the traditional working age population is projected to occur in the age 55–64 group.[9]

6. *New attitudes toward aging and retirement as baby boomers reach retirement age.* Baby boomers have a different attitude towards retirement than did prior generations. Two perspectives on the upcoming retirement age seem to permeate the literature. First, employers may see an "exodus" of baby boomers moving to retirement. Over 50 percent of baby boomers will be able to retire "comfortably" financially.[10] Second, baby boomers also have a greater need financially than previous generations. Coupled with a longer lifespan (expected to be 83), baby boomers could outlive their financial resources.[11]

7. *Rise in the number of individuals and families without health insurance.* More and more people are becoming uninsured. In 2004, uninsured Americans totaled 45.8 million. This is an 800,000-person increase.[12] Employers are increasingly finding the costs of health care to be prohibitive. With baby boomers retiring, companies are decreasing the availability or coverage of postretirement coverage.[13]

8. *Increased identity theft.* Identity theft is increasing as technology is increasing. Additional policies and procedures have been enacted by many employers to help prevent identity theft. HR.com suggests the following for companies:
   - Make certain to mark confidential information with a "confidential" stamp and keep it locked under secure access available only on a need-to-know basis.
   - Use a crisscross shredder to shred all personnel documents.
   - Be careful about giving out information to third parties, including anybody who claims that they are investigating a credit card application, home loan mortgage, financial aid obligations, etc.
   - If an employee raises a concern, conduct a prompt and thorough investigation to protect not only that employee, but perhaps others as well.[14]

9. *Work intensification as employers try to increase productivity with fewer employees.* In a recent study by Accenture, some employees experience a higher level of stress as workload increases, while others have decreased stress or actually claim to have no stress.[15] Upon further investigation, this stress seemed to be correlated to income rather than to other demographic information.[16]

10. *Vulnerability of technology to attack or disaster.* Many organizations are relying on electronic communications, computers, and other technology as a way of doing business. If attacked, some businesses would not be able to operate. For example, if the computer systems were to stop working, could the company still function? Is there an alternate work plan, which would allow the continuation of operations given such a disaster? A prepared organization would

have responses to the above questions. Recently, the U.S. Department of Commerce addressed this issue by implementing a program known as Continuity of Operations (COOP). It is a plan and a program that ensures that the essential functions will continue in the event of any disruptive activity focused on the Department, its personnel, or its facilities that is generated by man or by natural causes.[17]

See also Homeland Security; HR Strategy; Human Capital; Work-Life Balance

NOTES

1. Society of Human Resource Management, http://ezinearticles.com/What-You-Need-To-Know-About-Human-Resource-Trends-For-2007 (accessed April 3, 2008).

2. Ibid.

3. Information found at http://www.nchc.org/facts/cost.shtml (accessed August 20, 2008).

4. Karyn-Siobhan Robinson, "HR Needs Larger Role in Off Shoring," *HR Magazine,* May 2004.

5. Christan M. Thomas, "Achieving Balance Important for Individuals and Businesses," *Johnson City Press,* July 13, 2006.

6. Information found at http://www.dol.gov/esa/whd/fmla/ (accessed August 20, 2008).

7. Information found at http://hr.cch.com/news/hrm/012808a.asp (accessed August 20, 2008).

8. *The Aging of the U.S. Workforce: Employer Challenges and Responses* (New York: Ernst & Young, January 2006).

9. Ibid.

10. Information found at http://www.aarp.org/research/work/retirement/inb154_income.html (accessed August 20, 2008).

11. Ibid.

12. Information found at http://www.cbpp.org/8-30-05health.htm (accessed August 20, 2008).

13. Information found at http://www.hreonline.com/HRE/story.jsp?storyId=8401540 (accessed August 20, 2008).

14. Information found at http://www.hr.com (accessed August 20, 2008).

15. Information found at http://www.digitalforum.accenture.com/DigitalForum/Global/ViewByTopic/TechnologyCareers/0612_harried_employees.htm (accessed August 20, 2008).

16. Ibid.

17. Information found at http://dms.osec.doc.gov/cgi-bin/doit.cgi?204:112:f83a25ec27d4064b2 c4952b4a50f32ed83828f0a9288fb7d328906e343eddc87:155 (accessed August 20, 2008).

Paul Shelton and Jerry W. Gilley

HUMAN CAPITAL

To most people, capital means money in the bank, a hundred shares of Berkshire Hathaway stock, oil refineries in Texas, or steel plants in the Great Lakes region. These are all forms of capital in the sense that they are tangible assets that yield income and other useful outputs over long periods of time. But these tangible forms of capital are not the only ones. The term "human capital" refers to the inventory of productive skills and technical knowledge embodied in labor. Many early economists, such as Adam Smith, refer to it simply as labor. Smith initially defined capital to include (1) useful machines, instruments of the trade; (2) buildings as the means of procuring revenue; (3) improvements of land; and (4) human capital. Smith saw human capital as skills, dexterity (physical, intellectual, psychological, etc.) and judgment.

Human experience over time also has an impact on human capital. Furthermore, human capital can be acquired through formal schooling and on-the-job training. Formal education, a computer training course, leadership development initiatives, expenditures for medical care, and lessons on the virtues of ethics and honesty also are capital because they increase earnings, maintain and improve health, or add to a person's productive abilities over much of his lifetime. Therefore, economists regard expenditures on education, training, medical care, and so on as investments in human capital. These expenditures affect human capital because people cannot be separated from their knowledge, skills, health, or values in the way that they can be separated from their financial and physical assets. Investments in education and training may be the most important contributions to maintaining and/or increasing the value of human capital. Simply stated, human capital means people.[1]

Human Capital Management

Organizations employ a diverse, knowledge-based workforce composed of individuals with a broad spectrum of technical and process skills and institutional memory. They are the organization's human capital, its greatest asset. To attain the highest level of performance and accountability, organizations depend on three enablers: people, processes, and technology. The most important of these is people, because an organization's people determine its character and its ability to perform.

Social, economic, and technological changes have become a constant in our global society. These changes impact the ways in which organizations approach their work. Leaders' awareness of how much they rely on their human capital to achieve results is paramount to their survival. To meet the changing environment, organizations need to elevate human capital to a much higher priority than ever before and modernize their human capital policies and practices. In a tight labor market, they must become more competitive in attracting and retaining new employees with critical skills; create the kinds of performance incentives and training programs that motivate and empower employees; and build management-labor relationships that are based on common interests. Modern human capital policies and practices offer organizations a means to improve their economy, efficiency, and effectiveness to better serve their customers, both internal and external.

There are, however, two key principles that are central to the human capital idea. First, people are assets whose value can be enhanced through investment. As with any investment, the goal is to maximize value while managing risk. As the value of people increases, so does the performance capacity of the organization, and therefore its value to clients and other stakeholders. Second, an organization's human capital policies must be aligned to support the organization's "shared vision"—that is, the mission, vision for the future, core values, goals and objectives, and strategies by which the organization has defined its direction and its expectations for itself and its people. All human capital policies and practices should be designed, implemented, and assessed by the standard of how well they help the organization pursue its shared vision. In most organizations, the lion's share of operating costs is devoted to the workforce. For this reason, employees traditionally have been viewed through the budgetary lens, and therefore they have often been viewed as costs to be cut rather than as assets to be valued and enhanced. However, high-performance organizations in both the private and public sectors recognize that an organization's people largely determine its capacity to perform. These organizations understand that the value of the organization is dependent on the value of its people.

Enhancing the value of employees is a win-win goal for employers and employees alike. The more an organization recognizes the intrinsic value of each employee, the more it recognizes that this value can be enhanced with nurturing and investment. The more an organization recognizes that employees vary in their talents and motivations, and that a variety of incentive strategies and working arrangements can be created to enhance each employee's contributions to organizational performance, the more likely the organization will be to appreciate the variety of employee needs and circumstances and to act in ways that will make sense in both business and human terms.

One of the emerging challenges for leaders and managers will be to add to their traditional policy portfolios an understanding of the importance of performance management issues—including human capital issues—to the accomplishment of their agencies' policy and programmatic goals. If high performance and accountability depend on the three enablers—people, process, and technology—then it is useful, first and foremost, for any organization to have a clear and fact-based understanding of its human capital situation. There is no single recipe for successful human capital management. However, there are basic human capital elements and underlying values that are common to most high-performance organizations.[2]

See also HRIS; Performance Management: An Overview; Training

NOTES

1. Gary S. Becker, *Human Capital: A Theoretical and Empirical Analysis, with Special Reference to Education* (Chicago: University of Chicago Press, 1993).

2. David M. Walker, *Human Capital: A Self Assessment Checklist for Leaders* (Washington, DC: GAO, 2000).

Merwyn L. Strate

INNOVATION IN HUMAN RESOURCES

Competition is a primary driving force behind organizational change and innovation. In order to ensure continued success, organizations emphasize human resource development and apply progressive, or innovative, human resource management practices. No longer is innovation the sole domain of the research and development department. Innovation is driven by the creative ideas and actions of all employees. Innovation is cultivated in work environments that encourage and provide opportunities that generate creativity. Further, innovation requires a focus on attracting, retaining, and developing talent in organizations. This is the role of HR. More and more, there are examples of the drive for innovative HR practices in organizations, both in the private sector and in government.

Recently, the Office of Personnel Management (OPM) issued new regulations and processes for staffing, compensation, and performance management. Federal government agencies have been able to achieve their goals through flexible practices.[1] Agencies have begun to call some of their more innovative programs "reinvention labs."[2] The primary change has been to create more flexible rules and procedures as it pertains to employment practices. Further, the OPM has sponsored "demonstration projects,"[3] which provide a structure for testing and introducing ideas and interventions for the purpose of transformation change.

In general, HR has an opportunity to promote innovative practices through five areas: (1) recruitment and selection, (2) the design of flexible work arrangements, (3) employee development, (4) culture, and (5) partnering with line managers to influence culture and management practices. While all of the practices have the potential to have a positive impact on the organization's they serve, it should be noted that they must be implemented in conjunction with each other. Integration of all HR practices is critical. None can have a significant impact as a stand-alone practice.

Recruitment and Selection

Recruitment and selection efforts place emphasis on identifying potential employees who can "think outside the box." In other words, selection assessments should include an examination of people's creative capacity. Interviews that incorporate role play exercises and other cognitive-based tests that assess an individual's capacity to challenge the status quo, degree of inquisitiveness, and ability to influence change have been exemplified as innovative HR practices.

Employee Development

Employee development programs that teach creative problem-solving skills and teamwork are primary vehicles to innovation. Further, mentoring has been identified as having a significant impact on cultivating creativity.[4] Partnering a seasoned employee who has exemplified creative thought and action with newly hired employees is seen as a viable mentoring practice that can drive innovative results.

Flexible Work Arrangements

Organizations that are able to change quickly in response to the external market do so through flexibility. Flexibility is becoming the key ingredient with regard to human resource practices; specifically, flexibility in terms of where and how work is completed. Telecommuting, job sharing, and flexible schedules are becoming increasingly popular. More and more, organizations are creating policies and providing resources for flexible work arrangements. As a result, many have found productivity increases, as well as increased retention.

Culture

Culture is a set of beliefs and practices that guide the actions and behaviors of people in an organization. Such beliefs and traditions accumulate over time and become norms. Fostering a culture that is conducive to creativity is imperative to an organization's ability to remain competitive. HR, in partnership with line management, has an influence creating a culture that promotes, acts on, and rewards creativity. This is done through creating a space that is conducive to creativity and allowing the time necessary for creative thought and experimentation. Setting up facilities or meeting rooms dedicated as "creative spaces" and creating policies that enable a percentage of time to be dedicated to creative efforts are practices that, over time, become cultural norms.

Management Practices

Innovation requires the dedication of resources, including human, to an uncertain future. In general, employees prefer certainty and the status quo. They are not automatically willing to take risks without the assurance that the organization supports such efforts. Employees need to be assured that if they try new things and make mistakes, they will not be punished.

HR can work with managers on communication strategies that assure employees that failure is anticipated as part of the process. More importantly, managers can take actions that suggest the same. Both are critical to creating and sustaining creativity. Further, HR can work with line managers to create practices that reward and recognize employee behaviors such as questioning the status quo and purposively testing out new work process and procedures.

Conclusion

Employees have a significant role in contributing to organizational innovation. HR supports employees in this endeavor by establishing innovative HR practices that encourage employee creativity. Specifically, HR practices consist of using progressive techniques to hire creative talent; creating flexible work arrangements that assist with the retention of talent; providing developmental opportunities focused on creativity and teamwork; and implementing policies, and partnering with management to implement practices, that create a culture supportive of creative thought and action.

See also Culture; Employee Development: An Overview; Job Design; Job Sharing; Staffing: An Overview

NOTES

1. Office of Personnel Management, "HR Toolkit," U.S. Government, http://www.opm.gov/ (accessed April 15, 2008).

2. Ibid.

3. Ibid.

4. C. Brooke Orr and Nancy R. Lockwood, "Innovative Mentoring Programs in the Global Marketplace," Society for Human Resource Management, (2007). http://www.shrm.org (accessed April 1, 2008).

Pamela Dixon

INTERNATIONAL HUMAN RESOURCE MANAGEMENT

International human resource (IHR) management has become one of the most dynamic organizational capabilities needed for competing in a global marketplace. Business today has been dramatically changed by globalization, and so has the job of managers in multinational organizations. Corporate strategies must be set at the global enterprise level, coordinated into regional operations plans and executed at a market level in a way that serves a broad array of customer needs. Thus, human capital must be built, sustained and deployed within an evolving global context—creating the next frontier for human resource management.

Human resource management has been defined as the policies and practices needed to carry out the "people" or human resource aspects of managing a business, including recruiting, screening, training, rewarding, and appraising.[1] International (or global, in this entry) is described in this context as commerce between countries. Together, IHR is about supporting commerce between countries using the activities within the realm of the HR discipline.

While the above definition is important, it is essential that the human resource function contribute at the highest strategic level to ensure business success in a global economy. What appears to be the challenge is that domestic businesses are getting used to HR having good traditional processes, policies, and structures that are well institutionalized and are now beginning to focus time on strategic work. However, when moving to international locations, the IHR professional in some regard has to step back to foundational elements and ensure the basics are implemented before moving to strategic issues. The following perspective considers the level of contribution delivered by an HR function to the business:

- Level One: Transactions and information
- Level Two: Functional services (recruit, develop, compensate, etc.)
- Level Three: Workforce productivity
- Level Four: Competitive advantage via people, practices, and management
- Level Five: Strategic HR applied to business problems and opportunities[2]

A common challenge that IHR practitioners face is managing the wide variation in capability and contribution levels of HR in different geographies around the world. For example, while HR policies and practices in established markets might allow the HR function to contribute at a strategic level, in emerging markets the IHR practitioner may be required to step back and address foundational elements to ensure HR basics are implemented prior to moving into strategic issues.

The above model has relevance for the human resource discipline, especially for the IHR professional considering where to start as his company expands beyond its domestic framework.[3] Ensuring Levels One through Four are essential, although they must be grounded in Level Five, strategic planning, which takes into account the complexity and variation of global business. The IHR professional will be asked to craft strategies that utilize global talent, maximize knowledge transfer, minimize labor cost, and optimize cultural diversity. These are not capabilities commonly found or easily developed in traditional HR functions.

What Factors Have Accelerated The Global Business Landscape?

The speed of internationalization has accelerated dramatically in the last decade. The impact of such rapid and dramatic change has been met as an opportunity to some organizations and considered a threat by others. Following are some insights to the factors that have flattened the global business landscape so quickly:

1. Open borders as the walls came down between countries.
2. The new age of connectivity with a Web-enabled globe.
3. Workflow software providing standardized ways to connect and work.
4. Power of communities for natural subject matter idea generation.
5. Outsourcing of standardized work content.
6. Off-shoring of specific work content now that talent is available everywhere.
7. Supply-chaining that can deliver to any location.

8. Insourcing of work never dreamed possible before.
9. In-forming through various search engines (Google, Yahoo, etc.).
10. Digital, mobile, and virtual devises that move information to the individual.[4]

These factors have created a world in which work content can be done 24 hours a day, seven days a week, from anywhere. IHR professionals must understand these key themes when considering human capital strategies to drive business performance and global competitiveness for their organizations.

Strategic Work Streams for Next Level Contributions

Based on benchmark data from organizations that have expanded outside their domestic markets and drawing upon our own experience, six key elements are necessary in a successful people agenda for international business expansion.

1. *Human capital strategy:* A defined three- to five-year plan to deliver organizational excellence through leadership, talent, structure, competency, and capability.
2. *Talent generation:* Business-based workforce planning that delivers talent that provides sustained competitive advantage in innovation, quality and cost. In short, knowing the business imperatives and finding the best people in the world to execute them.
3. *Talent mobility:* System capability to know, grow, connect, and deploy a global workforce. This is a critical dimension to the organization's ability to attract and retain top international talent. Employer branding is critical to attract talent, while internal engagement activities are central to keeping attrition rates below local labor market norms.
4. *Performance management:* Establishing clear reporting relationships with focused priorities aligned to the business strategy, while implementing complimenting reward structures that reward and reinforce accountability for execution.
5. *Organizational capability:* Well-defined competency models combined with standardized processes and systems to ensure work is accomplished while reducing cycle time, confusion, and redundancy.
6. *Company values:* A global culture indicative of what the organization is or wants to become. Communicating values and a code of conduct is paramount as the organization expands into new regions.

Conclusion

The IHR professional has a significant strategic contribution to offer, no matter the global maturation of the organization. The world has changed, and with it the opportunity for the people component to have a profound impact on the success or failure of global organizations. For the IHR professional, the consideration is not *if* one's work will eventually include international elements or accountability, it is about *when*. Some are already on the way to experiencing the challenges and rewards of operating in an international business. For those still waiting to do so, we offer some closing ideas:

- Consider the needs of your business and look for solutions outside of your domestic location.
- Join an IHR organization
- Consider IHR education/certification.
- Seek global learning opportunities; become part of a global project team, if possible.
- Read international publications to build your global business acumen.
- Explore the globe via personal travel, the Internet, or by developing relationships locally with people from other cultures.

Sustained competitive advantage is the quest for the modern global business. Reaching this outcome can come only through outstanding people. Active IHR professionals leadership can expand business possibilities by accessing a broader, global pool of talent. You can literally make a world of difference.

NOTES

1. G. Dessler, *Human Resource Management,* 8th ed. (Upper Saddle River, NJ: Prentice-Hall, Inc, 2000).
2. J. Sullivan, *Rethinking Strategic HR* (Chicago: CCH Incorporated, 2004).
3. Ibid.
4. T.L. Friedman, *The World Is Flat* (New York: Farrar, Straus and Giroux, 2006).

Tim Reynolds and Robert Paxton

INTERNS

An intern is one who works in a temporary position with an emphasis on on-the-job training rather than merely employment, making it similar to an apprenticeship. Interns are usually college or university students but can also be other adults seeking skills for a new career. Student internships provide opportunities for students to gain experience in their field, determine if they have an interest in a particular career, create a network of contacts, and possibly gain school credit.

An internship may be paid, unpaid, or partially paid. The issue regarding pay must be carefully considered based upon the type of organization (for profit or not for profit), the type of work the intern is performing, whether school credit is being earned, and Department of Labor regulations. Internships can be full time or part time and are typically performed over a predetermined and agreed-upon period of time, such as summer breaks for college students.

Benefits of an Internship Program

An internship can provide benefits to the company as well as the intern. In a sense, they form a type of partnership based upon a mutually beneficial scenario, and each agrees to give and to take from this relationship.

Benefits to the Organization

Improving the talent pool is one of the top three priorities of a high-performing company.[1] The war for talent has forced companies to seek opportunities to source and identify upcoming talent as well as ways to engage its current employees. Interns can support this objective and provide companies with the following benefits:

- A pipeline of talent to the organization
- A "flex staff" to utilize at points of heightened business needs (e.g., seasonal variations)
- Proved job enrichment to traditionally medial or repetitive tasks
- Valuable "on campus" exposure and endorsements from current and previous interns
- Positioning of the company in a positive light within its community.

Benefit to the Intern

Internships also provide interns with valuable benefits that will pay dividends once they enter the business world. Such benefits include:

- Insight and direction into their career interests and abilities
- A real perspective of the working world
- Marketable work experience
- Valuable business contacts
- Income and possible school credit.

Successful Internship Programs

Interns come to an organization with a different set of expectations and knowledge/skills/abilities (KSAs) than a non-intern would. Therefore, special attention must be paid to them. The following rules for successful internship program are as follows:

- Consider carefully what qualifications you want your interns to have. To entrust an intern with meaningful work, you need to consider what kind of credentials the intern will need to perform. Specify whether an intern should have completed specific course work or a certain number of years of college.
- Keep an eye on expenses. Although interns are not usually as costly as regular employees, there are expenses involved. Recruiting can be costly, especially if you need to attend job fairs at various colleges.
- Be aware of the legalities. Most interns qualify as employees under various employment laws and are subject to minimum wage and overtime laws, worker's compensation coverage, and possibly unemployment compensation. You may want to consult your human resources staff to structure or revise benefit plans to exclude interns from benefits that are not mandatory.
- Ensure ahead of time that office supplies, computer access, and work spaces are available.
- Plan for time to supervise your interns. An intern is not a solution to your work overload if you do not have the time and energy to oversee the work that a successful internship requires.
- Set aside time to provide ongoing feedback and to conduct a formal performance review.
- Ask your human resources department for ongoing support. It is important that the human resources department be available for interns who have encountered problems and for managers who are handling issues with interns.[2]
  Additional consideration should be given to:
- Preparing to manage the unique attributes of the interns. Attention should be paid to potential generational and diversity differences that exist between the intern and her manager as well as the additional time and attention that come with the internship.
- Formulating a communication plan to address key stakeholders and peers of the interns.
- Deciding whether you will offer the intern a full-time/permanent position at the end of the internship.
- Having a clear purpose and goal for the program.
- Matching the right person to the job.
- Monitoring the intern's progress and engagement.
- Providing the intern with meaningful work.
- Providing the intern with a learning experience.

Conclusion

The numerous benefits to the company and to the intern provide a great deal of motivation to formulate a program. To ensure these benefits come to fruition, careful attention must be given to the planning and preparation stages, as companies can be blindsided and/or disillusioned by the variety of issues that may arise when attempting an intern program.

See also Recruiting and Selection; Employee Development; Compensation, Benefits, and Insurance; Employment Law

Resources:
Society for Human Resource Management. http://www.shrm.org.
  Wikimedia Foundation. "Intern." http://en.wikipedia.org/wiki/Intern.

NOTES

1. Ed Michaels, Helen Handfield-Jones, and Beth Axelrod, *The War for Talent* (Boston: Harvard Business School Press, 2001).
2. Amy Maingault, "A Few Rules for Successful Internships," Society for Human Resource Management, http://www.shrm.org (accessed March 8, 2008).

Pat Schneider

JOB ANALYSIS

Job analysis is a human resource (HR) practice that serves as a fundamental component of most HR-related decisions. Through the collection of job data regarding the nature of the work, worker requirements (e.g., level of skills and behaviors), and work environment, job analysis informs the complex decision making for HR practices.[1] A variety of methods are used to conduct a job analysis, which can be categorized as work-oriented, worker-oriented, multi-methods approach, and job analysis for managerial jobs.

Uses of Job Analysis

While not exhaustive, what follows is a comprehensive list of organizational purposes that are served by job analysis. Purposes covered in this entry include:
- The creation of job descriptions
- Human resource requirements
- Legal requirements
- Job classification
- Performance appraisals
- Job evaluation
- Job design
- Workforce planning
- Career development
- Selection exams
- Training and development

Job Descriptions

Jobs consist of a group of related duties and are typically performed by more than one person (e.g., nurse). A job description includes the title and other classifying information. Also, a job description typically provides a role summary, the essential duties and tasks, and minimum education and experience required. Further, it may contain other pertinent information such as reporting relationships, and equipment used on the job.

Human Resource Requirements

HR requirements consist of criteria and standards that job applicants must meet in order to qualify for or successfully perform a job. Minimum and preferred requirements to perform a given job include knowledge, skills, and abilities, as well as other specifications such as level of education and type and length of job-related experience.

Legal Requirements

Employment-related laws apply to decisions with regard to selection and hiring, pay, promotions, training, termination, and others. Federal and state agencies (e.g., Equal Employment Opportunity Commission [EEOC]) have established guidelines for which employers must comply. Job analysis is used to ensure employment decisions do not result in unlawful discrimination.

Job Classification

Job classification is a process whereby like-jobs are grouped together into job families (e.g., Helpdesk Analyst I, II, and III). Job families are typically based on duties and responsibilities of the jobs. Classification of the job will also determine a pay range and criteria for selection.

Performance Appraisals

The purpose of conducting performance appraisals is to provide feedback to an employee regarding his performance. Also, the appraisal process is used to make decisions on salary increases. Job analysis serves as a mechanism to link the criteria and standards established in the appraisal to the performance on the job.

Job Evaluation

The purpose of job evaluation is to ensure fair and competitive pay for a given job and to establish the value of one job compared to another within the company. Typically, job evaluation results in a job being placed in a pay grade based on organization-specific, compensable factors (e.g., level of complexity, decision-making authority, supervision).

Job Design

Job design is a function of creating a new job or redesigning a job. Job design entails identifying the collective tasks necessary to produce specific outcomes for a job. Redesign parses tasks in order to create a new job. Job redesign is done for a variety of reasons; to increase efficiency or worker motivation, or to achieve different job outcomes due to a change within the organization's business strategy.

Workforce Planning

Workforce planning consists of decisions made based on an organization's future needs for jobs as well as qualified people to fill those jobs.

Career Development

Career development focuses on designing a career ladder that promotes skill development and progressive job movement (either promotional or lateral). For example, companies may establish a career ladder for leadership careers and a ladder for technical careers. Another analogy frequently used in organizations that tend to have a flattened structure is the career "lattice," which suggests that careers can progress both vertically and laterally.

Selection Exams

Selection exams are utilized to assess the fit between a job and applicants for that job. Examples of selection exams include formal review of applications and resumes, performance assessments, cognitive assessments, and behavioral interviews. Job analysis plays a key role in establishing and validating the criteria that links job-related tasks to the above mentioned selection exams.

Training and Development
While people are hired because of the knowledge, skills and abilities they bring to the job, ongoing training and development are also needed. Job analysis illuminates the KSAs required for developmental assignments, or changes that occur in the job over time.

Job Analysis Methods

There are a multitude of job analysis methods. The list below is not exhaustive, but will provide an overview of the more prominent methods traditionally used in organizations. The methods can be categorized as work-oriented, worker-oriented, multi-methods approach, and job analysis for managerial jobs.

Work-oriented Methods
Methods used to describe the tasks and outcomes of worker actions are considered to be work-oriented methods of job analysis. There are four primary types of work-oriented methods: time and motion studies, functional job analysis, task inventories, and the critical incident technique.[2]

Worker-oriented Methods
Worker-oriented methods emphasize the attributes that people must possess in order to successfully perform a given job. Methods used within this category include the job element method (JEM), the position analysis questionnaire (PAQ), cognitive task analysis, and a variety of trait-based Methods.

Multi-methods Approach
The multi-methods approach incorporates multiple types of data, and is designed by combining various features of different job analysis methods. Examples include the combination job analysis method (CJAM), the multi-method job design questionnaire, and the use of O*Net (Occupational Information Network). The content found on O*Net consists of a wide-ranging set of job descriptors that include requirements for work and experience as well as worker characteristics and a variety of other occupational specific descriptors.

Job Analysis for Managerial Jobs
Managerial jobs differ from other types of jobs in terms of behavior and task content. Responsibilities and tasks that make up the managerial job include planning, coordinating work, and supervising others. Job analysis methods that are typically used for managerial jobs include functional-oriented analyses and other trait-based approaches such as assessment centers. One of the foremost used instruments is the Management Position Description Questionnaire (MPDQ), a self-report instrument that focuses on cognitive, technical, and people-related tasks. The MPDQ also has a section for knowledge, skills, and abilities (KSAs) associated with the job.

Conclusion

Job analysis consists of a rigorous and quantifiable process that informs HR-related decisions through the collection of job data regarding the work, worker requirements, and work environment. This entry described uses for job analysis and some of the more well-known methods used to conduct a job analysis. These methods are categorized as work-oriented, worker-oriented, multi-methods approach, and job analysis for managerial jobs.

See also Job Description; Job Design

NOTES

1. George Bohlander, Scott Snell, and Arthur Sherman, *Managing Human Resources* (Cincinnati, OH: South-Western, 2001).

2. Michael T. Brannick and Edward L. Levine, *Job Analysis: Methods, Research, and Applications for Human Resource Management in the New Millennium* (Thousand Oaks, CA: Sage Publications, 2002).

Pamela M. Dixon

JOB DESIGN

Job design is the fundamental design activity that maximizes performance. At the heart of job design are the organization's strategic business goals and objectives, which focus on performers' activities. Jobs that do not help an organization achieve its strategic business goals and objectives cease to be of value. It is extremely important, therefore, to link all job design activities to these goals and objectives.

Each job within an organization is housed within a business process, which is a subpart of an organizational function. In an organizational context, these are commonly referred to as departments or business units within organizations. Job design examines the smallest component parts of the component chain. Therefore, breakdowns or improvements in the interface between business processes will ultimately impact organizational performance capacity. Thus, job design activities should uncover opportunities for performance improvement. Once business process interfaces have been identified, four interrelated components require examination. They are performance outputs, performance activities, performance standards, and competency maps.[1]

Performance Outputs

Performance outputs are the tangibles and intangibles employees are paid to produce. As such, these outputs define an employee's job. Performance outputs can be the number of successful sales calls made by telemarketing representatives, the number of sales made per month by sales personnel, the service claims satisfied by customer service representatives, the number of proposals written each month, the number of packages delivered per day by postal workers, and so on. Outputs represent the hourly, daily, weekly, monthly, quarterly, and/or yearly expectation of employees in a specific job classification.[2]

Performance Activities

Performance activities are the steps in which employees engage to create performance outputs. Each performance activity consists of micro tasks, which collectively form the steps of an employee's job.[3] Once completed, these micro tasks become a way of describing the way a job is performed, commonly known as a *job description.*

Job descriptions demonstrate the relationship between performance outputs and activities. Therefore, they should be written to clearly identify performance outputs for each job, performance activities required by employees to produce these deliverables, and the relationship between activities and outputs. Moreover, each performance action or collection of activities produces one or more performance outputs. Consequently, a job description is simply a written document that describes an employee's performance activities and deliverables.[4]

Performance Standards

Performance standards represent excellence criteria used to measure product and service quality and worker efficiency.[5] Performance standards provide measures against which employees compare their actions and output to determine whether they are performing at acceptable levels. Performance standards represent the targets used to measure the quality of employee outputs and the efficiency of their performance activities.[6]

Identifying performance standards permits employees to regulate the quality of their productivity, which helps them to avoid needless mistakes, and maintains consistency. This ultimately leads to better organizational results. Performance standards also help managers determine acceptable performance levels and help them determine when performance outputs are at acceptable levels. Without performance standards, managers and employees lack the ability to ascertain whether they have created performance outputs or executed performance activities acceptable to internal and external stakeholders.[7]

Performance standards are based on performance outputs rather than on the way employees do their jobs, are achievable, easily understood by managers and employees, and specific and measurable. They are also time-based, written, and subject to change.[8]

Performance standards encourage employees to continue to produce at an acceptable level. Consequently, they will do their jobs and know when they are doing them well.[9]

Competency Maps

Once performance outputs, activities, and standards are identified, HR professionals and managers isolate the competencies (e.g., skills, knowledge, and attitudes) employees need to accomplish them. Competency maps can be very complex and detailed, since they represent the culmination of the knowledge, skills, behaviors, and attitudes an employee must possess to complete job tasks that comprise performance activities. They are also useful in:

1. Recruiting and selecting employees for given job classifications.
2. Determining the growth and development activities in which employees must participate to master performance.
3. Revealing employee strengths and weaknesses, thereby guiding formulation of career development activities as well as performance growth and development plans.[10]

See also Job Analysis; Job Descriptions

NOTES

1. Jerry W. Gilley, *Improving HRD Practice* (Malabar, FL: Krieger Publishing Co., 1998), 91.
2. Ibid., 97–98.

3. Jerry W. Gilley, Nathaniel W. Boughton, and Ann Maycunich, *The Performance Challenge: Developing Management Systems to Make Employees Your Organization's Greatest Asset* (Cambridge, MA: Perseus Publishing, 1999).

4. Gilley, *Improving HRD Practice.*

5. Gary Rummler and Alan Brache, *Improving Performance: How to Manage the White Spaces and the Organizational Chart* (San Francisco: Jossey-Bass, 1995).

6. Jerry W. Gilley and Steve A. Eggland, *Marketing HRD within Organizations: Improving the Visibility, Credibility, and Image of Programs* (San Francisco: Jossey-Bass Inc., 1992).

7. Ibid.

8. George B. Berke, *How to Conduct a Performance Appraisal* (Alexandria, VA: ASTD Press, 1990).

9. Gilley, *Improving HRD Practice.*

10. Gilley, Boughton, and Maycunich, *The Performance Challenge.*

Jerry W. Gilley

KNOWLEDGE MANAGEMENT

Knowledge management (KM) is a relatively new term used to define the process of gathering, organizing, analyzing, and sharing organizational knowledge.[1] Knowledge management focuses on a firm's knowledge assets and capabilities, along with the development and cultivation of channels through which knowledge flows. Critics argue that knowledge management is simply information management.[2] Proponents claim that the challenge is to translate knowledge into meaningful, usable information.

Technically, knowledge management as a practice has always existed. For example, knowledge has been shared via organizational training and development programs, through apprenticeships, during on-the-job instruction, and in employee orientations, to name a few. The impact of technology, specifically computers, however, has hastened and refined the process of and need for knowledge management.

Why Manage Knowledge?

Organizations create knowledge management programs to enhance efficiency and effectiveness, capitalize on market opportunities, and gain competitive advantage through learning and knowledge creation systems. KM adds value to an organization by
— Contributing to the firm's intellectual capital
— Enabling more informed decisions
— Encouraging the free flow of ideas and information
— Improving customer service and efficiency
— Enhancing productivity
A knowledge management plan involves an examination of corporate goals in light of the tools necessary to fulfill the organization's knowledge-sharing needs. The challenge is to convert knowledge into explicit, meaningful information for organizational members.

Phases of Knowledge Management

The four phases of knowledge management are gathering, organizing, refining, and disseminating.[3]

1. *Gathering*—includes data entry, OCR and scanning, voice input, pulling information from multiple sources, and searching for appropriate information to include.
2. *Organizing*—involves cataloging, indexing, filtering, and linking information.
3. *Refining*—entails contextualizing, collaborating, compacting, and mining data.
4. *Disseminating*—concerns flow, sharing, alert, and push.

Knowledge management occurs before, during, and after knowledge-related actions, with varying degrees of success. Given the relative newness of the concept, the complexity of business, and the challenges of communicating, many organizations struggle with adequately managing knowledge in any phase.

How to Manage Knowledge

Organizational knowledge management responsibilities may be housed in a centralized KM office or may be the domain of existing departments, usually human resources or IT. Knowledge management may be facilitated via KM of information management software, knowledge bases, document management systems, the Internet, Web conferencing, e-mail lists, blogs, and more. People are active participants in knowledge management through their participation in coaching and mentoring, job shadowing, groups, teams, communities of practice, and so forth.

See also Communities of Practice; HRIS; Knowledge Transfer; Learning Organizations

NOTES

1. Michael Stankosky, *Creating the Discipline of Knowledge Management: The Latest in University Research* (Burlington, MA: Elsevier Butterworth-Heinemann, 2004).
2. T.D. Wilson, "The Nonsense of Knowledge Management," *Information Research* 8, no. 1 (2002), http://informationr.net/ir/8-1/paper144.html (accessed August 20, 2008).
3. Jeff Angus, Jeetu Patel, and Jennifer Harty, "Knowledge Management: Great Concept...But What Is It?" *Information Week Online,* March 16, 1998. http://informationweek.com.

Ann Gilley

MERGERS AND ACQUISITIONS

With the advent of international competition in the marketplace, an increasing number of organizations are merging or being acquired by domestic and international corporations. A merger is the combining of two organizations, whereas an acquisition involves the purchase of one organization by another.[1] Before execution, mergers and acquisitions proceed through an extensive "due diligence" in which financial, product-line, business-strategy, and operational decisions are copiously evaluated. However, the people side of the business is often only a footnote, at least until real issues arise after the merger or acquisition. This phenomenon can be partly explained by the complexity and unpredictability of people issues. Studies suggest that two-thirds of mergers fail to achieve their objectives due largely to cultural impacts and other human factors.[2]

In a joint study by the Society of Human Resource Management and Towers Perrin Inc., executives were surveyed about their organizational expectations of merger or acquisition synergies. The survey revealed that the primary reason for entering into a merger or acquisition was to grow market share and profitability.[3] This study also detailed the gaps between expectations and ultimate results. The gaps were defined as the inability to overcome predetermined objectives. Schmidt suggests that three of the five areas of ultimate concern in the SHRM/Towers Perrin study were vested in the human resources arena, and the inadequate preparation for "the back end of the deal."[4]

Understanding Culture and Change

Change within organizational operations is an inevitable force in today's marketplace in order to survive. Change is implemented to gain operational efficiencies, to increase market share, to adjust sales to customer demands, to adapt to new technology, to introduce new products, to engage new competitors, and a host of other reasons. However, despite the legitimacy of the need for dynamic change, the impact on people within an organization is often a source of stress, disruption, and uncertainty.[5]

Understanding how individuals within the organization will react and adapt to change is something executives need to critically assess in mergers or acquisitions. Evaluating the likely cultural acceptance of the change enables careful formulation of communication strategies that will favorably impact organizational acceptance. Therefore, first auditing the leadership style and culture within the existing separate organizations provides a working framework necessary to evaluate compatibilities.[6] Notifying executives of a critical culture mismatch prior to the merger or acquisition could avert a disaster. In many cases, the retention of outside experts (consultants) in organizational behavioral would be prudent.

Engaging Stakeholders

Engaging stakeholders is pivotal to the success of a merger or acquisition. Employees, distributors, vendors, and customers all have a perspective and a vested interest in the change that a merger or acquisition may bring. Stakeholders may have valuable information about alternative procedures, systems, and operational factors essential to the success of the merger or acquisition.[7] Therefore, stakeholders should be included, as appropriate, in certain decisions in which their input would have a genuine bearing on the merger or acquisition. There is much to be gained by the inclusion of stakeholders as partners rather than bystanders. Solicitous and patronizing inquiries should be avoided because they are not authentic, and will only breed distrust and resentment. However, utilizing a full breadth of information that includes key stakeholders may positively impact the success of a merger or acquisition.

Communication

The communication plan regarding the merger or acquisition needs to be developed specifically for each stakeholder group, such as employees, customers, suppliers, and the media.[8] Although the substantive nature of the merger or acquisition announcement will be consistent for each stakeholder group, the communication approach may vary based on the needs and interests of each. Certainly, the informal employee grapevine will impact change communication. Therefore, is it critical that the organization send a clear, consistent message regarding upcoming changes.[9]

The initial concern for employees is likely to be job security. Understanding the obvious employee concerns in the context of a merger or acquisition requires managers and human resource professionals to accept strong leadership roles in framing the content, method, and timing of announcements. Timing of communication is often the most sensitive topic.[10] Furthermore, organizational leaders should wait to communicate plant closings and layoffs to stakeholders until definitive plans are in place to avoid confusion about impending changes.[11]

Leaders, managers, and human resource professionals should consider how to respond to the following questions.
- What is going to take place, and who will be affected by the changes? [12]
- Why are the changes taking place?
- What methods should be used to communicate change and to respond to stakeholder questions, such as e-mails, intranet postings, presentations, and one-on-one communication?[13]
- What are the advantages of mergers and acquisitions to stakeholder groups and to the organization?[14]

An authentic concern for employee welfare must be an integral part of the communication process. Honest, straightforward communication about the needs of the business and the competitive environment is an essential part of the communication strategy. Additionally, when lost jobs are likely going to be an outcome, the human resources department should define appropriate severance package or buyout strategies and actively assist employees with outplacement assistance.

Roles in Mergers and Acquisitions

Management and HR can have a significant, ongoing role as strategic business partner within the merger or acquisition process, as outlined in Figure 9.1.[15] Integral functions often associated with classic human resources responsibilities have a substantial impact on the ultimate success or failure of merger or acquisition activity. Leaders, managers, and human resource professionals should collaboratively formulate a comprehensive merger/acquisition integration plan for each factor shown in the table based on each of the issues and resistance factors.[16] Together, the merger or acquisition management team must act proactively by anticipating and articulating the issues most likely to arise, which include:

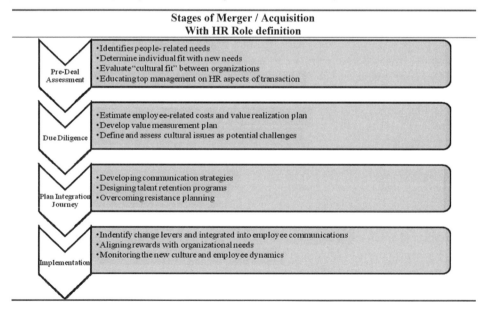

Figure 9.1   Adapted from Roles and Stages of Mergers/Acquisitions. Source: Jeffrey A. Mello, *Strategic Human Resource Management,* 2nd ed. (Mason, OH: Thomson South-Western, 2006), 262.

- Incompatible cultures
- Lower morale and productivity
- Union and nonunion workforces
- Layoffs
- Reward and compensation issues
- Performance management
- Incompatible corporate policies
- Seniority considerations
- Benefit differentials
- Workplace safety
- Affirmative action
- Employee discrimination issues

Conclusion

Mergers and acquisitions force organizations to thoroughly embrace the change process, identify and engage stakeholders, drive a well-defined communication strategy, and identify value areas where success is dependent on effective leadership and management. Further, constituent groups must be empowered to accept the necessity for change for the organization to survive and prosper. Cultural integration issues inherent in mergers and acquisitions pose the greatest threat to their success. Predictable employee resistance to change during the merger of conflicting styles from distinct employee cultures calls for action throughout the process.

NOTES

1. Thomas G. Cummings and Christopher G. Worley, *Essentials of Organization Development and Change,* 8th ed. (Cincinnati, OH: South-Western, 2005).

2. Jeffrey A. Mello, *Strategic Human Resource Management,* 2nd ed. (Mason, OH: Thomson South-Western, 2006).

3. Jeffrey A. Schmidt, "The Correct Spelling of M&A Begins with HR," *HR Magazine* 46, no. 6 (June 2001): 102–8.

4. Ibid.

5. Mello, *Strategic Human Resource Management.*
Schmidt, "The Correct Spelling of M&A Begins with HR," 102.

6. Margareta Barchan, "Humanity in a Merger," *Training & Development* 60, no. 2: 16.

7. Ibid.

8. Cummings and Worley, *Essentials of Organization Development and Change.*

9. William Bridges, *Managing Transitions: Making the Most of Change* (Cambridge: MA: Perseus Publishing, 2003).

10. Barchan, "Humanity in a Merger."

11. Bridges, *Managing Transitions: Making the Most of Change.*

12. Cummings and Worley, *Essentials of Organization Development and Change;* and Bridges, *Managing Transitions: Making the Most of Change.*

13. Cummings and Worley, *Essentials of Organization Development and Change.*

14. Ibid.

15. Ibid.

16. Ibid.

Lisa Scott Brinkman and Everon Christina Chenhall

ORGANIZATIONAL DESIGN

Organizational design is the creative process for designing and aligning elements of an organization to efficiently and effectively deliver the purpose of an organization. At its most basic, organizational design is concerned with accomplishing the work to implement the strategy. This involves alignment and integration of people, processes, structures, systems, and culture. Leadership in an organization should be as concerned about organizational design as they are about strategy, since the best strategy without implementation does not deliver business results.

Form Follows Function

Organizations deliver exactly what they are designed to deliver. If there is a lack of understanding or intentionality in the design, what is delivered may not be what is desired. Organizational design is not a simple task, since an organization is an open system and must respond to the environment, internal realities, and change while maintaining balance and a sense of stability. Foundational elements of the design may be stable, but other elements should be redesigned continuously to respond to the dynamics of the environment and strategy.

Design Elements

Many theorists have proposed methods to design organizations (see Table 9.2 and the Resources section of this entry). Although most theories focus on a different aspect of the design problem, there is a great deal of overlap of key elements and choices. Most of the approaches acknowledge that strategy drives the design. The elements that need to be considered and integrated are:

- *People:* The members of the organization, their capabilities, attraction, development, and retention.
- *Processes:* The information and workflows that deliver value to the customer, maintain the business, or enable other processes.
- *Systems:* Information/knowledge, communication, and measurement systems.
- *Structures:* Configurations and connections of roles, responsibilities, accountabilities, and relationships to share knowledge, make decisions, take action, and learn.
- *Culture:* Shared values, assumptions, and approaches to cope with external adaptation and internal integration that are reinforced through norms, artifacts, stories, and rewards.

Design Choices

There are many points of tension in designing an organization. Finding the balance that optimizes the integrated performance of the above elements is the goal. Key design choices involve:

- Location of power and authority for decision making and resource allocation (e.g., centralized vs. decentralized)
- Task differentiation vs. coordination
- Departmentalization—unit form and alignment (e.g., functional, product/service, geographic, matrix, networked, self-managing teams, cellular)
- Responsiveness vs. stability/consistency
- Perspective and optimization of the whole vs. the parts

Design Approaches

Table 9.2 contains a comparison chart of some of the organizational design theorists:

Table 9.2   Comparison of Organizational Design Theories

Approach/Theorist	# Design Elements	Design Elements	Focus/Point	Key Points or Differentiator
Five Star, Galbraith	Five categories of decision	• Strategy • Structure • People • Rewards • Processes	Strategy	Organization is an information processing entity dealing with uncertainty as it achieves its strategy. Organization's design is a critical leadership role. Matching, linking, coordinating all the categories.
McKinsey 7-S, Waterman and Peters	Seven connected circles	• Strategy • Structure • Systems • Skills • Staff • Style • Shared values	Strategy	Most strategic. Looking for sustainable competitive advantage. Most traditional, top down.
Strategic Management, Tichy	Six elements 3 x 2	3 System aspects • Technical • Political • Cultural Aligned to management tools • Mission/strategy • Organization Structure • HR management	Alignment of systems and tools	Multi-perspective look at change and response needed. Fit of technical, political, and cultural systems to management tools.
Congruence Model, Nadler et al.	Four organizational components	• Informal Organization • Formal Organization • Work • People	Fit	Organization as an effective system that transforms an input to an output through four components that fit.

Collaborative Organizational Design, Gelinas and James	Seven integrated circles	• Core goals and values • Strategy • Work processes • Structure • Systems • People • Culture	Core goals of future at design team level	Design teams use this model to both create their vision and design their organization. Goals are measurable, while values are the "how." It is used for unit level design.
Six Box Model, Weisbord	Six boxes	• Purpose • Structure • Relationships • Helpful mechanisms • Rewards • Leadership	Purpose and leadership	Clarity and balance are important. The model helps the client to visualize his organization as a systemic whole without the use of strange terminology.
Chaordic Design, Hock and Getzendanner	Six lenses	Purpose Principles Participants Organization concept Constitution Practices	Purpose and principles	High commitment, whole-system, boundaryless organizations. Iterative so all elements inform, support, and balance each other. Departure from rationalist tradition results focus.

See also Culture; HR Competencies

Resources:

Ashkenas, Robert, David Ulrich, Tom Jick, and Steve Kerr. *The Boundaryless Organization: Breaking the Chains of Organizational Structure.* San Francisco: Jossey-Bass Publishers, 1995.

Galbraith, Jay. *Designing Complex Organizations.* Reading, MA: Addison-Wesley Publishing Co., 1973.

Galbraith, Jay. "Designing the Innovating Organization." http://www.jaygalbraith.com/resources/designing_innovating_org.pdf.

Gelinas, Mary, and Roger James. "Collaborative Organizational Design." http://www.gelinasjames.com/what.html.

Hock, Dee. "Birth of the Chaordic Age." *Executive Excellence* 17, no. 6 (2000): 6–7.

Miles, Raymond, Charles Snow, John Mathews. Grant Miles, and Henry Coleman. "Organizing in the Knowledge Age: Anticipating the Cellular Form." *Academy of Management Executive,* 1997, 7–19.

Nadler, David, Marc Gerstein, and Robert Shaw. *Organizational Architecture: Designs for Changing Organizations.* San Francisco: Jossey-Bass Publishers, 1992.

Nadler, David, and Michael Tushman.. *Competing by Design: The Power of Organizational Architecture.* New York, Oxford University Press, 1997.

Pasmore, William A. *Designing Effective Organizations: The Socio-technical Systems Perspective.* New York: John Wiley & Sons, 1988.

Simons, Robert. *Levers of Organizational Design.* Boston: Harvard Business School Press, 2005.

Schein, Edgar. "Organizational Culture." *American Psychologist,* 1990, 109–19.

Waterman, Robert H., Jr., Thomas J. Peters, and Julien R. Phillips. "Structure Is Not Organization." *Business Horizons* 23, no. 3 (1980): 14–27.

Gina Hinrichs

PHR/SPHR DESIGNATIONS

Professional certifications are one way in which professionals in a field are able to assess and promote their level of qualification. The Human Resource Certification Institute (HRCI) is an affiliate of the Society for Human Resource Management (SHRM). HRCI is the organization that develops and delivers the human resources–credentialing programs that validate an individual's expertise in the HR field.

The Professional in Human Resources (PHR) and Senior Professional in Human Resources (SPHR) designations are professionally recognized and respected certifications that experienced HR professionals can attain through the HRCI certification testing process. Although some employers may require certification for their human resources staff, testing for the PHR or SPHR is a voluntary certification. One must meet certain work experience requirements and demonstrate knowledge of the human resources body of knowledge in order to achieve the certification. Once certified, an individual is issued a certificate confirming that he has met the standards and is entitled to use the initials PHR or SPHR after his name.

Professional in Human Resources

In order to sit for the PHR certification exam, an individual is required to have a minimum of two years of exempt-level professional HR experience. However, it is recommended that she have between two and four years of experience.

HRCI describes the recommended profile of a PHR candidate with the following characteristics:[1]

- Focuses on program implementation.
- Has tactical/logistical orientation.
- Has accountability to another HR professional within the organization.
- Has two to four years of exempt-level generalist HR work experience, but because of career length, may lack the breadth and depth of a more senior-level generalist.
- Has not had progressive HR work experience by virtue of career length.
- Focuses his or her impact on the organization within the HR department rather than organization wide.
- Commands respect through the credibility of knowledge and the use of policies and guidelines to make decisions.

Senior Professional in Human Resources

In order to sit for the SPHR certification exam, an individual is required to have a minimum of two years of exempt-level professional HR experience. However, it is recommended that she have between six and eight years of progressive HR experience.

HRCI describes the recommended profile of a SPHR candidate with the following characteristics:[2]

- Designs and plans rather than implements.
- Focuses on the "big picture."
- Has ultimate accountability in the HR department.
- Has breadth and depth of HR generalist knowledge.
- Uses judgment obtained with time and application of knowledge.
- Has a generalist role within organization.
- Understands the effect of decisions made within and outside of the organization.
- Understands the business, not just the HR function.
- Manages relationships; has influence within overall organization.
- Commands credibility within organization, community and field by experience.
- Possesses excellent negotiation skills.

Exam Overview

The PHR and SPHR exams are administered by computer and consist of 200 scored questions plus 25 unscored pretest questions, for a total of 225 questions. The test format is multiple choice, where four possible answers are provided for each question. One answer is the best-choice answer. Individuals are required to complete the exam in four hours.

HR Body of Knowledge

Both the PHR and SPHR certifications use the same HR body of knowledge focus areas in the examination test. These areas include strategic management, workforce planning and employment, human resource development, total rewards, employee and labor relations, and risk management. The percentage of questions from each focus area does differ between the PHR and SPHR exams. The PHR has a strong focus on the workforce planning and employment, where as the SPHR has its strongest focus on strategic management. Table 9.3 shows the percentage of questions taken from each area.

Exam Results

Both the PHR and SPHR tests are based on a scaled score. The highest possible score is 700; the minimum passing score is 500. When taking the exam, individuals will receive

Table 9.3   PHR and SPHR Exam, Percentage from Each Focus Area[3]

Focus Area	*PHR*	*SPHR*
Strategic Management	12%	29%
Workforce Planning and Employment	26%	17%
Human Resource Development	17%	17%
Total Rewards	16%	12%
Employee and Labor Relations	22%	18%
Risk Management	7%	7%

a preliminary pass/fail notice at the end of the exam. However, official results will take two to three weeks and will arrive by mail.

Conclusion

The PHR and SPHR certifications are professional designations that validate an individual's experience level and mastery of the HR body of knowledge. Professional achievement, public recognition, personal goal accomplishment, and career advancement are some of the many reasons why individuals become certified.

See also HR Competencies

NOTES

1. Human Resource Certification Institute, *2007 PHR-SPHR-GPHR Certification Handbook,* (Alexandria, VA: Human Resource Certification Institute, 2007).

2. Ibid.

3. Ibid.

Shanan M. Mahoney

PROJECT MANAGEMENT

Project management is a method and set of techniques based on the accepted management principles of planning, organizing, directing, and controlling. Each of these principles is used in combination to reach a desired end result, on time, within budget, and according to established specifications.[1] Further, project management is a way of thinking that keeps desired results in focus. Effective project managers achieve specific objectives using proven tools and techniques such as critical paths (charts), scheduling technologies (Gantt charts), goal and risk analysis, stakeholder analysis, controlling techniques, and project diagrams. Employees are organized and their efforts directed toward achievement of desired results. Finally, project management requires evaluation of project objectives against measurable criteria useful in determining the quality of the outcomes produced via the project.

What Is a Project?

One of the best ways to understand project management is to identify the characteristics of a project. Project management involves planning objectives and activities for successful results; organizing people to get things done; directing people to keep them focused on achieving desired results; and measuring progress to provide useful feedback.

Let us consider a common example: building a home. Home construction comprises literally thousands of activities and steps, each of which can be assigned to individual workers such as carpenters, bricklayers, electricians, plumbers, roofers, drywallers, painters, and finish carpenters. Each of these individuals is responsible for activities in his area of expertise. The building contractor (project manager) schedules and coordinates work activities in what is deemed a logical, efficient manner. In this way, a large, nearly unmanageable project (building a home) can be broken down into manageable subprojects assigned to specialized workers (subcontractors). If managed correctly, the project should be completed by the deadline, under or at budget, and at quality specifications. Simply put, work packages are groups of activities or tasks that, when linked together, produce a projected outcome.

In HRM, projects vary in size and scope, from a simple one-day training activity to a comprehensive organizational development redesign. A project is an organized effort with planned activities and schedules; it has specific time-bound results, multiple tasks and roles, a series of specific yet interdependent tasks, and it is a onetime effort that involves many people, usually across functional areas in the organization.[2]

The first task facing a project manager is to separate the project into parts and subparts that form sets of interrelated "work packages." A work package is a group of tasks that are continuous activities, each of which is assignable to a single individual.[3] Deliverables for each work package are clearly defined and measurable according to established standards and project controls. Each work package has a scheduled start date and end date for each task included. Finally, work packages are designed in such a way that preceding and succeeding work packages are identified. In other words, a logical flow exists for completing activities.[4]

Successful projects exhibit eight characteristics. Accordingly, successful projects:

1. Consist of a solid, conceptual plan leading toward the production of desired results.
2. Contain goal and objective statements that should be specific, measurable, agreed upon, realistic, and timely (SMART).
3. Are broken down, measurable, and clear, which helps reduce large projects to micro projects that are much easier to manage and control.
4. Consist of discrete steps, with observable results.
5. Maintain sufficient resources (material, financial, and human) needed to accomplish the desired objectives.
6. Assemble project team members who are focused on the desired outcomes.
7. Assemble competent, qualified, and cooperative team members.
8. Require constant monitoring of outcomes, with proper feedback given to project team members.[5]

Project Constraints

Projects are often constrained by the organization's need to maintain service, quality, and positive human relations within the firm. Obviously, constraints can hinder progress and/or achievement of desired outcomes. Consequently, effective project managers must guard against overzealousness, always realizing that internal political pressure and politics must be understood and managed.

On the surface, project management seems relatively simple. Unfortunately, some constraints make the process difficult and often lead to less-than-ideal project outcomes.

Accordingly, scheduling constraints include:
• Unavailability of a particular resource during a project
• Demands on resource needs for other, present, or future projects
• Different or conflicting demands by project managers for other resources
• Desire to avoid extensive work overloads for a particular individual
• Lack of resource availability to complete a particular task
• Budgetary constraints
• Desire to lessen write-offs or budget overruns
• Integration and use of other projects using the same resources
• Not enough time for doing activities that are uncertain

- Technical constraints that may need extra time
- Difficulties inherent in scheduling far in advance[6]

Any or all of these constraints can prevent project managers from producing projects on time, within budget, and up to quality standards. Consequently, these constraints should be taken into consideration prior to beginning any project.

Project Managers' Characteristics

Selecting a project manager requires consideration of an individual's experience, capabilities, qualifications, and competence in achieving project results in a timely fashion, within budget, and according to quality specifications.[7] Therefore, effective project managers motivate, inspire, and coach their team members. Active listening skills, as well as the ability to provide meaningful performance feedback, help ensure successful project completion. Such managers are assertive, not aggressive or submissive, in their interactions with team members and project support groups. Quite simply, they confront poor performance while maintaining the self-esteem of team members or support personnel. Interpersonal conflicts over financial and material resources waste precious time and thus should be minimized.

Effective project managers have the leadership and strategic expertise to design, coordinate, control, and implement plans. Such individuals have the ability to create a vision of the project and communicate it to all members of the project team. They have the ability to ask thought-provoking questions that help team members understand their roles and responsibilities. Thus, they delegate the appropriate responsibility and authority to team members to ensure successful project completion and create reporting and control systems that will alert team members to potential problems. Finally, effective project managers remain flexible while performing their multiple roles.

See also Goal Setting; HR Strategy

NOTES

1. Jerry W. Gilley and Ann Maycunich Gilley, *Strategically Integrated HRD: Six Transformational Roles in Creating Results Driven Programs* (Cambridge, MA: Perseus Publishing, 2003).

2. Ibid.

3. Jerry W. Gilley and Amy J. Coffern, *Internal Consulting for HRD Professionals: Tools, Techniques, and Strategies for Improving Organizational Performance* (New York: McGraw-Hill Professional Publishing, 1994).

4. Gilley and Gilley, *Strategically Integrated HRD.*

5. Gilley and Coffern, *Internal Consulting for HRD Professionals.*

6. Gilley and Coffern, *Internal Consulting for HRD Professionals;* and Gilley and Gilley, *Strategically Integrated HRD.*

7. Gilley and Gilley, *Strategically Integrated HRD.*

Jerry W. Gilley and Ann Gilley

SAFETY

Safety is one of the most important aspects of any business and thus a focus of governmental regulatory agencies. Workplace safety and health are overseen by three

Department of Labor (DOL) agencies: the Occupational Safety and Health Administration (OSHA); the Mine Safety and Health Administration (MHSA); and the Employment Standards Administration's Wage and Hour Division.[1] OSHA is responsible for the administration and enforcement of safety and health laws in most private industries subject to the Occupational Safety and Health Act. The MHSA administers and enforces the Mine Safety and Health Act of 1977, which applies to all mining and mineral processing operations in the United States. The DOL's Employment Standards Administration's Wage and Hour Division enforces the Fair Labor Standards Act (FLSA). The FLSA protects youth via its restrictions on minimum age, times of day during which young people may work, and the jobs they are legally able to perform.

Workplace safety programs are designed to prevent employee injury and illness on the job. A safe workplace:

- Reduces employee accidents, injuries, and illnesses
- Reduces expenditures for health insurance claims and benefits
- Reduces workers' compensation claims and payments
- Reduces the need for temporary help or overtime for existing employees
- Reduces employee stress
- Increases morale
- Reduces potential fines for noncompliance with safety laws.

Safety Programs

Workplace safety programs are as varied as the organizations that create them. In spite of the vast array of manufacturing and service firms that exist, workplace safety programs have common goals—to promote and reward safe practices in the workplace, and to reduce work-related illnesses, injuries, and fatalities.[2] Safety programs establish safe work practices, procedures, and guidelines, mandate training, assess job hazards and risks, detail responsibilities of managers and employees in the event of an occurrence, and provide guidelines for documentation.

Ways to Increase Safety

Workplace safety initiatives begin with communication of information about safety and specific ways to create and maintain a safe working environment, including

- Closing and locking doors, file cabinets, desks, and vehicles.
- Replacing burned-out interior and exterior lights.
- Teaching all employees the use of proper lifting techniques.
- Providing adjustable workstations.
- Redesigning work to eliminate repetitive motions.
- Creating a buddy system for workers.
- Installing alarms, signs, and warning signals.
- Limiting exposure to hazards.
- Using the proper tools for the job.[3]
- Seeking continual feedback from employees regarding workplace safety.
- Making safety part of the culture of the firm.
- Involving employees in design and implementation of safety programs.
- Rewarding safe practices.

- Mandating wearing of safety clothing such as boots, gloves, eye and ear protection, harnesses, and so forth.
- Maintaining clean work areas.
- Measuring and reporting company safety statistics.

Implications for Managers and HR

Safety in the workplace is everyone's responsibility, from the frontline manager to the HR professional who designs safety training programs. Creating and maintaining a safe work environment benefits employees, management, and the organization by preventing costly, dangerous illness and accidents.

See also Fair Labor Standards Act; Occupational Safety and Health Administration

NOTES

1. http://www.dol.gov..
2. http://nonprofitrisk.org/tools/workplace-safety/tutorials.shtml (Accessed May 13, 2008).
3. Ibid.

Ryan Skiera and Ann Gilley

WORK-LIFE BALANCE

The attainment of work-life balance continues to be the mythical quality standard for individuals in the workforce and the organizations that employ them. In the 2007 Society for Human Resource Management's (SHRM) Job Satisfaction Survey Report, "flexibility to balance life and work issues" ranks as "very important" for 52 percent of all respondents and 48 percent of HR professionals. For individual workers, work-life balance ranked fourth in importance, behind compensation, benefits, and job security, each of which can be argued as a contributor to achieving work-life balance. Despite ranking as "important" or "very important" in each satisfaction survey since 2002, SHRM reports that the responsiveness of organizations to these issues has only increased slightly from 2006.[1]

Traditionally considered a "mommy issue," work-life balance is now considered a standard for any individual desiring to be successful at work while also maintaining a personal life separate from it, despite marital or parental status. The terms work-life conflict (negative interactions between roles) and work-life enrichment are often used interchangeably with work-life balance, but are actually subsets of it.

Work-life Balance

Work-life balance has traditionally been defined in terms of equilibrium. A person achieved balance when equal time, energy, and enjoyment was expended and/or gained from both the work and family roles.[2] Recently, however, this definition has been expanded to move beyond "equality" as the determinant of balance. In this updated definition, balance occurs when an individual is actively engaged in both roles, without sacrificing one for the benefit of the other. Balance becomes a true interaction between roles, rather than a battle between them.[3]

Work-life Conflict

Work-life conflict occurs when the demands in one role interfere with an individual's effectiveness in the other role. Bidirectional in nature, work can interfere with life and life can interfere with work.[4] The three types of conflict that have been identified are time-based, strain-based, and behavioral-based. Time-based conflict is considered the most prevalent type of conflict and occurs when the amount of time spent in one role takes away from the amount of time available for the other role, or when preoccupation with one role impairs the ability to function in the other role. This phenomenon is also commonly referred to as "presenteeism."

Strain-based conflict occurs when the strain (or stressors) felt in one role make it difficult to perform in the other role and is based on the idea of fatigue and irritability created from one role affecting the activities in the other role. Work-related strain has been related to stressful events at work or job burnout that result in fatigue or depression in the family role. Life-based strain conflict primarily occurs when spousal career and family expectations are not in congruence.

Behavioral-based conflict occurs when the behaviors required in one role are incompatible with the behaviors required in the other role. For example, behaviors that are expected in the family role, like nurturing or emotional sensitivity, are viewed as inappropriate at work, or aggressive behaviors that may be required at work are considered inappropriate at home.

Work-life Enrichment

Known by a variety of terms (e.g., facilitation, enhancement, integration or positive spill-over) work-life enrichment is considered the positive side of the work-life interface, and occurs when the experiences in one role improve an individual's functioning in the other role.[5] Increases in function occur (1) when gains (e.g., monetary, knowledge, skills, or abilities) in one role directly improve the functioning in the other role, or (2) when gains in one role indirectly increase functioning in the other role due to overall improvements in behavior or attitudes.[6]

HR's Opportunities: Work-life Initiatives

In an environment characterized by a scarcity of resources, work-life issues can be a deciding factor in an employee's employment choices, and an opportunity for HR to make a contribution to the bottom line. Work-life initiatives have become part of the corporate response to provide work-life balance for employees. Work-life initiatives generally fall into one of the following categories: (1) health and wellness programs, (2) flexible work arrangements, (3) paid/unpaid time off, (4) child/elder care assistance, and (5) financial support assistance.

Implementing work-life initiatives is not as simple as it may seem. Key to the adoption of a successful set of work-life initiatives is a clear understanding of what is important to employees, as well as an analysis of organizational culture. A well-crafted set of work-life initiatives must be adequate, available, accessible, and affordable in terms of financial and personal costs. Work-life balance can have a strategic impact on organizational outcomes, including job satisfaction, organizational reputation, employee commitment, recruitment and retention, productivity, and organizational efficiency and profitability.

See also Benefits; Flex-Time; HR Metrics; Job Sharing; PTO (Paid Time Off) Bank

NOTES

1. Stephen Miller, "Job Satisfaction: Workers, HR Pros Have Varying Views," Society for Human Resource Management, http://www.shrm.org/rewards/library_published/benefits/nonIC/CMS_022089.asp (accessed November 12, 2007).

2. Jeffrey H. Greenhaus, Karen M. Collins, and Jason D. Shaw, "The Relation Between Work-Family Balance and Quality of Life," *Journal of Vocational Behavior,* December 2003, 510–31.

3. Joseph G. Grzywacz and Dawn S. Carlson, "Conceptualizing Work-Family Balance: Implications for Practice and Research," *Advances in Developing Human Resources,* November 2007, 455–71.

4. Jeffrey H. Greenhaus and Nicholas J. Beutell, "Sources of Conflict Between Work and Family Roles," *Academy of Management Review* (January 1985): 76–88

5. Jeffrey H. Greenhaus and Gary N. Powell, "When Work and Family are Allies: A Theory of Work-Family Enrichment," *Academy of Management Review,* January 2006, 72–92.

6. Dawn S. Carlson, K. Michelle Kacmar, Julie H. Wayne, and Joseph G. Grzywacz, "Measuring the Positive Side of the Work Family Interface: Development and Validation of a Work-Family Enrichment Scale," *Journal of Vocational Behavior,* January 2006, 131–64.

Heather S. McMillan and Lisa Scott Brinkman

WORKPLACE JUSTICE

Workplace justice can be viewed from the perspective of the perceived fairness of management decisions and treatment of employees. Employees may confront unjust situations such as pay inequities, unsafe working conditions, or discrimination based on race or sex. These unjust situations have a negative impact on employees' ability to perform and, ultimately, their commitment to the organization. In practice, workplace justice emphasizes a just outcome, as well as a fair procedure for realizing that outcome. In order to ensure workplace justice, organizations must take steps that ensure pay equity and establish policies and management practices that do not, either intentionally or unintentionally, result in discrimination and that maintain a safe work environment. Further, organizations must put in place a process by which employees can bring forward complaints and resolve issues.

Workplace Justice Strategies

In order to ensure workplace justice, organizations develop and implement formal strategies that include policies and procedures to resolve employees' work-related complaints. Strategies can be implemented at the organizational level (e.g., policies and procedures) as well as the management level (e.g., management practices and interactions with employees).

Organizational Strategies

At an organizational level, strategies used to ensure workplace justice include employee grievance processes, which are designed to provide employees procedural due process or procedural fairness.[1] Employee grievance processes ensure employees receive procedural due process in the resolution of complaints by (1) identifying workplace issues that can be grieved, (2) providing appeal steps, (3) providing a process to expedite serious cases, and (4) including a final review step by a neutral third-party arbiter.[2] Effective employee grievance processes depend on the degree to which they are accepted as reasonable by employees. Also, perceptions of fairness of the grievance process relate to the degree of reprisal against employees who initiate a grievance. Negative consequences associated with bringing forward a complaint will ultimately reduce the legitimacy of the process. Employees who fear reprisal from management will not utilize the process.

Management Strategies

Strategies focused on management practices include open communication, positive inter-personal relationships between employees and management, conflict management, and alternative dispute resolution (ADR), a form of cooperative problem-solving. These strategies focus on social process and encourage management and employees to work in a collaborative manner to solve problems and resolve disputes.

Effective management practices result in trust—employees trust that management decisions are just and fair. Mistrust occurs when management sends mixed signals; when words and actions are not consistent. ADR is increasingly being implemented in organizations. ADR is a cooperative problem-solving approach and is viewed as a viable alternative to the more adversarial grievance process.[3] ADR emphasizes employee involvement and requires empowerment on the part of managers. ADR has also resulted in higher grievance resolution and a reduction in the amount of time it takes to resolve complaints, and positive residual effects in the overall employee-employer relationship.[4]

Conclusion

Managers at all levels in an organization play a critical role in ensuring workplace justice. They do so by creating trusting working relationships with employees. Strategies used include establishing employee grievance processes that allow for procedural due process; and ensuring open communication, positive interpersonal relationships between employees and management, conflict management, and cooperative problem-solving approaches, such as ADR.

NOTES

1. Hoyt N. Wheeler and Jacques Rojot, eds., *Workplace Justice: Employment Obligations in International Perspective* (Columbia: University of South Carolina Press, 1992).
2. Ibid.
3. Dawn D. Bennett-Alexander and Laura P. Hartman, *Employment Law* (Boston: McGraw-Hill Irwin, 2007).
4. Ibid.

Pamela Dixon

WORKPLACE VIOLENCE

The issue of workplace violence is an emerging safety issue for many human resource professionals and organizations. Workplace violence can be defined as acts of harmful behavior to an employee occurring within a place of employment providing a service or product. Between 1993 and 1999, an average of 1.7 million violent assaults per year were committed in the U.S. against persons who were at work or on duty.[1] The Bureau of

Labor Statistics revealed in the *Census of Fatal Occupational Injuries* that 564 workplace homicides and 177 self-inflicted injuries occurred in 2005, accounting for 14 percent of the total 5,702 fatal work injuries in the United States.[2]

Types of Workplace Violence

Workplace acts of violence often include simple battery, aggravated assaults, sexual assaults, rapes, and homicides. More broadly defined, workplace violence can also include nonphysical actions such as aggression, harassment, and hostility. There are several categories for the types of workplace violence that can occur, including:

- Crime-motivated
- Personal relationships
- Customers or clients
- Coworkers

Many workplace violence acts occur during the commission of a crime such as robbery and theft. Additionally, employees' outside relationships are not isolated from their employment environment. Occurrences of domestic violence and stalking may also occur within the place of work. Customer violence could be the result of a client already prone to violence or someone who becomes volatile when triggered by a frustrating situation. Lastly, acts of violence and aggression can occur among coworkers on a peer-to-peer level, or employee to employer and vice versa.

Instances of workplace aggression and violence can have major economic costs to organizations, including loss of human life, decrease in performance and productivity, psychological distress, employee turnover, decline in attendance, fines, and negligence lawsuits. Thus, it is important for employers to create a proactive model to reduce the likelihood of workplace acts of violence. Following are several recommended areas for employers to develop prevention strategies:

1. Establishing a climate of respect
2. Reporting procedures and records
3. Evaluating security and work environments
4. Providing training and intervention resources
5. Employment screening
6. Crisis response planning

Establishing a Climate of Respect

Employers can establish a respectful and inclusive environment by developing a statement that embodies their desire for diversity and establishes their stances on elements of workplace acts of aggression. This includes posting the policy, identifying key individuals who will analyze the information, and creating a response strategy. These efforts can send a message to employees and customers that the organization is committed and intends to allocate resources to support these operational norms.

Initially, creating this supportive climate begins with employers providing just treatment of all employees through their fair employment policies, assessment of environmental conditions and stressors, and implementation of dispute resolution mechanisms. This includes being proactive rather than reactive when an act of aggression occurs at the employment site. An organization's commitment can be displayed by identifying a team of personnel to work on workplace violence procedures from senior management, legal counsel, security division, employee representatives, and human resource staffs. Furthermore, once the policies are developed, it is essential they be implemented in a timely, confidential, and fair manner.

Reporting Procedures and Records

Employees must be informed of the organization's procedures for reporting acts of aggression, hostility, and violence. It is crucial to know how to confidentially document instances and to whom to submit the reports. Organizations also must identify key personnel who will review the information and develop appropriate policies. In addition to developing reporting mechanisms, organizations need to identify what types of records are essential to review, such as:
• OSHA records
• Police reports, including crimes or disputes
• Worker compensation issues
• Attendance records
• Equal employment and opportunity investigations
• Accident reports
• Human resource reports of aggression complaints
• Grievance claims
• State and local laws/ordinances

Evaluating Security and Work Environments

Since many of the workplace acts of violence involve persons outside of the organization's employees, it is important for employers to assess their security practices. This includes examining safety measures like cameras monitoring the external and internal facilities, convenient locations of telephones for assistance calls, security alarms, landscaping, locked doors, and partition windows for customer service desks. It can also include providing after-business-hours precautions, security personnel, and plans for monitoring daily workplace safety. An additional strategy component is for employers to assess the workplace environmental conditions to specifically identify stress-inducing factors in order to reduce internal issues attributing to aggression.

Providing Training and Intervention Resources

A vital strategy component is employee training and the dissemination of information. In order to provide adequate employee support, an organization must effectively educate its workforce on the policies and available resources while documenting efforts and training attendance. Potential workshops could consist of these topics:
• New employee training on resources and statement
• Diversity and inclusiveness policies
• Substance abuse identification and resources
• Crime prevention strategies
• Self-defense tactics
• Sexual harassment training
• Dealing with interpersonal conflict

- Handling aggressive customers
- Emergency evacuation and crisis protocols
- Policies for reporting

Training also needs to be coupled with providing appropriate resources for staff personnel. At the core of this initiative is maintaining an employee assistance program (EAP) that provides support on emotional, health-related, legal, and financial matters. This venue will assist employees in dealing with external life stresses and issues such as domestic violence and substance abuse. Additionally, organizations can develop clearly defined and impartial employee grievance and dispute resolution processes.

Employment Screening

Nonphysical violence can be a warning sign for potential acts of future violence. Employers can review applicant materials for indicators of past history of violence. Evidence of an applicant's lack of control, resistance to authority, or failure to take responsibility may indicate potential future employment issues. Screening processes can include the following elements:

- Conduct thorough reference checks
- Structure situational interview questions
- Process background checks
- Provide drug testing

Lack of intervention for initial aggressive acts can lead to escalation. There is less likelihood for physical aggression among coworkers when an organization has set standards for appropriate behaviors and provides a consistent and fair process for aggressive behavior infractions.

Crisis Response Planning

The final point in an organization's workplace violence plan consists of developing an emergency response plan. In the unfortunate event of a violent act, employees must be versed in evacuation routes and safe locations for regrouping. Incorporated into this crisis protocol is employee-debriefing assistance, public relations procedures, emergency contact information for all staff, and available emotional/physical health resources.

See also Background Investigation; Emergency Preparedness; Employment Testing; Harassment; Safety

NOTES

1. Bureau of Justice Statistics, *Violence in the Workplace, 1993–99* (Washington, DC: U.S. Department of Justice, 2001).

2. Bureau of Labor Statistics, *National Census of Fatal Occupational Injuries in 2005* (Washington, DC: U.S. Department of Labor, 2006).

Lory-Ann Varela

Part IV
HR Policy

ARBITRATION

Arbitration is a method of alternative dispute resolution in which a neutral third party, the arbitrator, hears the dispute and makes a binding ruling that in most circumstances cannot be appealed. The parties control the process in that they agree to arbitration yet give control over the outcome to the arbitrator. Compared to litigation, arbitration is faster, simpler, cheaper, and allows for greater confidentiality. While it is a substitute for litigation, generally speaking it is still an adversarial process. There are, however, many variations, and some are more facilitative than others.

Arbitration can be either executory or ad hoc. In most cases it is *executory,* which means that an agreement to arbitrate any disputes is in place before the dispute occurs. This is typically the case in employment and various types of consumer arbitration. Arbitration is considered *ad hoc* when the parties agree to arbitrate after a dispute occurs. An example is when the parties involved in a car accident agree to arbitration.

Arbitration in Employment

In employment settings, arbitration is used in both union and non-union environments to settle a wide variety of employment disputes. It is a mainstay in unionized settings where it is commonly referred to as labor arbitration.

Grievance or "Rights" Arbitration

Grievance or "rights" arbitration is used to resolve disputes involving the interpretation and application of the terms of the contract that arise during the life of a collective bargaining agreement. It is the last step in the grievance procedure and virtually all collective bargaining contracts today contain an arbitration clause.

Interest Arbitration

Arbitration used to create a new employment agreement where the arbitrator determines the terms of the contract is called interest arbitration. Because the parties are essentially giving control over the terms and conditions of the contract to an arbitrator, it is not widely used in the private sector. One notable exception is professional sports, where it is used to set the compensation and benefits of athletes.

Employment Arbitration

Although arbitration has long been a mainstay in unionized settings, it is a relatively new phenomenon with non-union employers, where it is often referred to as employment arbitration. Increasingly, as a condition of employment employers are requiring employees to agree to arbitrate any disputes arising out of the employment relationship (e.g., sexual harassment, wrongful termination, discrimination) instead of filing a lawsuit. Such agreements to arbitrate are typically included in individual employment agreements, employee handbooks, and application forms. Initially there was some concern that courts would not enforce mandatory agreements to arbitrate, especially when there were alleged violations of equal employment opportunity laws. Subsequent court cases have, however, upheld their legality.

Arbitration Process

While there are different types of arbitration the process is fairly standard. The eight steps in the arbitration process are as follows.[1]

1. *Creating the arbitration contract*
   The arbitration contract spells out the subjects of arbitration, selection of an arbitrator, payment of the arbitration expenses, confidentiality, the procedures to be used, and the scope of the arbitrator's powers. This is often an executory agreement.
2. *Demanding/requesting arbitration*
   When there is an executory agreement to arbitrate, the party wishing to arbitrate typically makes a written demand for arbitration. If the other party does not contest whether the dispute is appropriate for arbitration, the process continues. For ad hoc arbitration this is done in conjunction with creating the arbitration contract.
3. *Selecting the arbitrator or arbitrator panel*
   The process for selecting an arbitrator is usually spelled out in executory agreements. Parties may request an arbitrator from the American Arbitration Association,[2] a private, nonprofit organization, or another professional association.
4. *Selecting a set of procedural rules*
   Parties may opt to abide by the rules of a professional association. For example, the AAA has rules and procedures that cover a variety of disputes including employment, healthcare, real estate, and commercial disputes. Parties may waive specific rules by mutual agreement.
5. *Preparing for arbitration*
   The process is similar to preparing for a court case, but less formal. It involves gathering evidence and witnesses and preparing to present the case
6. *Participating in the arbitration hearing*
   This is generally less formal than litigation, although the parties often have legal representation. There may be opening and closing statements and direct- and cross-examination. The arbitrator may ask questions and accept/reject evidence. The parties may also make comments on the case.
7. *Issuing the arbitration award*
   When the hearing is complete the arbitrator decides the outcome of the case, usually within 30 days. The decision is typically put in writing and an explanation of the arbitrator's award may be included if required by the procedural rules adopted.
8. *Enforcing the award*
   Unlike courts, arbitrators do not have enforcement powers. If one of the parties refuses to comply with an arbitrator's award, the other party must petition the court for enforcement. Refusal to comply could be considered a breach of the contract to arbitrate.

See also Collective Bargaining; Conflict Resolution; Grievance; Mediation

NOTES

1. Laurie S. Coltri, *Conflict Diagnosis and Alternative Dispute Resolution* (Upper Saddle River, NJ: Pearson Prentice Hall, 2004).

2. American Arbitration Association (2008), www.adr.org.

Beverly J. DeMarr

BARGAINING UNIT

Through collective bargaining, a group of employees (commonly referred to as a "bargaining unit") can elect a representative (e.g., a union) to negotiate on their behalf. In the United States there is tremendous diversity in the types of bargaining units that have evolved.[1] A bargaining unit may consist of workers of a particular department, several departments, an entire facility, several facilities, several companies, or the entire industry.

Determination of the Bargaining Unit

The composition of the bargaining unit is usually determined during the organizing process. A bargaining unit is an area in which the employer and the union make joint decisions concerning wages, hours, and working conditions.[2] Simply, it is the group of employees that will be represented collectively by a union. Through a union election, the employees of a bargaining unit grant the union the right to negotiate collectively on their behalf. The union becomes the exclusive representative for all members of the bargaining unit. The Labor-Management Relations Act (LMRA) explains:

> Representatives designated or selected for the purposes of collective bargaining by the majority of the employees in a unit appropriate for such purposes, shall be the exclusive representatives of all employees in such a unit for the purposes of collective bargaining in respect to rates of pay, hours of employment, or other conditions of employment.[3]

Typically, a union proposes the makeup of the bargaining unit. The makeup of an appropriate bargaining unit is frequently contested by the employer, requiring the National Labor Relations Board (NLRB) to decide who should be included.[4] This critical determination can decide the outcome of the representation election. The employer and union will argue for the bargaining unit to be defined in the most favorable manner for their individual position. When determining the appropriate bargaining unit, the NLRB considers the following factors:

- *Community of interests:* The mutuality of interests among employees in bargaining for wages, hours, and working conditions is frequently applied. These criteria are difficult to interpret because there is no benchmark used to define the degree of similarity necessary between employee groups. The NLRB considers whether the employees have sufficient common issues, or community of interest, so as not to create substantial conflicts in bargaining. Examples include whether employees with special craft skills and training should be separate from semiskilled workers in an industrial unit or whether production and maintenance workers should be grouped in a single unit with white-collar employees performing technical or clerical functions.

- *Geographical and physical proximity:* The more separate in distance two or more locations are, the more difficult it is for a single union to represent the employees. This factor may be given considerable weight when the employer's policies differ substantially across locations. An example might be a group of machinists working for a company with locations in Hawaii and Texas.
- *Employers' administrative or territorial divisions:* If labor relations or personnel management within a company is over a given territory, this unit rather than a single store or subset may be most appropriate. An example of this might be a group of eight hospitals located in close proximity, all sharing the same policies and practices.
- *Functional integration:* This factor relates to the degree that all potentially includable employees are required to maintain the company's major production processes. For example, in a clothing assembly process, it would make the most sense to keep all the people who make the pieces of a given article in one unit rather than break them apart into separate units (such as separating employees who sew trims and buttons and employees who sew zippers).
- *Interchange of employees:* If employees are frequently transferred across plants or offices, their community of interest may be more similar, leading the NLRB to designate a multiplant unit.
- *Bargaining history:* In applying this factor, the NLRB may take into account the past practices of the union and the employer (if it is a decertification or unit clarification election) or typical industry practices in bargaining.
- *Employee desires:* When the bargaining history involving several units exists, the NLRB may allow employees to vote for or against the units' inclusion in a more comprehensive unit. This is a function of how employees see themselves in an organization and with whom they want to be aligned.
- *Extent of organization:* The NLRB may consider, after the foregoing factors are analyzed, the degree of organization that has taken place in a given proposed unit (although this is not to be considered the prime factor). In this situation, the NLRB would evaluate how far along the process is and whether or not to cancel negotiations.[5]

See also: Collective Bargaining; Labor Unions; National Labor Relations Act

Resources:

Fossum, John A. *Labor Relations: Development, Structure, Process,* 6th ed. Chicago: Irwin, 1995.
Labor-Management Relations Act (Taft-Hartley Act). United States of America, 1947.
National Labor Relations Act (Wagner Act). United States of America, 1935.
Society for Human Resource Management. *The SHRM Learning System, Module 5* (2007).
Wortman, Max S., Jr., and George C. Witteried. *Labor Relations and Collective Bargaining.* Boston: Allyn and Bacon, 1969.

NOTES

1. Max S. Wortman, Jr., and George C. Witteried, *Labor Relations and Collective Bargaining* (Boston: Allyn and Bacon, 1969).
2. Ibid.
3. Labor-Management Relations Act, United States of America, 1947.
4. John A. Fossum, *Labor Relations: Development, Structure, Process* (Chicago: Irwin, 1995), 6.
5. *The SHRM Learning System, Module 5* (Society For Human Resource Management, 2007), 139–40.

Robert M. Sloyan

COLLECTIVE BARGAINING

Employees organize into unions to increase their bargaining power. Through collective bargaining, employees believe that they can obtain outcomes that are unavailable to them as individuals. Collective bargaining is the process by which management and union representatives negotiate employment conditions for a particular bargaining unit.[1] At the heart of collective bargaining is the collective bargaining agreement (CBA) or "contract." The CBA governs the day-to-day relationship of the employer and the employees in the bargaining unit for the period of time it specifies.[2] The CBA is a legal agreement regulating certain work-related issues.

Legal Issues (United States)

Since the Railway Labor Act became law in 1926, the federal government has consistently reiterated its support of free collective bargaining.[3] In the United States, the Wagner Act, also known as the National Labor Relations Act (1935), covers most collective bargaining agreements in the private sector. It was passed to protect and encourage the growth of the union movement. It guaranteed workers the right to self-organization, to form, join, or assist labor organizations, to bargain collectively through representatives of their own choosing, and to engage in concerted activities, for the purpose of collective bargaining or other mutual aid or protection.[4] It broadly forbade interference with employees' rights to be represented and to bargain, and allowed employees to have their labor organizations free from employer dominance, to be protected from employment discrimination for union activity, and to be free from retaliation for accusing the employer of an unlawful (unfair) labor practice.[5] The act requires employers to bargain with a union selected by a majority of the employees in an appropriate "unit" regarding wages, hours, and conditions of work. The Wagner Act also established the National Labor Relations Board to determine which, if any, union was the employees' choice to represent them and to hear and rule on alleged unfair labor practices.[6] In 1947, the Labor-Management Relations Act (LMRA), also known as the Taft-Hartley Act, amended the Wagner Act, further defining the collective bargaining process. The LMRA also established some union practices as unfair labor practices including intimidation, coercion, and physical violence.

Collective Bargaining Subjects

Bargaining subjects can be divided into three categories: mandatory, permissive, and prohibited. Mandatory subjects are required by law and must be negotiated at the request of either party. Mandatory subjects fall within the definition of wages, hours, and other terms and conditions of employment.[7] These include overtime, discharges, demotion, discipline, layoff, recall, seniority, promotion, transfer, safety, vacation, holiday, leave of absence, sick leave, grievances, and contracting out work. Permissive subjects are subjects that may be bargained but are not mandatory. These might include settlement of grievances, settlement of unfair labor practice charges, and neutrality agreements. Finally, prohibited subjects are those that are statutorily outlawed, such as discriminatory hiring and a union demand that the employer use only union-produced goods.

Good-Faith Bargaining

The NLRB and the courts ensure that collective bargaining proceeds with "good faith." Good-faith bargaining broadly means that both parties enter into negotiations with fair and open minds and a sincere desire to arrive at an agreement. As interpreted by the NLRB and the courts, the following may be considered in deciding if a violation of the good-faith bargaining requirement has occurred:

- *Surface bargaining*
  This involves merely going through the motions of bargaining with no real intention of completing a formal agreement.
- *Lack of concession*
  Although no one is required to make a concession, the courts' and the NLRB's definitions of good faith suggest that a willingness to compromise is an essential ingredient in good-faith bargaining.
- *Refusal to advance proposals and demands*
  The NLRB considers the advancement of proposals as a positive factor in determining overall good faith.
- *Dilatory tactics*
  The law requires that the parties meet and "confer at reasonable times and intervals." Obviously, refusal to meet at all with the union does not satisfy the positive duty imposed upon the employer.
- *Imposing conditions*
  Attempts to impose conditions that are so burdensome or unreasonable as to indicate bad faith will be scrutinized by the NLRB.
- *Bypassing the representative*
  An employer violates his duty to bargain when he refuses to negotiate with the union representative. The employer must deal with the statutory representative in conducting bargaining negotiations.
- *Commission of unfair labor practices during negotiations*
  Such practices may reflect poorly upon the good faith of the guilty party.
- *Not providing information*
  Upon request, information must be supplied to the union to enable it to understand and intelligently discuss the issues raised in bargaining.
- *Refusal to bargain*
  Refusal to bargain on a mandatory item (one *must* bargain over these) or insistence on a permissive item (one *may* bargain over these) is usually viewed as bad-faith bargaining.[8]

  See also: Bargaining Unit; Labor Unions; Labor-Management Relations (Taft-Hartley) Act; National Labor Relations Act

Resources:

Fossum, John A. *Labor Management: Development, Structure, Process,* 6th ed. Chicago: Irwin, 1995.
Labor-Management Relations Act (Taft-Hartley Act) United States of America, 1947.
National Labor Relations Act. United States of America, 1935.
Wortman, Max S., Jr., and George C. Witteried. *Labor Relations and Collective Bargaining.* Boston: Allyn and Bacon, 1969.

NOTES

1. *The SHRM Learning System, Module 5* (Society for Human Resource Management).
2. Ibid.
3. Max S. Wortman, Jr., and George C. Witteried, *Labor Relations and Collective Bargaining* (Boston: Allyn and Bacon, 1969).
4. Wagner Act, United States of America, 1935.
5. John A. Fossum, *Labor Relations: Development, Structure, Process* (Chicago: Irwin, 1995), 6.

6. Ibid.
7. *The SHRM Learning System,* 186–87.
8. Fossum, *Labor Relations: Development, Structure, Process.*

Robert M. Sloyan

COMPARABLE WORTH

Passed in the early 1960s, the Equal Pay Act and Title VII of the Civil Rights Act prohibited pay discrimination on the basis of gender by mandating the idea of "equal pay for equal work." Jobs with the same duties, similar working conditions, and requiring essentially similar knowledge, skills, and abilities must be paid the same wage.

Based on existing law, it is illegal for employers to mandate gender requirements in jobs (unless the employer can prove that gender is a bona fide occupational qualification) and pay men and women differently for performing the same job.

Despite four decades of legislative history, the gender wage gap still exists. Controlling for differences in working patterns, education, and so on, average wages for women are approximately 80 percent of the average wage for men across age groups.[1] This disparity drives the call for comparable worth: proponents maintain that any wage disparity is the result of gender-based discrimination. The doctrine of comparable worth extends the idea of equal pay presented in the Equal Pay Act and Title VII, but it maintains that jobs do not have to be equal in duties, only equal in "value" to the organization or society at large. Despite this call, Congress and the courts have been firm in their opposition to the comparable worth doctrine, primarily because of the practice of paying the same wages for completely different jobs.[2]

Implementing a Comparable Worth Pay Plan

Advocates of comparable worth maintain that jobs should be evaluated against a set of specific criteria, and all jobs with the same rating should be paid the same wages. In this system, completely different jobs would be required to pay the same if their ratings were the same. Implementing a comparable worth pay system typically involves four steps:

1. Adopt a job evaluation system for all jobs within the organization. Often a points system, it must be able to be used for every job in the organization, despite the specific duties of each job.
2. All jobs with the same evaluation score must be paid the same. Individual factors of each job can (and probably will) be different, but if the overall points are equal, pay must be equal.
3. Determine the gender representation within each job group. A job group is defined as all positions in the organization with similar duties and responsibilities, paid under the same schedule, and having similar preemployment qualifications and recruiting practices. Jobs are considered predominantly female if over 60 percent of the workers are female; male-dominated jobs occur when greater than 70 percent of workers are male.
4. Calculate a wage-to-job point ratio on all male-dominated jobs as they are assumed to be free of pay discrimination. All jobs within the group should be paid as if they were male-dominated jobs, as it is illegal under the Equal Pay Act and Title VII to lower wages to achieve equality.[3]

Criticisms to Comparable Worth Pay Systems

Opponents to the doctrine of comparable worth maintain that closing the wage gap through government mandates is not the answer. Wages are driven by market forces, primarily the idea of supply and demand. Those individuals with unique skills that are in high demand (for example, registered nurses) can demand higher wages than those with general skills sets suitable for a wide range of jobs (such as retail store clerks). Therefore, the answer to the wage gap is not to "penalize" organizations by forcing increased labor costs, but to encourage females to seek employment in traditionally "male-dominated" jobs through increased support for continuing education and training.

Additionally, opponents contend that the implementation of comparative worth systems could result in lower employee morale and productivity, violations of collective bargaining agreements, affirmative action plans, and state-mandated living wage laws.

Current Status of Comparable Worth Legislation

As previously noted, Congress and the courts have refused to mandate any sort of comparative worth legislation as they maintain it would be in violation of existing equal pay laws. However, numerous states are examining different forms of comparative worth legislation. Employers are advised to check the status of legislation in their state.

See also: Employment Law: An Overview; Equal Pay Act; Civil Rights Act of 1964 and 1991; Compensation: An Overview; Evaluation

NOTES

1. United States General Accounting Office, *Women's Earnings: Work Patterns Partially Explain Difference Between Men's and Women's Earnings* (Washington, DC: United States Government, October 2003).

2. SHRM Governmental Affairs Department, *Equal Pay/Comparable Worth* (Alexandria, VA: Society for Human Resource Management, July 2002).

3. George T. Milkovich and Jerry M. Newman, *Compensation* (Chicago: Irwin, 1996).

Heather S. McMillan

DISASTER RECOVERY PLAN

Disaster recovery is associated with the process of sufficiently restoring one's business or agency functions after a natural or human produced disaster. Natural disasters can include tornadoes, earthquakes, floods, and hurricanes. Human produced disasters can include terrorist attacks, industrial explosions, and computer viruses. Incorporated in disaster recovery is restoration of not only computer related software and hardware devices, but also the loss of key business or agency personnel to injury or death. Any good disaster recovery plan would allow one's business or agency, after a disaster, to continue operation without major interruptions through establishing a command center; implementing a comprehensive communication plan, including sources for employee assistance programs (EAPs) and information regarding alternate work arrangements; and ensuring computer system security.

Command Center

A command center which serves as the central source for decision-making and communication should be established. It is critical to establish a chain of command and enlist company-wide, top-down support whereby guidelines are established and used by people charged with the authority to make and act on decisions.

In many organizations the leadership responsible for decision making falls on the security and/or safety departments in conjunction with senior managers across the organization. Regardless of where the task falls, all departments and locations of an organization need to be involved.

Communication Plan

It is important to communicate early, often, and through numerous communication mediums in order to keep employees and others informed of operational plans, as well as plans for keeping employees healthy and safe. A comprehensive communication plan also takes into consideration multiple audiences, which may consist not only of active employees, but also include retirees, employees on leaves of absence, vendors, and benefits plan providers.

A company with an operating Web site can create an online space for employee communications. Information would include the company's expected hours of operation, temporary alternative work arrangements, and information on the status of pay, unemployment, and other benefits. Also, general notice should be provided regarding benefits through the posting of "legal notices" with newspapers of general circulation in the disaster area and in areas where employees may have relocated, including areas where government-sponsored shelters are being maintained.

Managers should be cognizant of the well-being of their current employees and communicate accordingly. Organizational staff can be frightened, overwhelmed, confused, or in great distress. Communication should include post-event notification of relatives regarding injuries and deaths, maintaining contact with displaced employees, and immediate post disaster summits, as well as crisis counseling for employees and options for alternate work arrangements.

Employee Assistance Programs

A catastrophic event might lead to injuries or loss of life within an organization. While the recovery effort for hardware, software, and data can be tenuous, the recovery from the loss of employees due to injury or death can be even more heart wrenching. Many employers have EAPs which provide counseling and support. These programs can be very effective when employees in a workplace have experienced a traumatic event.

Alternative Work Arrangements

Part of the disaster recovery plan must include alternative work schedules and suitable alternative work sites, including telecommuting arrangements. In certain cases, employers must give the workers advanced notice of plant closure. Applicable state laws should be consulted prior to the implementation of such measures.

Computer System Security

Computer technology is one of the most functionally important elements for any agency or business. If an organization loses hardware, software, and/or data due to disaster, the ability of that organization to function can be compromised to the point that its operations have to completely cease. The result can be not only loss of revenue, but also can harm the company's ability to maintain any semblance of reliability in the eyes of their clients and customers.

If an organization experiences a catastrophe, the statistics on recovery without a comprehensive plan are bleak. Of those suffering catastrophic data loss, only 6 percent survive and continue to operate, 43 percent never reopen, and 51 percent close their doors within two years.[1]

One of the keys to post-disaster organizational survival is the restoration of access to necessary data. This is often referred to as "time to data" (TTD) or "time to recovery" (TTR). The most efficient disaster recovery provides rapid time to recovery, assured continuous operations, and a minimization of data loss.[2]

Off-site Data Storage

Depending on the size of the organization and the monetary resources available, one can purchase a more expensive reliable system which can be cost prohibitive, or an inexpensive system which can give an organization security, but not infallible security. Reliable and often more expensive systems use remote mirroring of data to an alternate off-site storage facility. This allows the copied data to quickly be retrieved to replace lost data due to disaster.[3] A more cost effective option for some organizations is the regular data backup process wherein data is backed up to magnetic tape and stored at an off-site storage facility. However, magnetic tape backup, while more cost effective, lacks the real-time updating of more expensive systems.[4]

Conclusion

The key to disaster recovery involves preparedness. Organizations and agencies must be prepared to reduce agency interruption of normal operations during and after a catastrophic event. The ability to efficiently and effectively recover key hardware, software, and/or data in a timely manner is associated with whether one has invested in a remote mirroring or standard data backup system. While computer recovery strategies are very important, one must not lose sight of the human factor in disaster recovery efforts. Key personnel must be cognizant of vulnerable employees during times of tragedy and handle the temporary or long-term replacement of the injured and/or deceased employees with professionalism and dignity.

See also: Emergency Preparedness Plan; Safety

NOTES

1. Jim Hoffer, "Backing Up Business: Industry Trend or Event," *Health Management Technology,* January 2001, 1–2.

2. Ravi Chalaka, "Simplifying Disaster Recovery Solutions to Protect Your Data: Disaster Recovery," *Computer Technology Review,* December 2003, 1–3.

3. Ron Levine, "So-Called 'Small Disasters' Can Equal Big Trouble," *Disaster Recovery Journal,* Fall 2002, 76–77.

4. Rob Peglar, "Hurricane Preparedness: The Business Impact of Data Storage in Disaster Recovery," *Oil and Gas Financial Journal,* June 2007, 1–3.

Jason Karsky

DISCIPLINARY PROCEDURES

Regardless of the effort applied to recruit, select, train, and motivate employees, occasionally an employee will fail to meet performance expectations or will violate a company policy during his employment. When this occurs, the organization will need to have some method of disciplinary action, or a methodology that may lead to the individual's termination. Despite the best efforts of an organization to prevent a loss, terminating an employee can be a very difficult endeavor that requires careful planning, attention to detail, and often a paper trail to verify methods have been employed to positively prevent a wrongful termination.

The purpose of discipline is to point the way to more positive and productive behavior rather than to penalize the person for his mistakes.[1] Prior to any actual disciplinary action, organizational members should attempt to diagnose the problem to ensure that the employee is to blame for the incident and no other circumstances exist. While disciplinary procedures may be needed to facilitate termination, the real intent is to counsel and try to correct an employee's improper conduct. Initially, it should be determined if the misconduct resulted from a lack of understanding, lack of knowledge, or lack of motivation. Perhaps an employee does not understand why his or her behavior was inappropriate, or perhaps the employee is not aware of how to perform properly. Thus, counseling or training may be the remedy.[2]

While establishing a disciplinary policy is extremely important, the enforcement of this policy, across the organization, is even more paramount. By not following the established policy, some employees are failing to meet requirements established, while management will also lose credibility. Additionally, morale may suffer because of unfairly implemented policies or from the lack of upholding company policies and procedures. Therefore, a well-designed and well-communicated program that is applied fairly and equally throughout the organization and implemented with the intent of improving employee performance is the key to having a satisfied and motivated work force.

Employment-at-will Contract

In recent years, many organizations have implemented an "employment-at-will" contract or doctrine that states either an employee or employer could sever the employment relationship at any time. The release from employment could be for what has been termed "good cause," "no cause," or "bad cause."[3] Regardless of this signed agreement on the date of hire, and despite the fact that the employee handbook specifies there is an employment-at-will relationship, some employees that are fired sometimes will still sue their employers for wrongful discharge.

A wrongful discharge suit by an employee attempts to state that the discharge resulted in either a violation in an implied contract (the employer acted unfairly), or a violation of public policy (the employee refused to do something illegal, unethical, or unsafe). Courts holding the hearings have often been receptive to these cases, and employees have won settlements 70 percent of the time.[4] Thus, an unprepared organization that lacks the proper documentation displaying an effort to get the employee on the right path or lacks sufficient documentation and procedure to properly terminate an employee has often faced financial risk associated with a termination decision. Additionally, in recent years some employers have been faced with violence in the workplace as a result of a improperly handled termination. Therefore, it is necessary for organizations to develop a standardized, systematic approach to discipline and discharge of any employee, should it become necessary.

Procedural Justice

One of the key factors in any employee counseling process is fair and equal treatment to all. Employees are more likely to respond positively to any negative feedback given if they perceive that the counseling or appraisal process is fair and just. There are six determinants of procedural justice that every organization should follow in employee counseling and disciplinary actions:[5]

1. *Consistency*—the procedures are applied consistently across time and all personnel.
2. *Bias suppression*—the procedures are applied by a person who has a real vested interest in the outcome and no prior prejudices regarding the individual employee.
3. *Information accuracy*—the procedure is based on information that is perceived to be true.
4. *Correctability*—the procedure has built-in safeguards that allow one to appeal mistakes or bad decisions.
5. *Representativeness*—the procedure is informed by the concerns of all groups or stakeholders affected by the decision, including the individual being dismissed.
6. *Ethicality*—the procedure is consistent with prevailing moral standards as they pertain to issues like invasion of privacy or deception.

When a decision to terminate an employee is made, if the decision is explained well and implemented in a fashion that is "socially sensitive, considerate, and empathetic" it will help defuse some potential resentment that may result from an employee being discharged.[6] The organization that has a system which promotes procedural and interactive justice across the organization in an equal and fair manner will have more satisfied employees. There are four main elements to the process:[7]

1. *Explanation*—emphasize aspects of procedural fairness that justify the decision to discharge.
2. *Social sensitivity*—treat the individual with dignity and respect.
3. *Consideration*—listen to the individual's concerns.
4. *Empathy*—identify with the individual's feelings.

Progressive Discipline

Unless the violation is extreme, such as theft or violence for example, employees should not be terminated for a first offense. Should termination become necessary, it should be the result of a systematic discipline program. This systematic discipline program should consist of two primary components:

1. *Documentation*—specific publication of all work rules, procedures, and job descriptions in place prior to administering any discipline, and a detailed explanation of the violation thereof.
2. *Policy*—a progressive set of punitive measures that are clearly stated and established in an employee handbook. This policy should be fairly and equally practiced throughout the organization.

A progressive system may start with an unofficial warning (verbal) or a formal written warning, followed by a more stern written warning in conjunction with a suspension from work without pay. In fairness to the individuals with a suspension, the employer should also indicate that further violation may result in termination so that the individual is advised that further action should be avoided. In the end, should a problem employee require termination, the chance that he can prove wrongful discharge is minimized if the proper policy was followed and documentation exists that can demonstrate such action.

See also: Documentation; Performance Coaching; Performance Management: An Overview; Termination; Training

NOTES

1. H . John Bernardin, *Human Resource Management: An Experiential Approach, 4th ed.* (Boston: McGraw-Hill Irwin, 2007).

2. Steven E. Bers, "Defensive Discipline, Documentation, and Discharge," (2002), http://www.hr.com/servlets/sfs?t=/contentManager/onStory&e=UTF-8&i=1116423256281&l=0&ParentID=1119887457168&StoryID=1119650466890&highlight=1&keys=Disciplinary+%2Bprocedures&lang=0&active=no.

3. Raymond A. Noe, John R. Hollenbeck, Barry Gerhart, and Patrick M. Wright, *Human Resource Management: Gaining a Competitive Advantage,* 4th ed. (Boston: McGraw-Hill Irwin, 2003).

4. Ibid.

5. Ibid.

6. Ibid.

7. Ibid.

Frank E. Armstrong

DRESS CODE

Dress code is highly variable and entirely dependent upon each individual organization. The organization's product and type of labor will determine what type of dress code is appropriate. Getting employees to acquiesce with the dress code is important for the organization's representation as well as the individual employee's image and often, safety. Thus, a company's values may be seen in the dress of employees.[1]

Protective Attire Dress Code

Careers that involve occupational hazards require safety attire as part of the dress code. Some examples of protective attire that might be required in a position with occupational hazards are safety goggles to protect the eyes in a factory, plastic gloves in a laboratory, and nose and mouth masks in a medical facility.

Many hospitals in Florida are recreating dress codes.[2] The General Hospital in Tampa is adding color coordination to the dress code within different departments so that employees are easily distinguished to patients. Some hospitals are now even banning the use of perfumes, jewelry, and manicures as some patients may be sensitive to these products.

Casual Dress Code

Throughout the 1990s, the dress code trend in organizations shifted toward more casual attire. Many businesses adopted "casual Fridays" where employees dress down and often even wear jeans on Fridays. Results from casual dress codes often show improved communication.[3] In *Start Dressing Like a Pro,* Rocha states, "it started when many Silicon Valley firms found that their employees worked better in relaxed clothing than in stiffer, more traditional work wear, so they adopted this casual look as their daily attire. This slowly trickled down to other companies as they believed casual clothing would make employees more comfortable, and thus boost productivity."[4]

Current Dress Code Trend

While some research has suggested that a relaxed dress code makes for a more comfortable and therefore more productive staff, others argue the opposite. Some companies have observed a correlation between a more casual dress code and "increased tardiness, decreased productivity, and lack of focus and discipline."[5] Thus, a shift back towards more professional attire is the current trend. "According to the American Industry Dress Code Survey, in a national poll of 201 senior executives at companies with over $500 million in annual revenue, more than half of large businesses maintain a business attire policy —that means suit and tie for the gents and a suit or dress for the ladies."[6]

A survey created by Yahoo!, HotJobs, and Banana Republic in June 2006 found that less than half of men and women are employed at an organization where casual attire is an option. Moreover, 26 percent of employees reported that their organization has never had a "casual Friday."[7] One company, Computer Technology Solutions, has taken the dress code initiative even farther by recently sending out a memo to all employees advising them on the color of socks that are appropriate for their workplace.[8]

Generational Differences in Dress Code

Another important concern encompassing dress code is generational differences. The values and norms among the Baby Boomer generation (born between 1946 and 1964) are much different than those of the millennial generation (born 1980–2000). "Millenials" have grown up in an environment where tattoos and piercing have become socially acceptable. On the contrary, baby boomers first entered a work force in which sporting a suit to the office each day was customary. Approximately 77.5 million Americans make up the baby boomer population and currently hold more leadership positions than any other cohort.[9] Because baby boomers are essentially managing most millenials in the work force, it is crucial for the two groups to understand each other's motivations behind their wants and needs regarding dress code.[10]

Conclusion

Dress code is exceptionally important in the professional representation of organizations. Keeping abreast of current dress code trends as well as understanding generational differences will help organizations and their employees maintain a professional image.

NOTES

1. Jennifer Burkhart, *Understanding Organizational Culture* (State Library and Adult Education Office: Colorado State Department of Education, Denver, 1995).

2. Ibid.

3. Nicole Benkert, "Dress Code Trends," *Advance for Health Care,* July 1, 2004.

4. Ardella Ramey, *A Company Policy and Personnel Workbook,* 4th ed. (Central Point, OR: Oasis Press, 1999).

5. Roberto Rocha, "Start Dressing Like a Pro," *AskMen.com* http://www.askmen.com/money/ successful_100/105_success.html.

6. Benkert, "Dress Code Trends."

7. Raymond W. Neal, "Dealing with Dress Codes," *Looksmart FindArticles* (Media Central Inc., April 25, 2000), http://www.libsci.sc.edu/bob/class/clis724/SpecialLibrariesHandbook/neal.htm.

8. Kathy Gurchiek, "Comfort is the Main Criterion for Dress Attire" (Society for Human Resource Management, November 2, 2006), http://www.shrm.org.

9. Cindy F. Crawford, "Breaking the Dress Code," *Birmingham Business Journal,* April 16, 2007.

10. Deborah Gilberg, "Generation X: Stepping Up to the Leadership Plate," *CIO,* April 11, 2007, http://www.cio.com/article/103503/ (accessed June 1, 2007).

Meghan Clarisse Cave

E-MAIL/INTERNET POLICY

The Internet and e-mail have revolutionized the world's communication. They have allowed individuals and organizations alike to communicate more easily and efficiently, while crossing geographic and cultural obstacles.

Organizations should create and use Internet/e-mail policies to strategically outline proper use of employees' work time with the computer and to facilitate an efficient work environment.

Reasons for Email/Internet Policies

The government of the United Kingdom developed Internet and e-mail laws in their Data Protection Act in 1998. They list two major reasons to introduce policies for Internet and email use within an organization:
• To ensure that communications resources are not wasted and productivity does not suffer.
• To help protect the business from potentially damaging material being sent or received via the Internet or email and any possible resulting legal action.[2]

Suggestions for Creating E-mail/Internet Policies

When considering what policies should be created and implemented, organizations should customize policies and procedures that best fit with their goals and objectives. It does not hurt to get advice or view other organization's Internet policies for helpful ideas, but it is important for employers to know what will help their own organizations, and of course, have policies that are purposeful and pragmatic. A few suggestions to consider when creating Internet/e-mail policies are:
• Review your potential liabilities from Internet and e-mail misuse by writing policies that promote company privacy and productivity.
• Consider how you can maintain and police your policies.
• Think about how you can handle overuse of the phone, voicemail, email, or paging.
• Encourage employees to communicate their thoughts and ideas on Internet and e-mail policies to their managers, sponsors, and other stakeholders.
• Remember: policies should reflect the organization's culture relating to privacy.[1]

Understanding the Risks

Organizations want to be effective and successful. They will use any resources that will help them accomplish their mission and goals. Often they will obtain outside resources to keep their competitive "edge" in the market. The Internet is probably the most widely used resource, and it allows everyone to virtually communicate with almost anyone without wasting time, energies, or money. But as with any good commodity, one must understand the risks and safeguard oneself from liabilities and abuse. The most common risks include the following:

- Downloading files that contain viruses
- Obtaining copyrighted material such as music or films
- Transmitting valuable or sensitive business information without encryption
- Distributing or relaying offensive or abusive material via e-mail
- Generating junk email, or spam, via mass mailings
- Accepting files from people in online chat rooms which could bypass firewalls or e-mail filters

Further, organizations must avoid being overly dogmatic when executing guidelines. Applying a proper balance of common sense and thinking through potential risks will give employers the ability to have policies and procedures that work for instead of against their organizations. Trivial abuses of the system include transferring large file attachments or wasting work time on Internet surfing, personal e-mail or online chat rooms. More serious misconduct may result in disciplinary or even legal proceedings. This includes accessing or downloading pornography or other offensive material, libeling or defaming colleagues or even external business contacts via email, and using the Internet to commit fraud or other illegal acts.[2]

The Internet and e-mail are great tools that can help any organization to be productive and stay connected to employees and clients alike. But these tools can also be misused and become a hindrance. Organizations must be wise and accurately communicate their expectations and limitations of e-mail and the Internet. Then organizations should and must consistently monitor Internet and e-mail usage in order to maintain integrity and organizational standards.

NOTES

1. Darrel Raynor, *Internet & Email Policy Discussion,* Data Analysis & Results, Inc. 1999, http://www.dataanalysis.com.
2. *Introduce an Internet and Email Policy.* Guide developed with The National Centre, http://www.businesslink.gov.uk.

Roger Odegard

EMERGENCY PREPAREDNESS

Emergency preparedness plans and/or preparedness procedures are important to a business. Having plans or procedures in place will allow a company to be ready for the worst should an emergency occur. While it may not be often that an emergency arises, having a plan or procedure in place assists in the safety of the employees, safety of the customers, and the safety of vital assets or information of the business. Depending on the size of the business and the size of the emergency, the fate of the business can be sealed by how the employees react in an emergency. Emergencies can occur in different forms; therefore, it is important to have different plans and procedures in place for the different types of emergencies. Emergencies fit into the following categories: accidents, crime, natural hazards, and technological hazards.

Accidents

The best way to brace for an accident is to have plans or a set of procedures for employees to abide by. An accident can range anywhere from an employee injuring himself on company grounds, to a structural weakness of the building resulting in damage, to a process going wrong at the workplace causing damage. Enforcing proper OSHA (Occupational Safety and Health Administration) standards—many of which require an emergency action plan—and following the proper rules and guidelines will reduce the risk of an accident occurring. However, should an accident occur, following proper procedures and regulations should help reduce the amount of resulting damage.

Crime

Organizations must also be prepared for crime. While minor office theft is not an emergency, employees being held at gunpoint obviously is. Some companies will need emergency plans in place to prepare themselves for such acts. The company should also be braced to handle situations where data integrity is compromised and to respond to such violations.

Natural Hazards

Natural hazards that can occur include earthquakes, fire, floods, hurricanes, high winds, landslides, mudslides, sinkholes, thunderstorms, tornados, tsunamis, volcano eruptions, extreme cold, extreme heat, and winter storms/blizzards. Nature is unpredictable; having emergency plans or procedures in the event of severe weather will help prevent harm or the loss of employees' and customers' lives. Furthermore, having separate emergency plans to accommodate specific hazards is imperative. For example, an emergency plan to go underground for a tornado would not work in the event of a flood.

Technological Hazards

According to the Federal Emergency Management Agency (FEMA), "The number of technological incidents is escalating, mainly as a result of the increased number of new substances and the opportunities for human error inherent in the use of these materials." Depending upon the severity of the technological hazard occurring, employees might have to perform actions such as evacuating a small area of the business or a lockdown of the premises.

Conclusion

The four main types of hazards—accidents, crime, natural hazards, and technological hazards—can happen at any time. Organizations should be able to respond to these quickly and effectively with emergency preparedness plans and/or procedures in place detailing how to deal with each specific situation accordingly.

See also Disaster Recover Plan; Occupational Health and Safety Administration (OSHA); Safety

Resources:

Federal Emergency Management Agency (FEMA). "Are You Ready? An In-depth Guide to Citizen Preparedness," July 3, 2006. http://www.fema.gov/areyouready/ (accessed January 21, 2008).

FEMA. "Are You Ready? Technological Hazards," May 2, 2007. http://www.fema.gov/areyou-ready/technological_hazards.shtm (accessed February 8, 2008).

Occupational Safety and Health Administration (OSHA). "OSHA's Mission." http://www.osha.gov/oshinfo/mission.html (accessed February 8, 2008).

U.S. Department of Health and Human Services (HHS). "Disasters and Emergencies." http://www.hhs.gov/disasters/ (accessed January 21, 2008).

Chris Armstrong

EMPLOYEE ATTITUDE SURVEY

Also known as a climate survey or an employee engagement survey, an employee attitude survey (EAS) is a measurement of the attitudes, satisfaction, and commitment level of an organization's employees, as well as the effectiveness of managers, as seen by employees. It is generally administered by a neutral party, which could be either internal or external to the organization, and responses are kept confidential so that honest feedback can be obtained. Employee attitude surveys are used to find out whether action needs to be taken to make employees more satisfied. Although sometimes a one-time event, an EAS should be done regularly for maximum benefit.[1]

Typical EAS Questions

Employee attitude surveys typically consist of two types of questions: What parts of the jobs or rewards are motivating to the employee, and are employee needs being met?[2] Organizations like Wild Oats use employee attitude surveys as an indicator of how happy their employees are.[3] Typical questions include, "How happy are you with your job?" and "How do you feel about benefits, pay, and morale at your job?" Questions may also deal with management, for example, "Does your immediate manager involve you in planning the work of your team?" "Do you have sufficient authority to do your job well?" or "Does your manager provide a clear vision for your team?"[4] Questions can either use a rating scale or be open-ended to get more qualitative information. Comments by employees may be even more useful than rankings in some instances.

Administering and Giving Feedback on an EAS

Care should be exercised when administering an EAS, as merely conducting one raises employee's expectations that something will be done with the data.[5] Although it seems that asking employees what they think shows that the company cares about them, asking employees about their opinions and then not acting on those opinions may result in cynical employees and lower morale.

Data collected from the employee attitude survey should be shared with the company's employees, along with an action plan for dealing with any issues that arise from the analysis. Employees should also be given an opportunity to respond to both the data and the issues brought up by the survey and to have a role in addressing those issues.

From these surveys, employers can find out what is important to their employees, thus motivating them, and what needs to be done differently to avoid dissatisfaction.[6] As a result of concerns raised by its employees in their EAS, the Wild Oats company offered stock options, a wellness allowance, and retroactive raises to its employees.[7]

Conclusion

An EAS is a method used to find out what employee thoughts and attitudes are about an organization. It is administered confidentially to ensure honest responses. Once conducted, the data and analysis should be shared with employees, along with an action plan designed to address the issues brought up by the survey. If feedback does not occur, for example, when leaders do not like the results, employees often feel ignored, leading to lower morale. Surveys should be done regularly to assess progress and to keep the company informed of employee satisfaction.

See also Motivation; Retention

NOTES

1. Liz Simpson, "What's Going On in Your Company?" *Training,* June 2002: 30–35.
2. Sarah Coles, "Satisfying Basic Needs," *Employee Benefits,* October 2001: 3–7.
3. "Employee Surveys Get Results," *Leadership for the Front Lines,* December 2000: 7.
4. Mats Sundgren, Marcus Selart, Anders Ingergard, and Curt Bengston, "Dialogue-based Evaluation as a Creative Climate Indicator: Evidence from the Pharmaceutical Industry," *Creativity and Innovation Management,* March 2005: 91–92.
5. Simpson, "What's Going On in Your Company?" 30–35.
6. Coles, "Satisfying Basic Needs," 3–7.
7. "Employee Surveys Get Results," *Leadership for the Front Lines,* 7.

Barbara A. W. Eversole

EMPLOYEE HANDBOOK

Employee handbooks are guidelines for the relationship between employee and employer. Policy manuals, by contrast, are procedural, operations-focused, and typically are directed at supervisory and managerial staff.[1] Employee handbooks began as general statements on policies and procedures but now often include more general content such as organizational mission and vision.[1] Additionally, since the 1980s there has been a significant amount of litigation surrounding employee handbooks as guarantors of continuous employment and as contracts for continuing benefits. Human resource departments charged with creating employee handbooks would be wise to consult with an attorney to understand the complexity of the laws and precedents in their state prior to publishing a handbook or revisions to a handbook.[2]

Employee Handbook Contents

The contents included in employee handbooks can vary depending on the industry, size of the company, and number of employees.[3] Content will vary even more widely if the handbook must cover international issues.[4] It is strongly recommended that all handbooks be reviewed by an attorney and benchmarked against peer organizations. The language used must be carefully constructed to ensure that no employment contract is formed by developing the handbook or its policies.

A general framework for content includes the following sections: a welcome, employee expectations, workplace rules, compensation and benefits, professional development, expenses, emergencies, disclaimers, and acknowledgements.

A Welcome

A welcoming statement to new employees should be provided along with an explanation of the purpose of the handbook. A brief history of the company and the evolution of its products and services, as well as the organizational mission statement and vision statement could be included in this section.

Employee Expectations

Expectations of employees regarding a drug-free workplace, business ethics, Internet, computer use, and e-mail use, as well as statements of the organization's policies on equal opportunity employment, harassment, and affirmative action need to be given.

Workplace Rules

A list of conduct rules for employees should be presented in the employee handbook, including tardiness, absenteeism, lunch breaks, short breaks, smoking, dress code, use of company vehicles or property, anti-harassment rules, and consequences for rule infractions, including any progressive disciplinary procedure. An explanation of how complaints are handled, methods of resolving disputes, and other disciplinary issues should be addressed.

Compensation and Benefits

Payroll procedures, pay grades, rules and approvals governing overtime pay, work week hours, and time reporting procedures should be covered in the employee handbook. A summary of benefits including health insurance, life insurance, workman's compensation benefits, and retirement plans should also be included. Information on paid time off, holidays, vacation and/or sick leave, funeral leave, jury duty, military deployment, maternity leave, short term disability, and other leaves of absence, as well as who is eligible for leaves, how time may accrue, when vacation time must be taken, and the amount of time that may be carried forward from year to year, if any, should be included. Programs such as the Employee Assistance Program (EAP) and tuition reimbursement also should be outlined.

Professional Development

A description of the opportunities available for professional development and training and whether there are resources available internally for such development should be provided. Procedures for performance evaluation, transfer, and/or promotion within the organization should be offered. If the organization offers internal postings for jobs, those procedures should be presented as well.

Expenses

An explanation of the procedures surrounding reimbursement of expenses, travel arrangements, organizational credit card use, and petty cash should be outlined, including pre-approvals that may be required and customary time frames for reimbursement.

Emergencies

An explanation of the organization's crisis plan, media contacts, and employee procedures during internal emergencies should be outlined. Contact information for the families/partners of employees should be obtained, and employees should be provided with a person to contact in the organization in the case of a personal emergency. Safety and accident reporting rules also should be addressed.

Disclaimers

Disclaimers are a feature of employee handbooks that allow organizations to reserve certain rights, indicate that the handbook can be amended, and explain that the handbook is for informational purposes only and does not create a binding contract. Disclaimers may also include a statement about the handbook not overriding the at-will employee relationship. There should be a direct correlation between the disclaimers in the handbook and the acknowledgement of receipt of the handbook that employees sign.

Acknowledgments

Acknowledgments are signed by employees upon receipt of their employee handbook. The acknowledgment document is kept in the human resources office. Acknowledgments indicate that the employee has received the employee handbook and stipulates that the employee is required to read and understand the handbook. The acknowledgement should indicate that the handbook is not a contract or guarantee of continued employment and that the organization can change, eliminate, or supplement any provisions in the handbook, including benefits, workplace rules, organizational policies, and compensation and benefits. Procedures for how notification of these changes will be made should be included in the acknowledgement form. Acknowledgements may also indicate to whom employees should direct questions regarding the contents of the handbook.

See also Employment-at-Will; Employment Law: An Overview

Resources:

AELE Library of Case Summaries of Employment and Labor Law for Public and Safety Agents. http://www.aele.org/law/Digests/emplmenu.html.

AHI Employment Law Resource Center.: http://www.ahipubs.com/.

Society for Human Resource Management. www.shrm.org.

NOTES

1. "Do's and Don'ts for a Highly Effective Employee Handbook," *Compensation and Benefits for Law Offices,* September 2006: 2–5.

2. Kenneth A. Jennero, "Employers Beware: You May Be Bound by the Terms of Your Old Employee Handbooks," *Employee Relations L.J.* 20, no. 4 (Autumn 1994): 299–314.

3. "Employee Handbooks: Have You Updated Yours Lately?" *HR Focus,* July 2007: 5–6.

4. Dennis A. Briscoe, *International Human Resource Management* (Englewood Cliffs, NJ: Prentice Hall, 1995).

Debra Orr

EMPLOYMENT-AT-WILL

Employment-at-will is a common law doctrine that gives employers the right to hire, fire, demote, and promote whomever they choose, at any time, with or without prior notice, and for any reason unless there is a law or contract to the contrary.[1] It also gives employees similar rights—to quit a job at any time, with or without notice, for any reason. Employment-at-will is the general rule of employment in the United States, unless a formal agreement or contract stipulates a different relationship, such as a union labor contract.

Interpretation of the employment-at-will doctrine varies from state to state, and there are state and federal laws that may limit the employment-at-will relationship between employees and employers. Human resources professionals must be aware of the most common exceptions to the employment-at-will doctrine, and what guidelines employers should follow in order to protect their employment-at-will rights.

Exceptions to Employment-at-Will

The most common exceptions to employment-at-will include exceptions based on public policy, implied contract, or covenant of good faith and fair dealing.

Public Policy

The focus of all the public policy exceptions is the understanding that an employer cannot take negative action against an employee for fulfilling legal obligations or for exercising her legal rights. Public policy generally includes four main categories of conduct: (1) refusing to commit illegal or unethical acts, (2) performing a legal duty, (3) exercising legal rights, and (4) whistle-blowing.[2]

Public policy violations are the most widely recognized exceptions to the employment-at-will doctrine. Some examples of public policy exceptions include serving on military duty or jury service, reporting a workers' compensation claim, refusing to falsify company documents or commit perjury, reporting an employer's illegal actions, or filing a complaint of discrimination with the Equal Employment Opportunity Commission (EEOC).

Implied Contract

An implied contract exists when an agreement is implied from circumstances, even when there has been no formal written contract between the employee and employer. These implied contracts can prevent employers from treating their employees as at-will, because the implied contract has created obligations that the employer must follow. Some examples of implied contracts may include the following:

- An employee handbook that indicates employees will only be terminated for "just cause";
- Disciplinary action policies that promise a specific number of written warnings before termination; or
- A verbal promise made to an employee regarding job security.

Covenant of Good Faith and Fair Dealing

Some courts have held employers to an implied covenant of good faith and fair dealing. This means that a termination may not be justified if the employer did not act with honesty or has inflicted harm without justification.[3] The covenant of good faith and fair dealing assumes that there is an implied contract for every employment situation, which prevents an employer from terminating employment based on a decision made in bad faith. An example of this may be an employee who is fired shortly before becoming vested in the employer's retirement plan.

This is the least used exception to the employment-at-will doctrine because many courts are not willing to attempt to determine an employer's motive, and do not wish to circumvent the long-standing at-will employment standard.

Guidelines for Employers

Although the employment-at-will doctrine is well established in the United States, the majority of states have found circumstances that erode employers' rights to take action under an employment-at-will law. Because of this, it is important for companies to understand the employment-at-will doctrine and take action to protect its rights. The Society for Human Resource Management (SHRM) provides several suggestions for employers to follow:[4]

- Avoid representing the job as "permanent";
- List in job applications, offer-or-employment letters, and employee handbooks that employment is at-will;
- Require employees to sign an acknowledgement that they have received the employee handbook, that the handbook is not a contract, and that employment is at-will;
- Accurately and factually document performance appraisals, warnings, disciplinary actions, and discharge;
- Establish an internal conflict-resolution procedure; and
- Follow the organization's disciplinary process.
  See also Disciplinary Procedures; Employee Handbook

NOTES

1. Society for Human Resource Management, *The SHRM Learning System Module 5: Employee and Labor Relations* (2007), 21–23.
2. Ibid.
3. Ibid.
4. Robert J. Lanza and Martin Warren, "United States: Employment at Will Prevails Despite Exceptions to the Rule," *SHRM Legal Report,* October-November 2005, http://www.shrm.org/hrresources/lrpt_published/CMS_014415.asp#P-10_0 (accessed October 5, 2007).

Shanan M. Mahoney

EXEMPT-NONEXEMPT EMPLOYEE

In most situations, the Fair Labor Standards Act (FLSA) requires employers to pay employees at least the federal minimum wage for each hour worked, and it also requires overtime pay for any hours worked in excess of 40 hours per workweek. However, there are exemptions to these rules. The term "exempt" refers to employees who may be excluded from FLSA minimum wage and overtime requirements; "nonexempt" employees are covered by those requirements.

FLSA Exemption Requirements

The FLSA has identified three requirements, all of which must exist in order for an employee to be classified as exempt. The employee must earn a minimum salary level, must be paid on a salary basis, and must perform exempt duties.

Minimum Salary Level

The first requirement is that the employee must be paid a certain weekly minimum salary of $455 per week, or $23,660 per year; computer-related employees have a salary level requirement of $455 per week, or $18.20 per hour.[1] These amounts cannot be subject to reductions due to changes in the quantity or quality of work performed.

In most cases, if an employee does not earn the minimum of $455 per week, she cannot be considered exempt, even if she does meet the other requirements. However, outside sales employees are not subject to this salary level requirement.

Paid on a Salary Basis

The second requirement is that the employee must be paid on a salaried basis. This means that the employee is paid a predetermined set salary amount for each week of work, regardless of the number of hours worked. The employer cannot take improper deductions from the employee's pay. For example, the employer cannot take deductions from an employee's pay because the employee came to work late or left work early.

Perform Exempt Duties

The third requirement is that the employee must perform exempt duties. These duties can include executive, administrative, professional, computer, or outside sales duties. The FLSA has criteria to help define what types of duties are included under each category, and these are discussed below.

Exempt Duties Test

Executives, administrative, professional, computer, and outside sales employees are often referred to as "white-collar" employees and may be exempt from FLSA overtime and minimum wage regulations. It is important for employers to correctly identify employees who perform exempt duties. Job title alone is not sufficient to justify exempt duties. FLSA provides specific guidelines and criteria that must be met in order to meet the exempt duties requirements.

Executive Employees

In order to be considered an executive employee, an employee must
- have a primary duty involving management of an enterprise or a customarily recognized department or subdivision of the enterprise;
- customarily and regularly direct the work of two or more other full-time employees or their equivalent; and
- have the authority to hire or fire other employees; or the employee's suggestions and recommendations as to the hiring, firing, advancement, promotion, or any other change of status of other employees must be given particular weight.[1]

Administrative Employees

In order to be considered an administrative employee, an employee must have a primary duty of performing office or nonmanual work directly related to the management or general business operations of the employer. These duties must include the exercise of discretion and independent judgment with respect to matters of significance.

Professional Employees

Professional employees can be classified into two categories: learned professionals and creative professionals. The learned professional exemption is for employees who perform duties requiring advanced knowledge. The advanced knowledge must be in a field of science or learning and is generally acquired by a course of specialized intellectual instruction. Examples include lawyers, doctors, teachers, engineers, and pharmacists.

Creative professionals perform duties that require invention, imagination, originality, or talent in a recognized field of artistic or creative endeavor. Examples include actors, writers, musicians, and graphic artists.

Computer Employees

To qualify for the computer employee exemption, an employee's primary duties must fall into one of four categories:
- Application of systems analysis techniques and procedures
- Design, development, analysis, creation, testing or modification of computer systems or programs
- Design, documentation, testing, creation, or modification of computer systems related to machine operating systems
- A combination of these duties[2]

The computer employee exemption criteria do not require that the employee consistently exercise discretion and judgment and is not limited to computer employees who work in software functions.

Outside Sales Employees

As mentioned earlier, outside sales employees do not need to meet the minimum salary requirement in order to qualify for FLSA exemption. They do, however, need to meet certain criteria related to the job duties. Outside sales employees must have a primary duty of making sales or obtaining orders for contracts or services or for the use of facilities for which a consideration will be paid by the client or customer. They also must be customarily and regularly engaged away from the employer's place or places of business.

Safe Harbor

In 2004, the U.S. Department of Labor issued several revisions to the FLSA regulations that helped to define and clarify exempt status employees. One of these revisions was an update, referred to as the "safe harbor" regulation, which describes what could happen when an employer makes improper deductions from an exempt employee's pay. Under these new regulations, if an employer is shown to have an actual practice of making improper deductions, it could lose the exempt status for all employees in the same job classification.

The safe harbor provisions can also protect an employer from losing the exempt status for making improper deductions, regardless of the reason for the improper deduction, when the employer[3]
- has a clearly communicated policy that prohibits improper pay deductions and includes a complaint mechanism;
- reimburses employees for any improper deductions; and
- makes a good-faith commitment to comply in the future.

Because of the safe harbor provisions, employers should take action to ensure their employees are classified correctly, correct any past improper pay deductions, and review pay policies to ensure that they meet all FLSA exemption guidelines.

See also Fair Labor Standards Act (FLSA); Minimum Wage

NOTES

1. Camille Olson, Noah Finkel, and Russell Gore, "Overtime Exemptions for White-Collar Employees: New Regulations Clarify Status," *SHRM Legal Report,* June 2004, 6–9.

2. Society for Human Resource Management, *The SHRM Learning System Module 4: Compensation and Benefits* (2006), 9–17.

3. Ibid.

Shanan M. Mahoney

FLEXTIME

Flexible work schedules, also known as alternative work schedules, are alternatives to the traditional eight-hours-a-day, five-days-a-week work schedule. Flexible types of schedules are becoming more and more prevalent in today's workplace. By offering flexible work schedules, employers can help to better meet the changing needs and expectations of the workforce by providing employees with options that give greater flexibility in creating work schedules.

Flexible Work Schedule Options

As businesses become more focused on retention initiatives, employee motivation tools, and finding ways to meet employees' needs for a work/life balance, human resource professionals will need to be familiar with flexible work schedule options and know how to successfully implement them in the workplace. Flextime, job sharing, compressed work weeks, regular part-time, hoteling, and phased retirement are a few of the options employers and employees are using.

Flextime

One of the most popular flexible work schedules is known as flextime. In this option, employees have the ability to set their own hours while still covering core hours each day (hours that all employees must be at the workplace). For example, a company may still require employees to work eight hours a day, but the employees have the flexibility to work those hours anytime between 6:00 AM and 6:00 PM The core hours that all employees must be present at work would be between 9:00 AM and 3:00 PM (assuming each employee takes a one-hour lunch).

Flextime is especially useful for companies that operate in large metropolitan areas where heavy commuter traffic is an issue and for companies that provide services in multiple time zones.

Job Share

Job sharing allows two part-time employees to share responsibility for the hours and duties of one position within an organization. This type of flexible work schedule provides the company with full-time coverage for a position, while allowing the individual members of the job share to work a reduced number of hours during the week. The job share partners, sometimes referred to as partners in practice,[1] or PiPs, must have excellent communication skills between themselves and with customers, in order to be successful in the job share partnership.

Compressed Work Week

This option allows employees to work the required number of hours each pay period, but to do so in a limited number of days. The most common form of compressed work week is the "4/40" schedule where an employee works four 10-hour days in order to meet the required 40 hours per week.

Regular Part-time

Employees who are regularly scheduled, but work less than a full-time schedule, are usually considered to be at regular part-time status. The number of hours and scheduling varies from company to company. Employers also vary in the benefits packages that are offered to part-time employees versus full-time employees.

Hoteling

Hoteling is a flexible work schedule option that is most often used with employers who have a workforce that does not need on-site workspace for an entire day. Employees can reserve "an office," which generally includes a desk, phone, and computer equipment, for a specific time period. This allows one workspace to be utilized by many employees.

Phased Retirement

In phased retirement, an employee gradually reduces the number of hours worked, in preparation for full retirement. As the baby boomer generation prepares for retirement, a phased retirement system allows for a smoother transfer of knowledge and a more controlled succession plan.

Conclusion

The availability of flexible work schedules is one option that employers can use to increase workers' freedom and motivation. Flexible work schedules have been shown to decrease tardiness and absenteeism, increase employee company loyalty, and are viewed as a positive recruitment tool.[2]

See also: Job Sharing; PTO (Paid Time Off) Bank

Resources:

Society for Human Resource Management. *The SHRM Learning System Module 5: Employee and Labor Relations* (2007), 59–64.

NOTES

1. Pamela M. Dixon-Krausse, "Integration of Learning and Practice for Job Sharing Partnerships," in proceedings of *Academy of HRD* (Indianapolis: 2007).

2. David A. DeCenzo and Stephen P. Robbins, *Human Resource Management,* 6th ed. (New York: John Wiley & Sons, 1999), 111–15.

Shanan M. Mahoney

GRIEVANCE

The last 25 years has witnessed a significant decline in the percentage of unionized workers in the U.S. workforce, from 30 percent in 1975 to just under 14 percent today.[1] Despite this, unionization remains the norm in many industries, including services industries such as transportation, education, and hospitality, and unions are making concerted efforts to grow their membership base and organize employees in new industries.[2] Moreover, grievance procedure is a mandatory item in any collective bargaining agreement eventually reached between an employer organization and a collective bargaining unit as represented by a specific labor union. For these reasons, HR must be informed about the normative union grievance process.

Typical Grievance Procedure Steps

By definition, a grievance is a complaint from a unionized employee that has been formally documented and submitted. The grievance process is fairly normative across organizations and industries and includes the following progressive steps:[3]

- *Step 1: Discussion of written grievance*—the employee discusses the grievance with the union steward (the union's representative on the job) and the employee's supervisor.
- *Step 2: Meeting between union steward and supervisor's manager and/or HR manager*—if still unresolved, the union steward then elevates the grievance to a discussion with the supervisor's manager.
- *Step 3: Grievance committee consideration*—if still unresolved, the union steward elevates the grievance for consideration by the union's grievance committee, which in turn discusses the grievance with appropriate company managers.
- *Step 4: Meeting between national union representatives and executives of the company*—if still unresolved, the grievance committee elevates the grievance to the national union office, which in turn engages the executives of the company relative to the grievance.
- *Step 5: Grievance arbitration*—if still unresolved, the national union office elevates the grievance for adjudication by an impartial third party for ultimate resolution.

Grievance Procedure as Strike Aversion Tool

A well-designed and managed grievance procedure can help an organization avoid a costly and potentially disastrous strike situation. In the end, virtually all strikes are overwhelmingly costly for all involved, propagating collective bargaining as a zero-sum game. Thus, HR must proactively employ the grievance procedure as a catalyst for resolving employee complaints before they escalate to a strike.[4]

See also: Arbitration, Bargaining Unit, Collective Bargaining, Labor Unions

NOTES

1. U.S. Bureau of Labor Statistics, http://stats.bls.gov.
2. Stacy Hirsch, "Unions Reach Everywhere for New Members," *Baltimore Sun,* January 25, 2004.
3. Robert L. Mathis and John H. Jackson, *Human Resource Management* (Cincinnati, OH: South-Western College Publishing, 2000), 628.
4. Jeffrey A. Mello, *Strategic Human Resource Management* (Mason, OH: Thomson South-Western, 2006), 536.

Scott A. Quatro

INDEPENDENT CONTRACTORS

An organization must comply with Internal Revenue Service (IRS) regulations in its role as an employer. One of the responsibilities of an employer is the accurate categorization of workers as either employees or as independent contractors (IC), with the corresponding tax withholding and reporting functions inherent in either category of workers. Categorizing a worker as an IC exposes the organization to the greatest amount of risk since the IRS assumes that all workers are employees unless it can be documented otherwise. Failure to properly classify individuals can result in assessment of taxes, penalties, and interest.

Employee or Independent Contractor?

Organizations are responsible for determining the status of their workers for compensation, benefits, and tax purposes. The difference between employees and independent contractors proves critical.

Employees

Essentially, all individuals performing services for the organization for which they will be compensated are presumed to be employees unless they meet the criteria of independent contractor status discussed below.

Generally, current employees who perform additional services for which they will be compensated in addition to their regular duties will still be classified as employees. The following IRS questions provide additional guidance on determining employee status:

- Does the employee receive instructions on how the job is completed? (ICs do not receive instructions.)
- Does the employee receive training for the job? (ICs do not receive training.)
- Are the employee's services integrated into the business operations?
- Are the services rendered personally? (ICs can provide other employees to complete an assignment.)
- Does the employee work with assistants? (ICs hire, fire, and pay for their own assistants.)
- Is there a continuing relationship with the employer? (ICs do not have a continuing relationship.)
- Does the employee have set hours? (ICs set and control their own hours.)
- Is the work considered full time?
- Is the work completed on the organization's property? (ICs can complete the work any place they desire.)
- Is the work completed in a sequence set by the organization? (ICs have control over how a result is to be achieved.)
- Does the organization require regular or written reports?
- Is the employee paid by time rather than by the project? (ICs are typically paid by the job and not by time worked.)
- Is the employee reimbursed for expenses (for example, travel)? (ICs are paid by the job and generally not reimbursed for expenses.)
- Does the organization supply tools and materials? (ICs normally provide their own tools and materials.)
- Does the individual have an investment in the facilities or tools he is using? (ICs have a significant investment.)
- Can the individual realize a profit or loss?
- Does the individual work for more than one firm at a time? (ICs are free to work for more than one firm at a time.)
- Does the individual make his services available to the general public? (ICs make their services available to the general public.)
- Does the organization have the right to discharge the individual? (ICs can only be terminated for failure to comply with the terms of the agreement.)
- Does the individual have the right to quit the job? (ICs have a liability to complete the project to the satisfaction of the organization in accordance with the contract or agreement.)

The above questions are designed to determine who exercises control over the individual. If the organization has the legal right to control both the method and the result as to where, when, by whom, and how the work is to be performed, then the individual should generally be classified as an employee.

Another determining factor is which party is carrying the worker's compensation insurance? Most ICs carry their own worker's compensation insurance policy. They should provide the organization with a certificate of insurance before the work is completed.

Employees are paid through payroll and are subject to withholding of appropriate taxes. They will receive a W-2 at the end of the calendar year. ICs typically bill the organization for work or services rendered.

Independent Contractors

The general rule is that an individual is an independent contractor if the organization has the *legal right* to control or direct *only* the results of the work but not the means and method used in accomplishing the result. Generally, ICs hold themselves out in their own names as self-employed and make their services available to the public. Examples of individuals who might be considered for IC status include

a. Individuals providing professional services such as architects, accountants, attorneys, models, or medical providers; or
b. Consultants who routinely hold themselves out to the public and provide service for a fee.

Under certain circumstances, employees could be considered independent contractors if the following conditions are met:
• They operate a business outside the organization and offer their services to the public.
• They provide their own equipment and supplies.
• They complete the work on their own time and at their own discretion.

When paying an independent contractor, the organization typically completes a written agreement and a purchase order. The contract generally specifies work to be completed, time frame, and cost.

A Form W-9 "Request for Taxpayer's Identification and Certification" must be completed by the independent contractor and submitted to the organization to support the payment request to the accounts payable office. The Form W-9 can be found at http://www.irs.gov/pub/irs-fill/fw9.pdf.

Independent contractors are typically paid through accounts payable. Taxes are not withheld and the compensation will be reported to the individual at the end of the calendar year on an MISC 1099 for all amounts over $600.

See also: Exempt-Nonexempt Employee

Resources:
IRS Publication 15-A, "Employer's Supplemental Tax Guide" (Washington, DC: Internal Revenue Service, 2007), http://www.irs.gov/publications/p15a/index.html.

IRS Publication 15-B, "Employer's Tax Guide to Fringe Benefits" (Washington, DC: Internal Revenue Service, 2008), http://apps.irs.gov/publications/p15b/ar01.html.

Edward Dorman

LABOR UNIONS

Unions function as legal representatives of workers in many industries and are a way for the workers to have a voice within an organization. In the past, unions not only fought for better working conditions for employees but also higher wages and benefits. Because of these and similar issues, unions and management were, and sometimes still are, on different sides of the labor bargaining table.

History of Labor Unions

The labor/trade union can trace its history back to 1794 with the formation of the Federal Society of Journeymen Cordwainers (shoemakers), which was organized in Philadelphia.[1] What could be considered the first nationwide strike took place within the railroad industry in 1877. During this strike a large number of railroad employees lost their lives: this violence was a precursor of things to come.[2] After the national railroad strike, workers seemed ready to do anything to protect their way of making a living and earning the American dream. In these early years, union members committed murders, beatings, bombings and other terrorist-like actions in an attempt to make their point with management.

For their part, management was not totally innocent in these labor wars. Employers would sometimes hire armed guards to intimidate workers or engage in strong armed strategies to thwart a union movement or break up an existing union. Many times after an employee vote to strike, management would hire nonunion workers to cross the picket line and take over production. In many instances violence ensued.

Unions Today

The modern workplace has improved dramatically, with much of the credit attributed to unions. Unions continue to fight for improved working conditions, wages, benefits, and involvement in decision making, while yielding significant political clout.

Union membership reached a high in 1954 with over a quarter of the workforce—17 million out of a possible 60 million workers—represented by a union. As of 2006 that number had fallen to only 12 percent out of a possible 128.4 million employed, which equates to 15.4 million individuals belonging to a union.[3] This reduction is due to drastic declines in the number of workers at U.S. automobile and steel plants, an increase in the ability of nonunion companies to secure contracts and market share, rising health and benefit costs, and falling interest in unions on the part of workers. The largest U. S. labor unions today are the AFL-CIO and the Change to Win Federation, which split from the AFL-CIO in 2005. Most union gains have been in the service sector and education.

Union Legislation

Private sector unions are regulated by federal and state laws. At the federal level, the National Labor Relations Act (NLRA), passed in 1935, is administered by the National Labor Relations Board (NLRB), the overseeing body. Each state also has its own labor laws and labor board. Under the NLRA, even a vote from a minority of employees enables them to form a union, which can then represent the rights of only those who voted in favor of the union. Although once widely used, the minority model was abandoned when unions began to consistently win majority support. This "members only" model is being considered once again as unions lose employee support and labor laws curb workers' ability to organize.

Shops

Companies that employ union workers are described as closed, union, agency, or open shops. Closed shops employ only workers who are already union members; the company is required to recruit from the union membership. Union shops may hire nonunion workers but establish a time limit within which new employees must join the union. An agency shop allows nonunion works but requires them to pay a fee to the union for its services (for example, negotiating the contract). An open shop may have both union and nonunion employees, and does not require the nonunion workers to pay a fee to the union or contribute to the collective bargaining process. In some states, "right-to-work" laws mandate open shops.

Implications for Managers and HR

Unions represent the interests of their members in the workplace, which is an important consideration for all managers and HR personnel. Unions, for example, are responsible for negotiating employment wage ranges, annual pay increases, and benefits for all members. They also establish policies and procedures for hiring, promotion, termination, other employment actions, grievances, and due process. Union members view their representatives as a necessary buffer or layer of protection between themselves and management. Management and HR often perceive unions as intrusive entities that interfere with employer-employee relationships and business practices.

The challenge for managers and HR personnel is to develop successful working relationships that benefit employees and the company. Understanding labor laws and the company's specific union contract is the first step in effectively managing a unionized work force.

See also: Grievance; Labor-Management Relations Act; National Labor Relations Act

NOTES

1. Samuel Gompers, "Labor Unions: Facts and Figures," *American History* 7 (2006): 43.
2. Mark Rathbone, "Trade Unions in the USA," *History Review,* December 2005, 1–6.
3. Yoonsoo Lee and Beth Mowry, "Union Membership," *Economic Trends,* November 9, 2007, 16–17.

Ryan Skiera and Ann Gilley

LAYOFFS AND DOWNSIZING

Layoffs or downsizings are organizational interventions used to reduce the number of employees in an organization. These are typically associated with organizational conditions such as mergers and acquisitions, declines in market positions, reduction in revenue or capital position, technology and/or industry changes, or an implementation of new organizational structures.[1]

Though layoffs and downsizings are widely practiced, many potentially damaging effects can result when an organization chooses to reduce its workforce. The process by which an organization approaches layoffs and downsizings will have a dramatic influence on its short- and long-term successes.

Methods

There are times when an organization realizes a downturn in performance calls for a reconsideration of current employee size, structure, and strategy. If layoffs/downsizings are considered, they must improve the organization's financial condition and effectiveness and not just be perceived as an easy or quick fix. Several approaches can be used to administer layoffs or downsizings. Commonly these include offering employees voluntary retirement, severance and attrition, not backfilling positions, and employee sabbaticals. These offer employees an option of leaving the organization either permanently or temporarily.

Consequences

Most layoffs and downsizing efforts occur because organizations want to attain outcomes such as lower expense ratios, increased profits and return on investments, improved stock prices, lower overhead, better communication and productivity, and enhanced efficiency.[2] These goals, however, rarely actualize and, quite often, negative consequences stem from layoffs and downsizing efforts. Evidence from long-term evaluations of downsizing efforts shows that rarely are the results for productivity improvement, enhanced profitability, or expanded global competitiveness realized.

The negative consequences associated with layoffs and downsizings can be of individual/personal, organizational, and/or community natures.[3] Results for those let go, such as displacing employees and their families and psychological and emotional damage, are likely to occur. For the employees who remain in the organizations, feelings of guilt due to being retained are common. Furthermore, reduced performance, namely in the forms of reduced creativity, increased fatigue and stress, amplified resentment toward the organization, and intense risk of aversive choices and behavior, are often unforeseen and unaddressed.[4] Additionally, employees of organizations who experience layoffs and downsizings express feelings of job insecurity, loss of stability, lowered attachment to the organization, an invalidation of the psychological contract, and a higher intent to leave.

Organizations, often through the voluntary loss of gifted members who were initially retained, experience a reduction of experience, knowledge, skills, and abilities throughout.[5] Additionally, a reduced ability to be flexible, lowered morale, and less frequent instances of organizational citizenship behavior are often experienced. Furthermore, drain on the organization's learning efforts, lower customer satisfaction levels, and damage to the organization's reputation are also unanticipated results. Finally, and likely most importantly, a decline in performance is often the most telling effect of the downsizing or layoff effort.

Layoffs and downsizings can easily result in societal or community-based negative consequences as well. Lowered levels of attachment to organizations can occur because of downsizing experience with an organization. Additionally, lack of community support and a reduction in customer willingness to continue past purchase behavior often transpire.

There are also possibilities for positive consequences because of layoffs and downsizing efforts, though there has not been the empirical linkage of these in research to date. Employees who are retained in layoff/downsizing efforts may experience opportunities for career and personal growth, job enhancement, improvements such as better communication from a flattening of the organization, greater instances of teamwork, and a broader consideration of who the organizations' constituents or stakeholders are.

Advantages of Layoffs and Downsizing

The most important advantage of layoffs and downsizing is the immediate reduction in labor costs of the company. For many organizations their highest cost is labor, which includes salaries and benefits, and these can be cut dramatically in a layoff and downsizing effort. If a firm loses some of its profitability due to an increase in costs or a decrease in market share and sales, layoffs and downsizing will have an immediate, short-term benefit of improving the bottom line. This cost reduction has the added benefit of costing very little to implement and is very easy to accomplish. Another benefit is that processes are often improved, with employees able to do more with less, when layoffs and downsizing are combined with a reengineering effort. Some organizations found that, over time, they had built redundant or inefficient processes. Organizations that have gone through a layoffs and downsizing hope to be more flexible and adaptable to fluctuations in the market.[6]

Disadvantages of Layoffs and Downsizing

Although extremely popular at one point, layoffs and downsizing have recently been viewed more unfavorably. Layoffs and downsizing by making personnel cuts across the board without process improvement may mean that the organization loses many valuable workers. Many companies that have downsized have faced increased business without having enough human resource capacity to take advantage of the upturn.[7] Employees who are left behind after a layoffs and downsizing are often demoralized and overworked, leading to burnout and survivor guilt, along with poor customer service and quality.[8] Another disadvantage of layoffs and downsizing is that job seekers may see a downsized company as less attractive, unless layoffs and downsizing were accompanied by lots of support for and communication with employees.[9] Twenty-six percent of middle managers report that their organizations are mismanaged as a result of layoffs and downsizing.[10] Despite hopes to the contrary, stock prices have not been boosted as a result of layoffs and downsizing efforts by organizations.[11]

Considerations

If downsizing is implemented, there are several processes to follow for an improved chance at achieving the desired outcomes. Several things should be considered: short-term cost savings, costs related to severance and placement services, and the expenses associated with long-term workforce rebuilding needs. Additionally, a focus on the stakeholders, both internal and external, must occur. Similarly, customers' experiences should be kept in mind. Services for those who are retained, such as those that provide emotional support and recovery, are also necessary. Communication must be a primary focus of everyone from the leader of the organization to the immediate frontline managers.[12] A focus on being honest and transparent when handling all decisions and acting with integrity and ensuring that all promises that were made are kept should be priorities.

See also Organizational Development and Change: An Overview; Organizational Design; HR Strategy; Termination; WARN Act

NOTES

1. Wayne F. Cascio, "Downsizing: What Do We Know? What Have We Learned?" *Academy of Management Executive* 7 (1993): 95–104.

2. Kenneth P. De Meuse and Mitchell Lee Marks, *Resizing the Organization* (San Francisco: John Wiley & Sons, 2003).

3. Gail T. Fairhurst, Francois Cooren, and Daniel J. Cahill, "Discursiveness, Contradiction, and Unintended Consequences in Successive Downsizings." *Management Communication Quarterly* 15 (2002): 501–40.

4. Jeffrey E. Lewin and Wesley J. Johnston, "The Impact of Downsizing and Restructuring on Organizational Competitiveness," *Competitiveness Review* 10 (2000): 45–55.

5. Ibid.

6. Tahira M. Probst, Susan M. Stewart, Melissa L. Gruys, and Bradley W. Tierney, "Productivity, Counterproductivity and Creativity: The Ups and Downs of Job Insecurity," *The British Psychological Society,* September 2007, 479–97.

7. Henry Mintzberg, "Productivity is Killing American Enterprise," *Harvard Business Review,* July–August 2007, 25.

8. Philip Cheng-Fei Tsai, Yu-Fang Yen, Liang-Chih Huang, and Ing-Chung Huang, "A Study on Motivating Employees' Learning Commitment in the Post-downsizing Era: Job Satisfaction Perspective," *Journal of World Business,* June 2007, 157–69.

9. John Kammeyer-Mueller and Hui Liao, "Workforce Reduction and Job-Seeker Attraction: Examining Job Seekers' Reactions to Firm Workforce-Reduction Policies," *Human Resource Management* Winter (2006): 585–603.

10. Michael Laff, "Middle Managers Feel Squeezed," *Training and Development,* June 2007, 20.

11. Philip Cheng-Fei Tsai, Yu-Fang Yen, Liang-Chih Huang, and Ing-Chung Huang, "A Study on Motivating Employees' Learning Commitment in the Post-downsizing Era: Job Satisfaction Perspective," *Journal of World Business,* June 2007, 157–69.

12. James R. Morris, Wayne F. Cascio, and Clifford E. Young, "Downsizing After All These Years: Questions and Answers About Who Did It, How Many Did It, and Who Benefited from It," *Organizational Dynamics* 23, no. 1 (1999): 78–87.

Anne E. Herman and Barbara A. W. Eversole

MEDIATION

Mediation is a type of alternative dispute resolution, in which a neutral third party facilitates disputes between individuals, groups, organizations, communities, or governments in order to reach a negotiated and voluntary resolution.[1] Mediation utilizes a variety of techniques to initiate and/or enhance communication between parties in a dispute. For instance, parties involved in mediation are offered the chance to discuss the issues in a dispute, identify each other's concerns, clarify misinformation or misunderstandings, and discover common ground. In general, mediation assists people to agree on a mutually acceptable resolution.[2]

Mediation is an attractive form of conflict resolution because it increases cooperation and communication, while typically being free, fair, confidential, and empowering. Mediation also saves time and money, as well as helping avoid litigation.[3] Mediation can be utilized to prevent disputes and anticipate contentious issues before they occur. In general, mediation is used to help resolve disputes involving families, divorces, estates, workplace conflicts, environmental issues, landlord/tenant conflicts, and school conflicts. In relationship to human resource management, mediation can play a central role in resolving many conflicts. The most common HR-related conflicts for which mediation is regularly employed are EEO-related grievances and collective bargaining impasses.

In fact, both the EEOC (Equal Employment Opportunity Commission) and the NLRB (National Labor Relations Board) can be viewed as mediation agencies, both with the mission of assisting in the resolution of HR-related conflicts without involving judicial proceedings whenever possible.

Principles and Techniques

Mediation is founded on principles of respect for others' views, impartiality, voluntary participation, and the authority of the mediator.[4] Typically, a mediator does not directly resolve the dispute at hand, but instead begins by informing the interested parties about the process of mediation and that he is a neutral party in the dispute. A mediator must be aware of people's personalities and any behaviors not constructive to the process of mediation. During the mediation process, a mediator facilitates a discussion which evaluates the potential impacts of various solutions on the table and then offers opportunities to refine those solutions. A typical mediation includes the following steps:
- Introduce and establish credibility of the mediator
- Introduce the participants
- Establish mediator's role of authority in the mediation process
- Establish mediator's impartiality
- Emphasize the consensual nature of the mediation process
- Review the mediation process and outlining of procedures
- Establish trust that the mediation will be confidential
- Ensure people with authority to settle the dispute are present
- Clarify parties' willingness to mediate in good faith
- Engage in bargaining and negotiation
- Reach consensus and resolution
- Gain commitment to ensure resolution takes place[5]
    See also Arbitration; Conflict Resolution; Grievance; Negotiation

NOTES

1. U.S. Equal Employment Opportunity Commission, "Facts about Mediation," United States Government, http://www.eeoc.gov/mediate/facts.html (accessed December 8, 2007).
2. Ibid.
3. Ibid.
4. Marian Roberts, *Developing the Craft of Mediation: Reflections on Theory and Practice* (London and Philadelphia: Jessica Kingsley Publishers, 2007), 94–108.
5. Sharon C. Leviton and James L. Greenstone, *Elements of Mediation* (Pacific Grove, CA: Brooks/ Cole Publishing), 22–37.

Matt Neibauer

NEGOTIATION

Whether we realize it or not, we negotiate every day. We negotiate with family and friends, co-workers, supervisors, clients, providers, competitors, and the community. Negotiation is the communication between two or more people trying to agree on conflicting interests. Negotiation is "an interaction in which people try to meet their needs or accomplish their goals by reaching agreement with others who are trying to get their own needs met."[1]

The Negotiation Process

The negotiation process is more than just the meeting itself. What leads up to the actual negotiation meeting can be an important determinant of its success. Negotiation is a five-part process; the first three parts are pre-negotiation, which sets the stage for a successful negotiation:[2]

1. Defining the Problem—How does each party define the problem? Do they share an interest in seeing it solved? Are all members of a party on the same page?
2. Producing a Commitment to a Negotiated Settlement—Is negotiating better than living with the problem? Is the other party willing to negotiate in good faith? Is a fair settlement possible?
3. Arranging Negotiations—Setting the time, location, feasibility, who will be at the table, seating arrangements, and cultural considerations.
4. The Actual Negotiation—Coming together with effective communication to seek agreement.
5. Implementation—Parties should have a stake in implementing the agreement reached. Until the agreement is successfully implemented the negotiation itself is not a success.

Approaches to Negotiating

Negotiation styles can vary. Some people are hard negotiators, some are soft, and some fall in the middle. Negotiators sometimes stay fixed on their position and try to force the other party or parties into giving them their way. This hard stance approach is sometimes referred to as zero-sum, distributive, or positional bargaining. It is characterized by forcefulness, tricking, making smaller concessions than the other and claiming they are big, trying to out think the other and wearing them down;[3] basically playing hardball. There are those that favor this model where, "Negotiation then is primarily a process of splitting the pie."[4] Hard negotiating can have its drawbacks, however, because it erodes the relationship between the negotiators, making interaction strained and future negotiations less likely. Also, hard negotiators tend to see only limited resources and solutions, and thus he best solution possible may be overlooked altogether.

Some people want to avoid conflict or repercussions and simply give in to others' demands. Parties making quick concessions and agreements that do not meet their needs characterize this soft approach. People rarely get what they want with this method of negotiation, and it can be especially devastating when the other party participating is a hard negotiator. It also can set a precedent for future negotiations that may make it harder to accomplish goals and can foster feelings of exploitation and resentment against the other party.

Both the hard and soft approaches to negotiation can produce less than optimal results. There is another way, however. This approach has been called mutual gains, integrative, or interest-based.[5] It is a way of looking at interests rather than positions, sharing information, using creative problem solving, and looking for ways to enlarge the pie. Yes, there is a benefit to trying to get other party's needs met as well as one's own.

In *Getting to Yes,* this is called "principled negotiation" and a strong argument surfaces for this type of approach.[6] The following well-known story about an orange illustrates the possible benefits. Two children both wanted an orange, but there was only one.

They fought over who should have it and each ended up with half. This was the solution of positional bargainers. Each wanted the orange; that was their position. From this standpoint only one could truly get what she wanted, so they both failed to reach their goals. This is an example of splitting the pie versus expanding the pie for all. If only these children knew to discuss interests instead of positions they would have found that each wanted a different part of the orange: One, the peel for baking, the other the flesh for eating. They could have both had what they wanted without depriving the other, but instead neither got what she really wanted or needed.

Interests and Positions

What are positions and interests? "Your position is something you have decided upon. Your interests are what caused you to so decide."[7] Identifying positions is rarely difficult, although identifying interests can be. For example, a supervisor stating, "I wish that just once you would show up on time!" surely is letting you know her position. What is behind that statement? What does she need? Perhaps a deadline is looming and she is nervous about missing it? Maybe she has been reprimanded for her staff being late? These are a few examples of what the supervisor's interests may be underlying her position.

Tips and Pitfalls in Negotiation

Looking at interests rather than positions in a negotiation is just one way to strengthen your power in finding the best solution. The following lists provide a number of suggestions for what to do and what not to do.

Tips for Successful Negotiation

- Take into account not just our own needs, but the needs of the other party.
- Look for ways to expand the pie—"create value, expand options, develop win-win outcomes."[8]
- Be aware of and respectful of cultural differences.
- Don't take it personally
- Try to see the other's point of view, put yourself in her shoes.
- Be a good listener as well as a good speaker.
- Take both short- and long-term goals into account.
- Be creative, brainstorm.
- Look at the interests behind the positions: yours and theirs.
- Try to uncover shared interests.
- Look for uncommon interests that can be dovetailed.
- Separate the people from the problem.
- Be honest.
- Look to the future, not the past
- Know your Best Alternative to a Negotiated Agreement, or BATNA.[9]

Pitfalls to Successful Negotiation

- Having overconfidence.
- Not valuing other parties' concessions.
- Focusing only on positions.
- Making assumptions.
- Being dishonest.
- Being closed-minded.

- Seeing a fixed pie.
- Being stubborn.

Conclusion

"The goal of negotiators is to improve upon available alternatives to agreement and to do so in ways that push toward efficient, mutually beneficial deals."[10] Being a successful negotiator involves many elements. There are different approaches, and negotiators may define their successes differently. In many cases though, looking at interests rather than positions, seeing the issue from the other's point of view, and generating the greatest number of possible options can point one in the right direction for a successful negotiation.

See also: Arbitration; Conflict Resolution; Mediation

NOTES

1. Bernard S. Mayer, *The Dynamics of Conflict Resolution: A Practitioner's Guide* (San Francisco, CA: Jossey-Bass, 2000).

2. J. Wm. Breslin and Jeffrey. Z. Rubin, eds., *Negotiation Theory and Practice* (Cambridge, MA: Program on Negotiation Books, Harvard Law School, 1993.)

3. Deborah M. Kolb and Linda Putnam, "Through the Looking Glass: Negotiation Theory Refracted through the Lens of Gender," in *Workplace Dispute Resolution: Directions for the Twenty-first Century,* ed. S. Gleason (East Lansing: Michigan State University Press, 1997).

4. Ibid., 253.

5. Kolb and Putnam, "Through the Looking Glass."

6. R. Fisher and W. Ury, *Getting to Yes* (New York: Penguin Books, 1991).

7. Ibid., 41.

8. Mayer, *The Dynamics of Conflict Resolution,* 145.

9. Fisher and Ury, *Getting to Yes.*

10. Kolb and Putnam, "Through the Looking Glass," 231.

Sarah E. Asmus Yackey

OMBUDSMAN

Ombudsman is a noun with an etymological origin from the Old Norse word *umboths-mathr,* meaning "commission of man." The modern definition derives its meaning from Sweden or New Zealand and represents a government official who is "appointed to receive and investigate complaints made by individuals against abuses or capricious acts of public officials, or one that investigates reported complaints (as from students or consumers), reports findings, and helps to achieve equitable settlements."[1]

The term ombudsman may have derived from a Teutonic word usage characterized by an impartial agent tasked by an "aggrieved party" to collect payment on behalf of a client of another party.[2] The idea was to use an unbiased party who was known to hold legal abilities, possess impeccable integrity, could conduct an impartial investigation without political opinion, and would be charged with the task of investigating matters involving dispute.

The use of ombudsmen began during the early 1700s when the king of Sweden, Charles XII, was in exile in the Ottoman Empire due to the defeat of the Swedish Army at the battle of Poltava. During the period Charles XII was in exile, he commissioned an ombudsman, later called the Office of the King's Chancellor, to ensure statutes and civil servants were within the prescribed parameters of the kingdom. Within a hundred years, the Swedish parliament added the position of ombudsman to its constitution.

The ombudsman concept spread to North America in the 1960s and, although the Canadian national government did not adopt the concept, ten Canadian provinces created positions. Initiatives to gain official mandated Ombudsman positions within the United States failed during the mid 1960s and early 1970s. Nassau County, New York, became the first governmental agency within the United States to create an ombudsman position in 1966. As a result of the action in New York, several states followed suit, which caused rapid growth of the concept.

The Ombudsman Today

An ombudsman has five essential traits: first, status as an officer of the legislature rather than the executive branch of government; second, political and investigative independence; third, the lack of any ability to impose any remedy; fourth, an independent power to begin investigations; and finally, the ability to provide for direct, informal, speedy, and cheap resolution of appeals.[3]

Office of the National Ombudsman

By design and regulation, the National Ombudsman is an independent, impartial and confidential agent who investigates small business complaints (and comments) in the regulatory enforcement and compliance arena.[4] The Small Business Administration of the U.S. government has a functioning National Ombudsman. The National Ombudsman is housed in Washington, DC, in the Office of the National Ombudsman (ONO), which is a subagency of the U.S. Small Business Administration. (The mission of the SBA is to ensure a fair and timely business environment for small businesses.)

The ONO works closely with the Regulatory Fairness Board to review enforcement and regulatory issues, which may have an adverse impact on the millions of small businesses within the United States. The goal of the ONO is to remove or reduce small business impediments rather than force small businesses to circumvent federal mandates, rules, and requirements.

Building partnerships with small business is the goal of the ONO, which is designed to build and foster an atmosphere and environment of partnership by improving the regulatory requirements placed on small business in the spirit of cooperation and assistance. The Office of the National Ombudsman acts promptly and thoroughly on comments received from small businesses. The ONO sees the submission of comments as an excellent opportunity to foster and maintain a sound, working relationship with small businesses. Knowledge is gained in four important areas through the receipt of small business comments: first, these allow for a timely, high-level review of small business concerns; second, these allow the ONO to evaluate their field practices; third, small business comments give the ONO an avenue to evaluate the effectiveness of regulatory requirements; and, fourth, they provide the Federal Administration and Congress with a forum to address reforms. Efforts by the Office of the National Ombudsman and small businesses have realized social and political capital, allowing each to continue working in a friendly allied environment.

Implications for Managers and HR

Within organizations, the investigation of employee complaints typically falls within the domain of the HR or legal departments. The skill set of the HR practitioner may be richer than that of the ombudsman, with far greater reach and impact when applied to all of the environments in which results are a mainstay. The most important ombudsman skill possessed by managers and HR professionals is that of an impartial mediator who seeks consensus through negotiated resolution, cooperation, and reduction of conflict. Core competencies such as essential business knowledge and skills, communications, leadership, problem solving, and political navigation facilitate stakeholder problem resolution and equip internal professionals with a well-developed tool kit that exceeds that of the typical ombudsman.

See also Arbitration; Conflict Resolution; Mediation; Negotiation

NOTES

1. Merriam-Webster, Inc., *Merriam-Webster Dictionary* (Springfield, MA: Merriam-Webster, 2007).

2. N. Nemeth, *News Ombudsmen in North America, Assessing an Experiment in Social Responsibility* (Wesport, CT: Praeger, 2003).

3. Donald C. Rowat, *The Ombudsman Plan: The Worldwide Spread of an Idea* (Lanham, MD: University Press, 1985).

4. Small Business Administration, *Fostering a More Business Friendly Regulatory Enforcement Environment, FY 2000 Report* (Washington, DC: GPO, 2001).

Dean Nelson

OUTSOURCING

Today's global economy encompasses an expanded marketplace for products and services that has forever changed the competitive landscape. Organizations have turned to outsourcing as a means to sustain a competitive advantage. The decision to outsource is a strategic one, which must take into consideration several factors.

Definition

An organization represents a buyer of raw materials, which it subsequently transforms into finished products and services for another individual, the customer. "Customers, in turn, use, consume, or transform these outputs in their own processes."[1] A buyer may contract with a supplier to purchase raw materials in the form of products and services. In this type of an arrangement, the buyer provides the supplier with specifications and instructions on how to perform the work. A buyer may also choose to outsource a process to a supplier. In this situation, the outsourcing buyer communicates the desired results but surrenders control over how the supplier or outsourcing provider achieves those results. Peter Bendor-Samuel, CEO of the Everest Group and Outsourcing Center, explains, "It is the transfer of ownership that defines outsourcing."[2]

Organizations have opted to outsource aspects of their work to achieve growth and increase efficiency in their operations. Suppliers presumably have special expertise and economies of scale in the areas of work for which they assume responsibility and are held accountable. Economies of scale are achieved when the average cost per unit of a product or service decreases as more units are produced in a large-scale operation.[3]

Location

Location must be considered when deciding to outsource a particular process or function rather than keeping it inhouse. *Offshoring* by U.S. organizations involves outsourcing overseas to India, China, and other such countries. Outsourcing offshore has been widely debated in the media as a source of concern for the loss of domestic jobs. *Nearshoring* offers offshore locations but with outsourcing providers in neighboring countries, such as Canada. This option is sometimes perceived as less risky and less politically charged.[4] Domestic outsourcing is an alternative to establishing work abroad and should not be overlooked, especially by small to midsize businesses. Rural sourcing, for example, involves setting up operations in small towns and remote regions of the country instead of in large cities at a fraction of the cost. *Onshoring* within the United States is becoming attractive also for foreign-based outsourcing providers to better meet the needs of their American counterparts.[5] The local workforce where these new facilities are located benefit from employment and specialized training opportunities.

Additional Considerations

Outsourcing became popular in the early 1990s and was spurred even further after the bust of the "dotcom" bubble in 2001 and the economic recession that followed.[6] Organizations approached outsourcing as the solution to meet growing demands for higher quality products and services at lower costs. Unfortunately, some organizations' expectations were never fully realized because of cultural differences, language barriers, time zones, and so forth. Moreover, inefficient processes were being off-loaded in the hopes that lower wages in the offshore locations would offset the additional personnel needed to resolve the problems.[7] Yet, changing locations alone did not improve performance. These trials and pitfalls were not unique to the United States, as Asia, Europe, Latin America, and other regions around the world looked to position themselves in the global economy and compete for off-shoring work. Today executives recognize the need to consider the potential advantages and disadvantages of outsourcing more carefully, and make decisions that are deliberate and strategic. A thorough analysis of existing operations should be conducted before an outsourcing location is selected to define and understand the drivers and barriers of performance and cost.[8]

Reasons to consider outsourcing are numerous and include lowering costs, increasing efficiency, expanding geographical reach, harnessing talent, and catalyzing innovation. For small and midsize businesses, many outsourcing options exist today compared to just a decade ago. Reasons for them to consider outsourcing are more compelling than ever and include access to specialists on a part-time basis, low startup costs, reduced capital requirements, and fast startup time.[9]

Organizations must make staffing decisions about who to hire and where the individuals will work. Such determinations will affect not only the organizations but also the local and national economies over time. "Labor will be the driving factor that changes outsourcing in 2008"[10] and beyond. Organizations must balance risks and benefits concerning whether an outsourcing provider, perhaps located offshore, or their own inhouse staff should have direct contact with customers. Outsourcing was once reserved for nonessential activities, but today it pertains to these and core processes alike. Core processes are those key processes that are essential to the organization's success.[11] For example, the decision to outsource a call center is a critical one that could lead to either increased effectiveness of the service or decreased customer satisfaction.

Given today's competitive environment, organizations should consider adopting a global sourcing strategy according to current and future business demands. Companies that do not embrace outsourcing may lose ground to their competitors. Executives should evaluate the big picture and develop a performance improvement program[127] which incorporates performance measures to "establish the outsourcing relationship, measure progress, and support negotiations for renewals or contract changes."[13] The partnership should be actively managed such that the outcomes are not left to chance but rather are thoughtfully considered at each stage within the aspect of the work being outsourced and are results based not process based. Outsourcing can be a useful management tool with the proper planning and management structures to support its success.

See also Competitive Advantage; HR Strategy; Staffing: An Overview

NOTES

1. Arthur R. Tenner and Irving J. DeToro, *Process Redesign: The Implementation Guide for Managers* (Reading, MA: Addison-Wesley, 1997), 59.

2. "What is outsourcing?" *OutsourcingFAQ.com,* OutsourcingCenter, An Everest Group Company, http://www.outsourcing-faq.com/1.html (accessed March 29, 2008).

3. "Economies of scale," *Dictionary.com, The American Heritage Dictionary of the English Language, Fourth Edition* (Houghton Mifflin Company, 2004), http://dictionary.reference.com/browse/economies of scale (accessed March 29, 2008).

4. Jennifer Mears, "Offshoring Closer to Home," *Network World,* March 14, 2005, http://www.networkworld.com/news/2005/031405-nearshoring.html (accessed March 29, 2008).

5. Denise Dubie, "Outsourcing Moves Closer to Home," *Network World,* November 29, 2007, http://www.networkworld.com/news/2007/112907-nearshoring.html (accessed March 29, 2008).

6. "Offshoring Work: Business Hype or the Onset of Fundamental Transformation?" *Long Range Planning* 39, no. 3 (2006): 221.

7. Geraldine Fox, "Fix and Mix Approach to Offshoring," *Network World,* February 14, 2008, http://www.networkworld.com/news/2008/021408-fix-and-mix-approach-to.html (accessed March 29, 2008).

8. Ibid.

9. Dan Twing, "10 Reasons Why Small Businesses Should Consider Outsourcing," *Network World,* July 5,2006, http://www.networkworld.com/newsletters/asp/2006/0703out1.html (accessed March 29, 2008).

Peter Bendor-Samuel, "The Two Ways Offshoring Will Change Outsourcing in 2008," Outsourcing Center. An Everest Group Company, http://www.outsourcing-journal.com/nov2007-everest.html (accessed March 29, 2008).

10. Peter Bendor-Samuel, "The Two Ways Offshoring Will Change Outsourcing in 2008," Outsourcing Center. An Everest Group Company, http://www.outsourcing-journal.com/nov2007-everest.html (accessed March 29, 2008).

Arthur R. Tenner and Irving J. DeToro, *Process Redesign: The Implementation Guide for Managers* (Reading, MA: Addison-Wesley, 1997).

11. Arthur R. Tenner and Irving J. DeToro, *Process Redesign: The Implementation Guide for Managers* (Reading, MA: Addison-Wesley, 1997).

12. Fox, "Fix and Mix Approach to Offshoring."

13. Amy Schurr, "Study Shows Buyers Less Than Enamored with Their Outsourcers," *Network World*, August 21, 2007, http://www.networkworld.com/newsletters/asp/2007/0820itlead1.html (accessed March 29, 2008).

Alina M. Waite and Lisa Scott Brinkman

OVERTIME

Overtime is the amount of time an employee works in excess of his or her normal working hours. Due to changing demographics, societal trends, and globalization, overtime is becoming an increasingly confusing issue for many organizations regardless of the number of people employed.

Overtime laws were put in place by the Federal Fair Labor Standards Act (FLSA) of 1938. This law applies to employees who work in businesses and industries that engage in or produce goods for interstate commerce, which is virtually every firm. The FLSA established the standard 40-hour workweek and mandated additional pay of 1.5 times the worker's standard rate for hours worked in excess of 40.[1]

The intent of this statute was twofold: to reward individuals who put in long hours and to increase the level of employment within the United States. Framers of the law believed that it would be cheaper for an organization to hire more workers than it would be to pay existing ones the overtime rate. Although this idea was effective in 1938, companies today are finding that it is more cost effective to pay overtime rates to existing employees than to hire additional workers and pay the associated costs of health care and other benefits.

Two classes of worker are defined by the FLSA—exempt and nonexempt. Employees who are exempt from the law, and thus not entitled to overtime pay, include independent contractors and those who are not employees of the company, outside sales people, certain agricultural, live-in, and transportation employees, and certain administrative, professional, and executive (sometimes called salaried or white-collar) employees. To be exempt, administrative, professional, and executive workers must meet varying tests of salary and duties.[2]

Implications for Managers and HR

Organizational managers and HR professionals must understand the nuances of all employment laws, including the FLSA. Several trends challenge complying with overtime laws, including the increase in telecommuting, flexible work, global markets, and technology. For example, some employees prefer comparable time off (called "comp" or "compensation" time) in lieu of overtime pay. Although many managers are sympathetic to this preference and may see this as an opportunity to save the company money, they must understand that this practice is illegal in the private sector under the FLSA. (It is legal for the public sector.) Another common attempt to save money involves managers who require that their employees work "off the clock," which occurs in a variety of ways. Employees may be prohibited from "punching in" or recording actual time worked, or they may not be paid for mandatory travel, meetings, or training. Actions such as these violate the FLSA and may subject the organization to fines and penalties (or lawsuits by disgruntled employees).

HR professionals should stay abreast of employment laws and adequately inform their company's managers and supervisors of the law, its requirements, and consequences for noncompliance. Any questions regarding overtime requirements, the classification of employees, or other tenets of overtime can be answered at the Department of Labor Web site, www.dol.gov.

NOTE

1. U.S. Department of Labor, http://www.dol.gov.
2. Ibid.

Ryan Skiera

PTO (PAID TIME OFF) BANK

Paid time off (PTO) is generally considered a part of an employer's benefits package to its employees. It is a bank of hours that employees can use for absences from work.

How PTO Works

Most PTO banks are used as a replacement to the traditional vacation, sick, and personal days and holiday employee benefits. Employers establish an accrual system for employees to earn PTO hours; these accrual systems are most often based upon hours worked or a set amount per pay cycle. Table 10.1 shows a sample PTO accrual schedule.

Once the employee has earned PTO time, he may use the PTO hours to be paid for any time away from work, such as vacation, personal illness, caring for a sick dependent, personal days, or holidays. Most employers require that use of PTO be preapproved, except in the case of unforeseen circumstances.

Special Features

Some employers choose to offer special features associated with their PTO bank benefits. These may include the ability for employees to cash out unused PTO, donate PTO hours to another employee in cases of emergency, carry over PTO hours from year to year, or to go into a negative PTO balance with the expectation that the PTO will be earned in a future pay period. These types of special features vary from company to company and must have carefully created plan documents to administer.

Advantages of PTO

Employers are recognizing that there are many advantages of offering PTO. The use of PTO systems has been increasing over the past several years. In 1998, 25 percent of employers offered PTO, whereas in 2005, 67 percent of employers offered PTO benefits.[1]

Table 10.1   Sample PTO Accrual Schedule

Years of Service	PTO Earned per Hour (in hours)	Max PTO Earned per Pay Period (in hours)	Max PTO Earned per Year (in hours)
0–5 years	0.100	8.00	208
5–10 years	0.125	10.00	260
10+ years	0.150	12.00	312

One of the biggest advantages to companies is that PTO encourages employees to schedule time off, instead of having unplanned absenteeism. Being able to use their PTO bank for more vacation days rewards employees who rarely call off work due to illness. It also provides more control to employees in how they use their time off work and is seen as a positive recruitment and retention tool.

Disadvantages of PTO

There are some disadvantages of a PTO system that human resources professionals need to understand. One financial disadvantage that companies may be concerned about is that PTO systems can potentially cost more because employees who may not have used all of their previous sick hours will use all of their PTO hours. Another disadvantage is that employees can start to view all of their PTO hours as vacation hours, and will not call in sick at times when they should stay home.

Conclusion

As more employers are choosing to offer PTO plans in lieu of the traditional time off programs, human resources professionals will need to understand how PTO plans work, and the advantages and disadvantages of these plans.

See also: Benefits, Vacation/Holiday Policy

Resources:

F. John Reh. "Sick Leave vs. Paid Time Off." *Your Guide to Management.* http://management .about.com/od/conflictres/a/SickLvPTO1104.htm (accessed September 26, 2007).

NOTE

1. Steven F. Cyboran and Thomas M. Morrison, Jr., "Paid-Time-Off Programs: Giving Employees More Control Over Leave," http://www.shrm.org/rewards/library_published/benefits/nonIC/ CMS_018373.asp (accessed September 26, 2007).

Shanan M. Mahoney

SECURITY

Security can be defined as freedom from risk or danger; safety.[1] The terms security and safety are often used interchangeably, although security means protection from intentional, even malicious acts of others. Security is, therefore, essential to a business because the people and information contained within are exclusively the responsibility of the business itself. Security risks affect information about how the business operates such as the methods for production and/or services, financial information, customer data, and physical safety and records of employees.

If company, employee, or customer information should become compromised, stolen, or tampered with, or employee safety is at risk, the consequences to the firm could be grave. For example, public and private organizations—even the government—have experienced embarrassing and financially costly losses of assets and data, including inventory, laptop computers with sensitive information, and prototypes of new products. Computer viruses and the destruction and chaos they are capable of causing are nearly legendary.

And deliberate harm to employees, customers, students, or innocent bystanders by individuals bent on revenge, notoriety, or other purposes wreak havoc on those directly or indirectly impacted and drive demands for greater security.

Security Risks

The complexity of organizational competitive environments gives rise to numerous business, regional, national, and international security risks, including the following:
- Data/information security
- Computing/IT/network security
- Theft/fraud
- Physical security
- Financial security
- Home security
- Airport security
- Resource security (for example, food, water, oil, natural gas, steel, lumber, minerals, and so on)
- Homeland/public security/national security
- International security

Security is further defined by perils, risks, and threats. A peril or risk is a cause of loss, such as a fire, earthquake, flood, or theft.[2] A threat is a means by which an event is triggered, such as by a storm, thief, or terrorist. Organizations enhance their security by engaging in "risk management," which is the process of assessing current and potential threats to security (perils, risks) and formulating plans to minimize the threats of loss.

Minimizing Losses, Maximizing Security

Organizations have many tools at their disposal to enhance security for their companies, employees, customers, and any other stakeholders. Commonly deployed strategies include:
- Internal police/security guards
- Audio and video surveillance of employee work spaces, storage facilities, retail areas, and all other business grounds/property
- Insurance
- Employee training
- Establishment of security manuals, policies, and procedures
- Digitation and networking of internal control systems
- Continuous monitoring and enhancement of computer systems to prevent "hacking"
- Rewarding security actions (and punishing violators)

Managers and HR personnel are often heavily involved in security measures, which pervade all aspects of organizational life. HR personnel draft and execute employment letters and contracts that specify terms and conditions of employment, employee confidentiality and intellectual property agreements, policies regarding sharing of employee and company information, security clearance screenings, background and reference checks, and exit interviews, to name a few. Managers and HR professionals collaborate with company security personnel to identify current or potential risks along with possible courses of action to remedy security problems.

Nothing is more important than the security of an organization's people, products, customers, and information. Proper security measures prevent information from being stolen, protect company assets, and prevent harm of employees, customers, or other stakeholders.

See also Disaster Recovery Plan; Emergency Preparedness Plan

NOTES

1. "Security," *Dictionary.com Unabridged* (v1.1) (Random House, Inc.), http://dictionary .reference.com/browse/security (accessed December 1, 2007).

2. George E. Rejda, *Principles of Risk Management and Insurance,* 10th ed. (Boston, MA: Pearson/ Addison-Wesley, 2008).

Chris Armstrong and Ann Gilley

SEPARATION AGREEMENTS

Separation agreements, also known as termination agreements or severance agreements, serve as a contract between organizations and terminated employees detailing the relinquishment of the right to sue by the employee in exchange for monetary benefit. Separation agreements are most often used when a reduction-in-force occurs due to a merger, acquisition, or economic pressures. Rarely are separation agreements provided to employees who choose to leave the organization or who are fired for cause. Advocates of separation agreements maintain that, when constructed and presented correctly, they can serve as a reflection of an organization's desire to treat its employees fairly and with dignity.[1] Additionally, separation agreements can include clauses covering noncompete and nondisparagement agreements, thereby protecting the organization against additional litigation.

Rationale for Separation Agreements

Managers and HR professionals need to maintain separation agreements as they would any other HR policy, including yearly reviews and ad-hoc updating as necessary. While terminating an employee or planning a reduction-in-force are not events that any manager or HR professional relishes, a pre-prepared agreement can reduce some concerns. Additionally, having a standard policy and separation agreement in place can shield organizations from claims of discrimination because all terminated employees will receive the same information. Finally, because a standardized policy shows an organization's commitment to fair treatment of employees, equity is promoted among employees and the organization's reputation as a fair employer is maintained in the market, which is crucial for future recruiting efforts.[2]

Legal Concerns with Using Separation Agreements

While there are no federal mandates that specifically cover the utilization of separation agreements, employers should check with legal council to ensure compliance with state laws. The Age Discrimination in Employment Act and the Older Workers Benefit Protection Act legislate that employees over the age of 40 are guaranteed a longer review period before deciding whether to sign a separation agreement. Additionally, though not directly affected, separation agreements may be considered a benefit under the Employee

Retirement Income Security Act and should therefore be treated like any other benefit, for which employees have a defined procedure for filing claims, an identified plan administrator, and an appeal procedure for denials. Finally, although separation agreements are designed to protect organizations against lawsuits, employees can not sign away their right to file charges with the Equal Employment Opportunity Commission.[3]

When preparing a separation agreement, the wording should be clear and specific enough to prevent the possibility of future claims of "ignorance" by the employee regarding its contents. Additionally, employees should not be expected to sign the agreement on the spot. Suggesting that the employee consult his own legal counsel reinforces the organization's desire to treat employees fairly. Finally, employees should not be coerced into signing the agreement. Organizations are not required to pay out the financial benefits offered in lieu of a signed agreement if the employee chooses not to sign it.

See also Age Discrimination in Employment Act; Employment Law: An Overview; Retirement; Older Workers Benefit Protection Act; Termination

NOTES

1. John L. Hines, Jr. and Michael H. Cramer, "Protecting Your Organization's Reputation against Cybersmear," *SHRM Legal Report,* December 2006, c (accessed March 9, 2008).

2. Betty Sosnin, "Orderly Departures," *HR Magazine,* November 2005,: 74–78.

3. Condon A. McGlothlen, "Voluntary Separation Programs: A Safer Approach to Downsizing," *SHRM Legal Report,* December 2006, http://www.shrm.org/hrresources/lrpt_published/CMS_007247.asp (accessed March 9, 2008).

Heather S. McMillan

SUBSTANCE ABUSE

Substance abuse is the overindulgence in or dependence on a drug or chemical that harms one's physical and/or mental health or that of others. Those who abuse substances often experience adverse social consequences, including interference with work, family and social conflicts, or legal problems. Substance abuse often leads to addiction or substance dependence, despite the negative consequences. Tolerance occurs when an individual must use a larger amount of the substance to produce the same level of feeling (intoxication). Cessation or reduction of use of a substance may cause withdrawal, which can produce a range of reactions from anxiety or depression to hallucinations and seizures.

Organizations are concerned about substance abuse by employees and the resultant negative consequences for the individual, workforce, and company. Substance abuse leads to greater conflict and violence in the workplace, more accidents, and lower productivity.

Reasons for Substance Abuse

Individuals abuse substances for numerous, complex reasons. For some, abuse of substances is an attempt to self-medicate and improve one's state of happiness or pleasure, or relieve real or perceived pain. For others, abuse of substances may have been prevalent in the home and thus is seen as normal or expected, or behaviors may have been acquired through participation in a peer group (peer pressure may or may not have been an issue).

Regardless of the reason, the cost of substance abuse borne by society is high. Treatment programs, hospitalization, crime, jails, and prisons attest to the link between substance abuse and dysfunctional behavior.

Substances

Many substances are abused by members of society, including drugs, tobacco, and alcohol. Drugs include prescription, nonprescription, and illegal forms, many of which are inexpensive and easily obtained. Marijuana, LSD, cocaine (crack, coke), heroine, methamphetamines (meth, speed, crystal), and club drugs (ecstasy, GHB, and others) are commonly abused. The symptoms of withdrawal may range widely, from confusion and headaches to aggression and stroke.

Tobacco is addictive due to nicotine, although the host of chemicals contained within cigarettes damage health. People use tobacco to relieve depression, curb hunger, lose weight, heighten attention, and so on. Smoking is responsible for the deaths of nearly half a million people each year and related to direct and indirect health care costs estimated at $100 billion per year.[1] Withdrawal symptoms include headaches, sleep disturbances, anxiety, hunger, and depression.

Alcohol, like tobacco, is relatively inexpensive and legal—and therefore readily attainable. Although often used socially or perceived as an "upper," alcohol is actually a depressant. Alcohol lessens one's inhibitions and decreases muscle control and reaction time. Symptoms of withdrawal include anxiety, anger, irregular heartbeat, sleep disturbances, and hallucinations, among others.

Company Policies on Substance Abuse

Most organizations strive to maintain healthy, productive workplaces that are free from the illegal use, possession, or distribution of alcohol or controlled substances. Recently, more and more firms have restricted the use of tobacco products as well, citing workplace environmental quality concerns and the rising cost of health care. Written policies that address substance abuse and consequences must be clear and communicated to all personnel; training of all employees (including supervisors and managers) is highly recommended. Substance abuse policies must clearly specify that employees shall not use illegal substances or abuse legal substances in a manner that impairs work performance, organizational activities, or other stakeholders (employees, customers, vendors) in any way. Employees who violate substance abuse policies must be subject to specified corrective action, up to and including treatment or dismissal under applicable company policies and labor contracts.

Compliance with Federal or State Laws

Challenges to substance abuse policies are uncommon; however, employers must be aware of the laws to which they must abide. Some states have drug testing statutes, restrict testing, or specify procedures to be followed. Some also deem that a worker injured due to serious misconduct or abuse of substances is ineligible for workers' compensation benefits.[2]

The Americans with Disabilities Act prohibits discrimination against a "qualified individual with a disability...because of his disability." This definition does not include any applicant or employee who is currently abusing drugs or alcohol. The act does permit employers to adopt and enforce drug testing and drug-free workplace policies and to prohibit employees from using illegal drugs. A "qualified individual," however, may be someone who has successfully completed a rehabilitation program or is in such a program and no longer using illegal substances.

The Federal Drug-Free Workplace Act requires that all federal contractors or grant recipients of $100,000 or more must comply with its requirements. Drug testing is not required under the law.

These are but a sampling of the issues and laws relative to substance abuse. Employers must determine which laws exist in their states.

See also Americans with Disabilities Act; Drug-Free Workplace Act of 1990; Employee Assistance Programs; Wellness Programs

NOTES

1. eMedicineHealth, http://www.emedicinehealth.com (accessed April 8, 2008).
2. U.S. Drug Enforcement Agency, http://www.dea.gov (accessed April 8, 2008).

Ann Gilley

SUGGESTION SYSTEMS

A suggestion system process enables employees to voice concerns, make recommendations, or submit ideas regarding company processes, procedures, new ideas, working conditions, and benefits. A suggestion system is a traditional form of employee involvement. Recently they have shown amazing staying power, transitioning from "the box on the wall" to continuous improvement models, and further onto innovation and idea management systems involving wider areas such as creativity, innovation, employee communication, employee involvement, employee motivation, and ideas to improving customer service and to changing culture. Suggestion systems have many benefits, and companies can design a system that fits their culture and ties to company goals.

Benefits of Employee Suggestion Systems

"Companies that set up effective suggestion systems are finding that employees have ideas that can lower costs, increase revenues, improve efficiency, or produce greater quality," said Charles Martin, author of *Employee Suggestion Systems: Boosting Productivity and Profits.* For instance, a study of 47 companies with nearly 450,000 employees showed that employee ideas saved the organizations more than $624 million in 2003, according to the Employee Involvement Association (EIA), a Dayton, Ohio, based organization of professional managers of employment involvement programs. Companies that set up suggestion systems are also seeing an increase in teamwork as employees work together to submit an idea. In addition, employees begin to think more like managers, looking beyond the scope of their own jobs.

Essential Elements of an Employee Suggestion Program

For suggestion systems to be effective, seven key elements should be in place: senior management support, a simple, easy process for submitting suggestions, a consistent process for evaluating and implementing suggestions, a communication strategy for informing employees of the system and publicizing employee recognition, champions to sustain the system, a fair and motivating reward structure, and a program focused on key organizational goals.

For a suggestion system to be effective, senior management needs to support the system, have a say in the program's focus, and participate in the recognition. Senior management involvement can start with the appointment of an executive sponsor of the program who will be responsible for providing updates in executive meetings, and who can assure the appropriate approvals are being considered.[1]

Submitting ideas is easy with technology. Many companies have a link on their Web site to a form that employees can complete. If the company does not have a Web site or the program is being implemented in a single function of a company, the form can be distributed to the employees and submitted through email. If the program is through email, companies may need to have a box as well if employees want to remain anonymous.

A consistent process for evaluating and implementing the system is critical. Companies can create an evaluation committee and an implementation committee. Both committees should report to the executive sponsor and have a lead overseeing each committee. The committees usually consist of managers and an HR representative. In addition, the implementation committee should have a project manager on the team to ensure any new process identified through the suggestion system is created and completed.

A communication strategy is needed to inform employees about the system and to publicize employee recognition. Communication of the program and recognition can be covered in emails, posted on the company Website or in the newsletter, and announced in team meetings and town halls. In addition, some companies innovate by creating a catchy title for the program and providing employees information in a brochure or a company trinket.

Many suggestion systems are perceived poorly by employees because companies have not created a sustainable system. Having a fresh set of eyes can keep the program alive. This can be accomplished by monitoring the program to ensure it still meets the company's goals. Many companies utilize HR for this process. Rotating committee members and the executive sponsor annually, offering a 30-day special reward for a short-term lift, and asking employees for suggestions all contribute to a successful and well-received system.

Companies tend to be hesitant to start suggestion systems because of the cost. For a program to be fair and motivating it does not need to be expensive. Some companies do reward employees monetarily but many companies focus on the recognition and provide employees with a small gift, gift certificate, shirts with the company logo, or recognize the employee in the company newsletter.

Tying the program to organization goals has many benefits. The program supports the culture the company is creating; it can improve customer service and engage employees in the overall mission and vision of the company.

Suggestion programs are undergoing a new round of revitalization as more companies are looking for ways to involve and engage their employees. When companies truly value receiving input from employees on a regular basis, suggestion system programs are successful and companies have clear and valuable results to show for it.

See also Continuous Improvement Plan; Productivity Improvement Plan

NOTE

1. Susan J. Wells, "From Ideas to Results, To Get the Most from Your Company's Suggestion System, Move Ideas up the Ladder through a Formal Process," *SHRM F Whitepaper,* February 2005.

Cyndi Stewart

SURVEILLANCE

Surveillance is defined as "systematic ongoing collection, collation, and analysis of data and the timely dissemination of information to those who need to know so that action can be taken."[1] Surveillance is important as it allows for protection of a business, its employees, and its customers. In addition, surveillance can assist management to ensure work is being performed properly and in a timely manner.

Surveillance may occur via simple, low-technology methods such as observation or inspection, or via more sophisticated technology, including:

• Telephone tapping
• Eavesdropping or "bugs"
• Closed-circuit television or miniature cameras
• Directional microphones
• GPS tracking
• Electronic tagging
• Internet and computer monitoring
• Aircraft or satellite

Although surveillance is prevalent in our society and cannot be completely avoided, some question the methods or rationale used to support employee monitoring. Challenges to privacy rights surface when employees are uncomfortable with workplace monitoring, commonly as it relates to Internet and email privacy. Recent court rulings, however, have determined that employees should have no expectation of privacy when using employer email, computers, or other equipment. Federal and state laws do prohibit certain surveillance techniques; for example, the monitoring of telephone calls is prohibited without informing both parties (unless one has a warrant), and some states prohibit or regulate "bugs" and/or other surveillance devices. Further, employees do have a reasonable expectation of privacy in such places as locker rooms and bathrooms.

Benefits of Surveillance

Surveillance can protect a business, its employees, and its customers. A business utilizes surveillance to prevent theft, leakage of sensitive information, harassment and discrimination, and vandalism. If a person decides to steal money, information, or other assets, a video monitoring system will identify the individual or individuals responsible for the theft. Acts of vandalism or destruction of company property are also less likely to happen.

Surveillance systems protect employees from multiple harms, including workplace violence or hostility, harassment, false accusations, or injuries. Customers benefit when surveillance decreases shoplifting or stock shrinkage (due to internal or vendor theft) and keeps the cost of goods down. Customers also benefit when they are protected from false accusations (such as for breakage of stock or shoplifting) or injury while on the company's premises with no one nearby to assist—the chance of the patron being seen is improved because people monitoring the surveillance system are more apt to notice strange behavior. This will assist in customer safety as it will speed up the response time to a medically related incident.

Management Tool

A growing number of organizations are monitoring their employees' and customers' activities due to the low cost of modern technology. Surveillance can be a useful and effective management tool to ensure that work is being performed by the employees accurately and on time, to observe the efficiency (or lack thereof) of processes, and to document work actions. With the use of surveillance, managers have proof that their employees were not performing their duties to an acceptable extent. This information can then be shared with the employees and appropriate positive or corrective action taken.

Implications for Managers and HR

Organizations have a responsibility to maintain healthy, productive work environments for all of their members. One tool useful in protecting the company, its employees, and customers is surveillance. Managers already use their powers of observation to monitor employees, and the use of computer/Internet monitoring is commonplace. HR personnel should inform managers of legal and illegal monitoring methods, keep them apprised of changes in the law pertaining to surveillance, and clarify for all employees the responsibilities, benefits, and consequences of all surveillance.

Conclusion

Surveillance is important to businesses, their employees, and customers to ensure safety, enhance processes, protect information and assets, maintain customer satisfaction, and prevent theft. Surveillance can be used as an effective management tool by ensuring that employees are performing their duties, documenting malfunctions in processes, and reducing workplace violence. Managers and HR personnel are challenged to incorporate surveillance strategically while complying with applicable federal and state laws.

See also: Privacy Rights

NOTE

1. Glossary, "Managing Effective Risk Response: An Ecological Approach (MERREA)," http://www.merrea.org/glossary%20s.htm (accessed November 29, 2007).

Chris Armstrong

TELECOMMUTING

Commuting from the bedroom to the office and drinking morning coffee in pajamas sounds very appealing to today's workforce. In recent years, telecommuting has become second only to salary as the best way for attracting potential employees. In fact, according to a survey of 1,400 CFOs conducted by Robert Half International, 33 percent said telecommuting was *the* leading attraction.[1]

Telecommuting is defined as a work arrangement whereby employees for an organization or self-employed workers benefit from the flexibility in both working location and hours. Telework is a broader term that refers to the telecommunications aspect of working from a remote location, communicating via Internet, telephone, and so on. This allows for the employee to work from home, from a client's office, or on the road. As technology progresses, the need for organizations to house employees in a stationary work environment decreases. In fact, an increasingly popular motto is, "Work is something you do, not something you travel to."[2]

The Telework Movement

Coined in 1973 by physicist and engineer Jack Nilles, telecommuting or telework, began in the 1970s when mainframe computers paved the way for the first usage of telephone lines as a "network bridge."[3] Since then, telecommuting has gained popularity in the technological corporate community and increasingly in most government entities for federal employees as well.

The Evolution

Nilles, often referred to as the "father of telecommuting," published the first book on telecommuting in 1976,[4] outlining the benefits of telework as it relates to management and development in corporate America. With advances in technology, telecommuting increased. In fact, there were 4 million teleworkers in the United States alone in 1995[5] as compared to 19.6 million in 1999 and 44.4 million in 2004.[6] Therefore, as technology continues to advance, more people may find themselves in a virtual office environment over the traditional office in the future.

Future of Telework

Telecommuting has found a niche in some of the more traditional jobs, which includes data entry, word processing, and the accounting fields. However, more industries are finding that the virtual office can accommodate a wide range of occupations in various industries such as legal, medical, and engineering. As organizations evolve, so will the job market and the need to expand outside of the traditional office environment. According to John Edwards, president of the International Telework Association and Council, some areas in the country could have a telecommuting population as high as 60 percent in the near future.[7]

Telecommuting—Solution or Liability?

As the idea of telecommuting grows, many organizations are faced with deciding whether to join the proverbial bandwagon. How much of a cost savings is it? Will productivity increase or decrease? There are both pros and cons in allowing employees to work outside of the office, which have been analyzed and demystified.

The Virtual Office

When an employee telecommutes, generally there is a place in the home from which he or she can set up a computer and work. In doing this, the organization's overhead is reduced, which, in turn, reduces the need for office space. Both the employee and employer benefit from this situation as the employee is able to write off his/her work expenses and the employer is able to decrease overhead costs. Although there may be additional technological costs for the telecommuter, cost and availability of private networks, high-speed Internet, and so on have become quite reasonable in recent years.

The Accidental Employee

Teleworkers have flexibility compared to traditional office workers and increased productivity because of it. In fact, telecommuting employees are often 20 to 25 percent more productive than the traditional office worker and save employers an average of 63 percent on absenteeism.[8]

One of the disadvantages, however, is that fewer promotions may occur due to lack of visibility in a telecommuting role. Employers can easily take on an "out-of-sight, out-of-mind" mentality since their employees are not seen in the day-to-day operations. Therefore, it is important for teleworkers to effectively communicate using email, telephone, and so on, to exhibit a regular presence in the organization. Effective communication may also cut down on whether or not the teleworker feels social isolation as well.

For some teleworkers, another communication disadvantage is the increase in work load. Since most managers supervise their workers by observation and not by specific objectives, a noticeable increase in work can take place. This causes the teleworker to feel *more* overworked as a telecommuter than in a traditional office.[9]

Another communication issue having a negative impact on the teleworker is adapting to corporate culture. Although apparent in a traditional work environment, culture may be difficult for teleworkers to embrace due to the distance factor and lack of camaraderie with other employees. Therefore, it is management's responsibility for modifying this so they too can acclimatize within the organization.

Big-picture Effects

A recent measure introduced by Senators Ted Stevens and Mary Landrieu is called the Telework Enhancement Act of 2007.[10] This legislation aids in the decrease of pollution caused by commuter traffic, thus reducing greenhouse gas emissions and dependency on oil. In fact, not only is it "green" to telecommute, but there are tax incentives to telecommuting as well. Senator Rick Santorum introduced a tax break with the Telework Tax Inventive bill in June 2005. The introduction of the Parents' Tax Relief Act of 2007 by Senator Sam Brownback and Representative Lee Terry would establish a telecommuting tax credit for parents who telecommute at least 40 percent of the time.[11]

Confidentiality

Although decentralizing information has grown in recent years with the increase of technology, information shared within an organization still needs to follow strict protocol. Teleworkers usually have company data on their personal PCs or laptops, thus increasing the risk for data loss, compromising data integrity, and losing organizational control over the information. This also needs consideration prior to setting up an employee for telecommuting.

NOTES

1. The Telework Coalition, "Telework Facts," Washington, DC, http://www.telcoa.org/id33_m.htm (accessed July 2, 2007).

2. Woody Leonhard, *The Underground Guide to Telecommuting* (Reading, MA: Addison-Wesley, 1995)

3. Jack M. Niles, *Managing Telework: Strategies for Managing the Virtual Workplace* (New York: John Wiley & Sons, 1998).

4. Jack M. Niles, *The Telecommunications-Transportation Tradeoff: Options for Tomorrow* (New York: John Wiley & Sons, 1976).

5. The Telework Coalition, "Telework Facts," Washington, DC.

6. Katharine Hansen, "Making Your Case for Telecommuting: How to Convince the Boss," *Quintessential Careers,* http://www.quintcareers.com/telecommuting_options.html (accessed June 25, 2007).

7. Hope Deutscher, "Working from Home is Becoming a Trend," Prairie Public, http://www.prairiepublic.org/features/ebusiness/future/telecommuting.html (accessed June 25, 2007).

8. The Telework Coalition, "Telework Facts," Washington, DC.

9. The Telework Coalition, "Telework Facts," Washington, DC.

10. U.S. Senator Ted Stevens, "Senators Stevens and Landrieu Introduce Legislation to Promote 'Telework' for Federal Employees," http://stevens.senate.gov/public/index.cfm?FuseAction =NewsRoom.PressReleases&ContentRecord (accessed June 25, 2007).

11. Kristin Durbin, "Terry Introduces Parents' Tax Relief Act," Congressman Lee Terry, http://leeterry.house.gov/Article_Details.aspx?NewsID=1443 (accessed June 25, 2007).

Nicole Brown

TEMPORARY/SEASONAL EMPLOYEES

Many firms utilize a mix of full-time, part-time, temporary, seasonal, and contract workers to fulfill their long- and short-term staffing needs. A temporary/seasonal employee is a worker hired for a specific duration of time. Temporary workers are temporary employees that can work a specified duration of time, given local and state laws. Seasonal employees are workers that are hired for the duration necessary to perform during certain seasons, such as the autumn apple harvest.

Seasonal Employees

Seasonal employees are used in companies whose business fluctuates or is not stable throughout the whole year. Industries for seasonal work can vary from agriculture and entertainment to manufacturing and service. There are times in the year when food cannot be produced, theme parks are closed for the winter, or when a manufactured product will not sell (for example, a snow plow service is of little value in the summer). As such, different industries have seasonal employees on whom they rely during peak times, yet do not employ certain workers when demand is nonexistent.

Temporary Employees

An employee is considered a temporary worker if he or she is employed by a temporary employment agency and is placed in a temporary job at another company's work site. The work might be overseen by a supervisor from either the host company or the temporary agency.[1] Temporary workers are valuable when short-term projects or one-time projects are being undertaken by the company as it eases the workload of other employees or avoids hiring more full-time employees.

Costs and Benefits

Organizations derive numerous benefits from hiring temporary employees, including greater flexibility, cost savings, and the ability to engage and fully prescreen potential permanent workers. Firms commonly use temporary employees during peak times, for short-term projects, and to fill temporary vacancies. Employees who work on temporary assignments also enjoy greater flexibility, varied work engagements, the potential to learn new skills, and the ability to investigate the desirability of a potential permanent employer.

While hiring temporary workers may save a firm money, some studies show that the cost of hiring temporary workers is just slightly less or about the same as compared to hiring a full-time worker. Of the amount of wages paid, the temporary employee receives only a portion of what is charged by the agency to the host firm. The overage is markup over wages paid to cover the agency's administrative costs. Markups vary depending on the assignment, job specialty, experience required, and other special requirements as stipulated by the company. Markups can range anywhere from 25 percent to over 100 percent.[2] It is important to perform a cost/benefit analysis to determine whether temporary workers or full-time workers are preferred. Also, while benefits do not have to be paid to temporary workers, the questions of quality and reliability must be considered.

Legal Issues Involving Temporary Workers

Confusion sometimes arises as to whether a temporary worker is an independent contractor or a temporary worker. The IRS' test for determining a worker's employment status is called the "common law test." Three areas are used to determine how much control an employer has over an employee. The areas are behavioral control on the job, financial control, and the relationship with the employee.[3] The more control the employer has over an employee, the better the chance the employee is a temporary worker and not an independent contractor. Independent contractors have more freedom in how they perform their job duties and have more say in the amount they receive for duties performed, but often have to purchase their own supplies and work in their own manner.[4]

Conclusion

Seasonal employees work part of the year as their services are needed, while temporary employees work for a specified duration. Both seasonal and temporary workers benefit employers that need to fill talent gaps for the short-term, such as when a company has a one-time project or expects seasonal demand to peak. The additional cost of hiring temporary or seasonal employees must be considered and balanced in contrast to hiring additional full-time employees who may be more qualified or reliable.

See also Independent Contractor

NOTES

1. "Temporary Employees—Know Your Rights," Equal Rights Advocates, http://www.equalrights.org/publications/kyr/temporary.asp (accessed April 10, 2008).

2. "The Cost of Temporary Workers," AllBusiness, http://citationmachine.net/index.php?reqstyleid=2&reqsrcid=39&mode=form&more= (accessed April 11, 2008).

3. "Independent Contractors," IEEE, http://www.ieee.org/portal/pages/services/financial/tax/independentcontractors.html (accessed April 11, 2008).

4. "Independent Contractor—Pros of Working as an Independent Contractor," About.com, http://jobsearchtech.about.com/od/jobs/l/aa083099_2.htm (accessed April 11, 2008).

Chris Armstrong

TERMINATION

Terminations, the ending of employment relationships, present real challenges for human resource professionals and frontline managers. Whether the ending of the employment relationship is due to an economically motivated reduction in force, as is often the case for layoffs or downsizing, or "for cause" (based on specific performance deficits), careful attention to the protocols followed can make a difference in the impacts of termination on individuals and organizations.

Terminations during Layoffs or Downsizing

The way in which the reduction is done impacts the amount of bitterness or dissatisfaction felt both by the laid-off workers and survivors. Giving advance notice of downsizing can help reduce negative reactions. Providing outplacement programs for downsized workers is relatively common. A downsizing effort may be received more positively if an employer has attempted other alternatives such as worksharing, instituting a hiring freeze, or offering early retirement packages. When terminating a group of employees particular attention should be paid to potential adverse impacts on protected groups. For instance, does the layoff or downsizing impact older workers disproportionately? Failure to pay attention to the differential impacts on particular employee groups can lead to legal claims against the former employer.

When it comes to implementing a layoff, some commonsense guidelines can help. Here are some "dos:" (1) give as much warning as possible (and in the case of large layoffs legal protections such as WARN Act may apply), (2) if possible, deliver the termination information in a brief meeting in a private office or conference room, (3) provide information about any benefits associated with severance, (4) express appreciation for the individual's contributions, (5) control your emotions, and (6) encourage the employee to move forward in a positive direction.[1]

Involuntary Termination

Involuntary terminations take place for a number of reasons, such as poor performance, violation of organizational policies or procedures, absence, tardiness, or insubordination. While technically termination may be permissible for nearly any reason under employment-at-will conditions, a number of negative consequences can emerge for individuals and organizations if terminations are handled poorly.

A sound performance management system is a key to employee development and organizational success; if done well, it also lays the foundation for dealing with terminations if the need arises. Such a system has several characteristics including clear job expectations, ongoing supervisory feedback on job performance, regular formal performance appraisals which include goal setting for future performance and growth, and a well-designed and administered progressive discipline system.

Progressive discipline systems provide a series of steps designed to address and improve employee performance deficits. Typical steps in such systems include (1) oral counseling, (2) oral warning, (3) written warnings, (4) suspension or demotion, (5) final written warning and/or last chance meeting, and (6) termination.[2] By carefully following such a protocol the employee receives guidance and a time frame for improvement. The process also holds employees accountable and establishes plans for performance improvement.[3] Sound record keeping is imperative, since many claims are made against former employers each year, frequently resulting in lawsuits.[4] Careful documentation of performance appraisals and any disciplinary actions helps assure fair treatment of individuals while protecting the organization.

The Termination Process

There are many suggestions offered for how to proceed with terminations. In general the process should include careful preparation, a termination meeting, the exit process, and post-termination follow up.[5] Good preparation includes being current on state, federal, and local laws related to involuntary terminations. Preparation may also include an investigation that is thorough, complete, and well documented.[6] This can include a review of relevant disciplinary records, examination of all documentation, and a comparison with discipline used in similar situations in the past. Depending on the cause for termination, the investigation may include interviews with parties familiar with the situation. In many cases the decision to terminate follows a careful progressive discipline process as described earlier.

The termination meeting should adhere to five guidelines:

1. Present the situation clearly and concisely, without making excuses.
2. Avoid debates because this is not the time to have arguments about past performance.
3. Treat the employee with dignity and respect.
4. Show empathy but do not compromise.
5. Describe next steps.[7]

Next steps can include provision of a letter indicating any severance, benefits, or outplacement information. In cases where there are significant concerns about security, company officials may make arrangements for the employee's personal materials to be packed and given to the worker directly after the termination meeting.

Post-termination activities can include updating personnel files, documenting any agreements, and a review of job descriptions and workplace policies. This is done to determine if there are improvements that could be made in terms of hiring and performance management that could improve future staffing and organizational performance. Depending on the nature of the termination the employer may also administer ongoing insurance benefits.[8]

Claims of Wrongful Termination

A terminated employee may make a number of claims against a former employer. These may include claims of constructive discharge, retaliatory discharge, or coerced retirement.[9] Constructive discharge can cover a wide variety of complaints, often linked to perceived unfair labor practices, discrimination, or violation of the Americans with Disabilities Act. Such a claim may also occur if an employee is forced out of a job with an ultimatum to resign or face an unpleasant consequence such as intolerable working conditions, demotion, or reassignment.[10] Some courts have held that constructive discharge takes place if a reasonable person in the employee's place would have felt pressured to resign. A former employee may claim retaliatory discharge if he feels that he was punished for engaging in a protected activity, which can include opposing unlawful employer practices, filing a discrimination charge, or testifying, participating in or assisting in an investigation against an employer in situations such as those involving workers' compensation, OSHA, or unemployment compensation. Former employees may also claim that they were coerced to take retirement if demotion or dismissal were the other options provided. The former employee may seek to prove he was coerced due to age considerations. In addition to adhering to quality performance management approaches mentioned earlier, employers should carefully examine which workers (especially those in protected classes) will be impacted in a reduction, obtain valid waivers and releases, and in all cases treat workers, remaining or departing, with dignity.[11]

Conclusion

A sound performance management system is the foundation to both avoid unneeded terminations, and for protection of the worker and employer if termination occurs. Whether termination is for cause or is part of a layoff or downsizing, careful planning, clear communication, and purposeful follow-up are guidelines for handling these situations professionally and ethically.

See also Downsizings; Disciplinary Procedures; Documentation; Employment-at-Will; Separation Agreement; WARN Act; Wrongful Termination/Discharge

NOTES

1. *The SHRM Learning System: An Educational Resource for Today's HR Professional, Module Three: Staffing* (Alexandria, VA: Society for Human Resource Management, 1999), 74.

2. H. John Bernardin, *Human Resource Management: An Experiential Approach,* 4th ed. (New York: McGraw-Hill Irwin, 2007), 315; and Jane Gould, *The Fairness Factor: How to Manage Employee Termination to Minimize Legal Liability,* Film and Leader's Guide (Carlsbad, CA: CRM Films, 1998), 6.

3. Paul Falcone, "Employee Separations: Layoffs vs. Terminations for Cause," *HR Magazine,* October 2000, 189.

4. Paul Falcone, "A Blueprint for Progressive Discipline and Terminations," *HR Focus,* August 2000, 4.

5. Wendy Bliss and Gene Thornton, *The Employment Termination Source Book: A Collection of Practical Samples* (Alexandria, VA: Society for Human Resource Management, 2006), 5.

6. Francis T. Coleman, "Cardinal Rules of Termination," SHRM Legal Report, July 1995, reviewed June 2006, http://www.shrm.org/hrresources/lrpt_published/CMS_000943.asp.

7. Wayne F. Cascio. *Managing Human Resources: Productivity, Quality of Work Life, Profits,* 7th ed. (Boston, McGraw-Hill Irwin, 2006), 563–64.

8. H. John Bernardin, *Human Resource Management: An Experiential Approach,* 4th ed. (New York: McGraw-Hill Irwin, 2007), 319.

9. *The SHRM Learning System: An Educational Resource for Today's HR Professional, Module Three: Staffing,* 76.

10. Robert J. Paul and Kathryn Seebeger, "Constructive Discharge: When Quitting Constitutes Illegal Termination," *Review of Business,* Spring 2002, 23.

11. *The SHRM Learning System: An Educational Resource for Today's HR Professional, Module Three: Staffing,* 76.

Dave O'Connell

TRADE SECRETS (INTELLECTUAL PROPERTY)

Trade secrets and intellectual property, often termed proprietary information, are the terms used for the company specific information that is considered confidential or that may give the organization a competitive edge. Proprietary information defines the level of confidentiality that is given to a document or information of value to an organization. When a document or organizational information is termed "proprietary," the intent is to limit who can view it or become familiar with the contents. It further implies that the information is a "trade secret" or vital to the success of the organization's competitive edge.

According to the World Intellectual Property Organization, intellectual property are those items that are creations of the mind, or inventions, literary and artistic works, symbols, names, images, and designs used in commerce.[1] In a business setting, this may include such items as blueprints, product recipes, designs, formulas, financial information, research and development products, manufacturing information, or other such related information.

While technology has brought many innovations to the business world, it has also created a myriad of concerns. One of the major concerns is that of employee privacy and intellectual property rights. As computer attacks occur worldwide, one of the most severe security concerns is that of employee data confidentiality and the liability associated with the organization in the event of a security breach.[2] Additionally, protecting intellectual property is even more vital with today's emerging technology and research developments. Organizations are developing electronic communication policies that clearly define permitted electronic activities, use of employer computer systems, and the monitoring of email. Many organizations have banned the use of cellular cameras and instant messaging on computers due to the risk of intellectual property theft, and to prevent the intrusion of a virus or Trojan attack on the organization's computer network system.

The Economic Espionage Act of 1996

The Economic Espionage Act of 1996 (18 USC 1831–39) states that "trade secrets are all forms and types of financial, business, scientific, technical, economic or engineering information, including patterns, plans, compilations, program devices, formulas, designs, prototypes, methods, techniques, processes, procedures, programs, or codes, whether tangible or intangible, and whether or how they are stored, compiled, or memorialized physically, electronically, graphically, photographically, or in writing if:

- The owner thereof has taken reasonable measures to keep such information secret, and;
- The information derives independent economic value, actual or potential, from not being generally known to, and not being readily ascertainable through proper means by the public."[3]

There is no single or definitive standard used by an organization to discern what is proprietary or what may not be considered as proprietary, as it will vary by industry or organizational type. An organization that seeks to protect any information considered to be proprietary or a trade secret needs to have an economic value attached for the loss of this information, and therefore must take appropriate steps to maintain the confidentiality. The consideration of value must be instilled in the event that any legal recourse may be required in the event that proprietary information may be lost or disclosed. Organizations often require their employees sign noncompetition or proprietary information agreements to prevent employees from disclosing certain information during their employment, and to prevent them from disclosing information should they terminate employment. The organization can take further precautions by limiting employee access to computer files, maintaining secure areas where sensitive information is stored, and limiting visitor access to premises or certain areas within the facility. The Economic Espionage Act of 1996 is the first federal act dealing with the theft of trade secrets, which imposes severe penalties for stealing and disseminating trade secrets from an organization.

Licensing and Franchising

While expansion of the organization is always a desirable concept, there is the added concern of intellectual property and/or trade secret loss. Additional care is required to protect that intellectual property that is being shared, particularly for recipes, formulas, trademarks, brand names, methods, procedures, and the like. Both licensing and franchising are special arrangements in which the parent organization is required to provide technical information and assistance; however, the franchisee or licensee is obliged to use the rights responsibly and to additionally protect that intellectual property or information being shared.[3] Thus, sound written contracts and agreements must be put in place to bind the partnering organization to the parent organization in equal responsibility to protect intellectual property, trade secrets, and "proprietary information."

NOTES

1. World Intellectual Property Organization, "What Is Intellectual Property?" (n. d.), http://www.wipo.int/about-ip/en/.

2. H. John Bernardin, *Human Resource Management: An Experiential Approach,* 4th ed. (Boston: McGraw-Hill, Irwin, 2007).

3. Texas A&M Research Foundation, "Proprietary Information and Trade Secrets" (n. d.), http://rf-web.tamu.edu/security/secguide/S2unclas/Propriet.htm.

Frank E. Armstrong

TRAVEL

Traveling, in relation to business, encompasses the travel of employees from their home to work, employees moving around inside the company from one workstation or site to another, or going to a different business in which the employer either purchases or supplies products and/or services or travels to clients. Aside from the daily commute, traveling from one location to another requires a travel policy with clear details, enabling an employee a fair understanding of what company money is allocated to certain expenses for him to eat and sleep in a different location. Traveling, however, can occur inside a company itself, if the building is large enough or has multiple sites. Understanding the importance, relevance, and issues that ensue during travel will ensure that business operations progress smoothly.

Traveling to and from Work

For a business to operate, it must have employees perform job duties upon a daily basis on the designated days of operation. As such, the employees have to travel to and from work. The time spent traveling to and from work is not compensable, because the employee is not performing an essential job function by traveling to work. But upon arrival and situating himself, he is then capable of performing essential job functions and therefore must be paid for duties performed.

Travel Inside the Workplace

There are instances when employees will need to travel around the workplace. While the travel time may range from under a minute to multiple minutes, this time adds up in the scope of a year, which is money paid for travel time. This time is compensable as it may be required in the employee's job duty to travel from one station to another to perform his functions. However, it is to be noted that in some instances where it would appear that an employee should not be compensated, he is entitled to compensation. For instance, in the case of *IBP v. Alvarez,* a lawsuit was filed in which the workers were not getting paid for putting on and taking off their protective clothing. As was found by the Ninth Circuit and affirmed by the Supreme Court, time spent donning and removing the protective clothing essential to performing their job duties was compensable time.[1] This is enforceable under the Fair Labor Standards Act (FLSA Section 4) and by the Portal-to-Portal Act.[2] Not all time spent preparing for work is compensable, however. For example, if a particular uniform is available at work but not necessary to be worn to perform essential job functions, the individual is then not entitled to compensation pay for the time it takes him or her to put on the uniform. If any uncertainty exists as to whether or not the individual is to be compensated, it is best to use caution and pay the individual and research the laws for future reference.

Travel Policies

Some employees might be required to travel to other locations or other companies. As such, a company must have a travel policy established. When the decision is made to send an employee to another location, a travel budget must be made and approved. The considerations to be planned for involve method of travel, traveling time, lodging expenses, and dining and miscellaneous expenses allocation. Having a detailed expense policy will not only save the company money but will also help avoid confusion that the employee might have on how to spend the company's money.[3]

Conclusion

Overall, there are different applications of travel and while some traveling on behalf of the employee is not compensable, some travel is; the daily commute to and from work is not compensable, but time spent preparing for work in the workplace might be, depending upon the work. Thus, it is best for HR professionals to research and understand the laws regarding these issues. The more detailed and developed a travel policy is will result in less confusion and better accountability of expenses.

Resources:
"Travel," *Dictionary.com Unabridged (v1.1),* Random House, Inc.,http://dictionary.reference.com/browse/travel (accessed December 13, 2007).

Chris Armstrong

NOTES

1. David Walsh, *Employment Law for Human Resource Practice* (Mason, OH: Thompson Higher Education, 2007).
2. Charles Mataya, "Supremes Clarify Portal-to-Portal Act?" FindLaw for Legal Professionals, http://library.findlaw.com/2005/Dec/21/241505.html (accessed January 3, 2008).
3. "Developing a Travel Policy," AllBusiness, http://www.allbusiness.com/accounting-reporting/expenses-expense-accounts/1368-1.html (accessed April 2, 2008).

WORK ELIGIBILITY

Work eligibility provisions are in place to protect employees, whether they are United States (U.S.) workers or immigrant workers, from discrimination in hiring and firing practices based on national origin.[1] The provisions make sure that workers are able to earn the same wages regardless of their work status. According to the Immigration and Nationality Act, "Employers may hire only persons who may legally work in the United States (e.g., citizens and nationals of the U.S.) and aliens authorized to work in the U.S.[2] It is illegal for employers to knowingly employ workers who are not eligible to work in the United States.

Prevailing Wages

The United States' economy is not static as workers will continue to work for prevailing wages. The Department of Labor has established minimum wage requirements that cover a majority of workers who are not otherwise exempt.[3] The implications for not having some type of work eligibility are lower wages for all employees and higher unemployment for U.S. workers as jobs would be given to those illegal workers who are willing to work for lower wages.

Documentation and Rules for Workers

Employers are required to keep employment records on each employee, which include wages, time sheets, and verification of employment eligibility with an I-9 form and copies of the verifying documentation. Documents that can be used to show work eligibility include the following documents that show both the worker's identity and eligibility to work in the United States:

> U.S. Passport; Permanent Resident Card or Alien Registration Receipt Card (form I-551); an unexpired foreign passport with a temporary I-551 stamp; an unexpired Employment Authorization Documentation that contains a photograph of the person; or an unexpired foreign passport with an Arrival-Departure Record. If documents are not available that establish both the eligibility and identity of an employee there is a list of documents that establish the identity of a worker which include: Driver's license or ID card issued by a state; School ID card with photograph; voter's registration card; U.S. military card; Military dependent's ID card; U.S. Coast Guard Merchant Mariner card; Native American tribal document; Driver's license issued by a Canadian government authority; or approved documents for workers under the age of 18 and one of the following documents which verify employment eligibility including: U.S. Social Security card; Certification of Birth Abroad issued by the Department of State; original or certified copy of birth certificate; Native American tribal document; U.S.

Citizen ID card; ID card for use of Resident Citizen of the U.S. (Form I-179); or an unexpired document of employment authorization issued by DHS.[4]

The penalty to the organization for not having a completed and retained I-9 form is not less than $100 or more than $1,000 for each individual employee not in compliance.

Rules and regulations regarding work eligibility and the verification of seasonal or temporary foreign workers remains in flux with new rules being implemented continuously as economic pressures require. In February 2008, the U.S. Department of Homeland Security proposed a set of rule modifications that would increase the number of days that a foreign worker could stay in the United States after completing his current employment and decrease the number of days that workers would have to remain out of the country prior to reentry for temporary employment.[5]

Compliance Assistance

The U.S. Department of Justice has established the "Office of Special Counsel for Immigration Related Unfair Employment Practices" for the protection of the rights of all workers, U.S. citizens, and legal immigrants. This office investigates complaints from employees who think that they have been unfairly discriminated against and provides dispute resolution assistance and a community educational outreach component.[6]

NOTES

1. U.S. Department of Labor, http://www.dol.gov/compliance/guide/aw.htm#who (accessed February 16, 2008).

2. Ibid.

3. Fair Labor Standards Act of 138 (FLSA) as amended, http://www.dol.gov/compliance/guide/minwage.htm#who (accessed February 22, 2008).

4. Form I-9 Employment Eligibility Verification, http://www.uscis.gov/files/form/i-9.pdf (accessed February 16, 2007).

5. U.S. Homeland Security, "DHS Proposes Changes to Improve H-2A Temporary Agricultural Worker Program," http://www.dhs.gov/xnews/releases/pr_1202308094416.shtm (accessed February 16, 2008).

6. Office of Special Counsel for Immigration Related Unfair Employment Practices, U.S. Department of Justice, http://www.justice.gov/crt/activity.html#osc (accessed February 16, 2008).

Debora A. Montgomery-Colbert

Part V
Checklists and Tools

Contents

Change Management
    Change Audit
    Identifying Barriers to Change
    Responding to Change
    Comprehensive Model for Change
    Create an Environment of Change
    Myths and Realities of Change
    Popular Change Models
    Why Change Initiatives Fail

Strategy
    SWOT Analysis
    Problem-Solving Model
    Planning for Conflict and Resistance
    Strategic Planning
    Sample Vision, Mission, Goals
    S.M.A.R.T. (w). Criteria for Developing Goals
    Using the Balanced Scorecard
    Systemic Strategic HR Alignment
    Traditional HR vs. Strategic HR
    A Model for Contemporary HR Success

Performance
    Sample 360-Feedback Form
    Evaluation Problems—Halo and Horn Effects
    Concerns About Performance Appraisals
    Developmental Evaluations
    Developmental Appraisal Form
    Performance Growth and Development Plan
    Coaching
    Providing Performance Feedback
    Common Errors in Performance Evaluation
    Evolution of Leadership

Communications/Planning
    Creating a Strategic Communications Plan
    Summary of Effective Communication Techniques
    Assessment of Communication Effectiveness
    Disaster Planning
    Costs of a Disaster Protection/Business Continuity Plan
    Employee Safety Checklist
    Emergency Supplies Checklist

HR Practice
    Recognition and Reward Strategies
    Illegal/Legal Interview Questions
    Ineffective/Effective Interview Questions
    Major HRM Laws
    Designing Jobs
    Preparing for an Overseas Assignment
    Facilitating Effective Meetings
    New Employee Checklist
    Resignation/Termination Checklist
    Employee Exit Interview Form
    Death of an Employee
    Keys to Managing Sexual Harassment
    Major Motivators of Employing Internal vs. External Recruitment

Change Management

Change Audit

I. Historical Perspective of Change

In the past, what was the **culture** of the organization with respect to change (e.g., resistant, noncommittal, aggressive, successful, inconsistent, etc.)?

What types of change have occurred?

____Small (e.g., changes in policy, procedures, etc.)
____Moderate (e.g., new product, competitive challenges)
____Large-scale (e.g., merger, acquisition)

Specifically, describe the change initiatives:

Who was responsible for leading and implementing the change(s)?

Why was this particular person responsible?

When did the change effort occur?

How was the change implemented?
What were the **barriers** to change within the firm (e.g., culture, poor management, lack of/poor communications, insufficient resources, etc.)?

What were the results? Define based on
• Congruence with organizational goals, mission, and vision
• Impact on people
• Impact on processes/efficiency/service
• Impact on profitability
• Evidence that the changes were adopted and are now part of the daily workings of the firm
What would have been necessary for the change to have been (more) successful?

II. Current State of Readiness for Change

What is the current culture of the organization with respect to change (e.g., resistant, noncommittal, aggressive, successful, inconsistent, etc.)?

Is the firm in the midst of any current change(s)? If so, describe:

What types of change are occurring?

____Small (changes in policy, procedures, etc)
____Moderate (new product, competitive challenges)
____Large-scale (merger, acquisition)

Specifically describe the change initiatives:

Who is responsible for leading and implementing the change(s)?

Why is this particular person responsible?

How is the change being implemented?

Describe the level of **willingness** of people to change.
- Do they recognize the need to change?
- What is the level of predisposition (or resistance) to change?

Describe the ability of people within the organization to change based on their
- Knowledge of change
- Change skills
- Resilience

What barriers to change exist within the organization? Typical barriers include:
- Policies, procedures
- Organizational apathy or overconfidence
- Dysfunctional culture
- Poor leadership/management
- Insufficient resources
- Lack of rewards or consequences
- Etc.

What will be necessary for the change to be successful?

III. Action Plan

What must happen for change to occur successfully? How can willingness be enhanced? How can the gaps in ability be lessened? How can barriers be reduced or eliminated?

Describe the desired outcome of the change. How will we measure results? Define based on
- Congruence with organizational goals, mission, and vision
- Impact on people
- Impact on processes/efficiency/service
- Impact on profitability
- Evidence that the changes were adopted and are now part of the daily workings of the firm

Who should lead the change(s) and why? Who else must be involved?

How should the change be implemented? What is the timeframe?

What resources are needed?

How can we overcome the barriers to change?

How should we celebrate our successes?

Source: Ann Gilley, *Manager as Change Leader* (Westport, CT: Praeger, 2005).

Identifying Barriers to Change

List the most common barriers to change within your organization. Barriers occur at all levels and within all people. Identify the cause or source, and develop a strategy to address it. Common barriers include: lack of leadership; lack of organizational support; dysfunctional culture; poor communications; lack of information about the change; cumbersome policies/procedures; lack of rewards or consequences.

Barrier	Cause/Source	Strategy to Overcome

Source: Adapted from Ann Gilley, *Manager as Change Leader* (Westport, CT: Praeger, 2005).

Responding to Change

1. Identify the words and behaviors that reveal individuals' emotions and perceptions regarding an impending change.
2. Develop strategies to help individuals work through their issues and toward successful change (communication, involvement, and support are essential).

Words/Behaviors	Perception of Change	Strategy to Move Forward
"Don't worry, it won't happen." "This doesn't affect me."	Denial	Communications, information
"I hate this." "They can't make me."	Resistance	Communications, feedback, information, support, training
"I'll try it." "This might work."	Exploration	Support, communication, rewards
"I like this." "It's about time." "This works."	Commitment	Recognition, rewards, feedback

Source: Adapted from discussions by Cynthia D. Scott and D.T. Jaffe, "Survive and Thrive in Times of Change," *Training and Development Journal* 42, no. 4 (1988): 25–27.

Comprehensive Model for Change

1. Recognize that change is immensely complex; nonlinear.
2. Understand individual and organizational responses (resistance) to change, and how to deal with these responses.
3. Create a culture that supports change.
4. Establish a vision for change.
5. Build a guiding coalition for the change.
6. "Sell" the change to all levels of the organization; help individuals understand that the change is necessary, urgent; teach that change is good, desirable.
7. Remove barriers to action.
8. Involve employees at all levels in the change process (including planning, implementation, monitoring, and rewarding).
9. Communicate proficiently; solicit input and share information with those impacted by the change.
10. Prepare for and plan responses to resistance; treat resistance to change as an opportunity; understand that resistance is a symptom of a deeper problem (e.g., poor management or strategy, ineffective communication, etc.).
11. Deal with employees and their reactions individually, not as a group.
12. Execute the change in small increments.
13. Constantly monitor progress of the change initiative and refine/adjust as needed.
14. Reward individuals and groups for engaging in change.
15. Celebrate short- and long-term wins.
16. Solidify the change in the newly emerged culture.

Source: Ann Gilley, *Manager as Change Leader* (Praeger, 2005).

Create an Environment of Change

What	How
Hire individuals with a predisposition to change and high tolerance for ambiguity.	
Enhance your own change skills.	
Encourage and reward innovation, creativity, and risk-taking.	
Do not micromanage; be a resource, coach, partner, and guide.	
Identify and remove barriers to change.	
Fight for resources.	
Allow failure and encourage people to learn from their mistakes.	
Trust your people—and make certain they know it.	
Involve people at all levels in change.	
Engage in change frequently and incrementally.	
Promote the benefits of change and help people to see change as an opportunity.	
Help individuals assess how change will benefit them personally.	
Encourage people to work through change together.	
Provide forums for discussion; actively seek and act on feedback.	
Celebrate small victories and milestones.	
Reward those who change, both individually and in groups.	
Other:	
Other:	

Source: Ann Gilley, *Manager as Change Leader* (Westport, CT: Praeger, 2005).

Myths and Realities of Change

Myth of Change	Reality of Change
Organizations are rationally functioning systems that adjust strategically to changing conditions.	Organizations operate irrationally (because they're composed of people) and are wired to protect the status quo.
Employees operate in the best interests of the organization.	People act in their own best interests, often seeking to preserve or enhance number one. Further, they only want to know what's in it for them.
Individuals engage in change because of its merits.	Most people engage in change to avoid unnecessary difficulties or personal pain.
Change can occur without creating conflict in the system.	By definition, change upsets the current state and will always create some degree of conflict. Effective change management understands, allows, and prepares for conflict. Institutions are often unrealistic about the amount of conflict that occurs as a result of change, and naively expect change to be accepted wholeheartedly by employees.
Successful long-term change can be accomplished through short-term leadership.	Short-term leadership typically lacks the commitment and long-term foresight necessary to make change last—in essence, they don't have to live with the consequences of their decisions.
Change is easy.	Rarely. In fact, effective change processes are quite complex, as are the individuals required to embrace change.
Change is always good.	Not always. Change is often ill-conceived or poorly planned. Further, most institutions do not refer to their guiding principles and values when initiating change, but rather are reacting to external pressures such as changing regulations or the need for greater revenue.
Conflict is always bad.	Not always. A certain amount of conflict can be healthy, particularly when it acts as a catalyst for positive change.
Leadership/management always wants change while only employees resist.	Quite the contrary. Leaders have their own preferences and agendas, which don't always align with the proposed change.
People must be *forced* to accept change.	Although many fear change, the fault usually lies with management's failure to properly communicate the reasons for and benefits of change. Well-planned and communicated change may have advocates at all levels within the firm.
People opt to be architects of the change affecting them.	Most individuals do not participate in a pro-active manner in initiating change, preferring instead to be its victims.

Source: Ann Gilley, *Manager as Change Leader* (Westport, CT: Praeger, 2005).

Popular Change Models

Step	Lewin's Model	Gilley's 7-step Model	Ulrich's 7-step Model	Kotter's 8-step Model
1	Unfreeze	Communicate the Urgency for Change	Lead Change	Establish a Sense of Urgency
2	Movement	Provide Leadership	Create a Shared Need	Form a Powerful Guiding Coalition
3	Refreeze	Create Ownership and Support	Shape a Vision	Create a Vision
4		Create a Shared Vision	Mobilize Commitment	Communicate the Vision
5		Implement and Manage Change	Change Systems and Structures	Empower Others to Act on the Vision
6		Integrate Change into the Culture	Monitor Progress	Plan for and Create Short-term Wins
7		Measure and Monitor Change	Make Change Last	Consolidate Improvements and Produce Still More Change
8				Institutionalize New Approaches

Source: Adapted from Jerry W. Gilley and Ann Gilley, *Strategically Integrated HRD* (Cambridge, MA: Perseus Publishing, 2003); John Kotter, *Leading Change* (Boston: Harvard Business School Press, 1996); Kurt Lewin, *Field Theory in Social Sciences* (New York: Harper, 1951); and David Ulrich, *Human Resource Champions* (Boston: Harvard Business School Press, 1998).

Why Change Initiatives Fail

1. The change is ill-conceived.
2. No one is in charge of facilitating and managing the change initiative.
3. The change initiative plan lacks structure.
4. The change initiative plan lacks details.
5. The change initiative is under-budgeted.
6. Only the change initiative team is interested in the end result.
7. Insufficient resources are allocated to facilitate and manage the change initiative.
8. The change initiative is not tracked against its project plan.

9. The change initiative team is not communicating.
10. The change initiative strays from its original goals.
11. The change initiative is a solution in search of a problem.

Source: Adapted from Ann Gilley, *Manager as Change Leader* (Westport: CT: Preager, 2005).

Strategy

SWOT Analysis

Strengths and weaknesses are internal, and over which an organization has control. Opportunities and threats are external to an organization, yet create conditions to which a response may be required.

Strengths—list positives that the organization controls related to quality of products, company reputation and goodwill, research and development, leadership and workforce talent, facilities, processes, internal policies, customer service levels, customer satisfaction, distribution channels, technology, and so on.

Weaknesses—list negatives within the company's control, such as poor leadership/management, dysfunctional culture, policies, procedures, or processes, product quality issues, ineffective marketing or distribution, outdated technology, facilities, or equipment, financial position, and so forth.

Opportunities—list conditions beyond the organization's control that may positively impact the business, such as the economy, legislative environment, weather or natural disasters, war, consumer trends, changes in competitors' positions, global pressures, etc.

Threats—list conditions beyond the organization's control that may negatively impact the business such as the economy, legislative environment, weather or natural disasters, war, consumer trends, changes in competitors' positions, global pressures, etc.

Problem-Solving Model

1. **Findings:** Gather evidence (facts, data, statistics) regarding the problem, opportunity, or situation. Evidence in the form of quantifiable and qualifiable data will be housed in historical documents (company annual reports, department/division reports, human resource files) as well as with members of the organization (via observations, interviews, focus groups, and so forth).
2. **Problem(s) or Opportunity(ies):** Thorough analysis of the findings should reveal a problem(s) to be solved or opportunity(ies) to be pursued. Identify true causes of problems or opportunities, not merely symptoms.
3. **Alternatives** (to solve the problem or capitalize on the opportunity): Identify multiple alternative means by which to approach the problem or opportunity. The first alternative is always "no change." For each alternative, thoroughly assess its viability by determining the costs, benefits, pros, cons, timeframe, and viability (realistic assessment).
4. **Recommendation(s):** Following a thorough evaluation of alternatives, a recommendation(s) should logically flow.

Source: Adapted from Ann Gilley, *Manager as Change Leader* (Westport, CT: Praeger, 2005).

Planning for Conflict and Resistance

___Understand that conflict and resistance are natural human responses to change.

___Make no assumptions that "everyone is on board."

___Recognize that conflict can be healthy—it is not always negative.

___Resistance is a symptom of an underlying root cause; it provides an opportunity to address questions, concerns, and problems associated with change.

___Involve others in developing solutions to conflict and resistance.

___Discuss the potential for conflict or resistance with those who will be impacted by the change by asking, "How will this change impact you?" "What conflict(s) do you think will occur?" "How can we resolve the conflict?" "What will you as an individual need to work through this change?"

___Plan to share information in a timely, substantive fashion. Resistance is often the result of insufficient information regarding the impending change.

___Communicate in ways that meet individuals' needs (e.g., face-to-face, in writing, via e-mail, etc.).

___Change, resistance, and conflict are very personal. Treat people as unique.

___Share your feelings and strategies for overcoming your own resistance or conflicts.

___Encourage others to resolve their own interpersonal conflicts.

___Know when to intervene in others' conflicts and when to back off.

___Help create "win-win" situations; that is, benefits for all parties.

___Reward individuals and groups for resolving conflicts or overcoming resistance.

Source: Adapted from Ann Gilley, *Manager as Change Leader* (Westport, CT: Praeger, 2005).

Strategic Planning

1. Invite employees at all levels to contribute to the process.
2. Determine the strengths, weaknesses, opportunities, and threats (SWOT) of an organization via internal and external environmental analysis.
3. Identify organizational values and guiding principles.
4. Develop the organization's ideal vision.
5. Create the organization's mission.
6. Establish supporting organizational goals and objectives.
7. Develop action plans to achieve goals and objectives.
8. Locate places within the organization where readiness for change is acute.
9. Identify and enlist key organizational players to motivate action.
10. Establish a formal feedback system that gathers immediate reactions from decision-makers and employees.
11. Implement strategic plans in a timely, efficient manner.
12. Conduct formative and summative evaluations to determine the overall success of the strategic plan.
13. Recognize and reward employees appropriately.

Sample Vision, Mission, Goals

A vision statement broadly conveys the organization's desire to be the best, usually in one sentence, and drives the mission. A mission statement identifies stakeholders while supporting the vision. Goals and objectives specify how the organization will serve its stakeholders and achieve its mission (and, ultimately, vision).

Vision: To be the nation's leading provider of X.

Mission: To provide our employees with a healthy work environment, our customers with a quality product, our shareholders with a fair rate of return, and our community with a responsible employer.

Goals: Increase revenues to $1.5 million this year
Bring three new products to market this year
Reduce employee turnover to 5 percent
Reduce workplace accidents by 10 percent
Provide an 11 percent rate of return to our shareholders
Donate 2 percent of profits to local charities/the community

S.M.A.R.T. (w). Criteria for Developing Goals

Specific—Strategic goals that are well-defined and clear.
Measurable—Every strategic goal must be quantifiable—measured in some way (e.g., number/quantity, quality, time, percentage, and cost).
Agreed Upon—Members of the organization must agree on the strategic goals, which enhances buy-in and support.
Realistic—Goals must be attainable given the resources and time available. Unrealistic goals are demotivating, which is a precursor to frustration and failure.
Timely—All strategic goals must be tied to a timetable (e.g., six months, this fiscal year, December 31) to ensure their completion.
Written—All strategic goals should be documented to record desired outcomes. Written goals communicate importance of and commitment to their completion.

Source: Adapted from Jerry W. Gilley and Ann Gilley, *Strategically Integrated HRD* (Cambridge, MA: Perseus Publishing, 2003).

Using the Balanced Scorecard

The balanced scorecard is a strategic management tool that measures performance and links an organization's strategic objectives to certain comprehensive indicators. The balanced scorecard measures four key "hard" and "soft" perspectives, thus reflecting a more accurate "balance" than just financial measures. The four categories measured are:
— Financial (e.g., profitability, growth, and return on assets reflected by gross margins, sales, cash flows, revenue growth, cost reductions, working capital, etc.)
— Customer (e.g., customer acquisition, satisfaction, and retention as revealed by customer service, customer satisfaction, number of complaints, response time, market share, quality, etc.)
— Internal (e.g., improved core competencies, technologies, processes and morale as reflected by development/lead/cycle times, efficiency, reduction in waste, employee morale and suggestions, sales per employee, etc.)
— Innovation and learning (e.g., continuous improvement, new product development, and employee growth and development as reflected by number of new products brought to market, employee training hours, learning of strategic skills, ability to change, alignment of individual and organizational goals, etc.)

Using a balanced scorecard requires

1. Refining corporate strategy, key objective, and critical success factors.

2. Determining what to measure (financial, customer, internal, and/or innovation/learning).
3. Creating a plan to measure strategic, goals, and success factors.
4. Implementing the plan (involve, communicate, implement, monitor).
5. Share results regularly (e.g., daily, weekly, monthly, quarterly).
6. Use the results to improve performance.
7. Review and revise the plan.

Source: Adapted from: Robert S. Kaplan and David P. Norton, *The Balanced Scorecard: Translating Strategy into Action* (Boston: Harvard Business School Press, 1996); Robert S. Kaplan and David P. Norton, *The Strategy-focused Organization: How Balanced Scorecard Companies Thrive in the New Business Environment* (Boston: Harvard Business School Press, 2000).

Systemic Strategic HR Alignment

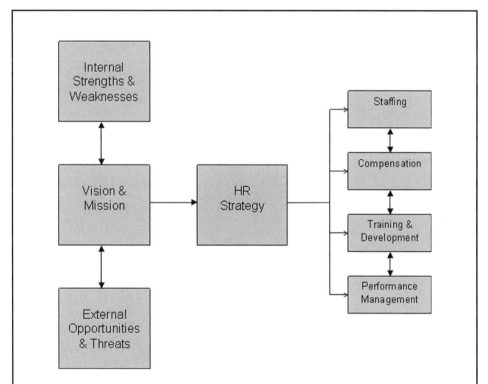

HR strategy must be designed and developed to reinforce the overall strategic vision and mission of the firm. This HR strategy is then reinforced via intentionally designed and implemented HR practices, which in turn are interdependent. That is, the Performance Management process reinforces the achievement of tasks in line with the firm's overarching strategic goals, and such achievements are then rewarded via the Compensation process. Significant shortfalls surfaced via the Performance Management process are addressed via subsequent Training and Development initiatives at both an individual employee and enterprise-wide level, or via Staffing through the hiring of external talent.

Source: Adapted from Jeffrey A. Mello, *Strategic Human Resource Management* (Mason, OH: Thomson South-Western, 2006), 171.

Traditional HR vs. Strategic HR

Traditional HR	Strategic HR
Personnel Administration	Human Capital Management
Specialist HR Roles	Generalist HR Roles
Compliance Focus	Business Focus
Support Function	Strategic Driver
Cost Center	Investment Center
Centralized Control of HR	Shared Ownership of HR
Transaction Focus	Value-Added Focus

Source: Adapted from Jeffrey A. Mello, *Strategic Human Resource Management* (Mason, OH: Thomson South-Western, 2006), 165.

A Model for Contemporary HR Success

Contemporary HR professionals must first establish credibility as a Business Partner to their client groups. This involves understanding both then ongoing and immediate business challenges of the groups. Once this understanding is developed the HR professional has earned the right to employ their HR expertise as an HR Consultant for their client groups, adding value in addressing the business challenges via HR practices. Lastly, after demonstrating a track record of value-added success, the HR professional can begin operating as a Change Leader, assertively advocating for necessary change within their client groups.

Performance

Sample 360-Feedback Form

Performance Assessment

Employee _____   Date _____
Supervisor _____

Indicate your relationship to the individual you are rating:

☐ Self
☐ Manager
☐ Colleague/peer
☐ Direct report (I am evaluating my manager)
☐ Internal customer (I am evaluating a colleague outside of my department)
☐ External customer
☐ Other

You have been identified by the person being rated in this evaluation as someone who can provide valuable input to the employee on his/her performance. Your responses will remain anonymous; only composite information will be provided to the employee. Please return this form to _____(supervisor)_____ by _____(date)_____.

How well does this person perform this competency? Please use the following scale for your evaluation. N is appropriate when you are unfamiliar with behavior in certain areas:

(5) **Exceptional**—This individual consistently exceeds behavior and skills expectations in this area.

(4) **High**—This individual meets most and exceeds some of the behavior and skills expectations in this area.

(3) **Meets**—This individual meets a majority of the behavior and skills expectations in this area for this job. There is generally a positive perspective toward responsibilities.

(2) **Low**—This individual meets some behavior and skills expectations in this area but sometimes falls short.

(1) **Poor**—This individual consistently fails to reach behavior and skills expectations in this area.

(N)—**"Not applicable"** or **"Not observed"**

Customer Service

Treats customers like business partners   N 1 2 3 4 5

Presents ideas simply and clearly   N 1 2 3 4 5

Listens actively to internal and external customers   N 1 2 3 4 5

Solicits and provides constructive and honest feedback   N 1 2 3 4 5

Keeps others informed   N 1 2 3 4 5

Balances requests with business requirements   N 1 2 3 4 5

Responds to appropriate needs of customers   N 1 2 3 4 5

Comments: _____

_____

_____

Teamwork

Supports team goals   N 1 2 3 4 5

Puts interest of team ahead of self   N 1 2 3 4 5

Builds consensus and shares relevant information   N 1 2 3 4 5

Builds and maintains productive working relationships   N 1 2 3 4 5

Treats others fairly   N 1 2 3 4 5

Actively seeks involvement/uses input from people   N 1 2 3 4 5
with different perspectives

Recognizes and respects the contributions and needs   N 1 2 3 4 5
of each individual

Comments: _____

_____

_____

Business and Individual Skills

Demonstrates broad business knowledge and skills   N 1 2 3 4 5

Acts to add value to the business   N 1 2 3 4 5

Recognizes problems and identifies underlying causes   N 1 2 3 4 5

Makes timely decisions   N 1 2 3 4 5

Coaches and develops others   N 1 2 3 4 5

Is trustworthy, open, and honest   N 1 2 3 4 5

Visualizes the present and future, and develops strategies to get there   N 1 2 3 4 5

Comments: _____
_____
_____

Professional and Technical Knowledge

Demonstrates professional/technical expertise   N 1 2 3 4 5

Shares expertise with others   N 1 2 3 4 5

Organizes work   N 1 2 3 4 5

Acts dependably to get things done right the first time   N 1 2 3 4 5

Improves existing processes and/or introduces new methods   N 1 2 3 4 5

Actively increases personal skills, knowledge, and technical base   N 1 2 3 4 5

Motivates others to achieve results through example and encouragement   N 1 2 3 4 5

Comments: _____
_____
_____

Manages Resources

Takes initiative to make things happen   N 1 2 3 4 5

Takes informed, calculated risks   N 1 2 3 4 5

Makes well-reasoned, timely decisions   N 1 2 3 4 5

Follows through to deliver results   N 1 2 3 4 5

Uses resources efficiently   N 1 2 3 4 5

Communicates a clear direction   N 1 2 3 4 5

Anticipates and prepares for change   N 1 2 3 4 5

Comments: _____
_____
_____

Overall comments regarding this individual and his/her performance/behavior: _____
_____
_____
_____

Evaluation Problems—Halo and Horn Effects

The **horn** and **halo** effects occur when a supervisor provides an overly favorable or harsh evaluation of an employee. Both biases may be overcome by:
• Conducting frequent/multiple evaluations throughout the year
• Involving a third party to evaluate the employee
• Having the employee complete a self-evaluation
• Using multi-rater (360-degree) feedback

The **halo effect** occurs when one overrates an employee, which occurs due to:
• *Recency*—allowing a recent positive event to distort judgment of the individual's entire performance
• *Blind spot effect*—overlooking performance deficiencies because the organization leader likes the employee for some reason
• *Compatibility*—overlooking negative performance because an individual is easy to work with, has a pleasing manner, or highly desired personality
• *Previous outstanding performance*—previous success overshadows current performance
• *Similar to me*—rating a person highly due to perceived similarities to oneself
• *Favoritism*—allowing poor performance to be overshadowed by qualities the organization leader personally finds appealing in the employee
• *Overemphasis*—giving too much weight to one outstanding factor, good or bad
• *No-complaint bias*—an average individual has received no negative criticisms or complaints (e.g., no news is good news)
• *One-asset person*—certain characteristics such as advanced degrees or impressive appearance may be ranked higher than work performance

- *High-potential effect*—persons who *could* achieve or accomplish a great deal are given undue consideration
- *Leniency*—some evaluators fail to adequately address poor performance by being too "forgiving"

The **horn effect** is the opposite of the halo effect and occurs when one rates an employee lower than circumstances justify, and occurs due to:

- *Recency*—allowing a recent negative event or poor performance to distort judgment of ones entire work
- *Grouping* (tarnishing or whitewashing)—painting all employees in a work group with the same perceptional brush
- *Prejudice*—allowing good performance to be overshadowed by an individual's traits or qualities that the organization leader finds unattractive
- *Guilt by association*—employees are prejudged due to the company they keep
- *Dramatic incident effect*—one recent mistake or poor performance offsets the entire year's achievements
- *Difficult employee effect*—irritating, contrary, or opposite personality characteristics overshadow actual performance
- *Maverick effect*—the nonconformist may be downgraded because he or she is different
- *Weak team effect*—exemplary performance may be downplayed because the individual belongs to an underachieving work group
- *Unrealistic expectations effect*—expectations that are too high are brought about by the evaluator's perfectionism
- *Personality trait effect*—faculty or staff members exhibit certain personality traits considered inappropriate
- *Self-comparison effect*—bias due to differentiation in the way the supervisor perceives a job should be carried out

Source: Adapted from Jerry W. Gilley and Ann Gilley, *Strategically Integrated HRD* (Cambridge, MA: Perseus Publishing, 2003).

Concerns about Performance Appraisals

Both managers and employees have concerns about performance appraisals, which should be addressed prior to the discussion.

Managers' Concerns

1. What is the employee doing well or need to improve?
2. What can I do to support my employee in his/her quest to improve?
3. How should I share negative information?
4. How will the employee respond?
5. How do I follow up with my employee to ensure improvement?
6. What is the best way to evaluate his/her work?
7. What changes are likely to occur in the organization in the months ahead that might impact this employee, his or her job, and performance?
8. How can I adequately reward/recognize my employee for change, improvement, and/or exemplary performance?

Employees' Concerns

1. How am I doing?

2. What is my raise?
3. How qualified is my supervisor to evaluate me and my performance?
4. What can I do to improve?
5. How will I be punished if I don't improve?
6. Do I have a chance for advancement?
7. What will be expected of me prior to my next performance appraisal?
8. How can my work be evaluated during this time?
9. What kind of help or attention can I expect from my performance coaches or supervisor?
10. What changes are likely to occur within the organization that affect my job and/or performance in the months ahead, and how will they affect me?

Developmental Evaluations

Developmental evaluations focus on improving employee performance. The Developmental Appraisal Form reviews goals and performance for the past period, while the Performance Growth and Development Plan looks to the future. To conduct a developmental evaluation:

1. Gather employee performance data.
2. Compare performance results with performance standards and expectations.
3. Share observations and opinions with the employee that includes perceptions of her strengths and weaknesses, record of performance, and abilities and attitudes toward performance activities.
4. Allow the employee to contribute and respond to manager's critiques.
5. Discuss manager and employee differences.
6. Discuss development opportunities that will enhance the employee's skills and abilities.
7. Identify, isolate, and eliminate performance interference.
8. Create a growth and development plan based on the employee's strengths.
9. Identify performance consequences that will motivate the employee to engage and produce at an acceptable or exemplary level.

Source: Adapted from Jerry W. Gilley and Ann Maycunich, *Beyond the Learning Organization* (Cambridge, MA: Perseus Publishing, 2000).

Developmental Appraisal Form

Employee _____   Date _____

Supervisor _____   For the period from _____ to_____

Goal for the Past Period	Accomplishment(s)	Shortfall(s)
1.		
2.		
3.		

Employee Signature _____   Date _____

Supervisor Signature _____

Source: Adapted from Jerry W. Gilley and Ann Maycunich, *Beyond the Learning Organization* (Cambridge, MA: Perseus Publishing, 2000).

Performance Growth and Development Plan

Employee _____ Date _____

Supervisor _____ For the period from _____ to_____

Goal	Completion Date	Supervisor Support/ Resources/Date
1.		
2.		
3.		

Date of follow-up/next meeting _____

Employee Signature _____ Date _____

Supervisor Signature _____

Source: Adapted from Jerry W. Gilley and Ann Maycunich, *Beyond the Learning Organization* (Cambridge, MA: Perseus Publishing, 2000).

Coaching

Benefits of Coaching to...		
Individuals	**Managers**	**Organizations**
Better relationship with manager	Better relationship with employees	Fewer complaints, grievances, lawsuits
Self-esteem	Understanding of employees' strengths & weaknesses	Better communication among all levels
Job satisfaction	Motivated, productive workforce	Capacity, productivity, resilience, and superior results
Advancement/career opportunities	Superior results through their people	Enhanced collaboration, teamwork, and competitiveness
Individualized attention	Enhanced interpersonal and managerial skills	Improved culture and work environment
Treatment as a unique being	Opportunities to serve personnel	Organizational learning
Personal and professional growth and development	Career opportunities	Competitive advantage through people

Source: Jerry W. Gilley and Ann Gilley, *The Manager as Coach* (Westport: CT: Preager, 2007).

Providing Performance Feedback

1. Provide timely feedback, immediately after the event if possible.
2. Use the "+" "−" "+" rule, which means start with brief positive feedback, address the negative, and end on a positive note. For example, "...your work is typically of high quality (+)..., however, your recent interactions with certain colleagues has caused conflict that has hindered team performance and must be addressed (−)..., I'm confident in your ability to... (+)."
3. Tell the employee exactly what was done incorrectly and the resulting consequences.
4. Offer tangible evidence of the poor performance.
5. Allow the employee to respond to feedback; listen to the employee's response and pay attention to his or her nonverbal behavior.
6. Describe the appropriate performance that the employee must demonstrate, which may include exact steps to be followed, changes to be made, or means by which to enhance quality.
7. Provide examples of ways to improve performance and ask for the employee's ideas.
8. Identify the skills and/or knowledge necessary to improve performance.
9. Communicate to the employee the penalties and consequences of poor performance (discipline, suspension, termination, etc.) and the reward for adequate or exemplary work.
10. Make sure the employee understands it is his responsibility to correct performance and that he is accountable for solving of the performance problem.
11. Express your confidence in the employee's skills and ability to improve.

Source: Adapted from: Jerry W. Gilley and Ann Gilley, *Strategically Integrated HRD* (Cambridge, MA: Perseus Publishing, 2003)

Common Errors in Performance Evaluation

Type of Error	How to Correct
Bias/stereotyping—showing partiality or prejudice due to preconceived opinions and/or attitudes regarding a person or group.	Training of evaluators; provide evaluation guidelines; employee self-evaluation Forced ranking or distribution technique; employee self-evaluation
Central tendency—avoids high and low ratings; ranks all employees as average.	Forced ranking or distribution technique; employee self-evaluation
Halo effect—consistently overrates employees due to overemphasis of a single positive trait, skill, or behavior.	Use multi-rater (e.g., 360-degree) feedback
Horn effect—consistently underrates employees due to overemphasis of a single negative trait or behavior.	Use multi-rater (e.g., 360-degree) feedback
Leniency/severity—rating groups of employees as all high or all low performers.	Use multi-rate (e.g., 360-degree) feedback; forced ranking or distribution technique; employee self-evaluation
Recency—assessing employees either favorably or negatively based on their most recent performance rather than performance for the entire period.	Frequent evaluations over the entire performance period; employee self-evaluation
Similarity/contrast—bias due to perceived similarity or contrast between work behaviors of the rater and employee.	Training of evaluators; provide evaluation guidelines; multi-rate and/or employee self-evaluation

Evolution of Leadership

Leaders and organizations have and continue to evolve. Traditional leadership has its roots in the industrial revolution, when organizations were suddenly faced with the challenge of managing a large, previously agricultural workforce.

Contemporary leaders are described as "servant," "learning," and "developmental" based on the focus of their actions. Servant and learning leaders focus on their organizations by improving the talent and quality of their workforces. Developmental leaders focus on employees' growth and development, and recognize that the organization will ultimately benefit.

|----------------|------------------|----------------|----------------|----------|----------------|--→
Traditional   Charismatic   Transactional   Transformational   Servant   Learning   Developmental

Traditional—Hierarchical, bureaucratic, command/control; management makes all decisions; employees are paid to work, not provide input.

Charismatic—rely on personality (e.g., charming, persuasive, bullying) to influence others.

Transactional—view relationship with employees as a series of give and take (reward and punish) transactions.

Transformational—view change as critical; move the organization to the "next phase;" willing to downsize, rightsize, or outsource to meet organizational goals.

Servant—put the needs of employees and the organization first; fight to provide employees with the resources necessary to be successful; long-term focus.

Learning—recognize and model the importance of continuous learning at all organizational levels in order to grow (and occasionally reinvent) the organization.

Developmental—focus on employee growth and development in order to grow and develop the organization.

Communications/Planning

Creating a Strategic Communications Plan

I. Map the communications strategy.

1. Identify the target audience—who needs to know (e.g., shareholders, customers, community, vendors, employees—at what levels)?
2. What specific information should be shared?
3. How should the information be shared—by what method?
   a. Individually, face-to-face
   b. Group meeting
   c. Personal phone call
   d. Formal letter
   e. Company memorandum
   f. E-mail
      i. Personal
      ii. Group, department, or division
      iii. Company-wide
   g. Press release
   h. Other
4. When is the information necessary—pre-event, during, post?

II. Create a detailed communications time line.

Audience	Specific Information to be Shared	Method or Media	Timeframe/Date(s)

Source: Ann Gilley, *Manager as Change Leader* (Westport, CT: Praeger, 2005)

Summary of Effective Communication Techniques

Active Listening — Looking someone in the eye and concentrating on what is being said. The result is "hearing" and clearly understanding what is being communicated.

Clarifying — Building a clear understanding of others by asking them to elaborate or confirm.

Encouraging — Persuading others via statements or gestures that reveal your support.

Interpreting — Decoding or translating information to draw meaning and understanding.

Paraphrasing — Restating others' ideas or words to demonstrate your understanding.

Questioning — Using inquiry to gather additional information necessary for understanding.

Silence — Intentional quiet that enables meaning to resonate or adjust the pace of interaction.

Summarizing — Reviewing what has transpired in order to check levels of agreement and understanding by participants.

Reflecting — Imitating another's message content by stating your understanding of his or her feelings and attitudes.

Tentative Analysis — Drawing a conclusion based on initial testing of a thought or idea expressed by another.

Source: Adapted from: Jerry W. Gilley and Ann Gilley, *Strategically Integrated HRD* (Cambridge, MA: Perseus Publishing, 2003).

Assessment of Communication Effectiveness

- What effort do I make to genuinely understand others?
- To what degree does my personal history affect conversations?
- To what degree is my self-concept at risk?
- How threatened do I feel while communicating?
- How often am I misunderstood?
- How frequently do I misunderstand others?
- Do I hear others correctly?
- Do I really understand what others are saying?
- How threatened are others during interactions with me?
- How might I reduce defensiveness?
- Do I make any unjustified assumptions during interactions?
- Does my attitude toward others distort my perceptions?
- What are the interpersonal styles of those with whom I interact? How do they match my own?
- Do I consciously adjust to others to accommodate their interpersonal styles?
- What problems have resulted due to my communications methods or style?
- How can I improve my interpersonal interactions with others?

Disaster Planning

1. Build a disaster planning team—include personnel who represent security, facilities, human resources, management, and an experienced disaster planner (external resource if necessary).
2. Complete a risk assessment—identify vulnerabilities within your organization as well as external risks. Consider risks related to employees, products, customers, the industry, etc. Identify and align resources for future need, including surveillance and alarm systems, insurance coverage, storage facilities, IT backup, etc.
3. Develop a Disaster Plan—list:
   a. Location of off-site control center
   b. Key personnel and contact information, including after-hours
   c. Chain of command, include responsibilities and limits of authority
   d. Prioritized functions and activities
   e. Floor plans, evacuation routes and procedures
   f. Sources and locations of information, including off-site and after-hours
   g. Directory of vendors/suppliers of emergency equipment and supplies
   h. Prioritization and procedures for tasks to be completed during and after recovery
4. Test the Plan—engage in a real-life test run to assess the effectiveness of the plan and make modifications.
5. Implement the Plan—communicate the plan to employees, provide training, conduct routine emergency drills.
6. Review, Revise, and Improve the Plan—routinely revisit the plan and revise as necessary to maintain current with organizational realities and objectives; communicate all changes to employees.

Costs of a Disaster Protection/Business Continuity Plan

No Cost
- Establish a disaster protection/emergency preparedness team or committee.
- Meet with insurance provider to review current and needed coverages.
- Create evacuation and shelter procedures.

- Communicate disaster plan procedures and expectations to all employees.
- Create an emergency contact list for all employees.
- Create a list of critical business contactors and others to be called upon in an emergency.
- Analyze potential emergency threats and risks, both internal and external.
- Determine in advance what will happen if your building is unusable.
- Create a list of equipment, inventory, and files.
- Discuss alternatives and back-up options with utility service providers.
- Include emergency preparedness procedures information in new employee orientation, staff meetings, newsletters, Intranet, periodic emails and updates, etc.

Less than $500
- Purchase fire extinguishers and smoke alarms.
- Purchase emergency supplies for each unit/department.
- Establish a telephone call-tree, password protected web page, email alert, or call-in voice recording to communicate with employees during an emergency.
- Provide first aid and CPR training to key employees.
- Maintain up-to-date computer antivirus software and firewalls.
- Stabilize cabinets and equipment to walls or other stable equipment; place heavy or breakable objects on low shelves or in easily accessible areas.
- Elevate valuable machinery, equipment, and files in case of flooding.
- Back up records, files, and critical data; keep a copy off-site.
- Conduct routine safety drills.

More than $500
- Purchase additional insurance to cover business interruptions, flood, or earthquake.
- Install a back-up generator and/or provide for other alternative utility back-up options.
- Install automatic sprinklers, fire hoses, and fire resistant doors and walls.
- Hire a professional engineer to evaluate your buildings' wind, fire, and seismic resistance; update facilities if necessary.
- Engage a security professional to evaluate and/or create a disaster preparedness plan.
- Provide training for safety and key emergency response personnel.
- Provide first aid and CPR training to most or all employees.

Employee Safety Checklist

XYZ, Inc.

These guidelines have been established to ensure safe working conditions. You will be informed of any changes or additions in safety regulations as they arise and are included in company policy and the Employee Handbook.

- ☐ Safety Rules
- ☐ Emergency Response Team
- ☐ Safety Committee
- ☐ OSHA Hazard Communication Standards
- ☐ Smoking and Tobacco Policy
- ☐ Accident or Injury on the Job
- ☐ First Aid
- ☐ Serious Injury/Emergency Procedures
- ☐ Fire Evacuation Routes and Procedures
- ☐ Tornado Procedures
- ☐ Earthquake Procedures

The safety section of the Employee Handbook has been discussed with me and I intend to follow the regulations and procedures as outlined.

_____
Employee Signature   Date

_____
Human Resources Representative   Date

Emergency Supplies Checklist

Recommended emergency supplies include the following:
- ☐ Water—store at least one gallon of water per person per day
- ☐ Food—at least a three-day supply of nonperishable food
- ☐ Can opener
- ☐ Battery-powered radio and extra batteries
- ☐ Flashlight and extra batteries
- ☐ First aid kit
- ☐ Whistle (to signal for help)
- ☐ Matches or lighter
- ☐ Dust or filter masks
- ☐ Moist towelettes
- ☐ Wrench or pliers
- ☐ Plastic sheeting or duct tape
- ☐ Garbage bags and plastic ties
- ☐ Blankets, towels, rags

HR Practice

Recognition and Reward Strategies

Monetary Rewards	Nonmonetary Rewards
Individual bonuses	Appreciation ("thank you")
Conference/workshop attendance	Interesting work or special project
Group/team bonuses	Challenge
Gift certificates	Involvement
Company stock	Vacation, leisure time
Company product(s) or discounts	Responsibility and authority
Percent of cost savings for new ideas	Recognition certificates or plaques
Gift for children or spouse	"Employee of the month" award
Individual or group lunches	Flexible work schedule
Etc.	Freedom and independence
	Fun
	Special privileges (e.g., close parking space, first use of new technology)
	Etc.

Managers who effectively provide recognition and rewards...
• Describe the employee's specific desirable/exemplary behavior.
• Explain the benefits of the desirable behavior.
• Express appreciation for the employee's continued efforts.
• Continually monitor employee efforts and follow-through with additional rewards to encourage continued positive behavior.

Illegal/Legal Interview Questions

Topic	May Not Ask	May Ask
Age	What is your date of birth?	Are you 18 or older?
	How old are you?	
	When did you graduate from high school?	
	When do you plan to retire?	
Citizenship	Are you a U.S. citizen?	Are you legally able to work in the United States?
	What country are you from?	
	Do you have a "green" card?	
Credit Rating	What is your credit score?	May we have your permission to run a credit report?
	Have you ever declared bankruptcy?	
Criminal Record	Have you ever been arrested?	Have you ever been convicted of a felony?
Disabilities	Are you disabled?	Are there any functions of this job that you would be unable to perform?
Gender	What is your sexual preference?	Don't ask.
Height/Weight	How tall are you?	Don't ask unless a BFOQ.
	How much do you weigh?	
Marital/family status	Are you married?	Don't ask.
	What will your husband/wife do if you take this job?	
	Do you have children?	

	Do you plan to have more children?	
	Who takes care of your children?	
	Are you pregnant?	
	You're engaged; do you still plan to work after getting married?	
Military Record	When were you discharged?	Are you a military veteran?
	Were you dishonorably discharged?	
	In what unit/branch did you serve?	
Organizations	What social organizations do you belong to (if would reveal individual's race, religion, etc.)?	Don't ask unless a BFOQ.
Race, national origin, or language	What country are you from?	What other languages do you speak (if a BFOQ)?
	What is your nationality?	
	What is your native language?	
	What language do you speak at home?	
	What organizations do you belong to?	
Religion	What is your religion?	Are you able to work any day/time?
	What church do you attend?	Are you unable to work any day/time?
	What religious organizations do you support?	
	Can you work on Sunday (or any other specific day that might reveal religious preference)?	

Ineffective/Effective Interview Questions

The following ineffective questions, while sometimes humorous, often fail to reveal a candidate's skills, behaviors, and appropriateness for the job. Carefully consider what you are attempting to measure and what job-related questions will enhance your ability to choose high performers.

Ineffective Questions

Ineffective questions allow an applicant to describe him or herself, yet fail to reveal knowledge, skills, and abilities necessary for a job. Examples of ineffective questions are:

- What kind of an animal would you be and why?
- What is your favorite color and why?
- An airplane crashes on the border of the United States and Mexico. Where should they bury the survivors?
- How many barbers are in Chicago?
- Give me two reasons why I should not hire you.
- What are your greatest strengths/weaknesses?
- What don't you want me to know about you?

Effective Questions

Effective questions focus on behaviors and what a candidate can do or has done, not how he/she says he can do. Ask a candidate to *describe, explain, show,* or *tell* you how he or she has handled a specific situation in the past. Look for behaviors and skills that will enable the individual to succeed in the job. For example:

- Describe a time when you encountered conflict with a coworker and how you handled that.
- How do you handle multiple tasks or competing demands?
- Sell this coffee mug to me (if interviewing a potential salesperson).
- Explain in detail how you handle an irate customer.
- Describe the process you go through when facilitating a department meeting.
- Tell me how you handle your employees' performance issues.

Major HRM Laws

Civil Rights Act (CRA) of 1964	Prohibits discrimination on the basis of race, religion, color, gender, or national origin; applies to employers with 15+ employees
Civil Rights Act (CRA) of 1991	Strengthened the CRA of 1964 by allowing compensation and punitive damages for discrimination
Age Discrimination in Employment Act	Prohibits discrimination against individuals who are age 40 or older; restricts mandatory retirement
Vocational Rehabilitation Act (VRA)	Prohibits discrimination on the basis of physical or mental disability
Americans with Disabilities Act (ADA)	Strengthened the VRA of 1973 by requiring employers to provide "reasonable accommodations" to disabled employees to allow them to work

Equal Employment Opportunity Laws

Equal Pay Act (EPA) of 1963	Requires that men and women be paid the same for equal work
Family and Medical Leave Act (FMLA)	Requires employers with 50 or more employees to provide up to 12 weeks of unpaid leave for certain family (e.g., birth or adoption of a child) or medical reasons

Compensation/Benefits Laws

Occupational Safety and Health Act (OSHA)	Established mandatory safety and health standards for organizations
Fair Labor Standards Act (FLSA)	Established the standard 40-hour workweek, and set requirements for minimum wage, overtime pay, child labor, and record keeping

Health/Safety Laws

Designing Jobs

The following steps assist in the design of effective jobs.

- Create a Competency Map consisting of the skills, knowledge, and attitudes needed to complete performance activities used to generate performance outputs. These are essential when recruiting and selecting employees for given job classifications.
- Identify Performance Activities (the steps or micro tasks) that collectively constitute an employee's job.
- Identify Desired Performance Outputs that represent the deliverables (tangible outcomes) that employees generate via their performance activities.

- Establish Performance Standards that measure the quality and efficiency of employee outputs and activities.
- Create Job Descriptions that demonstrate the relationship between performance outputs and activities; Job Descriptions clearly identifying performance outputs for each job, performance activities required by employees to create deliverables, and the relationship between activities and outputs.

Source: Adapted from: Gary Rummler and Alan Brache, *Improving Performance* (San Francisco: Jossey-Bass, 1995).

Preparing for an Overseas Assignment

1. Analyze the assignment; determine what job(s) is to be performed by who, where, and when.
2. Identify and compile sources of information (current employees in the foreign country, if any; U.S. embassy or consulate; Internet; *CIA World Factbook;* tourist handbooks, etc.)
3. Learn as much as you can about the country (languages, currency, customs, history, laws/rules/regulations, weather, politics, religions and holidays, etc.)
    a. Learn key words and phrases in the native language
    b. Become familiar with local currency
4. Understand the local culture, including
    a. Differences between the sexes
    b. Manners, hospitality, mealtime customs
    c. Language, humor, and gestures
    d. Money, tips
    e. Giving and receiving gifts
    f. Transportation
    g. Laws and police customs
5. Determine passport/visa/travel and inoculation requirements; make arrangements well in advance.
6. Plan for return to the United States (time frame, work responsibilities, next assignment)

Facilitating Effective Meetings

Meetings are a reality of organizational life, although they are not necessarily effective or efficient. Successful meetings enhance communications, improve decision-making, productivity, and motivation, and save time and money.

1. **Plan the meeting**—topic, desired outcomes, facilitator, attendees, time, place, refreshments.
2. **Develop an agenda**
    a. Prioritize items to be covered
    b. Indicate time to be devoted to each item
    c. Start with discussion of your responsibilities (e.g., time manager, facilitator) and meeting rules (e.g., no interruptions, respect opinions, no personal attacks, etc.)
    d. Include "review" or "wrap-up" in final 2–5 minutes
3. **Start on time**—do not delay the start of the meeting for any individual or group who is/are late. Delays punish those who arrived on time and send the message that they are less important than those who are late.
4. **Stick to the agenda**
    a. The facilitator must be the time manager!
    b. Manage attendees—do not allow violation of meeting rules
    c. If a topic exhausts assigned time, "table" it to the next meeting or force a decision

5. **Wrap-up**
   a. Review decisions made, assignments for next time, date and time of next meeting. Thank attendees for their participation.
6. **End on time!**
7. **Assess meeting effectiveness**—Make notes/initial plans for next meeting.

New Employee Checklist

Name		Start Date
Position	Department	Insurance Effective
Employee #	SSN	

- ☐ Offer acceptance date _____
- ☐ Send welcome letter (include employment verification documentation list) specifying when and where to report on first day.
- ☐ Post internal welcome
- ☐ Create agenda for first day (HR information, meet with department manager, tour)
- ☐ Create training schedule
- ☐ Skills profile

Orientation Packet	
Receipt of handbook	Safety orientation materials
Training schedule	Benefits summary
Security form	Health plan comparison
Employee data sheet	Prescription drug list
I-9	Dental plan summary
W-4	Vision plan summary
Time card	COBRA notice
Pay period information	Long-term disability info sheet
Additional information sheet and handouts	Health Plan enrollment form
Retirement plan info	Dental enrollment form
Vacation/personal day information	Vision enrollment form
Skills profile	Long-term disability enrollment form

CHECKLISTS AND TOOLS   595

Forms for Employee Completion	Forms for Human Resources
Employee information sheet	Personnel change notice
W-4	Eight-week orientation notice
I-9	I-9
Receipt of handbook	New-hire report
Security form	Enter birthday/anniversary
Benefit enrollment form	COBRA notice to employee's home
Health plan enrollment form	New-hire forms to payroll
Dental enrollment form	Benefit enrollment forms
Vision enrollment form	Vacation notice
Long-term disability enrollment form	
First-year vacation options/notice	

Resignation/Termination Checklist

Name		Date Last Employed
Position	**Department**	
Employee #	**SSN**	

Forms to be Completed by HR	
	Date Sent
Information letter to employee –COBRA continuation options, retirement plan distribution, etc.	
Exit interview and form, if applicable	
Personnel change notice to Payroll	
COBRA/HIPAA	
Receipt of employee keys/key card	
Benefits status change—notify vendor	
Remove from internal systems—notify IT	

Form to be Completed by Employee	
	Date Received
Retirement Plan Distribution Request	

Employee Exit Interview Form

Name		Date Last Employed
Position	Department	
Employee #	SSN	

Indicate completion of the following, including date if required:

_____ Accounting (cash advances, company credit card, etc.)
_____ Telephone operations (password, voice mail, phone bill, etc.)
_____ Library (books out, unpaid fees)
_____ Keys (employee is responsible for returning keys to facilities)
_____ E-mail cancelled (and any other Web-based access)
_____ W-4 change (address, exemptions)
_____ Direct deposit (continue or close account?)
_____ Last regular check (does not include vacation)
_____ Unused vacation payoff (approximately _____ hours)
_____ Sick leave payoff (**retirement only,** approximately _____ hours)
_____ Security/ID card—notify security
_____ Parking permit (return to public safety or HR)
_____ COBRA information sent on _____/_____/_____
_____ Insurance coverage ends on _____/_____/_____

My signature on this form certifies that I understand all of the above information, which has been discussed with me. I understand it is my responsibility to satisfy, or make arrangements to satisfy, all debts and obligations with XYZ, Inc. prior to my last official date of employment.

_____   _____
Employee's Signature   **Date**

_____   _____
HR Representative Signature   **Date**

Death of an Employee

Name		Date Deceased
Position	Department	
Employee #	SSN	

Beneficiary/representative _____

Complete all of the following items:

_____ Discuss with beneficiary/dependents the date that insurance coverage will end and any other related issues (e.g., beneficiary changes, settlement options, continuing health plan coverage, etc.).

_____ Explain insurance continuation eligibility through COBRA. Date of COBRA notification to dependents: _____

_____ Obtain certified copy of Death Certificate to process life insurance claim. Discuss amount of policy with **named beneficiary only.**

_____ Notify employee's retirement plan and health care provider(s) of death.

_____ Contact Payroll to determine status of last paycheck and payment of vacation/sick leave to beneficiary.

_____ Notify Social Security Office.

Notify Departments to do the following:

_____ Complete Employee Change Notice (copy to home department and HR).

_____ Change employee's voicemail.

_____ Change computer passwords and stop e-mail access (IT/help desk).

_____ Coordinate with beneficiary/family members to pick up/deliver personal items.

_____ Secure keys, ID card, parking permits.

_____ Send gift to family (HR).

_____ Schedule memorial if applicable (home department with HR).

Keys to Managing Sexual Harassment

- Develop and disseminate clear policies relative to sexual harassment, including examples of unacceptable behavior and summaries of applicable laws.
- Delineate how sexual harassment policies are anchored in the culture of the organization.
- Investigate all complaints thoroughly and promptly.
- Document all process steps and discussions.
- Openly consider both sides of the dialogue, ensuring that both the complainant and the accused are afforded equitable due process.
- Achieve resolution of all complaints as expeditiously as possible, including all necessary actions.
- Require that both the complainant and the accused sign written statements attesting to the accuracy of the documented specifics.
- Ensure consistency in all actions.

Source: Adapted from Jeffrey A. Mello, *Strategic Human Resource Management* (Mason, OH: Thomson South-Western, 2006), 165.

Major Motivators of Employing Internal vs. External Recruitment

External Recruitment Motivators	Internal Recruitment Motivators
New perspective	Insider knowledge
Applicable new skills	Directly relevant skills
Change stimulus	Stability reinforcement
Talent acquisition	Talent development
Market-driven	Meritocracy-driven
Reinforces vitality	Reinforces loyalty
Culture enhancement	Culture congruence

Part VI
Resources

Articles

Abrahamson, Eric. "Change without Pain." *Harvard Business Review,* July/August 2000, 75–79.

Amundson, Norman E. "Mattering: A Foundation for Employment Counseling and Training." *Journal of Employment Counseling* 30 (1993): 146–52.

Ashton, Chris, and Lynne Morton. "Managing Talent for Competitive Advantage." *Strategic Human Resources Review,* July/August 2005, 28–31.

Becker, Brian E., and Mark A. Huselid. "Strategic Human Resource Management: Where Do We Go from Here?" *Journal of Management* 32, no. 6 (2006): 898–925.

Beer, Michael, R.A. Eisenstat, and B. Spector. "Why Change Programs Don't Produce Change." *Harvard Business Review,* November/December 1990, 158–66.

Boyle, Matthew. "Happy People, Happy Returns." *Fortune* 153, no. 1 (2006): 100.

Branine, Mohamed. "Job Sharing and Equal Opportunities under the New Public Management in Local Authorities." *The International Journal of Public Sector Management* 17, no. 2 (2004): 136–52.

Breaugh, J.A., and M. Starke. "Research on Employee Recruitment: So Many Studies, So Many Remaining Questions." *Journal of Management* 26, no. 3 (2000): 405–34.

Brookfield, Steven D. "Analyzing a Critical Paradigm of Self-Directed Learning: A Response." *Adult Education Quarterly* 36, no. 1 (1985): 60–64.

Butler, Kelley. "EAP Benefits Worth More Than Their Price Tag." *Employee Benefit News,* September 2007, 9.

Capozzoli, Thomas. "How to Succeed with Self-Directed Work Teams." *Supervision,* February 2006, 25–26.

Carmeli, Abraham. "The Relationship between Emotional Intelligence and Work Attitudes, Behaviors and Outcomes." *Journal of Managerial Psychology* 18, no. 8 (2003): 788–813.

Cheng-Fei Tsai, Philip, Yu-Fang Yen, Liang-Chih Huang, and Ing-Chung Huang. "A Study on Motivating Employees' Learning Commitment in the Post-Downsizing Era: Job Satisfaction Perspective." *Journal of World Business,* June 2007, 157–69.

Coles, Sarah. "Satisfying Basic Needs." *Employee Benefits,* October 2001, 3–7.

Cote, S., and M. Miners. "Emotional Intelligence, Cognitive Intelligence, and Job Performance." *Administrative Science Quarterly* 51, no. 1 (2006): 1–28.

Dean, Peter J. "Examining the Practice of Human Performance Technology." *Performance Improvement Quarterly* 8, no. 2 (1995): 68–94.

Deci, Edward L., and Richard M. Ryan. "The 'What' and 'Why' of Goal Pursuits: Human Needs and the Self-determination of Behavior." *Psychological Inquiry* 11, no. 4 (2000): 227.

Denning, Steve. "Transformational Innovation." *Strategy & Leadership* 33 (2005): 11–16.

Deutschman, A. "Change or Die." *Fast Company,* May 2005, 54–62.

Fairhurst, Gail T., Francois Cooren, and Daniel J. Cahill. "Discursiveness, Contradiction, and Unintended Consequences in Successive Downsizings." *Management Communication Quarterly* 15 (2002): 501–40.

Falcone, Paul. "Employee Separations: Layoffs vs. Terminations for Cause." *HR Magazine,* October 2000, 189.

Frase-Blunt, Martha. "Short-Term Executives: Companies That Need an Executive for a Special Purpose—To Launch a Project, To Fill In During an Absence—Are Hiring Temps for the Job." *HR Magazine,* June 2004, 6.

Furnham, A., and K.V. Petrides. "Trait Emotional Intelligence and Happiness." *Social Behavioral and Personality* 31, no. 8 (December 2003): 815–24.

Gan, Marie, and Brian H. Kleiner. "How to Write Job Descriptions Effectively." *Management Research News* 8, no. 28 (2005): 48–54.

Gardner, Randy, Julie Welch, and Brooke Grechus. "Choosing the Right Retirement Plan for a Self-Employed Individual." *Journal of Financial Planning,* February 2004, 28–32.

Gibson, Jane Whitney, and Dana V. Tesone. "Management Fads: Emergence, Evolution, and Implications for Managers." *Academy of Management Executives,* November 2001, 122–33.

Gilley, Jerry W., and Michael W. Galbraith. "Examining Professional Certification." *Training and Development Journal* 40, no. 6 (June 1986): 60–61.

Grossman, Robert. "The Under-Reported Impact of Age Discrimination and Its Threat to Business Vitality." *Business Horizons* 48, no. 1 (2005): 71–78.

Grossman, Robert J. "New Competencies for HR." *HR Magazine,* June 2007, 58–62.

Hackman, J. Richard, and Ruth Wageman. "A Theory of Team Coaching." *Academy of Management Review* 30 (2005): 269–87.

Hallock, Daniel E., Ronald J. Salazar, and Sandy Venneman. "Demographic and Attitudinal Correlates of Employee Satisfaction with an ESOP." *British Journal of Management,* December 2004, 321–33.

Hurtz, G.M., and J.J. Donovan. "Personality and Job Performance: The Big 5 Revisited." *Journal of Applied Psychology* 85, no. 6 (2000): 869–79.

Huselid, Mark A. "The Impact of Human Resource Management Practices on Turnover, Productivity, and Corporate Financial Performance." *Academy of Management Journal* 38 (1995): 635–72.

IBM. "Expanding the Innovation Horizon: The Global CEO Study." *IBM Global Business Services,* 2006.

Judge, T.A., C.A. Higgins, and D.M. Cable. "The Employment Interview: A Review of Recent Research and Recommendations for Future Research." *Human Resource Management Review* 4 (2000): 383–406.

Kammeyer-Mueller, John, and Hui Liao. "Workforce Reduction and Job-Seeker Attraction: Examining Job Seekers' Reactions to Firm Workforce-Reduction Policies." *Human Resource Management,* Winter 2006, 585–603.

Karsen, Rudy. "Calculating the Cost of Turnover." *Employment Relations Today,* Spring 2007, 33–36.

Kerr, Steven. "On the Folly of Rewarding A, While Hoping for B." *Academy of Management Executive* 9, no. 1 (1995): 7.

Kluger, Avraham N., and Angelo DeNisi. "The Effects of Feedback Interventions on Performance." *Psychological Bulletin* 119, no. 2 (1996): 254.

Kotter, John P. "Leading Change: Why Transformational Efforts Fail." *Harvard Business Review,* March/April 1995, 59–67.

Laff, Michael. "Middle Managers Feel Squeezed." *Training and Development,* June 2007, 20.

Latham, Gary P., and Craig C. Pinder. "Work Motivation Theory and Research at the Dawn of the Twenty-first Century." *Annual Review of Psychology* 56, no. 1 (2005): 485.

Levering, Robert. "Creating a Great Place to Work: Why It Is Important and How It Is Done." *Corrections Today,* 66, no. 5 (2004): 86–88.

Lewin, Jeffrey E., and Wesley J. Johnston. "The Impact of Downsizing and Restructuring on Organizational Competitiveness." *Competitiveness Review* 10 (2000): 45–55.

Lockwood, Nancy R. "Talent Management Driver for Organizational Success." *HR Magazine,* June 2006, 1–11.

Maltbia, Terrence. "Diversity's Impact on the Executive Coaching Process." *Proceedings of the Academy of Human Resource Development,* February 2005, 221–28.

Mintzberg, Henry. "Productivity is Killing American Enterprise." *Harvard Business Review,* July–August 2007, 25.

Morris, James R., Wayne F. Cascio, and Clifford E. Young. "Downsizing after All These Years: Questions and Answers about Who Did It, How Many Did It, and Who Benefited from It." *Organizational Dynamics* 13, no. 2 (1999): 78–87.

Nadler, David A., and Michael L. Tushman. "Beyond the Charismatic Leader: Leadership and Organizational Change." *California Management Review,* Winter 1990, 77–97.

Norhia, N., W. Joyce, and B. Robertson. "What Really Works." *Harvard Business Review* 81 (2003): 43–52.

Orenstein, Ruth L. "Executive Coaching: It's Not Just about the Executive." *Journal of Applied Behavioral Science,* September 2002, 355–75.

Paulas, P.B., and H. Yang. "Idea Generation in Groups: A Basis for Creativity in Organizations." *Organizational Behavior and Human Decision Processes* 82, no. 1 (2000): 76–87.

Pereira, Gloria M., and H.G. Osburn. "Effects of Participation in Decision Making on Performance and Employee Attitudes: A Quality Circles Meta-Analysis." *Journal of Business Psychology,* July 2007, 145–53.

Preskill, Hallie. "The Use of Critical Incidents to Foster Reflection and Leaning in HRD." *Human Resource Development Quarterly* 7, no. 4 (1996): 335–47.

Probst, Tahira M., Susan M. Stewart, Melissa L. Gruys, and Bradley W. Tierney. "Productivity, Counterproductivity and Creativity: The Ups and Downs of Job Insecurity." *The British Psychological Society,* September 2007, 479–97.

Rathbone, Mark. "Trade Unions in the USA." *History Review,* December 2005, 1–6.

Ready, Douglas A., and Jay A. Conger. "Make Your Company a Talent Factory." *Harvard Business Review,* June 2007: 68–77.

Robinson, Karyn-Siobhan. "HR Needs Larger Role in Off Shoring." *HR Magazine,* May 2004.

Rynes, S.L., K.G. Brown, and A.E. Colbert. "Seven Misconceptions about Human Resource Practices: Research Findings Versus Practitioner Beliefs." *Academy of Management Executive* 16, no. 3 (2002): 92–103.

Schmidt, F., and J.E. Hunter. "The Validity and Utility of Selection Methods in Personnel Psychology: Practical and Theoretical Implications of 85 Years of Research Findings." *Psychological Bulletin* 124, no. 2 (1998): 262–74.

Scott, Cynthia D., and D.T. Jaffe. "Survive and Thrive in Times of Change." *Training and Development Journal* 42, no. 4 (1988): 25–27.

Sisk, Michael. "Reward Systems That Really Work." *Harvard Management Update* 10, no. 9 (2005): 1.

Thach, Liz, and Tom Heinselman. "Executive Coaching Defined." *Training and Development Journal,* March 1999, 34–40.

Thompson, L. "Improving the Creativity of Organizational Work Groups." *Academy of Management Executive* 17, no. 1 (2003): 96–111.

Turner, A.N. "Consulting Is More Than Giving Advice." *Harvard Business Review* 61, no. 5 (1983): 120–29.

van Mierlo, H., C.G. Rutte, J.K. Vermunt, M.A.J. Kompier, and J.A.M.C. Doorewaard. "Individual Autonomy in Work Teams: The Role of Team Autonomy, Self-Efficacy, and

Social Support." *European Journal of Work and Organizational Psychology* 15, no. 3 (2006): 282–99.

Witherspoon, Robert, and Randall P. White. "Executive Coaching: A Continuum of Roles." *Consulting Psychology Journal: Practice and Research,* Spring 1996, 87–95.

Wong, Chi-Sum, and Kenneth S. Law. "The Effects of Leader and Follower Emotional Intelligence on Performance and Attitude: An Exploratory Study." *The Leadership Quarterly* 13, no. 3 (2002): 243–74.

Yukl, G., and C.M. Fable. "Influence Tactics and Objectives in Upward, Downward, and Lateral Influence Attempts." *Journal of Applied Psychology* 75, no. 3 (1990): 133.

Books

Ahlrichs, Nancy S. *Competing for Talent: Key Recruitment and Retention Strategies for Becoming an Employer of Choice.* Palo Alto, CA: Davies-Black, 2000.

Allen, David. *Getting Things Done: The Art of Stress-Free Productivity.* New York: Viking Books, 2001.

Anderson, D., and L.A. Anderson. *Beyond Change Management: Advanced Strategies, for Today's Transformational Leader.* San Francisco: Pfeffer, 2001.

Argenti, P.A., and J. Forman. *The Power of Corporate Communications: Crafting a Voice and Image of Your Business.* New York: McGraw-Hill, 2002.

Argyris, Chris, and Donald Schon. *Organizational Learning II: A Theory of Action Perspective.* Reading, MA: Addison-Wesley, 1996.

Armstrong, Michael. *Performance Management: Key Strategies and Practical Guidelines.* London: Kogan Page, 2006.

Bacon, Terry R. *Effective Coaching.* Durango, CO: International Learning Works, 1997.

Bakke, D.W. *Joy at Work.* Seattle: PVG, 2003.

Baldwin, Timothy T., William H. Bommer, and Robert S. Rubin. *Developing Management Skills: What Great Managers Know and Do.* New York: McGraw-Hill/Irwin, 2008.

Bass, Bernard. *Bass and Stogdill's Handbook of Leadership.* New York: The Free Press, 1990.

Becker, Brian E., Mark A. Huselid, and Dave Ulrich. *The HR Scorecard.* Boston: Harvard Business School Press, 2001.

Beer, Michael, and Nitin Nohria. *Breaking the Code of Change.* Boston: Harvard Business School Press, 2000.

Bell, Chip R. *Managers as Mentors: Building Partnerships for Learning.* San Francisco: Berrett-Koehler, 2002.

Bellman, G.M. *Getting Things Done When You Are Not in Charge.* San Francisco: Berrett-Koehler, 2001.

Bennis, Warren. *On Becoming a Leader.* Cambridge, MA: Perseus, 1989.

Berger, Lance A., and Dorothy R. Berger, editors. *The Compensation Handbook: A State-of-the-Art Guide to Compensation Strategy and Design,* 4th ed. New York: McGraw-Hill, 1999.

Bernardin, H. John. *Human Resource Management: An Experiential Approach,* 4th ed. New York: McGraw-Hill/Irwin, 2007.

Berns, Gregory. *Satisfaction.* New York: Holt, 2005.

Biech, Elaine. *The Pfeiffer Book of Successful Team-Building Tools: Best of the Annuals.* New York: John Wiley, 2001.

Bliss, Wendy, and Gene Thornton. *The Employment Termination Source Book : A Collection of Practical Samples* Alexandria, VA: Society for Human Resource Management, 2006.

Block, Peter. *The Empowered Manager: Positive Political Skills at Work.* San Francisco: Jossey-Bass, 1987.

———. *Flawless Consulting: A Guide to Getting Your Expertise Used,* 2nd ed. San Diego: Pfeiffer, 1999.

———. *Stewardship.* San Francisco: Berrett-Koehler, 1992.

Bohlander, George. and Scott Snell. *Managing Human Resources,* 14th ed. Mason, OH: Thomas South-Western, 2007.

Bolles, Richard. *What Color is Your Parachute?* Berkeley, CA: Ten Speed Press, 2001.

Bolman, L.G., and Terrance Deal. *Reframing Organizations: Artistry, Choice, and Leadership,* 3rd ed. San Francisco: Jossey-Bass, 2003.

Bolton, Robert. *People Skills: How to Assert Yourself, Listen to Others, and Resolve Conflicts.* New York: Simon & Schuster, 1986.

Bolton, Robert, and Dorothy Grover Bolton. *People Styles at Work: Making Bad Relationships Good and Good Relationships Better.* New York: AMACOM, 1996.

Boudreau, John W., and Peter M. Ramstad. *Beyond HR: The New Science of Human Capital.* Boston: Harvard Business School Press, 2007.

Boverie, Patricia E., and Michael S. Kroth. *Transforming Work: The Five Keys to Achieving Trust, Commitment, and Passion in the Workplace.* Cambridge, MA: Perseus, 2001.

Bredin, Alice. *The Virtual Office Survival Handbook.* New York: John Wiley, 1996.

Brinkerhoff, Robert O., and Steven Gill. *The Learning Alliance.* San Francisco: Jossey-Bass, 1994.

Brinkerhoff, Robert O., and A.M. Apking. *High Impact Learning: Strategies for Leveraging Business Results from Training.* Cambridge, MA: Perseus, 2001.

Broad, Mary, and John Newstrom. *Transfer of Training. Action-Packed Strategies to Ensure High Pay-off from Training Investment.* Reading, MA: Addison-Wesley, 1992.

Buckingham, Marcus, and Donald O. Clifton. *Now, Discover Your Strengths.* New York: The Free Press, 2001.

Buckingham, Marcus, and C. Coffman. *First, Break All the Rules: What the World's Greatest Managers Do Differently.* New York: Simon & Schuster, 1999.

Buckman, R.H. *Building a Knowledge-Driven Organization.* Boston: McGraw-Hill, 2004.

Burke, Warren W. *Organization Change: Theory and Practice.* Thousand Oaks, CA: Sage, 2002.

————. *Organizational Development: A Process of Learning and Changing.* Reading, MA: Addison-Wesley, 1992.

Business: The Ultimate Resource, 2nd ed. Cambridge, MA: Basic Books, 2006.

Cascio, Wayne F. *Managing Human Resources: Productivity, Quality of Work Life, Profits.* New York: McGraw-Hill, 2005.

Clifton, Donald, and Paula Nelson. *Soar with Your Strengths.* New York: Delacorte, 1992.

Cloke, K., and Joseph Goldsmith. *Resolving Conflicts at Work: A Complete Guide for Everyone on the Job.* San Francisco: Jossey-Bass, 2001.

Codling, Sylvia. *Benchmarking.* Brookfield, VT: Grower, 1998.

Collins, Jim. *Good to Great: Why Some Companies Make the Leap...and Others Don't.* New York: Harper Collins, 2001.

Conger, Jay A., and Beth Benjamin. *Building Leaders: How Successful Companies Develop the Next Generation.* San Francisco: Jossey-Bass, 1999.

Conner, Donald. *Managing at the Speed of Change.* New York: Villard Books, 1992.

Cooperrider, David, and Suresh Srivastava. *Appreciative Inquiry in Organizational Life.* Greenwich: JAI Press, 1987.

Cummings, T.G., and C.G. Worley. *Organizational Development and Change,* 8th ed. Cincinnati, OH: South-Western College Publishing, 2005.

Dana, D. *Conflict Resolution.* New York: McGraw-Hill, 2000.

Dawson, Roger. *Secrets of Power Negotiating,* 2nd ed. Franklin Lakes, NJ: The Career Press, 2001.

————. *Secrets of Power Persuasion: Everything You'll Ever Need to Get Anything You'll Ever Want.* Eaglewood Cliffs, NJ: Prentice Hall Press, 2001.

Deci, Edward. *Intrinsic Motivation.* New York: Plenum, 1975.

Deluca, Matthew J. *Best Answers to the 201 Most Frequently Asked Interview Questions.* New York: McGraw-Hill Professional Publishing, 1996.

De Meuse, Kenneth P., and Mitchell Lee Marks. *Resizing the Organization* San Francisco: John Wiley & Sons, 2003.

Dessler, Gary. *Human Resource Management.* Upper Saddle River, NJ: Pearson Prentice Hall, 2005.

Deutsch, M., and P.T. Colemen. *Handbook of Conflict Resolution: Theory and Practice.* San Francisco: Jossey-Bass, 2000.

Dixon, N.M. *Common Knowledge: How Companies Thrive by Sharing What They Know.* Boston, MA: Harvard Business School Press, 2000.

Dotlich, David L., and Peter C. Cairo. *Action Coaching: How to Leverage Individual Performance for Company Success.* San Francisco: Jossey-Bass, 1999.

Drucker, Peter. *The Effective Executive.* New York: Harper Collins, 2002.

———. *Management Challenges for the 21st Century.* New York: Harper Collins, 1999.

Edwards, Mark R., and Ann J. Ewan. *360° Feedback: The Powerful New Model for Employee Assessment & Performance Improvement.* New York: AMACOM, 1996.

Ehrlich, C.J. "Human Resource Management: A Changing Script for a Changing World." In *Tomorrow's HR Management: 48 Thought Leaders Call for Change,* edited by David. Ulrich, M.R. Losey, and G. Lake. New York: Wiley & Sons, 1997.

Eichinger, R., and David Ulrich. *Human Resource Challenges.* New York: The Human Resource Planning Society, 1995.

Fisher, Roger, William Ury, and Bruce Patton. *Getting to Yes: Negotiating Agreements without Giving In.* New York: New Rutherford, NJ: Penguin, 1991.

Fitz-enz, Jac. *The ROI of Human Capital: Measuring the Economic Value of Employee Performance.* New York: Amacon, 2000.

Flannery, T.P., D.A. Hofrichter, and P.E. Platten. *People Pperformance and Pay: Dynamic Compensation for Changing Organizations.* New York: The Free Press, 1996.

Fleischer, Charles. *HR for Small Business.* Naperville, IL: Sourcebooks, 2005.

Fombrun, Charles J., and Mark D. Nevins. *The Advice Business: Essential Tools and Models for Management Consulting.* Upper Saddle River, NJ: Pearson/Prentice Hall, 2003.

Fossum, John A. *Labor Relations: Development, Structure, Process.* Chicago: Irwin, 1995.

Fournies, Ferdinand F. *Coaching for Improved Work Performance.* New York: McGraw-Hill, 2000.

———. *Why Employees Don't Do What They're Supposed To Do: And What To Do About It.* New York: McGraw-Hill, 1988.

Francis, Huw, and Michelyne Callan, *Live and Work Abroad: A Guide for Modern Nomads.* Cincinnati, OH: Seven Hills Book Distributors, 2001.

French, Wendell L., and Cecil H. Bell, Jr. *Organizational Development: Behavioral Science Interventions for Organizational Improvement.* Englewood Cliffs, NJ: Prentice-Hall, 1999.

Fulmer, Robert M., and Marshall Goldsmith. *The Leadership Investment: How the World's Best Organizations Gain Strategic Advantage through Leadership Development.* Washington, DC: AMACOM, 2000.

Gerdes, S. *Navigating the Partnership Maze: Creating Alliances That Work.* New York: McGraw-Hill, 2002.

Giaclone, Robert A., and Carole L. Jurkiewicz, editors. *Handbook of Workplace Spirituality and Organizational Performance.* Armonk, NY: M.E. Sharpe, 2003.

Gibson, James L., John M. Ivancevich, James H. Donnelly, Jr., and Robert Konopaske. *Organizations: Behavior, Structure, Processes,* 12th ed. New York: McGraw-Hill/Irwin, 2006.

Gilley, Ann. *Manager as Change Leader.* Westport, CT: Praeger, 2005.

Gilley, Jerry W. *Improving HRD Practice.* Malabar, FL: Krieger Publishing, 1998.

Gilley, Jerry W., and Nathaniel W. Boughton. *Stop Managing, Start Coaching!* Chicago: Irwin Professional Publishing, 1996.

Gilley, Jerry W., Nathaniel W. Boughton, and Ann Maycunich. *The Performance Challenge: Developing Management Systems to Make Employees Your Organization's Greatest Asset.* Cambridge, MA: Perseus Books, 1999.

Gilley, Jerry W., and Amy J. Coffern. *Internal Consulting for HRD Professionals: Tools, Techniques, and Strategies for Improving Organizational Performance.* New York: McGraw-Hill Professional Publishing, 1994.

Gilley, Jerry W., and Steven A. Eggland, *Marketing HRD Programs within Organizations: Improving the Visibility, Credibility, and Image of Programs.* San Francisco: Jossey-Bass, 1992.

Gilley, Jerry W., Steven A. Eggland, and Ann Maycunich Gilley. 2002. *Principles of Human Resource Development,* 2nd ed. Cambridge, MA: Perseus, 2002.

Gilley, Jerry W., and Ann Gilley. *The Manager as Coach.* Westport, CT: Praeger, 2007.

———. *Organizational Learning, Performance, and Change: An Introduction to Strategic HRD.* Cambridge, MA: Perseus, 2000.

Gilley, Jerry W., and Ann Maycunich, *Beyond the Learning Organization: Creating a Culture of Continuous Growth and Development through State-of-the-Art Human Resource Practices.* Cambridge, MA: Perseus Books, 2000.

Goleman, Donald. *Emotional Intelligence.* New York: Bantam Books, 1995.

———. *Working with Emotional Intelligence.* New York: Bantam Books, 1998.

Greene, Robert. *The Art of Seduction.* New Rutherford, NJ: Penguin Putnam, 2003.

———. *The 48 Laws of Power.* New Rutherford, NJ: Penguin Putnam, 2000.

Greenleaf, Robert K. *On Becoming a Servant Leader.* San Francisco: Jossey-Bass, 1996.

Grote, Dick. *The Complete Guide to Performance Appraisal.* New York: AMACOM, 1996.

Guba, E.G., and Y.S. Lincoln. *Effective Evaluation: Improving the Usefulness of Evaluation Results through Responsive and Naturalistic Approaches.* San Francisco: Jossey-Bass, 1988.

Guirdham, Maureen. *Communicating Across Cultures.* West Lafayette, IN: Purdue University Press, 1999.

Hale, Judy. *The Performance Consultant's Fieldbook: Tools and Techniques for Improving Organizations and People.* San Francisco: Jossey-Bass and Pfeiffer, 1998.

Hamel, Gary. *Leading the Revolution.* Boston, MA: Harvard Business School Press, 2000.

Hammer, Michael, and J. Champy. *Reengineering the Corporation: A Manifesto for Business Revolution.* New York: Harper Business, 1993.

Heneman, Robert L., and Jon M. Werner. *Merit Pay—Linking Pay to Performance in a Changing World,* 2nd ed. Charlotte, NC: Information Age Publishing, 2005.

Holbeche, Linda. *Aligning Human Resources and Business Strategy.* Woburn, MA: Butterworth-Heinemann, 1999.

Holden, Philip. *Ethics for Managers.* Brookfield, VT: Grower, 2000.

Holton, Edward. F., III, Tim. T. Baldwin, and Sharon Naquin. *Managing and Changing Learning Transfer Systems.* San Francisco: Berrett-Koehler, 2004.

Hudson, Frederic M. *The Handbook of Coaching: A Comprehensive Resource Guide for Managers, Executives, Consultants, and Human Resource Professionals.* San Francisco: Jossey-Bass, 1999.

Ivancevich, John M., Robert Konopaske, and Michael T. Matteson. *Organizational Behavior and Management.* Boston: McGraw-Hill, 2008.

Jamison, Kay R. *Exuberance: The Passion for Life.* New York: Knopf, 2004.

Jay, Ros *Ultimate Book of Business Creativity: 50 Great Thinking Tools for Transforming Your Business.* Oxford: Capstone, 2001.

Kaner, Sam, Lenny Lind, Catherine Toldi, Sarah Fisk, and Duane Berger. *Facilitator's Guide to Participatory Decision-Making.* British Columbia: New Society Publishers, 1996.

Kanter, Rosabeth M. *The Change Masters.* New York: Simon & Schuster, 1983.

Kaplan, Robert S., and David P. Norton. *The Balanced Scorecard.* Boston: Harvard Business School Press, 1996.

Katzenbach, J.R., and D. Smith. *The Wisdom of Teams.* Boston: Harvard Business School Press, 1993.

Kaye, Beverly L. *Up Is Not the Only Way: A Guide to Developing Workforce Talent.* Palo Alto, CA: Consulting Psychologists Press, 1997.

Kaye, Beverly L., and Sharon Jordan-Evans. *Love 'Em or Lose 'Em: Getting Good People to Stay.* San Francisco: Berrett-Koehler, 1999.

Kissler, G.D. *The Change Riders: Managing the Power of Change.* Cambridge, MA: Perseus, 1991.

Knowles, Malcolm. *Self-Directed Learning.* New York: Association Press, 1975.

Kotter, John. *Leading Change.* Boston: Harvard Business School Press, 1996.

Kotter, John P. *Power and Influence.* New York: Free Press, 1985.

Kouzes, James M., and Barry Z. Posner, *The Leadership Challenge: How to Get Extraordinary Things Done in Organizations.* San Francisco: Jossey-Bass, 1991.

Kreitner, Robert. *Foundations of Management: Basics and Best Practices.* Boston, MA: Houghton Mifflin, 2005.

Kroth, Michael. *The Manager as Motivator.* Westport, CT: Praeger, 2007.

Kroth, Michael, and Patricia E. Boverie. *Transforming Work.* Cambridge, MA: Perseus, 2002.

LaFasto, Frank M., and Carl E. Larson. *When Teams Work Best: 6,000 Team Members and Leaders Tell What It Takes to Succeed.* Thousand Oaks, CA: Sage, 2001.

Larson, Carl E., and Frank M.J. LaFasto. *Teamwork: What Must Go Right, What Can Go Wrong.* Newbury Park, CA: Sage., 1989.

Lawler, Edward E. *Rewarding Excellence: Pay Strategies for the New Economy.* San Francisco: Jossey-Bass, 2000.

Leas, S.B. *Discover Your Conflict Management Style.* Washington, DC: Alban Institute, 1998.

LeBoeuf, Michael. *Getting Results: The Secret to Motivating Yourself and Others.* New York: Berkeley Books, 1985.

Leed, David. *The 7 Powers of Questions: Secrets to Successful Communications in Life and at Work.* New York: Perigee Books, 2000.

Lencioni, Patrick. *Silos, Politics and Turf Wars.* New York: Jossey-Bass, 2006.

Levitt, Julie G. *Your Career: How to Make It Happen,* 4th ed. Florence, KY: South-Western Educational Publishing, 1999.

Lewicki, R.J., B. Barry, D.M. Saunders, and J.W. Minton. *Essential Negotiation,* 3rd ed. New York: McGraw-Hill/Irwin, 2003.

Lewin, Kurt. *Field Theory in Social Science.* New York: Harper, 1951.

Locke, E., and G. Latham. *A Theory of Goal Setting and Task Performance.* Englewood Cliffs, NJ: Prentice Hall, 1990.

Lomax, Stan. *Best Practices for Managers and Expatriates: A Guide on Selection, Hiring, and Compensation.* New York: John Wiley, 2001.

Lussier, Robert N. *Management Fundamentals: Concepts, Applications, Skill Development,* 4thd ed. Mason, OH: Thomson South-Western, 2009.

Mager, Robert F. *Preparing Instructional Objectives.* 2nd ed. Belmont, CA: Fearon, 1975.

Marquardt, Michael J. *Action Learning in Action: Transforming Problems and People for World-Class Organizational Learning.* Palo Alto, CA: Davies-Black, 1999.

Martin, C.L., and R.E. Kidwell. *HRM from A to Z.* New York: McGraw-Hill, 2001.

Maurer, Robert. *Beyond the Wall of Resistance: Unconventional Strategies That Build Support for Change.* Austin, TX: Bard Books, 1996.

Mayer, John D., and Peter Salovey. "What Is Emotional Intelligence?" In *Emotional Development and Emotional Intelligence: Implications for Educators,* edited by Peter Salovey and D. Sluyter, 3–31. New York; Basic Books, 1997.

Mayer, John D., Peter Salovey, and David Caruso. "Models of Emotional Intelligence." In *The Handbook of Intelligence,* edited by R.J. Sternberrg, 396–420. New York; Cambridge University Press, 2000.

McDonnell, Sharon. *You're Hired! Secrets to a Successful Job Search.* New York: Macmillan, 1999.

McLagan, Patrica, and N. Christo. *The Age of Participation.* San Francisco, CA: Berrett-Koehler, 1995.

Mello, Jeffrey A. *Strategic Human Resource Management.* Mason, OH: Thomson South-Western, 2005.

Michaels, Ed, Helen Handfield-Jones, and Beth Axelrod. *The War for Talent.* Boston: McKinsey & Company, 2001.

Mink, Oscar G., P. W. Esterhuysen, Barbara P. Mink, and Keith O. Owen. *Change at Work: A Comprehensive Management Process for Transforming Organizations.* San Francisco: Jossey-Bass, 1993.

Mink, Oscar G., Keith Owen, and Barbara Mink. *Developing High-Performance People.* Cambridge, MA: Perseus, 1993.

Mitroff, Ian I. *Managing Crises Before They Happen.* New York: AMACOM, 2000.

Myers, Isabel Briggs, with Peter B. Myers. *Gifts Differing: Understanding Personality Type.* Mountain View, CA: Davies-Black, 1980.

Nadler, David. *Champions of Change.* San Francisco: Jossey-Bass, 1998.

Nilson, C. *The Performance Consulting Toolbook: Tools for Trainers in a Performance Consulting Role.* New York: McGraw-Hill, 1999.

Nkomo, S., M. Sottler, and R. B. McAfee. *Human Resource Management Applications Cases, Exercises, Incidents, and Skill Builders.* Mason, OH: Thomson South-Western, 2008.

Northouse, Peter G. *Leadership Theory and Practice.* Thousand Oaks, CA: Sage, 2007.

O'Hair, Dan, Gustav W. Friedrich, and Lynda Dee Dixon, *Strategic Communication in Business and the Professions,* 5th ed. Boston, MA: Houghton Mifflin, 2005.

O'Shaughnessy, Lynn. *Retirement Bible.* New York: Hungry Minds, 2001.

Parker, G. M. *Team Players and Teamwork: The New Competitive Business Strategy.* San Francisco: Jossey-Bass, 1990.

Patterson, James. *Coming Clean about Organizational Change.* Arlington, VA: American Association of School Administrators, 1997.

Peterson, David. B., and M. D. Hicks. *Development First: Strategies for Self-Development.* Minneapolis: Personnel Decisions International, 1995.

———. *Leader as Coach: Strategies for Coaching and Developing Others.* Minneapolis: Personnel Decisions International, 1996.

Pettinger, Richard. *The Learning Organization.* Oxford, UK: Capstone, 2002.

Pfeffer, Jeffrey. *Competitive Advantage Through People.* Boston: Harvard Business School Press, 1994.

Pfeffer, Jeffrey, and Robert I. Sutton. *The Knowing-Doing Gap.* Boston: Harvard Business School Press, 2000.

Phillips, Barty. *The Home Office Planner.* San Francisco: Chronicle Books, 2000.

Porter, Lyman A., Gregory A. Bigley, and Richard M. Steers, editors. *Motivation and Work Behavior.* Boston: McGraw-Hill/Irwin, 2003.

Porter, Michael E. *Competitive Advantage: Creating and Sustaining Superior Performance.* New York: The Free Press, 1985.

———. *On Competition.* Boston, MA: Harvard Business School Publishing, 1998.

Proctor, Tony. *Creative Problem Solving for Managers.* New York: Routledge, 1999.

Raines, C. *Connecting Generations: The Sourcebook for a New Generation.* New York: Crisp Publications, 2003.

Ramey, Ardella. *A Company Policy and Personnel Workbook,* 4th ed. Central Point, NY: Oasis Press, 1999.

Reardon, Kathleen K. *The Secret Handshake: Mastering the Politics of the Business Inner Circle.* New York: Doubleday, 2001.

Reilly, Peter. *Flexibility at Work: Balancing the Interests of Employer and Employee.* Burlington, VT: Ashgate, 2001.

Rejda, G. E. *Principles of Risk Management and Insurance,* 10th ed. Boston, MA: Pearson/Addison-Wesley, 2008.

Rigsbee, E. *Developing Strategic Alliances.* New York: Crisp Publications, 2000.

Roberts, Marian. *Developing the Craft of Mediation: Reflections on Theory and Practice.* London and Philadelphia: Jessica Kingsley Publishers, 2007.

Robinson, Dana G., and James. C. Robinson. *Moving from Training to Performance: A Practical Guide.* San Francisco: Berrett-Koehler, 1998.

———. *Performance Consulting: Moving Beyond Training,* 2nd ed. San Francisco: Berrett-Koehler, 2008.

Rogers, Everett. *Diffusion of Innovations,* 5th ed. New York: The Free Press, 2003.

Rosenberg, Deanne. *A Manager's Guide to Hiring the Best Person for Every Job.* New York: John Wiley, 2000.

Rosenberg, Marc J. "Human Performance Technology: Foundation for Human Performance Improvement." In *The ASTD Models for Human Performance Improvement: Roles, Competencies, and Outputs,* edited by William Rothwell. Alexandria, VA: American Society for Training and Development, 1996.

Rossett, Allison. *First Things Fast: A Handbook for Performance Analysis.* San Francisco: Pfeiffer, 1998.

Rothwell, William. *Beyond Training and Development: State-of-the-Art Strategies for Enhancing Human Performance.* New York: AMACOM, 1996.

Rummler, Gary A., and Alan P. Brache. *Improving Performance: How to Manage the White Spaces on the Organizational Chart.* San Francisco: Jossey-Bass, 1995.

Russo, J. Edward, and Paul J. Schoemaker. *Winning Decisions: Getting It Right the First Time.* New York: Doubleday, 2001.

Ryan, Kathleen D., and Daniel K. Oestreich. *Driving Fear Out of the Workplace: Creating the High-Trust, High-Performance Organization.* San Francisco: Jossey-Bass, 1998.

Schein, Edgar H. *The Corporate Culture Survival Guide.* San Francisco: Jossey-Bass, 1999.

Schon, Donald A. *Educating the Reflective Practitioner: Toward a New Design for Teaching and Learning in the Professions.* San Francisco: Jossey-Bass, 1987.

Schuler, Randall S., and Susan E. Jackson. *Strategic Human Resource Management,* 2nd ed. San Francisco: Blackwell, 2007.

Senge, Peter M. *The Fifth Discipline: The Art and Practice of the Learning Organization.* New York: Doubleday, 1990.

Shell, G.R. *Bargaining for Advantage: Negotiation Strategy for Reasonable People.* New Rutherford, NJ: Penguin Books, 2000.

Simonsen, Peggy. *Promoting a Development Culture in Your Organization: Using Career Development as a Change Agent.* Palo Alto, CA: Davies-Black, 1997.

Sims, Ronald R. *Changing the Way We Manage Change.* Westport, CT: Quorum Books, 2002.

———. *Human Resource Management: Contemporary Issues, Challenges, and Opportunities.* Charlotte, NC: Information Age Publishing, 2007.

Sims, Ronald R., and Scott A. Quatro, editors. *Leadership: Succeeding in the Private, Public, and Not-for-Profit Sectors.* Armonk, NY: M.E. Sharpe, 2005.

Smalley, Larry R. *Interviewing and Selecting High Performers.* San Francisco: Jossey-Bass, 1997.

Spector, Paul E. *Industrial and Organizational Psychology: Research and Practice.* Hoboken, NJ: John Wiley, 2006.

Stolovitch, Harold D., and Erica J. Keeps. *Handbook of Human Performance Technology: Improving Individual and Organizational Performance Worldwide.* San Francisco: Jossey-Bass, 1999.

Straus, D., and T.C. Layton. *How to Make Collaboration Work: Powerful Ways to Build Consensus, Solve Problems, and Make Decisions.* San Francisco: Berrett-Koehler, 2001.

Tenner, Arthur R., and Irving J. DeToro. *Process Redesign: The Implementation Guide for Managers.* Reading, MA: Addison-Wesley, 1997.

Thomas, Kenneth W. *Intrinsic Motivation at Work: Building Energy and Commitment,* 1st ed. San Francisco: Berrett-Koehler, 2000.

Thompson, Leigh L. *Making the Team: A Guide for Managers.* New Jersey: Pearson Prentice Hall, 2004.

Thorne, J.D. *A Concise Guide to Successful Employment Practices.* Chicago: CCH Incorporated, 2000.

Tinder, G. *Political Thinking: The Perennial Questions,* 6th ed. New York: Longman, 2003.

Tisch, James. *The Power of We: Succeeding Through Partnerships.* New York: Wiley, 2004.

Treacy, Michael, and Fred Wiersema, *The Discipline of Market Leaders.* New York: Basic Books, 1995.

Turner, Chris. *All Hat and No Cattle.* Cambridge, MA: Perseus, 2000.

Ulrich, David. *Human Resource Champions.* Boston: Harvard Business School Press, 1998.

Ulrich, Dave, and Wayne Brockbank. *The HR Value Proposition.* Boston: Harvard Business School Press, 2005.

Ulrich, David, James Zenger, and N. Smallwood. *Results-Based Leadership: How Leaders Build the Business and Improve the Bottom Line.* Boston: Harvard Business School Press, 1999.

Ury, William L. *Getting Past No: Negotiating Your Way from Confrontation to Cooperation.* New York: Bantam, 1993.

Vaile, Peter. *Learning as a Way of Being.* San Francisco: Jossey-Bass, 1996.

Vengel, A. *The Influence Edge: How to Persuade Others to Help You Achieve Your Goals.* San Francisco: Berrett-Koehler, 2001.

Vicere, Albert A., and Robert M. Fulmer. *Leadership by Design.* Boston, MA: Harvard Business School Press, 1998.

Vroom, Victor H. *Work and Motivation.* New York: Wiley, 1964.

Watling, Brian. *The Appraisal Checklist: How to Help Your Team Get the Results You Both Want.* Philadelphia , PA: Trans-Atlantic Publications, 2000.

Waugh, William L. *Living with Hazards, Dealing with Disasters: An Introduction to Emergency Management.* New York: M.E. Sharpe, 2000.

Wendelton, Kate. *Job-Search Secrets.* New York: Five O'Clock Books, 1997.

Westgaard, Odin. *Tests That Work: Designing and Delivering Fair and Practical Measurement Tools in the Workplace.* San Francisco: Jossey-Bass/Pfeiffer, 1999.

Wheatley, Margaret J. *Leadership and the New Science.* San Francisco: Berrett-Koehler, 1999.

Wilson, G.K. *Business and Politics: A Comparative Introduction,* 3rd ed. Chatham, NJ: Chatham House, 2003.

Yate, Martin J. *Great Answers to Tough Interview Questions.* Dover, NH: Kogan Page, 2001.

Zachary, Lois J. *The Mentor's Guide: Facilitating Effective Learning Relationships.* San Francisco: Jossey-Bass, 2000.

Zeitz, P. *The Art and Craft of Problem-Solving.* New York: Wiley, 1999.

Journals and Magazines

Academy of Management Executive
Academy of Management Journal
Academy of Management Review
Administrative Science Quarterly
Advanced Management Journal (SAM)
American Psychologist
Applied Psychology
Assessment Journal
Association Management
British Journal of Management
Business Communication Quarterly
BusinessWeek
California Management Review

Career Development International
Compensation and Benefits Review
Compensation and Working Conditions
Creativity and Innovation Management
Disaster Prevention and Management
Disaster Recovery Journal
Employee Benefits Journal
Entrepreneur
Fast Company
Forbes
Fortune
Harvard Business Review
HR Focus
HR Magazine
Human Performance
Human Resource Development Review
Human Resource Development Quarterly
Human Resource Management
Human Resource Management Review
Inc.
Industrial Relations
International Journal of Coaching
International Journal of Innovation Management
International Journal of Management Practice
International Journal of Strategic Change Management
Journal of Applied Behavioral Science
Journal of Applied Psychology
Journal of Behavioral Decision Making
Journal of Business and Leadership
Journal of Business Ethics
Journal of Change Management
Journal of Communication Management
Journal of Innovation Management
Journal of Knowledge Management
Journal of Leadership and Organizational Studies
Journal of Management
Journal of Management Development
Journal of Management Education
Journal of Management Studies
Journal of Managerial Psychology
Journal of Organization Behavior
Journal of Organization Behavior Management
Journal of Organizational Change Management
Journal of Organizational Excellence
Journal of Workplace Learning
Leadership and Organizational Development Journal
Leader to Leader
Leadership Quarterly
Management Decision
Management in Practice
Management Today

McKinsey Quarterly
OD Practitioner
Organization Development Journal
Organizational Dynamics
Organization Management Journal
Performance Improvement Quarterly
Personnel Management
Personnel Psychology
Personnel Review
Psychometrika
Public Manager (The)
SAM Advanced Management Journal
Sloan Management Review
Strategic Change
Strategic Direction
Strategic Management Journal
Strategy + Business
Strategy and Leadership
Supervision
Team Performance Management
Training
Training & Management Development Methods
Workforce

Organizations

Academy of Human Resource Development
College of Technology
Bowling Green State University
Bowling Green, OH 43403-0301
419-372-9155
http://www.ahrd.org

Academy of Management
235 Elm Road
P.O. Box 3020
Briarcliff Manor, NY 10510-8020
914-923-2615

American Association for Affirmative Action
P. O. Box 14460
Washington, DC 20044
800-252-8952
http://www.affirmativeaction.org

American Benefits Council
1212 New York Avenue NW, Suite 1250
Washington, DC 20005
202-289-6700
http://www.americanbenefitscouncil.org

The American Coaching Association
P.O. Box 353
Lafayette Hill, PA 19444
610-825-4505

American Creativity Association (ACA)
P.O. Box 5856
Philadelphia, PA 19128
888-837-1409
http://www.amcreativityassoc.org

American Federation of Coaches
http://www.americanfedcoaches.org

American Institute for Managing Diversity
50 Hurt Plaza, Suite 1150
Atlanta, GA 30303
404-302-9226
http://www.aimd.org

American Institute of Stress
124 Park Avenue
Yonkers, NY 10703
914-963-1200
http://www.stress.org

American Management Association
1601 Broadway
New York, NY 10019
212-586-8100 or 800-262-9699
http://www.amanet.org

American Payroll Association
660 North Main Avenue, Suite 100
San Antonio, TX 78205-1217
210-226-4600
http://www.americanpayroll.org

American Productivity and Quality Center
123 N. Post Oak Lane, 3rd Floor
Houston, TX 77024
800-776-9676
http://www.apqc.org

American Psychological Association
750 First Street, NE
Washington, DC 20002-4242
202-336-5580
http://www.apa.org

American Society for Payroll Management
P.O. Box 117
Stormville, NY 12582
800-684-4024
http://www.aspm.org

American Society for Training and Development
1640 King Street
Box 1443
Alexandria, VA 22313-2043
704-683-8103
http://www.astd.org

American Staffing Association
277 South Washington Street, Suite 200
Alexandria, VA 22314
703-253-2020
http://www.staffingtoday.net

Association of Internal Management Consultants
http://www.aimc.org

Association for Strategic Planning
12021 Wilshire Boulevard, Suite 286
Los Angeles, CA 90025
866-816-2080
http://www.strategyplus.org

The Center for Creative Leadership
1 Leadership Place
P.O. Box 26300
Greensboro, NC 27438-6300
336-545-2810
http://www.ccl.org

Center for the Study of Work Teams
University of North Texas
Terrill Hall 343
P.O. Box 311280
Denton, TX 76203-1280
940-565-3096
http://www.workteams.unt.edu

Employment Conditions Abroad
One Rockefeller Plaza, Suite 325
New York, NY 10020
212-582-2333
http://www.eca-international.com

Hay Group
101 Hudson Street
Jersey City, NJ 07302
201-557-8400
http://www.haygroup.com
Provides comprehensive business information, including best practices, salaries, benefits, etc.

Human Resource Planning Society
317 Madison Avenue, Suite 1509
New York, NY 10017
212-490-6387
http://www.hrps.org

Institute of Management and Administration (IOMA)
29 West 35th Street, 5th Floor
New York, NY 10001-2299
212-244-0360
http://www.ioma.com

International Association of Career Coaches
P.O. Box 5778
Lake Havasu City, AZ 86404
866-226-2244
http://www.iaccweb.org

International Association of Management
P.O. Box 64841
Virginia Beach, VA 23467-4841
757-482-2273
http://www.aom-iaom.org

International Communication Association
1730 Rhode Island Avenue NW, Suite 300
Washington, DC 20036
202-530-9855
http://www.icahdq.org

International Public Management Association for Human Resources
1617 Duke Street
Alexandria, VA 22314
(703) 549-1700
http://www.ipma-hr.org

International Society for Performance Improvement
1400 Silver Spring Street, Suite 260
Silver Spring, MD 20910
301-587-8573
http://www.ispi.org

International Telework Association and Council
401 Edgewater Place, Suite 600
Wakefield, MA 01880
202-547-6157
http://www.telecommute.org

National Commission on Entrepreneurship
444 North Capital Street, Suite 399
Washington, DC 20001
202-434-8060
http://www.ncoe.org

Organization Development Network
71 Valley Street, Suite 301
South Orange, NJ 07079-2825
973-763-7337
odnetwork@ODNetwork.org
http://www.ODNetwork.org

The Outsourcing Institute
Jericho Atrium
500 N. Broadway, Suite 141
Jericho, NY 11753
516-681-0066
http://www.outsourcing.com

Risk and Insurance Management Society
655 Third Avenue, 2nd Floor
New York, NY 10017
212-286-9292
http://www.rims.org

Society for Business Ethics
Management Department, School of Business Administration
Loyola University Chicago
820 N. Michigan Ave.
Chicago, IL 60611
312-915-6994
http://www.luc.edu/depts/business/sbe

Society for Human Resource Management
1800 Duke Street
Alexandria, VA 22314
800-283-SHRM
http://www.shrm.org

Society for Personality Assessment
6109H Arlington Boulevard
Falls Church, VA 22044
703-534-4772
http://www.personality.org

U.S. Citizenship and Immigration Services
800-375-5283
http://www.uscis.gov
A division of the U.S. Department of Homeland Security

U.S. Department of Homeland Security
Washington, DC 29528
202-282-8000
http://www.dhs.gov

U.S. Department of Labor
Frances Perkins Building
200 Constitution Ave, NW
Washington, DC 20210
866-487-2365
http://www.dol.gov

U.S. Equal Employment Opportunity Commission
1801 L Street, NW
Washington, DC 20507
202-663-4900
800-669-4000
http://www.eeoc.gov

U. S. Office of Personnel Management
1900 E Street, NW
Washington, DC 20415
202-606-1800
http://www.opm.gov

Work in America Institute
700 White Plains Road
Scarsdale, NY 10583
914-472-9600
http://www.workinamerica.org

Web Sites
http://www.advisorteam.com/user/ktsintro.asp
The Keirsey 70-question personality assessment

http://www.ahrd.org
Academy of Human Resource Development

http://www.apa.org
American Psychological Association

http://www.apqc.org/best
APQC's Benchmarking and Best Practice site

http://www.astd.org
American Society for Training and Development

http://www.balancedscorecard.com
Gives access to a version of the Balanced Scorecard

http://www.benchmarkingnetwork.com
Comprehensive benchmarking site

http://www.benchmarkingplus.com
Benchmarking information

http://www.benefitslink.com
Benefits information and links

http://www.bls.gov
U.S. Bureau of Labor Statistics

http://www.bls.gov/ncs/ebs
Employee benefits statistics from BLS data

http://www.business.com

http://www.business.gov
Information on starting and managing a business, business law, government forms

http://www.capt.org
Center for Applications of Psychological Type

http://www.careerbuilder.com Job search resource; list of interview questions (legal and illegal)

http://www.careercity.com
Career information

http://www.careermag.comInformation on career strategies, resumes, job listings, and placement

http://www.coachingnetwork.org
Coaching and Mentoring Network

http://www.compensationlink.com
Information on pay programs, articles, links, etc.

http://www.content.monster.com
Tough interview questions

http://www.cpp.com
Consulting Psychologists Press; employment tests including the Myers-Briggs Type Indicator
(MBTI), the Parker Team Player Survey, and others

http://www.creativitypool.com
Database for creative problem-solving.

http://www.cvandresumetips.com
Resume and curriculum vitae advice

http://www.disabilityinfo.gov
Information on disability programs, services, laws, and benefits.

http://www.dhs.gov
U.S. Department of Homeland Security

http://www.dol.gov
U.S. Department of Labor; provides labor statistics, salary data, forms, minimum wage guidelines, etc.

http://www.dol.gov/elaws
Employment law information

http://www.eeoc.gov
U.S. Equal Employment Opportunity Commission; provides information regarding EEO laws, harassment, discrimination, filing charges, etc.

http://www.entrepreneur.com
Information for small business owners

http://www.ethics.org
Ethics Resource Center

http://www.equalemployment.com
Links to companies committed to EEOC

http://www.fema.gov
U.S. Federal Emergency Management Agency

http://www.findlaw.com
Information on employment and business law

http://www.globalassignment.com
An e-newsletter for expatriates

http://www.gohome.com
Advice on home offices

http://www.govbenefits.gov
Information on government benefit and assistance programs

http://www.hr.blr.com
A comprehensive-membership, fee-based site that lists HR resources, tools, sample forms, checklists, salary finders, etc.

http://www.haypaynet.com
Subscription access to Hay's PayNet databases of pay rates in more than 60 countries

http://www.healthyplace.com/site/tests/psychological.asp
Online personality tests

http://www.humanresources.about.com
HR guides, forms, checklists, resources

http://www.humanresources.com
Professional information, HR job postings, and related information

http://www.hr.com
HR.com

http://www.hr-guide.com
HR Internet guide; provides hundreds of links to HR-related Web sites

http://www.hrtools.com
Registration required: forms, and training resources

http://www.hrvillage.com
HR resources, advice, forms

http://www.hrzone.com
HR articles, news, legal information

http://www.humanresources.org/
National Human Resources Association

http://www.innonet.org
Innovation Network

http://www.inc.com
Magazine for entrepreneurs

http://www.inquiryinc.com
Center for Inquiring Leadership

http://www.ioma.com
IOMA Report on Salary Surveys (monthly report)

http://www.ipma-hr.org
International Public Management Association for Human Resources

http://www.ispi.org
International Society for Performance Improvement

http://www.ivillage.com
Job search help

http://www.jobhuntersbible.com
Job search help, salary information, etc.

http://www.jobstar.org
JobStar Central

http://www.kmresource.com
Knowledge management resources

http://www.leadersdirect.com
Tips for leaders and managers

http://www.leadershipcoachacademy.com
Leadership Coach Academy

http://www.learnaboutcultures.com
Information on cultures of different countries

http://www.mentoring.org
The National Mentoring Partnership

http://www.mentoringgroup.com
The Mentoring Group

http://www.monster.com
Resource for help with resumes, cover letters, job searches

http://www.opm.gov
Office of Personnel management; provides an "HR Tool Kit," salary/wage data, information for job
    seekers, etc.

http://www.obmnetwork.com/
Organization Behavior Management Network

http://www.odnetwork.org/
Organizational Development Network

http://www.opm.gov
U.S. Office of Personnel Management

http://www.opm.gov/perform/teams
Links to articles, tools, and measures for teams

http://www.osha.gov
U.S. Occupational Safety and Health Administration

http://www.outsourcing.com
Site for the Outsourcing Institute

http://www.overseasjobs.com
Information on employment overseas

http://www.personalitypage.com
Online personality profile, small fee

http://www.prometheon.com
Training resource site: articles, surveys, etc.

http://www.psychtests.com
Online psychological tests

http://www.ready.gov
Department of Homeland Security–sponsored site

http://www.recruitersnetwork.com
Recruiters Network

http://www.recruitersonline.com/index.phtml
Recruiters Online Network

http://www.regulations.gov
Information on government regulations

http://www.relo-usa.com
U.S. relocation information

http://www.relocationcentral.com
Relocation Central, a relocation directory.

http://www.resume.com
Sample resumes

http://www.resume.monster.com
Resume-writing information

http://www.retireplan.about.com
About.com's site for retirement planning

http://www.rileyguide.com/salguides/html
The Riley Guide to Salaries

http://www.salary.com
For national, regional, and local salary information

http://www.salarycenter.monster.com
Salary information

http://www.salariesreview.com
Salary and cost-of-living information

http://www.shldirect.com
Practice tests and advice from SHLDirect, a test publisher

http://www.shrm.org
Society for Human Resource Management

http://www.smartbenefits.com
Benefits information and links

http://www.stress.org
The American Institute of Stress

http://www.teamspirit123.com

http://www.testpublishers.org
Association of Test Publishers

http://www.tjobs.com
Telecommuting jobs

http://www.usa.gov
Government information by topic, federal forms, and other business/HR information

http://www.uscis.gov
U.S. Citizenship and Immigration Services; a division of Homeland Security.

http://www.workforce.com
An online HR magazine

http://www.workindex.com
Lists work-related Web sites, human resource tools, and other HR information

http://www.worldatwork.org
Information for HR managers

Index

ability inventories, 7–9
absences, 155–56
absenteeism, 400
Accenture study, 452
accidental employee, 546
accidents, preparation for, 507
accommodation, 106, 386
ACES leadership model, 329–32
acknowledgment document, 511
action plan, for employee development, 42–44
action research, 374–75
ADA. *See* Americans with Disabilities Act
Adamson Act (1916), 302
adaptability, 41, 371, 389. *See also* change
ADEA. *See* Age Discrimination in Employment Act
adjusted gross income (AGI), 289
administrative employees, 514
affirmative action, 225–26, 290–91, 393
Age Discrimination in Employment Act (ADEA), 216, 221, 227–29, 299, 305, 440; BFOQs and, 232; disparate treatment and, 241; illegal and legal questions in, 223; Older Workers Benefit Protection Act, 207, 287, 538; retaliation and, 308
agency shop, 522
agile organization, 380–81
aging workforce, 393
alcoholism, 540. *See also* substance abuse
alternative dispute resolution, 484
alternative work arrangements, 499
Amendments. *See* Constitutional Amendments
American Civil Liberties Union, 279
American Council of Education, 63
American Industry Dress Code Survey, 504
American Management Association, 324
Americans with Disabilities Act of 1990, 216, 221, 229–31, 235, 302; discharge and, 550; drug tests and, 540–41; employment testing and, 17, 18; illegal and legal questions in, 223; job descriptions and, 23; reasonable accommodations and, 230–31, 302–3, 314–15; record retention laws and, 305; retaliation and, 306; Title I, 440; undue hardship and, 230, 311–12, 315

Analytical, Conceptual, Emotional and Spiritual (ACES) leadership model, 329–32
anticipatory socialization, 106
applicant tracking software, 31
appraisal documentation, 135
appraisals, 23, 117, 244. *See also* evaluation; performance appraisals
appreciative inquiry, 44–45
apprenticeship, 91, 382; interns, 460–61. *See also* on-the-job training
arbitration, 300, 491–92
Arbitration Act of 1888, 300
assessments, 42, 126; multi-rater, 146; work behavior inventory, 13. *See also* evaluation
assimilation, 397. *See also* on-boarding
AT&T, 9
attitude, personality and, 86
attitude surveys, 508–9
attribution theory, 385
Austermuehle, Paul, 3, 4
authority, 154
autonomy, 403
average indexed monthly earnings (AIME), 309
avoidance, conflict and, 386
Avon Products, 338
awareness stage, 99, 100–101

Babson College, 338
baby boomers, 452, 504, 517
background investigation, 11–12, 26, 36
balanced scorecard, 189
Baldrige criteria, 98
Ball v. United States, 255
bargaining, good faith in, 267, 495–96

bargaining unit, 493–94. *See also* collective bargaining
Beazley, Hamilton, 405
behavior, feedback and, 124
behavioral approaches, to innovation, 371
behavioral interviewing, 6, 20
behavior inventory, 12–13
behavior level, in training evaluation, 112
benchmarking, of salary, 200–203
Bendor-Samuel, Peter, 531
benefits, 89, 92, 156–58, 510; cafeteria benefit plans, 160–61; child and elder care, 161–63; domestic partner, 168–69; employee assistance programs, 170; employee stock option plan, 166, 171–72; gain sharing and profit sharing, 175–77; legally-required, 164–65; medical leave and, 254; persons with disabilities and, 304; as recruiting/retention tool, 162; social security, 157, 165, 166, 169; statements of, 289; unemployment compensation, 158, 211–12; workers' compensation, 158, 165, 319–23. *See also* insurance; pension plans
Ben & Jerry's, CEO search at, 25
Bernard Hodes Group, 15
best practices training, 111
Bloodborne Pathogen Standard, 285
bona fide occupation qualification (BFOQ), 222, 231–32; Civil Rights Act of 1964 and, 231, 232; Hooters restaurants and, 37, 295–96
bona fide seniority system, 296
bonuses, 158–60, 189
brand, 4
bridge employment, 200
broad-based option plans (BBOPs), 190
budget, forecasting and, 433–34
Bureau of labor Statistics, 348, 484–85
Burger, Warren, 18
burnout prevention, 46–47
Bush, George H. W., 287, 311
Bush, George W., 288, 310
business ethics, 401. *See also* ethics
business principles and practices, 446
business staffing plan, 4–5
buyer, outsourcing and, 531

cafeteria benefit plans, 160–61
California Public Utilities Commission, 263
campus recruiting, 13–14
Canada, Employment Equity Act in, 291
Canadian Modernization of Benefits and Obligations Act (C-23), 168

Careerbuilder.com, 31
career development, 48–51, 145, 463
career planning, 23, 47–51, 53, 118
career resource center, 52–53
casual dress code, 503–4
Census of Fatal Occupational Injuries, 485
CEO (chief executive officer) search, 25. *See also under* executive
change, 362–66; audits of, 362–63; culture and, 469; facilitation and management of, 368–70, 448–49; implementation of, 363–66; models of, 370; organizational culture and, 389; people and, 364–66; phases of response to, 364–65; transitional, 371; types of, 362. *See also* adaptability
change champion, 115
charitable/tax-exempt organizations, 290
Charles XII, king of Sweden, 529–30
Checking ABI/Inform (database), 98
child and elder care, 161–63
child labor law, 232–34, 252, 480
Circle of Conflict model, 385
Citizenship and Immigration Service, 271, 272
Civil Rights Act of 1964, 234–35; four-fifths rule and, 257; illegal and legal questions in, 223. *See also* Title VII (Civil Rights Act of 1964)
Civil Rights Act of 1991, 221, 235–36; illegal and legal questions in, 223
Civil Service Commission, 17
closed shop, 522
coaching programs, 42, 53–55, 84, 116; executive, 335–36; 116, performance, 54–55, 95–98, 116, 344. *See also* mentoring
COBRA (Consolidated Omnibus Budget Reconciliation Act), 157, 186, 208, 236–38
Code of Federal Regulation (CFR), 244
collaboration, 386, 404. *See also* teams and teamwork
collective bargaining, 283, 494–96, 525; bargaining unit and, 493–94; grievance and, 517–18
colleges and universities: corporate, 61–63; recruitment at, 13–14, 30–31
College Savings Plans, 290
Collyns, Napier, 345
combination job analysis method, 464
commission, 163, 188
commitment, 144, 448; to change, 365, 369; rewarding, 151–52
common law test, 548
Commonwealth Fund study, 181–82
communication, 403, 432; in agile organization,

381; barriers to, 352; corporate culture and, 390; in disasters, 499; electronic, 552 (*See also* e-mail; Internet); Employee Right-to-Know law and, 244–45; in job sharing, 79; managerial, 407–8; on mergers and acquisitions, 469–70; strategic, 350–52; verbal *vs.* written, 351–52; wrongful termination and, 325–26
community of interests, 493
community of practice, 382–84
company values, 459. *See also* value
comparable worth, 497–98
compensation, 149–53, 163–66, 510; benchmarking of, 200–203; commission, 163, 188; deferred, 165–66; for eminent domain claims, 256; merit pay, 186–87; organizational goals and, 152–53; pay for performance, 187–90; payroll, 190–92; recognition and, 145; rewards and, 149–53; severance pay, 207–9; skill-based pay, 209–11; strategies for, 150–52; traditional, 149–50; workers', 158, 165, 319–23; for work-related injuries, 320–21. *See also* salary; wages
compensation reviews, 118
competencies, 205, 438–39
competency maps, 466
competition, 455, 533; conflict and, 386; corporate culture and, 389; strategies for, 353
competitive advantage, 25, 333–35, 381, 443
composition, 444
compressed work week, 516
compromise, conflict and, 386
computer-based training (CBT), 56–58
computer employees, 515
Computer Matching and Privacy Act of 1988, 297
computer systems, 452; employers and, 262; security of, 499–500, 536, 552. *See also* Internet
Computer Technology Solutions, 504
confidentiality, 178, 323–25. *See also* privacy
conflict, 432; arbitration and, 491–92; role management and, 107; time-based, 482
conflict resolution, 384–86; mediation and, 525–26
Congress, railroad legislation and, 302
consensual relationships, 417
consistency, 502; in awards, 130
Consolidated Omnibus Budget Reconciliation Act (COBRA), 157, 186, 208, 236–38
Constitutional Amendments: Fifth Amendment, 255–56; First Amendment, 240; Fourteenth

Amendment, 259–61; Fourth Amendment, 261–63
consulting/consultants, 348–49; internal/external, 372–74; performance, 135–37
Consumer Credit Protection Act (CCPA), 177, 178
consumer-directed health plan (CDHP), 181–82
contingency theory, of leadership, 341
Continuity of Operations (COOP), 453
continuity planning, in disaster, 437
continuous improvement plan, 41, 58–61
contract, implied, 512
contracting, in good faith, 267
cooperation, 151. *See also* teams and teamwork
Cooperrider, David, 44
corporate culture, 388–90, 546. *See also* organizational culture
Corporate Leadership Council study, 438
corporate strategy, 431–32, 457
corrective action, 398–99
cost leadership, 334
costs, 444, 451; forecasting, 434; layoffs and downsizing, 524
creativity, 371, 456; rewarding, 150–51
credibility, 439, 446
credit reports, 12, 224, 249–50
crime, preparation for, 507
criminal history, 12
crisis management, 387–88
crisis response plan, 487
critical infrastructure, 436
cross-training, 64–66
culture, 456; change and, 469; continuous improvement, 61; corporate, 388–90, 546; human values and, 406. *See also* organizational culture
customer focus, 101

daily operations, documentation of, 428–29
data collection, 410
data collection interviews, 21
decision making, 86, 190, 389
defamation, 223, 238–40
deferred compensation, 165–66
defined benefit plans, 196–97, 199, 289
defined contribution health plan (DCHP), 181
defined contribution plans, 196, 197, 199–200
delegation, 67–68
Deming, W. Edwards, 59, 411
denial, change and, 365, 369

Department of Commerce, 453
Department of Defense, 280
Department of Education, 418
Department of Justice, 17, 301, 556
Department of Labor (DoL), 17, 285, 312, 460,
    515; ADEA and, 227; Bureau of Labor
    Statistics, 202, 258–59; child labor and, 232,
    233; *Dictionary of Occupational Titles,* 23;
    Employment and Training Administration,
    310; Employment Standards Administration,
    314; Field Operations Handbook, 177;
    Office of Contract Compliance Programs,
    314; TAA benefits and, 310–11; Wage and
    Hour Division, 251, 281, 282, 480, 555
Department of Veterans Affairs, 291
depth skill plans, 210
design, organizational, 472–74
development. *See* employee development
developmental change, 362. *See also* change
developmental organizations, 390–92
developmental planning, 118
development goals. *See* goal setting
Dictionary of Occupational Titles (DOT), 23
differentiation, 334–35
disability, 167, 293. *See also* Americans with
    Disabilities Act
disability income benefits, 310
disability insurance, 166–68, 185
disaster, 317, 436; recovery plan for, 498–500
discharge. *See* termination
disciplinary procedures, 501–3; termination
    and, 501, 549, 550
disclaimers, 511
discrimination, 219, 245; four-fifths rule and,
    257–59; illegal, 294–96; unintentional, 220.
    See also Equal Employment Opportunity
    Commission (EEOC)
disengagement, 400
disparate treatment/disparate impact, 220,
    240–41
diversity, 393–94
Diversity Management and Equal Employment
    Opportunity, 291
documentation, 325–26, 427–29, 550;
    appraisal, 135; discipline and, 502;
    electronic, 78; Employment Eligibility
    Verification (I-9 form), 272–74, 275; OSHA
    guidelines, 286; worker eligibility, 555–56.
    See also record keeping
domestic partner benefits, 168–69
downsizing. *See* layoffs and downsizing
dress code, 503–4
Drucker, Peter, 404

Drug-Free Workplace Act (DFWA), 242, 541
drug testing, 540–41. *See also* substance abuse
due diligence, 468
due process: Fifth Amendment and, 256;
    Fourteenth Amendment and, 260–61
Duke Corporate Education, 338
dysfunctional culture, 377

earnings test, 310
East India Company, 418–19
Economic Espionage Act of 1996, 552–53
Economic Growth and Tax Relief Reconciliation
    Act of 2001 (EGTRRA), 288–89
economies of scale, 531–32
education: diversity and, 394; formal, 42;
    investments in, 454. *See also* training
educational history, 12
Edwards, John, 545
EEOC. *See* Equal Employment Opportunity
    Commission
efficiency, 190
EI. *See* emotional intelligence
e-learning (web-based training), 109
electronic appraisal, 135
electronic communications, 552. *See also* e-mail
    communication; Internet
Electronic Communications Privacy Act, 263
electronic documents, 78
electronic job boards, 31
elimination period, 167
e-mail communication, 324, 352, 505–6, 542
emergency preparedness, 436, 437, 506–7, 511.
    See also disaster
eminent domain, fair compensation and, 256
emotional intelligence (EI), 69–71
Emotion Quotient Inventory, 69
employee assistance programs, 170, 499
employee attitude survey (EAS), 508–9
employee-at-will contract, 501–2, 511–13
employee benefits. *See* benefits
employee champion, 449–50
employee development, 41–112, 456; action
    plan for, 42–44; appreciative inquiry and,
    44–45; burnout prevention, 46–47; career
    planning and, 47–51; career resource center,
    52–53; coaching, 42, 53–55, 84, 95–98;
    computer-based training, 56–58; continuous
    improvement plan, 58–61; corporate univer-
    sity, 61–63; cross-training, 64–66; delegation
    and, 67–68; emotional intelligence and, 69–
    71; goal setting in, 71–73; human resource
    development, 73–75; job sharing, 77–81;
    mentoring, 42, 83–85; Myers-Briggs Type

Indicator, 85–87; needs hierarchy and, 81–83; new employee orientation, 87–90; performance aids for, 93–98; productivity improvement plan, 98–102; professional certification and, 102–4; socialization, 105–8; types of, 41–42. *See also* training

employee enlistment, 16

employee handbook, 440, 509–11

Employee Involvement Association, 541

Employee Polygraph Protection Act of 1988 (EPPA), 27–29, 243

employee preparedness, 437

employee referral programs (ERPs), 15–16

employee relations, 397–400

Employee Retirement Income Security Act (ERISA), 168, 248–49, 306, 538–39; benefits and, 157; pension benefit guarantee corporation and, 192–94

Employee Right-To-Know (ERTK) law, 243–45

employees: empowerment of, 395–97, 414; independent contractors and, 519–20; monitoring of, 324; screening of, 222–24; temporary/seasonal, 547–48

employee stock option plan (ESOP), 166, 171–72, 189–90

employee suggestion systems, 541–42

Employee Suggestion Systems (Martin), 541

employer branding, 4

Employer Credit Cafeteria plans, 160

employer liability, 270

employment actions, 428

employment agencies, 30, 429–30

employment arbitration, 491–92

employment-at-will, 511–13

employment-based health insurance (EBHI), 179, 181

employment documentation. *See* documentation

Employment Eligibility Verification (I-9 form), 272–74, 275

Employment Equity Act (Canada), 291

employment law, 219–326; affirmative action, 225–26, 290–91, 393; child labor, 232–34, 252, 480; COBRA, 157, 186, 208, 236–38; Constitutional Amendments, 255–56, 259–63; defamation, 223, 238–40; Drug-Free Workplace Act, 242, 541; ERISA, 157, 168, 192–94, 248–49, 306, 538–39; FOIA, 263–65; four-fifths rule, 257–59; good faith doctrine, 266–68, 318, 495–96, 512; on harassment, 268–70; I-9 (employment eligibility verification), 272–74, 275; Immigration Reform and Control Act, 221, 223, 274–76,

427; list of major, 221(table); polygraph testing, 27–29, 243; prima facie, 294–96; Privacy Act of 1974, 296–98; Railway Labor Act, 300–302; reasonable accommodations, 230–31, 302–4; record retention, 304–6; right-to-know, 243–45; Social Security Act of 1935, 212, 308–10; Vocational Rehabilitation Act of 1973, 221, 223, 299, 314–15; whistle-blowing, 318–19; wrongful termination, 325–26. *See also specific laws*

employment loss, WARN Act and, 315–18

employment records, 304–6. *See also* documentation; record keeping

employment screening, 487

employment shock, 106

employment testing, 17–19

empowerment, employee, 395–97, 414

Enron corporation, 319

environmental analysis, 356–57

EPPA (Employee Polygraph Protection Act of 1988), 27–29, 243

Equal Employment Opportunity Act of 1972, 225, 299, 525

Equal Employment Opportunity Commission (EEOC), 235, 247, 418, 440; ADA rights and, 231, 314–15; ADEA and, 228; employee selection and, 17, 37; employment law and, 219–20; mediation and, 526; pregnancy discrimination and, 292; prima facie and, 295; procedure, 245–46; reasonable accommodation and, 315; retaliation cases and, 306–7; separation agreements and, 539; wellness plans and, 215. *See also* Age Discrimination in Employment Act of 1967; Americans with Disabilities Act; Title VII (Civil Rights Act of 1964)

Equal Pay Act (1963), 164, 221, 246–47, 440; comparable worth and, 497–98

Equal protection clause, 14th Amendment, 220, 260

equity, stakeholder, 205

Erdman Act (1898), 300

ERISA. *See* Employment Retirement Income Security Act

esprit de corps, 382

esteem needs, 82

ethics, 401–2, 414, 502

evaluations, 116–21, 463; developmental, 116–19; forced ranking, 126–29; merit pay and, 186; pre-training, 92; reliability and utility of, 121; training, 110–12; validity of, 120–21

exclusive provider organization (EPO), 180

executive, short-term, 347–49
executive coaching, 335–36
executive employees, 514. *See also* managers;
    management
Executive Order 13164 (Bush), 303
executive search firm, 25, 430–31
exempt-nonexempt employee, 513–15
exiting process, 400
exit interviews, 21, 122–23, 400
expenses, 510. *See also* costs
experiential-based training, 109
exploration, change and, 365, 369
external job posting, 24–25

Fair and Accurate Credit Transactions Act, 305
fair comment on public interest, 239
fair compensation, 256. *See also* compensation
Fair Credit Reporting Act (FCRA), 249–50
fair dealing, 512
Fair Labor Standards Act of 1938 (FLSA), 164,
    251–53, 480, 515, 554; child labor and,
    232–33; Equal Pay Act and, 247; minimum
    wage and, 251–52, 513; overtime and, 534
fairness issues, 10
Family and Medical Leave Act of 1993 (FMLA),
    157, 162, 221, 253–55, 305; military leave
    and, 254, 281
FCRA. *See* Fair Credit Reporting Act
Federal Emergency Management Agency, 507
Federal Mediation and Conciliation Service, 278
Federal Trade Commission, 297
Federal Unemployment Tax Act (1939), 212,
    305
feedback, 117, 399, 502; continuous, 134;
    360-degree, 109, 134, 146–47; exiting
    process and, 400; guidelines for effective,
    124–25; performance analysis, 131–32;
    performance coaching and, 95, 96; retention
    and, 145
field human resource needs, 431–32
Fifth Amendment, 255–56
FIOA. *See* Freedom of Information Act
First Amendment, 240
flexibility, in work arrangements, 456; flextime,
    516–17; job sharing, 77–81, 516;
    telecommuting, 544–46; training and, 57
flexible spending amounts, 160
FMLA. *See* Family and Medical Leave Act
FOIA. *See* Freedom of Information Act
follow-up reviews, 134
forced ranking evaluation, 126–29
Ford Motor Company, 127
forecasting, 433–34, 443

foreign suppliers. *See* offshoring
form and function, 472
Fortune magazine, 14, 126, 411
four-fifths rule, 257–59
401(K) plans, 166, 172–75, 198, 289
Fourteenth Amendment, 220, 259–61
Fourth Amendment, 261–63
franchising, 553
freedom and independence, 154
Freedom of Information Act (1966), 263–65
fringe benefits, 292. *See also* benefits
Frost, Carl, 204
full retirement age (FRA), 199
fun, 154–55
functional integration, 494

gainsharing, 175–77, 189, 203–5
Galbraith, Jay, 473
garnishments, 177–78
gatekeeping, change and, 365–66, 377
gay partner rights, 266; domestic partner
    benefits, 168–69
Gelinas, Mary, 474
General Electric (GE), 59, 127, 337
Gerhart, Barry, 502
Gerstner, Lou, 110, 111
Getting to Yes (Fisher & Ury), 527
GLBT. *See* gay partner rights
globalization, 393, 413, 457–60
global sourcing, 533
goals and objectives, 354, 358, 359–60, 394;
    organizational, 114, 152–53
goal setting, 71–73
Golden Rule, 413
good-faith bargaining, 267, 495–96
good faith doctrine, 266–68, 512;
    whistle-blowing and, 318. *See also* bona fide
    occupation qualification
Google, rewards at, 130
gradual retirement, 200
grievance procedure, 491, 517–18
Griggs v. Duke Power Co., 18
group discussion, leaderless, 10
group health insurance. *See* COBRA
    (Consolidated Omnibus Budget
    Reconciliation Act)
group incentives, 154. *See also* teams and
    teamwork
group pay for performance, 189

Hagel & Company, 442
Hamburger University, 62, 63
hands-on learning, 405

harassment, 268–70; sexual, 417–18
Hart, Karen, 4, 16
Hazard Communication (HAZCOM), 243–45
headhunter (search firm), 25, 430–31
health care costs, 451
health care plans, 179–82; wellness programs, 215–16
health coverage tax credit (HCTC), 311
health insurance, 183–84, 215; under COBRA, 157, 186, 208, 236–38; disability insurance, 166–68, 185; as domestic partner benefit, 169; people without, 452; pregnancy-related conditions and, 293. *See also* Medicare
Health Insurance Portability and Accountability Act (HIPAA), 157, 183–84, 216, 305
health maintenance organization (HMO), 180
health reimbursement arrangement (HRA), 181
health savings account (HSA), 181
Hewitt Associates report, 52, 182, 393
high deductible health plans, 181
high potential, 14
hiring, 6, 8; confidentiality in, 323–24; of managers, 344; negligent, 26; pregnancy discrimination and, 291–92; short-term executives, 349
Hock, Dee, 474
holiday policies, 213–14
Hollenbeck, John R., 502
homeland security, 272, 435–37
Homer, *Odyssey* of, 83
H1B visas, 270–72
Hooters restaurants, 37, 295–96
horizontal skill plans, 210
hostile work environment, 268–69, 417. *See also* violence, workplace
hoteling, 517
human capital, 453–55, 459. *See also* human resources
human process interventions, 375–76
Human Resource Certification Institute (HCRI), 475
Human Resource Competency Study, 438–39
human resource development (HRD), 73–75; leadership and, 332–33
human resource management (HRM), 23, 441; evaluation and, 119–21; international, 457–60; interventions in, 376; professional certification and, 102–4; retention, 144–45, 146
human resource planning, 118
human resource policy. *See* policy, human resource
human resources (HR): competencies, 438–39;

compliance with, 440; field *vs.* corporate, 431–32; innovation in, 455–57; job analysis and, 462–65; job sharing and, 80; metrics, 6–7, 443–45; strategy, 445–50; talent management and, 419; trends in, 451–53
human resources information systems (HRIS), 441

IBM, 419; training evaluation at, 110–12
IBP v. Alvarez, 554
identity, 204–5
identity theft, 250, 452
immigrant visa (IV), 270–72
Immigration and Nationality Act (INA), 271
Immigration and Naturalization Service, 276
Immigration Reform and Control Act of 1986, 221, 223, 274–76, 427
immune systems, 365–66, 376–78
implied contract, 512
Improshare plan, 176, 203
improvement stage, 99, 100–101
in-basket/in-box, 10
incentives, 154, 163
income, 444. *See also* compensation; salary; wages
indemnity plans, 179
independent contractors, 518–20, 548
index, 445
individual leadership development process (ILDP), 338–39
individual performance management, 114, 138
individual retirement accounts (IRAs), 206, 288
I-9 (Employment Eligibility Verification), 272–74, 275
information devices, 262
information-gathering function, 86
information industries, 435
information technology (IT), 78, 110, 111, 441
injury, work-related. *See* workers' compensation
innocent dissemination, 239
innovation, 41, 455–57; behavioral approaches to, 371; change and, 364, 370–72; cognitive approaches to, 371
in-service distributions, 289
inspection failure, 96
insurance, 184–86; disability, 166–68. *See also* health insurance
insurance companies, 436; workers' compensation and, 322, 323
intellectual capacity/curiosity, 14
intellectual capital, 80, 371
intellectual property, 551–53
interactive video training (IVT), 76–77

interest arbitration, 491
internal job posting, 24
Internal Revenue Code, 160–61, 172
Internal Revenue Service (IRS), 169, 197, 518, 548; ERISA and, 248; 401(k) plans and, 172, 173, 174
internal searches, 5
international human resource management, 457–60
International Labor Affairs Bureau (ILAB), 233
Internet, 324, 338; e-learning, 109; exit interviews, 122; job postings on, 25, 31, 34; policy, 505–6
interns, 460–61
interviewing, 19–21; behavioral, 6, 20; data collection in, 21; exit interviews, 21, 122–23, 400; selection and, 36; simulation of, 10
investment, 454
IRAs (individual retirement accounts), 206, 289
IRCA. See Immigration Reform and Control Act of 1986

James, Roger, 474
job analysis, 462–65
job classification, 463
job description, 21–23, 465–66
job design, 463, 465–66
job experience, 42
job fairs, 30–31
job functions test, 19
job history, 35. See also resumes
job interviews. See interviewing
job posting, 24–25
job satisfaction, 70, 402–3, 481
job security, 144, 403. See also retention
job sharing, 77–81, 516
job specifications, 22
Johnson, Lyndon B., 219, 234
judging, 86. See also decision making
Jung, Carl, 85
jury duty leave, 276–77
justice, workplace, 483–84, 502

Kasse, Margie, 16
knowledge management database (KMD), 7–9
knowledge management (KM), 100, 467–68; ability inventories and, 7–9
knowledge/skills/abilities (KSAs), 461
knowledge transfer (KT), 404–5
Kotter, John P., 363
Kovacevich, Dick, 393

Labor Department. See Department of Labor

labor relations law. See National Labor Relations Act
labor unions, 283, 284, 520–22; grievance and, 517–18; Scanlon plan and, 176, 204; shop types, 522; unfair labor practices by, 278
layoffs and downsizing, 522–25, 549
leader member exchange (LMX) theory, 341
leadership, 329–60; ACES model, 329–32; in agile organization, 381; barriers to change and, 366; competitive advantage and, 333–35; contemporary HR and, 332–33; costs and, 334; development of, 337–39; ethics and, 401–2; executive coaching, 335–36; managerial malpractice and, 342–45; rewarding, 151; scenario planning and, 345–47; short-term executive, 347–49; strategic communication and, 350–52; strategic planning and, 100, 353–54, 358; strategy and, 329–60; succession planning and, 8, 354–55; support for, 394; SWOT analysis and, 354, 356–57; theories of, 339–42; transformational, 341–42
leadership development trainee programs, 14
learning level, in training evaluation, 112
learning organization, 391, 406–7
Leave and Liberty (DoD), 280
legal issues, 10, 463; in collective bargaining, 495; in employment testing, 17; independent contractors and, 520; selection and, 37; in separation agreements, 538–39; severance pay and, 207; temporary workers and, 548. See also employment law
leisure time, 154
Lewin, Kurt, 363, 370
liability, 26, 435; harassment and, 270
libel, 238
licensing, 553
lie detector tests. See polygraph test
life insurance, 184–85
long-term solutions, rewards for, 152
loyalty, rewarding, 151–52

macrophages, 366, 377
managed care plans, 180, 185
management: barriers to change and, 366; innovation and, 457; performance standards and, 142; project, 477–79; surveillance and, 544; workplace justice and, 484
management consultants, 372–74
management trainee programs, 14
managerial job analysis, 464
managers, 400; communication and, 407–8; job sharing and, 81; malpractice, 342–45;

mergers and acquisitions and, 470–71; organizational culture and, 389–90; overtime pay and, 534

market focus, 101

market range assignment, 192

Martin, Charles, 541

Mary Kay, rewards at, 130

Maslow's hierarchy of needs, 81–83

Massachusetts Institute of Technology, 204

mass layoff, WARN Act and, 317, 318

master-apprenticeship relationships, 382–83

Material Safety Data Sheets, 285–86

maternity-related leave, 292–93

Mayer Salovey Caruso Emotional Intelligence Test, 69

McDonald's Corporation, 62

McKinsey & Company study, 418

mediation, 525–26

medical care, 454; costs in, 451

medical leave. *See* Family and Medical Leave Act of 1993

medical records, 307

Medicare, 157–58, 198, 308, 309–10

Medicare Modernization Act (2003), 198

mental models, 406

mentoring, 42, 83–85, 405

mergers and acquisitions, 390, 468–71

merit pay, 186–87, 188

MetLife, 338

metrics, 443–45; implementation and, 6–7

military leave, 254, 280–81

millennial generation, 504

Mine Safety and Health Administration, 480

minimum wage, 251–52, 281–82, 513, 555

mission statements, 330, 354, 358, 454

Monster.com, 31

Moody, R. Wayne, 16

motivation, 129–30, 153, 405; intrinsic *vs.* extrinsic, 99; religion/spirituality and, 414–15. *See also* rewards

movement, change and, 363, 370

multiemployer pension plans, 193

multirater assessment, 146. *See also* 360-degree feedback

Multitrait Emotional Intelligence Assessment, 69

mutual aid, 283

Myers-Briggs Type Indicator (MBTI), 85–87

Nadler, David, 473

narrative evaluation, 134, 135

National Association of Colleges and Employers, 13

National Association of Manufacturers, 278

National Coalition on Health Care study, 451

National Compensation Survey, 202

National Council on Disability, 314

National Defense Authorization Act (2008), 254, 281

National Fraud Alert System, 250

National Guard, 280, 314

National Institute on Disability and Rehabilitation Research, 315

National Labor Relations Act (1935), 277–79, 282–83, 493, 495, 521

National Labor Relations Board (NLRB), 279, 282, 521, 526; bargaining unit and, 493, 494; collective bargaining and, 495–96

National Mediation Board, 301

natural disasters, 317, 436; recovery plan for, 498–500

natural hazards, 507

nearshoring, 532

needs analysis, 409–10

needs hierarchy, 81–83

negligent hiring, 26

negotiation, 526–29. *See also* collective bargaining; conflict resolution; mediation

new employee, 68, 510; orientation of, 87–90; placement of, 105–6

Newland, Ted, 345

new skills, application of, 152. *See also* innovation

New York Times v. Sullivan, 240

Nilles, Jack, 545

NLRB. *See* National Labor Relations Board

Noe, Raymond A., 502

nonprofit organizations, 319

Nordstrom (retailer), 334–35

Norris-Laguardia Act (1932), 284–85

Northouse, Peter, 339

OASDHI. *See* Old Age, Survivors, Disability, and Health Insurance Program

objectives. *See* goals and objectives

objectivity issues, 10

Occupational Classification System Manual (OCSM), 202

Occupational Information Network database (O*Net), 23, 202, 464

Occupational Safety and Health Act of 1970, 221, 285–87, 305–6, 320

Occupational Safety and Health Administration (OSHA), 244, 285–87, 435, 507

ODC. *See* organizational development and change

Odyssey (Homer), 83
Office of Child Labor, Forced Labor, and
    Human Trafficking (OCFT), 233
Office of Child Support Enforcement, 178
Office of National Ombudsman (ONO), 530
Office of Personnel Management (OPM),
    455–56
Office of Strategic Studies, 9
offshoring, 532
off-site data storage, 500
Oklahoma City bombing, 435
Old Age, Survivors, Disability, and Health
    Insurance Program (OASDHI), 308–10
Older Workers Benefit Protection Act
    (OWBPA), 207, 287–88, 538
O'Leary, George, 32
ombudsman, 529–31
on-boarding, 6, 397–98
online applications, 31, 34
online databases, 98, 135, 147. *See also* Internet
onshoring, 532
on-the-job (OJT) training, 90–92, 397–98, 454,
    460–61
open shop, 522
open systems framework, 375
opinion, defamation and, 239
oral presentation, 10
organizational behavior, 379–443; agile
    organization and, 380–81; community of
    practice and, 382–84; conflict resolution and,
    384–86; crisis management and, 387–88;
    employee empowerment and, 395–97;
    employee relations, 397–400; ethics and,
    401–2; overview of, 379–80
organizational capability, 459
organizational culture, 105–6, 371, 384, 388–
    90; corrective action and, 398; leadership
    development and, 331–32; managers and,
    389–90; subcultures and, 389
organizational design, 472–74
organizational development and change (ODC),
    361–78; action-research foundations of, 374–
    75; barriers to change, 366–67; change
    implementation, 363–66; change manage-
    ment and, 368–70; immune system and,
    365–66, 376–78; innovation and, 370–72;
    internal/external consulting and, 372–74;
    interventions in, 375–76; principles of,
    362–63
organizational goals, 114, 152–53
organizational learning, 391, 406–7
organizational performance management, 138
organizational strategies, justice and, 483–84

OSHA. *See* Occupational Safety and Health
    Administration
outside sales employees, 515
outsourcing, 451, 531–33; of payroll, 191–92
outstanding stage, 100–101, 102
overtime pay, 252, 534–35

paid time off (PTO) policies, 214, 535–36
Parents' Tax Relief Act (2007), 546
partial disability, 167
participation, 205
partner, 68
partnerships, 530
path-goal theory, 341
pay, skill-based, 209–11
pay for performance, 187–90
pay grades and ranges, 164
Payless ShoeSource, 20
payroll, 190–92
payroll records, 305
peer review, 134
peer support, 405, 539
pension benefit guarantee corporation (PBGC),
    192–95
pension plans, 166, 195–98, 206; defined
    benefit, 165; defined contribution, 196, 197,
    199–200. *See also* retirement plans
Pension Protection Act of 2006, 288–90
perceiving, personality and, 86
performance: activities, 465–66; aids to,
    93–95; bonuses and, 159; deferred
    compensation and, 166; goals, 72–73; good
    faith in, 267–68; outputs, 465; standards for,
    22, 421
performance analysis, 131–32, 137
performance appraisals, 23, 117, 132–35, 224;
    employment actions and, 428; job analysis
    and, 463; management of, 187
performance coaching, 95–98, 116, 344. *See also*
    coaching programs
performance consulting, 135–37
performance management, 113–47, 398, 459,
    549; advocate for, 115–16; benefits of, 139;
    360-degree feedback and, 134, 146–47;
    developmental evaluations and, 116–19;
    evaluation and, 119–21; exit interviews and,
    122–23; feedback in, 124–25; forced ranking
    evaluation and, 126–29; individual *vs.*
    organizational, 138; ineffective, 139–40;
    learning-centric, 110; motivation and, 129–
    30; performance analysis, 131–32, 137; per-
    formance appraisals, 132–35; performance
    consulting, 135–37; promotion and, 143–44;

retention and, 144–46; roles in, 115–16; systems for, 137–40

performance standards, 140–42, 145, 466

performance tests, 222

persistent conduct, harassment and, 269

personal files, privacy and, 323–25

personality, culture and, 388

personality characteristics, 14

personal mastery, 407

personal protective equipment, 286

personnel file, 89

pervasive conduct, harassment and, 270

Peters, Thomas J., 473

phased retirement, 517

physiological needs, 82

piece rate, 188

placement, of new employees, 105–6

Plan, Do, Check, Act (PDCA) model, 59, 111

plant closing, WARN Act and, 316, 317

point of service plan (POS), 180, 185

policy, human resource, 398, 491–556; arbitration, 491–92; collective bargaining unit, 493–96; comparable worth, 497–98; disaster plans, 498–500; disciplinary procedures, 501–3; dress code, 503–4; e-mail/Internet, 505–6; emergency preparedness, 506–7; employee attitude survey, 508–9; employee handbook, 440, 509–11; flextime, 516–17; grievance procedure, 491, 517–18; independent contractors, 518–20; labor unions, 520–22; layoffs and downsizing, 522–25; mediation, 525–26; negotiation, 526–29; ombudsman, 529–31; outsourcing, 531–33; paid time off (PTO), 214, 535–36; separation agreements, 538–39; suggestion systems, 541–42; temporary/seasonal employees, 547–48; trade secrets, 551–53; travel, 553–55; work eligibility, 555–56

polygraph test, 27–29, 243

Portal-to-Portal Act of 1947, 252, 554

poverty of time, 383–84, 444

practice, community of, 382–84

preferential treatment, 290–92

preferred provider organization (PPO), 180, 185

Pregnancy Discrimination Act of 1978, 221, 292–94; illegal and legal questions in, 223

presenteeism, 482

prima facie, 294–96, 308

priorities, 447

privacy, protection of, 26, 323–25; Fourth Amendment and, 261–63; health information, 183–84; surveillance and, 543–44

Privacy Act of 1974, 296–98

privilege, defamation and, 239

Privileges and Immunities Clause (14th Amendment), 260

problem solving, 44

procedural justice, 502

process management, 101

productivity improvement plan, 98–102, 452

professional certification, 102–4, 475–77

professional development, 154, 510

professional employees, 514–15

Professional in Human Resources (PHR), 475, 476–77

profit sharing, 175–77, 189

progressive discipline, 502–3

project management, 8, 477–79

Project RAISE, 84

promotion, 143–44, 145; managerial, 344

proprietary information. See trade secrets

protected classification, 298–300

protective attire dress code, 503

PTO. See paid time off (PTO) policies

public figures, defamation and, 239–40

Public Interest Research Group, 250

public policy, 512. See also policy, human resource

quality, 4, 395, 444

quality circles, 410–12

quid pro quo harassment, 417

Railway Labor Act (RLA), 300–302

RAND Corporation study, 181

rapid continuous improvement (RCI), 59–61

rate and ratio, 444

rating form, 135

RBL Group, 438

reaction level, in training evaluation, 112

reasonable accommodations, 230–31, 302–4, 315

recognition, 399, 403, 542; compensation and, 145, 153

record keeping, 252–53; confidentiality in, 323. See also documentation

record retention laws, 304–6

recruiting and selection, 3–39, 222–24, 456; ability inventories in, 7–9; assessment center, 9–11; background investigation, 11–12; behavior inventory, 12–13; benefits and, 162; at colleges and universities, 13–14, 30–31; employee referral programs, 15–16;

employment testing, 17–19; internal *vs.* external recruitment, 29–31; interviewing, 19–21; job description, 21–23; job posting, 24–25; metrics and implementation, 6–7; polygraph test, 27–29; references, 31–33; resumes, 33–35; selection, 17–18, 35–37, 220, 257; talent inventory, 37–39

reengineering, 447

reference checks, 223

references, 12, 31–33

refreezing, 363, 370

regular part-time, 517

Rehabilitation Act of 1973, 302, 305

Rehabilitation Services Administration, 314

relationships, job description and, 22

religion and spirituality, 412–15

Rensselaer Polytechnic Institute, 63

resistance, to change, 365, 369

respect, climate of, 485–86

responsibilities and duties, 22, 154

restricted stock grants, 166

results level, in training evaluation, 112

results strategy, 447–48

resumes, 33–35; online, 31, 34

retaliation, 294, 306–8, 550

retention, 108, 144–46, 394, 399–400; benefits as tool for, 162; job sharing and, 80; promotion and, 143

retirement benefits, 308–9, 452

retirement plans, 166, 198–200; baby boomer, 452, 517; 401(K) plans, 166, 172–75, 198, 289–90; phased, 517. *See also* Employee Retirement Income Security Act (ERISA)

rewards: bonuses, 158–60; compensation and, 149–53; evaluations of, 118; extrinsic, 129–30; noncash incentives, 153; performance and, 96; strategies for, 150–52, 153; training and, 92

"rights" arbitration, 491

rising star, 68

risk sharing, 187–88

Robert Half International survey, 544

Rocha, Roberto, 503–4

Rogers, Everett M., 364

role management socialization, 107

role-play exercises, 10

rookie, 68. *See also* new employee

Ross School of Business, 438

Roth IRAs, 289

Royal Dutch/Shell Oil, 345–46

Rucker plan, 175, 176, 203

rural sourcing, 532

safe harbor, 515

safety, in workplace, 26, 82, 479–81. *See also* Occupational Safety and Health; workers' compensation; security concerns

salary, 163, 192, 513–14; benchmarking of, 200–203; merit pay and, 186; minimum, 513; surveys of, 202

Saratoga Institute survey, 399

Savings Incentive Match Plan for Employees (SIMPLE), 206

Scanlon Plan, 175, 176, 203–5

scenario planning, 345–47

Schmidt, Jeffrey A., 469

Schutte Self-Report Emotional Intelligence Test, 69

SDWT. *See* self-directed work teams

search and seizure, 261–62

search firms, 25, 430–31

seasonal employees, 547–48

security concerns, 435–37, 486, 536–38; computer systems, 499–500, 536, 552

selecting. *See* recruiting and selection

selection exams, 463–64

self-actualization, 82

self-assessment, 134

self-directed work teams (SDWTs), 415–16

self-incrimination, 255–56

Senge, Peter, 406

seniority systems, 296

Senior Professional in Human Resources (SPHR), 475, 476–77

separation agreements, 538–39

severance pay, 207–9

severe conduct, as harassment, 269

sexual harassment, 417–18

shared corporate knowledge bank, 111

shared vision, 406, 454

Shewart, Walter, 59

short-term executive, 347–49

SHRM. *See* Society for Human Resource Management

simplified employee pension (SEP) plans, 206

single-employer pension plan, 193

situational interviewing. *See* behavioral interviewing

situational leadership theory, 340–41

skill-based pay, 209–11

skills, opportunities to use, 403

skills analysis, 49

skills theory, of leadership, 340

skill transfer, 109, 152

slander, 238

Small Business Administration, 530

SMART (specific, measurable, achievable, results-oriented, time-based) criteria, 72, 73, 359
Smith, Adam, 453
socialization, 105–8
social needs, 82
social networking, 405
social security, 157, 165, 166, 199; survivors' benefits, 308–9. *See also* Medicare
Social Security Act of 1935, 212, 308–10
Society for Human Resource Management (SHRM), 103, 397, 468–69, 475, 513; diversity and, 393, 394; Job Satisfaction Survey Report, 402, 481; trends identified by, 451–53
sourcing, 4–5, 394; outsourcing, 191–92, 451, 531–33
Southwest Airlines, 156, 334
Spectrum Human Resource Systems Corporation, 442
spot awards, 189
Srivastva, Suresh, 44
staffing, 3–4, 434; planning discussions for, 5. *See also* recruiting and selection
stakeholder engagement, 469
stakeholder equity, 205
stakeholder reaction, 444
Start Dressing Like a Pro (Rocha), 503–4
stock option plan (SOP), 166, 171–72, 189–90
strategic communication, 350–52
strategic interventions, 376
strategic planning, 100, 353–54, 358
strengths, weaknesses, opportunities, and threats (SWOT), 354, 356–57
stress, burnout and, 46, 452, 482
strikes, 278, 279, 284, 521; grievance procedure and, 518
style theory, of leadership, 340
substance abuse, 539–41
succession planning, 8, 354–55
success sharing, 187–88
suggestion systems, 541–42
Sullivan, John, 15, 87
Supreme Court, U.S., 18, 240
surveillance, 543–44
survivors' benefits, 310–11
SWOT analysis. *See* strengths, weaknesses, opportunities, and threats (SWOT)
systems thinking, 407

Taft-Hartley Act. *See* National Labor Relations Act (1935)
talent, 439; generation and mobility, 459;

inventory of, 37–39; management of, 354, 418–20; training and, 108
tax-exempt organizations, 290
team-based pay, 163, 189
teams and teamwork, 420–21; cross-functional/cross-divisional, 110–11; incentives, 154; learning, 407; rewarding, 151; self-directed, 415–16; virtual, 421
Technical Assistance Research Program, 99
technological hazards, 507
technology, 57; career development and, 53; job sharing and, 78; vulnerability of, 452. *See also* computer systems
technostructural interventions, 376
telecommuting, 544–46
Telework Enhancement Act (2007), 546
Telework Tax Incentive Act (2005), 546
temporary/seasonal employees, 547–48
termination, 224, 549–51; confidentiality and, 324; disciplinary procedures and, 501, 549, 550; due to pregnancy, 294; involuntary, 549–50; layoffs and downsizing, 522–25, 549; severance pay, 207–9; wrongful, 325–26, 501, 550–51
Terry v. Ohio, 262
testing, 17–19; selection and, 36, 463–64
360-degree feedback, 109, 134, 146–47
time, poverty of, 383–84, 444
time-based conflict, 482
time-off policies, 213–14, 535–36
Title VII (Civil Rights Act of 1964), 220, 306, 440; ADEA compared, 227; affirmative action and, 225; BFOQs and, 231, 232, 235; discrimination and, 299; preferential treatment and, 291; Pregnancy Discrimination Act and, 221, 292, 293; prima facie and, 295–96, 307; sexual harassment and, 417; testing and, 17, 18
tobacco, 540
total quality management, 395, 411
Towers Perrin Inc., 468–69
Toyota Motor Company, 59, 60
Trade Adjustment Assistance Act of 2002, 310–11
trade secrets, 551–53
traditional organization, 390–91
traditional stage, 100–101, 102
training, 8, 14, 108–9, 444; computer-based, 56–58; cross-training, 64–66; delivery methods for, 108–9; development and, 464; diversification and, 394; evaluation of, 110–12; experiential-based, 109; federal law and, 244; interactive video, 76–77; intervention

resources and, 486–87; on-the-job, 90–92, 397–98, 454, 460–61; opportunities for, 145; web-based, 109

Trait Emotional Intelligence Questionnaire, 69–70

trait-factor theory, 339

transformational change, 371

transformational leadership theory, 341–42

transformational learning, 406

Transportation Act of 1920, 301

travel policy, 553–55

Triangle of Satisfaction model, 385

Truman, Harry S., 279

truth, defamation and, 239, 240

turnover, 399, 422–23

Ulrich, Dave, 3, 363

undue hardship, 230, 311–12, 315

unemployment compensation insurance, 158, 211–12

unfreezing, 363, 370

Uniform Commercial Code, 267

Uniformed Services Employment and Reemployment Rights Act (USERRA), 280, 312–14

Uniform Guideline on Employee Selection, 17–18, 220, 257

unionization, 278, 517. *See also* labor unions

union shop, 522

United Benefit Advisors, 215

United Health Group, 63

United Nations Children's Fund, 233

United Technologies, 63

universities and colleges: corporate, 61–63; recruitment at, 13–14, 30–31

USERRA. *See* Uniformed Services Employment and Reemployment Rights Act

utility, of evaluations, 121

vacation, 154

vacation policies, 213–14

value, 455

value-chain activities, 334

value creation, 447–48

verbal *vs.* written communication, 351–52

vertical skill plans, 210

Veterans' Benefits Improvement Act of 2004, 280

video training, 76–77

violence, workplace, 484–87, 501

virtual office, 545. *See also* telecommuting

virtual teams, 421

vision, shared, 406, 454

vision statements, 330, 354, 357–58

Vocational Rehabilitation Act of 1973, 221, 299, 314–15; illegal and legal questions in, 223

volume, output and, 444

Wack, Pierre, 345–47

wages, 163, 548; comparable worth doctrine and, 497–98; minimum, 251–52, 281–82, 513, 555. *See also* Equal Pay Act (1963)

Wagner Act, 278–79, 495

WARN Act of 1988, 207, 315–18

Waterman, Robert H., Jr., 473

wellness programs, 215–16

West's Encyclopedia of American Law, 267

whistle-blowing, 318–19

Wild Oats survey, 508

Wilson, Woodrow, 301

Wong Law Emotional Intelligence Scale, 69

work behavior inventory, 12–13

work eligibility, 555–56

Worker Adjustment and Retraining Notification (WARN) Act of 1988, 207, 315–18

worker bee, 68

workers' compensation, 158, 165, 319–23

workforce focus, 100

work history, 12, 35

work intensification, 452

work-life balance, 403, 452, 481–82

work-life flexibility, 80, 145

work performance standards. *See* performance standards

workplace justice, 483–84, 502

workplace privacy, 323–25. *See also* privacy, protection of

workplace rules, 510

workplace safety. *See* safety, in workplace

workplace violence, 484–87, 501

work planning evaluations, 117–18

work-related injury. *See* workers' compensation

work schedule, flexibility in, 516–17

world economy, 413. *See also* globalization

World Intellectual Property Organization, 552

World War II, 179; assessment centers in, 9

Wright, Patrick M., 502

written case analysis, 10

wrongful termination/discharge, 325–26, 501, 550–51

Wyatt, Watson, 432

"yellow dog" contracts, 284, 300

About the Editors and Contributors

Ann Gilley is an Associate Professor of Management at Ferris State University. Formerly on the faculty at Colorado State University, she is author and co-author of several books, including *Manager as Change Leader; The Performance Challenge; Beyond the Learning Organization;* and *Organizational Learning, Performance, and Change,* and she is the recipient of the Academy of Human Resource Development book-of-the-year award in 2000.

Jerry W. Gilley is a Professor of Organizational Development and Change at Colorado State University and the President of the Academy of Human Resource Development (AHRD). Dr. Gilley has authored and/or co-authored 18 books, which include *Manager as Coach, Manager as Political Navigator; Strategically Integrated HRD; Principles of Human Resource Development; The Manager as Change Agent: Philosophy and Practice of Organizational Learning, Performance, and Change;* and *Organizational Learning, Performance, and Change: An Introduction to Strategic HRD,* which was selected the HRD Book of the Year (2000) by the Academy of HRD.

Scott A. Quatro is Associate Professor or Management in the Department of Business Administration at Covenant College, a selective liberal arts college in the Reformed Christian tradition. Dr. Quatro's teaching, consulting, and research activities are focused on systemic human resource management practices, holistic leadership development, and organizational purpose/spirituality. His consulting clients have included both Fortune 500 firms and small to mid-sized organizations, including Chattem, Merrill Lynch, Payless ShoeSource, DriveTime, Cold Stone Creamery, and Meritage Homes. He has authored or co-authored four books and a total of 13 articles and chapters that have appeared in a wide variety of scholarly and practitioner publications. Dr. Quatro serves as a peer reviewer for *Human Resource Development Review* and the *Journal of Business Ethics.* He received a BA in English from Pepperdine University and an MBA from the College of William and Mary, and he holds a Ph.D. from Iowa State University.

Pamela Dixon is an Assistant Professor of Business Administration at Wayne State College. Pamela has over 15 years of experience as a practitioner in Human Resources and Organizational Development. She holds a Ph.D. in Organizational Performance and Change from Colorado State University, an M.Ed. in Instructional Technology, with an emphasis in Adult Learning, and a BA in Organizational Studies.

Chris Armstrong is a graduate student at Ferris State University where he is pursuing a Master of Science in Information Systems Management with a concentration in Information Security and Networking Management. He earned his Bachelor of Science in Management with minors in Research Methods and Applications and Computer Information Systems.

Frank E. Armstrong is an adjunct Professor of Management at Ferris State University, a professor at the University of Phoenix, and a professor at California National University for Advanced Studies. He is the author of several articles published in *Quality Digest* and *Quality* magazine. Frank has been in the quality arena of manufacturing for the past 20 years, is an RAB Auditor and a certified IATCA Quality Auditor.

James Steven Beck has his MBA from Centenary College of Louisiana and is a CPA with over 30 years of experience in the manufacturing and service industries. He is currently the Vice President of Administration for Eltron Research and Development, Inc., located in Boulder, Colorado, and is a Ph.D. candidate in the Organizational Performance and Change program at Colorado State University in Fort Collins, Colorado.

Dana M. Borchert is an Industrial/Organizational Psychology doctoral student at Saint Louis University. She is an integral part of the research team at Saint Louis University. Her specific interests are focused in the constructs of Emotional Intelligence and Work Affect. She presented a paper entitled *Are They Blind: Emotional Intelligence and the Recognition of Ethical Violations* at the Midwest Academy of Management Conference in the fall of 2007.

Shay Bright is an assistant director in the office of Conflict Resolution and Student Conduct Services at Colorado State University. She provides conflict resolution services to students, faculty, and staff, coordinates the Restorative Justice Program, and conducts training throughout campus. She has a master's from the Institute for Conflict Analysis and Resolution at George Mason University and is currently pursuing a Ph.D. in Organizational Performance and Change at Colorado State University.

Lisa Scott Brinkman is a Ph.D. candidate in the College of Applied Human Science in Organizational Performance and Change at Colorado State University and a freelance business consultant. She provides change management, process, and performance metrics consulting, facilitates procedures and policies sessions for organizations and designs and facilitates aligning employees with organizational strategy.

Nicole Brown is a recent graduate of Colorado State University's Master program in Organizational Performance and Change. Home-based in Denver, she has spent the last seven years working in the medical field as a liaison between medical insurance carriers and attorneys representing clients in workers' compensation claims. She aspires to do more freelance writing as well as teaching business in an adult education forum.

Jim Byrne is a police detective as well as principle speaker and trainer for Rocky Mountain Training Group. His focus is on organizational communication issues in the private and public sectors.

Meghan Clarisse Cave is a Financial Aid Administrator at the Colorado School of Mines. In 2003 she earned her BS in Natural Resource, Recreation and Tourism and in 2007 her M.Ed., both from Colorado State University. As a student, she was highly involved in the student chapter of the Society for Human Resource Management, and in 2007 she was awarded the SHRM Graduate Student Leader Scholarship.

Everon Christina Chenhall is a Ph.D. student in the College of Applied Human Science in Organizational Performance and Change at Colorado State University.

Thomas J. Chermack is an assistant professor in the Organizational Performance and Change program at Colorado State University. Formerly a consultant with Personnel Decisions International, his research focuses on the effects of scenario planning in organizations and on theory building methods in applied disciplines. He also manages Chermack Scenarios (www.thomaschermack.com), a scenario planning consultancy through which he has consulted with organizations such as General Mills, Saudi Aramco, and Motorola. Chermack's research has focused on the outcomes of scenario planning and has appeared in scholarly publications such as *Futures, Futures Research Quarterly, Human Resource Development Review, The Academy of Strategic Management Journal,* and the *Journal of Leadership and Organizational Studies.*

Teresa K. Cook is an Assistant Professor of Accounting at Ferris State University. She is a Certified Management Accountant and has nearly 20 years of experience in the corporate world, much of which covered benefit plan administration.

Julianne Daniels works in health care and holds a master's degree in Communications.

Beverly DeMarr is a Professor of Management and currently teaches courses in Negotiation, Organizational Behavior, Human Resource Management, and Compensation. Dr. DeMarr holds a Ph.D. from the School of Labor and Industrial Relations at Michigan State University and is active in the Academy of Management and Organizational Behavior Teaching Society. She is also a board member and volunteer mediator for the Westshore Dispute Resolution Center and is currently writing two textbooks on negotiation and dispute resolution, which will be published by Prentice-Hall.

Laura Dendinger is an Associate Professor of Business at Wayne State College and a member of the Nebraska State Bar Association. She teaches in the area of business communication, law, ethics and alternative dispute resolution.

Victoria T. Dieringer is a Program Manager for Raytheon Intelligence and Information Systems. A retired Lieutenant Colonel in the USAF Reserves, she has over 24 years of experience in government service. She is a doctoral candidate in the Organizational Development and Change program at Colorado State University.

Edward Dorman is a faculty member of accounting and the former Director of Accounting Services for Ferris State University.

Linda S. Dorré has been a Human Resources professional for over 20 years. She recently received her M.Ed. from Colorado State University in the area of Organizational Performance and Change.

Teresa Dwire has taught high school social studies and German for the past seven years and recently received her M.Ed. from Colorado State University's Organizational Performance and Change program. She currently is the Operations Manager for the Western Colorado Math and Science Center.

Amanda Easton is an Employee Relations Specialist for Easton Consulting. Easton provides employee relations consulting, writes personnel policies, designs and facilitates harassment prevention training, and conducts independent human resources investigations.

Barbara A. W. Eversole is an Assistant Professor at Indiana State University. She is the Founder and Senior Consultant of Transformations Unlimited Associates, an organizational consulting firm specializing in executive, management, and organization development. Dr. Eversole has 20 years of experience in management, training and development, and coaching, and recently she conducted research on CEOs for her dissertation. Her Ph.D. is in Organizational Performance and Change from Colorado State. She also holds an MBA and an MA in Counseling, and has received charter certification to administer the Myers-Briggs Type Indicator.

Jen Fullerton is a Ph.D. student in the Organizational Performance and Change program at Colorado State University. She is a former compensation professional who worked at Level 3 Communications as a Compensation Analyst and played a critical role in a company-wide job evaluation and market analysis using benchmark jobs.

Marisha L. Godek is the Associate Research Director of the Orthopaedic Bioengineering Research Laboratory at Colorado State University. Her research and publications focus on physiological responses to surgically placed biomaterials. Specific research regarding the immune system and collaborations with leading academic and business leaders have yielded relevant correlations between the body and organizations.

Igor Golovatyy is a graduate student at Colorado State University with the Organizational Performance and Change program.

Michael J. Gundlach is an Associate Professor of Management at California State University, Chico. Dr. Gundlach specializes in human resource management and received his Ph.D. in organizational behavior and human resource management from Florida State University. He has published research in outlets such as *Academy of Management Review; Journal of Management; Human Relations; Journal of Leadership and Organizational Studies;* and *International Journal of Selection & Assessment.* He also has published work in books and edited series and has presented research at international conferences. His research and consulting include areas such as teamwork, training and development, and whistle-blowing.

Jessica Haas is a recent graduate of the Organizational Performance and Change Master program at Colorado State University. Her background includes marketing communications, training implementation, branding, and marketing program development.

Lea Hanson is the Associate Director of Admissions at Colorado State University and a Ph.D. candidate in the university's Organizational Performance and Change program. She earned her master's degree in Higher Education from CSU and her undergraduate degree in Psychology from the University of North Dakota.

Derrick E. Haynes is the owner of AIJH Consulting Group and is pursuing his Ph.D. in Organizational Performance and Change at Colorado State University.

Maureen S. Heaphy is a Fellow of the American Society for Quality and a faculty member in the College of Business Graduate Program at Ferris State University. She teaches classes for the Master of Business Administration degree.

Douglas G. Heeter is a management professor at Ferris State University, where he teaches graduate and undergraduate courses in insurance and business management. He holds professional and educational designations including the Chartered Life Underwriter (CLU) and the Chartered Property and Casualty Underwriter (CPCU) and has taught professional insurance courses leading to the IIA/INS and CLU designations. Dr. Heeter consults for lawyer groups that require insurance research, has edited textbooks for McGraw-Hill Publishing, and created the National Exam for Insurance Agent Qualification—1998–2002 for the ASI Group—Educational Testing Service. The Michigan Association of Insurance Agents honored Dr. Heeter with Presidential Awards in 1996 and 2000, and he was inducted into the Michigan Insurance Hall of Fame in September 2003.

Anne E. Herman serves as a Research Consultant in the Kenexa Research Institute and has consulting experience in organizational assessment and change, organizational strategy, creativity and innovation, employee selection and promotion, performance management, program evaluation, and statistical methodology. She has spoken at many conferences and her research has appeared in several publications. She is also a member of the Society of Industrial and Organizational Psychology, Academy of Management, American Psychological Association, and the Organization Development Network. She holds a Master of Arts degree in psychology and is currently a doctoral candidate in Industrial and Organizational Psychology at the University of Nebraska.

Gina Hinrichs is president of Hinrichs Consulting LLC and an adjunct professor for Benedictine University, Capella University, and Lawrence Tech University. She is author and co-author of several articles and chapters on the topic of teams, whole systems change, and organizational design.

Brad M. Jensen is a Ph.D. candidate in the Organizational Performance and Change program at Colorado State University and the director of a 1,200-member nonprofit organization in Fort Collins, Colorado.

Lynda Kemp is pursing an Ed.D. in Organizational Performance and Change at Colorado State University. She recently completed an M.Ed. in Human Resource Development with an emphasis in Counseling and Career Development and currently advises business students at the University of Colorado. Previously, she spent nearly 20 years working as a city planner.

Jason Karsky is an Associate Professor in the Department of Sociology, Psychology, and Criminal Justice at Wayne State College. He authored the new curriculum in emergency management and serves on the campus Disaster Planning Group. Over the years, he has traveled to many conferences and presented on various emergency management related topics. He has secured grant funding and developed two large-scale multi-agency mock disaster scenarios. One involved a bus accident with over 50 victims, while another involved an airplane crash into a fertilizer chemical company. He is the 2006 George Rebensdorf Teaching Excellence Award Winner for the Nebraska State College System.

Steven J. Kerno Jr. is a doctoral candidate at St. Ambrose University (Davenport, Iowa) in business administration. He is also employed full-time as a parts cross-reference analyst at John Deere PDC in Milan, Illinois. He has written feature articles on the changing nature of non-management careers for trade/occupation magazines such as *Mechanical Engineering; Resource; P; IE; Welding; Modern Materials Handling; Appliance;* and *Inbound Logistics* and will be contributing a chapter to be titled "Protean Professionalism and Career Development" to the forthcoming book *Career Development in Bioengineering and Biotechnology.* He resides in Rock Island, Illinois, with his wife, Tammy, and four children (Brett, Stephanie, Scott, and Andrew).

Martin Kollasch is the Manager of International Operations at the National Board of Chiropractic Examiners and a Ph.D. candidate in Organizational Performance and Change at Colorado State University.

Robin R. Labenz is a student at Wayne State College, majoring in Business Administration and minoring in Human Resource Management.

Henry H. Luckel Jr. is a bi-vocational minister working at Hewlett-Packard as an Informational Technology Support Specialist. He is the Pastor of Prairie Church in Yoder, Colorado, and is the president of the Southern Baptist Bi-Vocational Ministers Association. He is currently working toward his doctorate in Education and Human Resources Studies (Organizational Performance and Change) at Colorado State University.

Shanan M. Mahoney has over 15 years of experience in human resources and is an owner and Senior Consultant at the HR consulting firm, NorthPoint, LLC. Shanan received her bachelor degree in business administration from Ohio University in Athens, Ohio, and earned her Master of Science in Management from Regis University in Denver, Colorado. Shanan is a member of the Society for Human Resource Management (SHRM) and is certified as a Senior Professional in Human Resources (SPHR).

Jennifer A. Majkowski is a human resource professional and former corporate recruiter who specializes in recruitment and benefit/compensation strategies.

Douglas Maxwell has a 25-year career in human resources administration with rural and urban nonprofit healthcare systems and national healthcare companies. He is a principle with Diversity Roadmap, LLC, whose purpose is to advance the Diversity Roadmap Model as the transformational process to spotlight individual and organizational value through learning and development change process. Doug is an adjunct professor of Management at Grand Canyon University, Maricopa Community College District, and a faculty member of the Arizona Healthcare Leadership Academy. He is the author of the article "Workforce Diversity: HR's Call to Leadership" in *The American Society for Healthcare Human Resources* (Winter 2006) and coauthored a chapter, "Ethics in Diversity Management Leadership," in *Executive Ethics: Ethical Dilemmas and Challenges for the C-suite,* edited by Scott A. Quatro and Ronald R. Sims (2008).

Elizabeth A. McCane is a Registered Environmental Manager (REM) and a Registered Environmental Assessor (REA) currently working as the Environmental Compliance Program Manager for the Colorado Army National Guard. She previously worked as an environmental protection specialist for the Colorado Air National Guard; the Department of the Army (Fort Irwin, California); and as an Environmental, Safety and Health specialist for the National Aeronautics and Space Administration (NASA) Goldstone Deep Space Communication Complex, Barstow, California.

Scott McDonald is a Program Director with the Office of Continuing Education at the University of Illinois at Urbana-Champaign. Scott is also a Ph.D. student in the area of Organizational Performance and Change at Colorado State University.

Heather S. McMillan is an Assistant Professor of Management at Southeast Missouri State University. Certified as a Professional in Human Resources (PHR) by the Society for Human Resource Management, she has eight years of progressive experience in corporate human resource management. Her primary research interests are in the areas of work-life balance, HR metrics, and practitioner development.

Fred Miles spent 26 years with Motorola and retired in 2001. His career in Human Resources included numerous assignments in staffing, employee relations, training and development, and organizational effectiveness. Fred is Principle of The Miles Alliance, which provides Human Resources Solutions, and is an Adjunct Faculty member teaching various human esources classes in undergraduate and graduate programs throughout the valley for Grand Canyon University. Retired as a USAF Lt. Colonel in 1992, he spent six years on active duty and 19 in the reserves.

Carol Miller is a faculty member of Business, Management and Marketing, and program chair of Business, Accounting and Economics at the Community College of Denver. She is pursuing her Ph.D. in Organizational Performance and Change through Colorado State University.

Debora A. Montgomery-Colbert has a Master of Science of Management degree from Regis University and is currently completing a Ph.D. in Organizational Performance and Change at Colorado State University. She has spent over 11 years working in the field of Distance and Continuing Education and is the Director of Online/Distance

Learning for Colorado State University Division of Continuing Education. She resides in Colorado with her husband, Jonathan, and three children (Robert, Kathryn, and Curtis).

Michael Lane Morris is a 2005–2006 William B. Stokely Faculty Scholar and an Associate Professor/Program Director of Human Resource Development in the Department of Management, College of Business Administration at The University of Tennessee. He serves as President of the Academy of Human Resource Development. In 2004 and 2005, he served as the Program Chair and Proceedings Editor of the Academy of Human Resource Development (AHRD) Conferences and Proceedings. In 2005, he was elected a member of the AHRD Board of Directors and is a member of numerous top-tier editorial boards. His research interests include various work/family/life issues, promotion of health and wellness, and evaluation strategies.

Matt Neibauer is a Research Associate for the Colorado Water Resources Research Institute at Colorado State University. He has co-authored *Linking Public Attitudes with Perceptions of Factors Impacting Water Quality and Attending Learning Activities; Land and Water Inventory Guided for Landowners in Areas of Coal Bed Methane Development; Water Conservation In and Around the Home;* and *Glossary of Water Terminology.*

Dean Nelson is a doctoral student in the Organizational Performance and Change program at Colorado State University.

Lori Nicholson is an Assistant Professor of Computer Science at Wayne State College in Wayne, Nebraska.

Betsy Nolan is currently employed in the metal manufacturing industry as the Assistant Controller and Assistant HR Manager of Metal Components. She is a graduate of Ferris State University.

Dave O'Connell is an Associate Professor of Management at St. Ambrose University. He holds a DBA in Organizational Behavior from Boston University. He teaches courses in HR and Organizational Behavior at the undergraduate, master, and doctoral levels. Dave has published articles in the *Journal of Management Education; Journal of Leadership and Organizational Studies; Leadership and Organizational Development Journal;* and *The CASE Journal.* His research has focused on contingent employment, team development, leadership competencies, adaptability, and case pedagogy. Currently, he is exploring the development and dissemination of organizational vision. Prior to doctoral studies, he served with the Public Service Company of New Mexico in a number of communications and research capacities from 1979 through 1993.

Al O'Connor is President of O'Connor HR CareerCoaching, a career consulting company whose mission is to assist human resources professionals in enhancing their careers through new opportunities. He has over 40 years of combined human resources and career management experience.

Roger Odegard is a Ph.D. student in Organizational Performance and Change at Colorado State University.

Brenda E. Ogden is a full-time instructor in the College of Business at Colorado State University. She teaches strategic communication, general management, and leadership courses at the undergraduate level and as an adjunct professor in the Distance MBA program. She spent 15 years in organizations before pursuing a teaching career and currently consults with organizations on issues in communication, change, and time management. She has co-authored articles on communication and technology, values-based management, and a communications resource book. Her research focus is on communication and change management with emphasis on intercultural, gender, generational, and team issues.

Debra Orr is an assistant professor of Organizational Leadership at Roosevelt University in Chicago. As a scholar-practitioner, she consults in organization development, teaches, and writes.

Robert Paxton is Vice President, Human Resources, for Whirlpool's global talent acquisition, talent management, and employee engagement activities. He has held various HR leadership roles in North America, Europe, and Asia. Bob holds an MBA from the University of Houston-Victoria and an undergraduate degree in Human Resources Management from Ohio University. He is a certified Senior Professional in Human Resources (SPHR) from the Human Resources Certification Institute and the Society for Human Resource Management.

Kevin F. Preston is a doctoral student in Colorado State University's Organizational Performance and Change program. Kevin is also a learning professional at a large national healthcare provider where he focuses on learning technology, governance, design, and community.

Tim Reynolds is Vice President of Human Resources for Whirlpool Corporation's Global Design, Technology and Sourcing Organization. His work is focused on the delivery of global human capital strategies and tactics to build a profit growing culture and customer loyalty centric enterprise. He holds a Master degree in Labor and Human Resources and a BBA in HRM/MGT. He has served as a member of the HRM Advisory Board and is a current member of the Executive Advisory Board for the College of Business at Ohio University. Tim has published articles in HR/OD journals and has been a regular speaker at national conferences.

Cynthia Roberts is an Associate Professor and Chair of the Business and Organizational Leadership departments at Purdue University North Central where she teaches leadership, team development, organizational behavior, ethics, and diversity. She holds dual M.S. degrees from Loyola University Chicago in training as well as organizational development and is nearing completion of her Ph.D. in Organizational Development at Benedictine University. Her research interests include leadership development, gender and leadership, and team development.

Stephanee Roessing, SPHR, is a Sr. Consultant, Talent and Organization Development at Level 3 Communications, Inc. She holds an M.Ed. in Organization Performance and Change from Colorado State University and a MA of International Studies from the University of Denver.

Paul Rosser has 25 years of experience in hospital-based business development and physician practice management. He also has extensive experience in development of hospital-based and freestanding outpatient diagnostic centers. For the past six years Mr. Rosser has taught in the Regis University MBA program. He is a candidate for a Ph.D. in Education and Human Resource Studies, specializing in Organizational Performance and Change, at Colorado State University.

Dean M. Savoca, CTACC, is a performance consultant, speaker, and trainer and holds a Master degree from Colorado State University in Organizational Performance and Change. He is principal of *SynergyLife LLC* partnering with entrepreneurs, sales professionals, and organizations to improve performance. He has over 13 years of experience in the performance improvement industry including 10 years with Maritz Performance Improvement and Maritz Travel Companies. He has extensive sales experience and served as general manager of a destination management company and is certified in Appreciative Inquiry and Emotional Intelligence. He serves on the Board of Directors of the Cherry Creek Chamber of Commerce in Denver, Colorado, and is a Results Coach with Anthony Robbins Companies.

Pat Schneider has over 16 years of business and human resources experience in various industries including hospitality, security services, and financial services. For the past 10 years he has held senior-level human resource positions with responsibility for providing leadership and strategic direction in the areas of organizational development, staffing, compensation, performance management, benefits, and employee relations. A Certified Professional in Human Resources (PHR) and a member of the Society for Human Resource Management (SHRM), he has a Bachelor of Art degree in Psychology with a minor in Human Resource Management from the University of Wisconsin–Eau Claire. He holds a Master degree in Education in Organizational Performance and Change from Colorado State University.

Brad Schroeder, SPHR, is the Director of Talent Management for Blue Cross Blue Shield of Nebraska. He has worked in various Human Resource positions over 10 years with Health Care Service Corporation, the parent company of the Blue Cross and Blue Shield plans of Illinois, Texas, New Mexico, and Oklahoma. He holds two degrees from the University of Illinois at Urbana–Champaign, including a Master degree in Labor and Industrial Relations with a specialty in Human Resource Management.

Kerry Schut is a Graduate of Ferris State University with a BS in Business Administration. She lives in the Grand Rapids, Michigan, area with her husband and two children.

Marie Shanle is a student at Wayne State College, majoring in Business Administration and minoring in Human Resource Management.

Paul M. Shelton is an Assistant Professor of Management at the University of Central Oklahoma. He spent 10 years working for the U.S. Immigration Service and the U.S. Department of Homeland Security as a Border Patrol Agent, Deportation Officer, Adjudications Officer, Congressional Liaison, and manager. He holds a Ph.D. in Organizational Performance and Change from Colorado State University and an MBA from Azusa Pacific University.

Ronald R. Sims is the Floyd Dewey Gottwald Senior Professor in the Mason School of Business at the College of William and Mary. He received his Ph.D. in Organizational Behavior from Case Western Reserve University. His research focuses on a variety of topics which include leadership and change management, HRM, business ethics, employee training/management/leadership development (e.g., human resource development), learning styles, and experiential learning. Dr. Sims is the author or co-author of 27 books and more than 80 articles that have appeared in a wide variety of scholarly and practitioner journals.

Ryan Skiera is currently performing adjunct duties for the Management Department of Ferris State University. He received his Bachelor of Science degree from Ferris State University and earned his MBA from Grand Valley State University. He has worked in a number of capacities for different chemical manufacturers, most notably Pfizer.

Robert M. Sloyan is currently the Vice President of Human Resources for a manufacturing organization located in the Midwest. He has negotiated and/or managed collective bargaining agreements with the Service Employees International Union (SEIU), the Communications Workers of America (CWA), and the International Brotherhood of Electrical Workers (IBEW). He holds an MBA in Finance (2001) and Human Resources (1994) from St. Xavier University. He is currently a Ph.D. candidate at Benedictine University. He lives in the Chicago area with his wife and three sons.

Matt Springer has served as a police officer with the Aurora Police Department, near Denver, Colorado, for four years. He is currently pursuing his Ph.D. in Organizational Performance and Change at Colorado State University.

Cyndi Stewart is currently Vice President of Human Resources for Lehman Brothers Mortgage Capital Division. Prior to Lehman Brothers, she held senior human resources positions for Citigroup and Hyatt. She holds a BS from the State University of New York–Utica and an MS in Organizational Performance and Change from Colorado State University.

Kyle B. Stone is a Ph.D. student in the Organizational Performance and Change program at Colorado State University and holds a Master degree in Adult Education and Training from Colorado State University. He has been working in manufacturing for over 17 years primarily in the role of plant and operations management. He has been actively involved in implementing continuous improvement, workforce development, organizational development, plant design, and startup in the automotive and utility truck industry.

Merwyn L. Strate is an Assistant Professor of Organizational Leadership at Purdue University. His research interests include complex adaptive systems, adaptive competence, intergenerational issues in the workplace, and qualitative research methods for business and industry.

Nancy Svoboda, SPHR, is the Senior Vice President of Human Resources at The Integer Group, LLC. She received a Bachelor of Science degree in Business Administration from Illinois State University and a Master degree in Education with a specialization in Organizational Performance and Change at Colorado State University. She has more than 20 years of business and human resources experience in various industries including childcare, retail, and advertising/marketing. For the past 12 years she has held senior-level human resources positions with responsibility for providing leadership and strategic direction in the areas of organizational development, staffing, compensation, performance management, benefits, and employee relations.

Susan Sweem is a senior human resources manager for Akzo Nobel, a global chemical/coatings company headquartered in The Netherlands. In this capacity, she is responsible for the coordination of HR activities in the United States which include compensation, benefits, expatriate administration, and mergers and acquisitions. Prior to joining Akzo, she worked in the home hardware and healthcare industries. She has a Bachelor degree in Sociology from Iowa State University and a Master degree in Industrial Relations from Loyola University and is currently a doctoral candidate in Organization Development at Benedictine University.

Alison Thero currently works for Hewlett-Packard as an Engineering Program Manager. She has 12 years of program and project management experience in implementations of enterprise-wide Forecasting and Planning Solutions with Advanced Micro Devices, Celestica, i2 Technologies, Amkor, and Hewlett-Packard. She holds a BA from the University of Texas at Austin and an MBA from Colorado State University. She is currently working toward a Ph.D. in Organizational Performance and Change at Colorado State University. Her spare time is spent with her family, running, and playing the harp.

Maria Valladares is a public relations professional and graduate of Ferris State University.

Adam VanDreumel is an Account Manager with Delios Computer Solutions, Inc., specializing in the technology needs of small to medium-sized businesses. He holds several technology-related certifications, a BS in Business Administration from Ferris State University, and is currently assessing postgraduate programs. He is married and has two sons.

Lory-Ann Varela has worked more than a decade in higher education in the fields of career services, multicultural affairs and residence life at both public and private universities. She completed her M.Ed. in Counselor Education from the University of Florida and an M.Ed. in Social Justice in Education from the University of Massachusetts–Amherst. She is currently enrolled in the Organizational Performance and Change Ph.D. program at Colorado State University.

Donald L. Venneberg, Ph.D., is Assistant Professor of Organizational Performance and Change at Colorado State University. He is also a former federal senior executive who led large organizations in the logistics and information technology fields.

Alina M. Waite is a full-time Instructor of Organizational Development and Change at Colorado State University. She teaches performance consulting, action research, and learning transfer courses at the graduate level both on campus and via distance learning. Her research focuses on performance improvement, process improvement, and analysis. She has over 15 years of experience working in the health care industry and has served in a variety of leadership capacities both in the United States and abroad. Prior to her current position, she was the Director of Research and Development of an international organization specializing in the design, development, and manufacture of medical devices.

Elizabeth Wheeler is the Human Resources Manager for a distance education school. She is responsible for all aspects of the human resources function.

Sarah E. Asmus Yackey owns Northern Colorado Mediation Institute, a division of Smiling Lab Communications, Inc. She has been working in the conflict resolution field for six years with an emphasis on mediation and restorative justice. Sarah has a master's in Conflict Resolution and is a professional member of the Association for Conflict Resolution (ACR) and the Colorado Council of Mediators (CCMO). She has worked in both the public and private sectors and has presented at regional conferences in her field. She teaches courses in restorative justice at Front Range Community College in Fort Collins, Colorado.

Suzanne Zivnuska is an Associate Professor at California State University, Chico, specializing in human resource management. Dr. Zivnuska's doctorate is in Organizational Behavior and Human Resource Management from Florida State University, and her major research interests in human resource management include the effects of impression management and politics on performance as well as work-family balance issues. Her work has appeared in journals such as *Human Relations; Journal of Applied Psychology; Journal of Organizational Behavior; Journal of Applied Social Psychology;* and *Leadership Quarterly.*